CALVIN

CALVIN

BRUCE GORDON

YALE UNIVERSITY PRESS
NEW HAVEN AND LONDON

For Rona

But if there be no certain knowledge for the present, and no constant and unhesitant persuasion for the future, who dare glory?

John Calvin on Romans 5:2.

For information about this and other Yale University Press publications, please contact:

U.S. Office: sales.press@yale.edu   www.yalebooks.com
Europe Office: sales@yaleup.co.uk   www.yalebooks.co.uk

Set in Minion by IDSUK (DataConnection) Ltd.
Printed in Great Britain by MPG Books Ltd, Bodmin, Cornwall

Library of Congress Cataloging-in-Publication Data

Gordon, Bruce, 1962–
   Calvin / Bruce Gordon.
      p. cm.
   Includes bibliographical references and index.
   ISBN 978–0–300–12076–9 (alk. paper)
   1. Calvin, Jean, 1509–1564. I. Title.

   BX9418.G63 2009
   284'.2092—dc22
   [B]

                                                                                    2008047642

A catalogue record for this book is available from the British Library.

10 9 8 7 6 5 4 3 2 1

Contents

Illustrations

Preface

JOHN CALVIN was the greatest Protestant reformer of the sixteenth century, brilliant, visionary and iconic. The superior force of his mind was evident in all that he did. He was also ruthless, and an outstanding hater. Among those things he hated were the Roman church, Anabaptists and those people who, he believed, only faint-heartedly embraced the Gospel and tainted themselves with idolatry. He saw himself as an instrument of God, and as a prophet of the Church he brooked no rivals. He never felt he had encountered an intellectual equal, and he was probably correct. To achieve what he believed to be right, he would do virtually anything. Although not physically imposing, he dominated others and knew how to manipulate relationships. He intimidated, bullied and humiliated, saving some of his worst conduct for his friends. Yet as he lay dying they gathered around the bed distraught with grief. There would be no other like him.

This is the story of a prodigious young boy from a provincial background and modest means who by sheer talent progressed through the elite world of the French Renaissance. He studied in Paris and the best universities under the leading figures of the day. Few would have had a better education, and few were intellectually equipped to make more of it. But the man behind the precocious talent was a difficult person and one with a troubled conscience. The religious ideas of the great French evangelicals as well as the revolutionary views of Martin Luther took hold of this impressionable young man and changed him for ever. The rest of his life was a coming to terms with that conversion.

But what made Calvin great? It may seem odd, but working on this biography has convinced me that the answer does not lie in the events of his life.

Nor is the question adequately addressed in terms of the numerous and diverse influences that shaped his mind. They were significant, as we shall see, but there is more. What made Calvin Calvin, and not another sixteenth-century writer, was his brilliance as a thinker and writer, and, above all, his ability to interpret the Bible. His coherent, penetrating and lucid vision of God's abiding love for humanity, expressed in some of the most exquisite prose of his age, has continued down the centuries to instruct and to inspire. Like all great writers he transcends his time.

Calvin was fully aware of his talents, which he regarded as part of his special calling by God. His journey was to find the appropriate vocation for that summons. Ultimately it was located in a relative backwater, Geneva, which he beheld much as Jonah did Nineveh. But Calvin understood his destiny to extend far beyond Geneva's walls: he was a man of the Church, and its unity was his deepest passion. Luther had brilliantly expressed what it meant to be saved by God. That discovery had changed Europe. Calvin's genius was to discover the Church, and teach what it was to be part of that body if one lived in a besieged city, under a capricious Tudor monarch or as a refugee facing persecution and exile.

Despite his dominant personality, Calvin rarely and reluctantly drew attention to himself in his writing. He spoke through the Bible and its major characters: Moses, David and the prophets. Above all, however, his model was the Apostle Paul, the great teacher and pastor who belonged to no one church and spoke to all. The identification was so complete that Calvin painted himself into his portrait of the Apostle, revealing his own thoughts, struggles and anxieties. Exile was his defining experience, freeing him from attachment to any particular place as he roamed across Swiss and German lands. And it endowed him with his most powerful and resonant message: the Christian is never alone, for the Christian is at home in God.

What, then, is the point of a biography? The simple, and unapologetic, answer is that Calvin led a fascinating life with the requisite elements of danger, tragedy, conflict and betrayal. There was also friendship, love and vision. In short, John Calvin was a human being who ate, slept and travailed under a broken body. Similarly, his brilliant mind and dazzling ability with the written and spoken word were not created *ex nihilo*. Calvin saw the Christian life in terms of a journey; in his own case this was physical, intellectual and spiritual. He travelled through France, the Holy Roman Empire, into Italy and across the Swiss Confederation for his studies, to flee persecution and in search of Christian unity. His ravenous appetite for knowledge made him a lifelong student utterly devoted to books and intellectual exchange, never for their own sake, but in the service of the Church. His mind continuously soaked up the teaching of ancient, medieval and contemporary writers and the result was an ever evolving intellect. Calvin reworked and revised the *Institutes of the Christian Religion* extensively between 1536 and 1559 to take account of his scriptural work, his reading of theological tradition, contemporary debates and his desire to find the correct and clearest order of argument. Likewise, the biblical commentaries were revised and reprinted. Utterly driven, Calvin laboured all the hours the day permitted to bring knowledge of God's saving action in Christ to the people and to combat those he believed to be opponents of the Gospel. To follow his path it is crucial to understand the contexts for his words and deeds. Despite his enduring renown, he was a man of the sixteenth century, and we have to enter that world.

That world was also populated by many other figures, and while the Calvin of legend stands alone, our story is very different. Friends, family, colleagues and students filled his life and not simply in walk-on parts. In person and through his networks of correspondence, which ultimately extended across Europe, Calvin was constantly in dialogue with others. That was how he defined both his theology and his role in the Church. The constant exchange of ideas and information was the very life blood of the Reformation and he came to see himself working with partners and linked churches. Most prominent were Philip Melanchthon and Heinrich Bullinger, but there were a host of others. These relationships could be complicated and might have to weather many storms, but no one worked harder than Calvin to preserve them. Much of the attention of this book will be focused upon the ebb and flow of his contacts.

The location of Calvin's grave is unknown, and that was the way he wanted it. Fully conscious of his fame and the spell he cast over his supporters, he feared being made an object of veneration. Nothing would have horrified him more than the monument to the Reformation in Geneva with its enormous image of the Frenchman. He deliberately wrote next to nothing about himself and his life. In the preface to his 1557 commentary on the psalms he provided a spiritual autobiography, but to the modern eye it is conspicuously short on facts. This is hardly surprising as its purpose was to stress the omnipotence of God and Calvin's providential calling. There are scattered fragments in the letters and tracts, but on the whole we search Calvin's writings in vain for much personal information. Yet it is important to note that this concealment is only partial, as is evident if we compare Calvin with Shakespeare. Both lives

are shrouded in mist, but, while for Shakespeare we know only what his characters thought, and how much they express the playwright's own views
continues to be debatable, we are in no doubt about what Calvin believed. For
our part, we will not have to discuss whether Calvin was a Protestant or
Catholic. He was a pedagogue dedicated to clarity of thought and expression:
essential tools of the Christian faith. Like many of his contemporaries, he did
not believe that details of his life and personality, profane ruminations that
they were, should in any way obscure that message. By concealing himself he
created space for the faithful to meet God directly.

    This biography will concentrate on the Calvin we can know, following the
events of his life and charting his thoughts through his letters and writings.
Problems abound, and the historian must plot a careful course. The letters,
our best source for what Calvin thought of the people and events of his day,
often reveal him at his most intemperate and thin-skinned as he fulminated
against the failings of others, including his closest friends. It would be easy to
sketch an overly negative view of the man, but that is by no means the intention here. However, he was a man, and misjudgements and errors were made.
His character needs to be read alongside those of the other reformers who
struggled, frequently in vain, against the often insurmountable obstacles
standing in the way of religious reform: fierce Catholic opposition, reluctant,
even hostile, political masters, and a laity often not at all persuaded of the
necessity of change. They lived in an age when events moved quickly and
information very slowly. Their actions and thoughts were profoundly shaped
by a world over which they had little control. That was precisely why Calvin's
teaching on predestination and providence found a receptive audience.

    The sources reveal a complex, volatile man who found relations with others
troubling, if not a burden. In the public arena Calvin walked and spoke with
stunning confidence. In private he was, by his own admission, shy and
awkward. He adored his wife and suffered greatly when his baby son died. He
worked ceaselessly on behalf of the refugees who came to Geneva and took an
especial interest in the well-being of widows and children. To his intimates he
was both a benevolent father and a bully, with opponents vindictive and even
cruel, and certainly he knew how to bend, or at least conceal, the truth when
circumstances demanded. At times he could be waspish and obsessed with self-
justification as if his reputation was the most important issue. When he made
up his mind about individuals he seldom wavered; for good or bad, their lot
was cast. This often resulted in conflict and a profound sense of betrayal.
Calvin demanded complete loyalty from his intimates. He could accept error

and ignorance, but never opposition. His confidence in his own judgement led to several critical miscalculations, such as with the German Lutherans, England and France. This is what made him human.

A few notes on terminology and usages. All labels for religious movements in the sixteenth century must carry health warnings, but I have chosen to use some and not others. I have avoided the term 'Calvinist' because it is both vague and misleading in our context. While Calvin lived there were no 'Calvinists'. I have preferred the name 'Reformed' for the theological tradition that arose out of the Swiss Confederation and which Calvin played a crucial role in shaping. I have, however, preserved the use of the terms 'Lutheran' and 'Zwinglian' as shorthand for what emerged from Wittenberg and Zurich. Similarly, I speak of the reform movement in France as 'evangelicals' to indicate that they held a wide body of views, but that their central point of cohesion was the Bible. Only in the 1550s, with the emergence of churches, can one talk of French Protestantism. For the sake of simplicity, I have not used the term 'Huguenot'. Finally, I speak of the Catholic and Protestant churches. Calvin would have hated the idea of Rome being called Catholic, but it is a modern convention that aids clarity. Church is used in the upper case to indicate its universal form. The choice of terms is not intended to indicate any confessional disposition, just to aid clarity. In quoting Calvin and other sources I have made use of good existing translations where possible; with the letters, however, I have reworked most of them in light of the Latin and French as the Bonnet translations can be quite misleading. Nevertheless, I have given the Bonnet references where possible for those who wish to read more. The interested reader should be aware that the dating of the Bonnet letters is frequently inaccurate.

This book is intended for those with an interest in John Calvin who may have little familiarity with either the reformer or the sixteenth century. I have tried as far as possible to provide sufficient background to events, persons and ideas without taxing the reader's patience. Where I could I have avoided overly technical language, such as in discussing theology, to avert confusion. In the Select Bibliography at the conclusion I point the reader to more specialist studies in English for further reading.

Acknowledgements

IT IS a pleasure to acknowledge the time, patience and expertise that enabled me to undertake and complete this project. From the start Heather McCallum of Yale University Press was a constant source of encouragement, persuading me that a biography for a wider audience could be written by a non-Calvin expert. As such I owe much to the kindness of others. I was extremely fortunate that Irena Backus, Ward Holder and David Whitford were prepared to read a draft and offer helpful criticism and corrections. David Whitford's class on Calvin at the United Theological Seminary in Dayton, Ohio, also read an early version and greatly helped to shape the text. To them, I express my thanks. Michael W. Bruening generously allowed me to see the text of his book on the Vaud before publication. My debt to that work is evident. I am particularly grateful to a reader for the Press who put an enormous amount of time and expertise into a report from which I benefited greatly. It was a model of professional and humane scholarship, a lesson to us all.

In St Andrews, Andrew Pettegree, Bridget Heal, Jane Stevens, Matthew McLean and Charles Drummond read the manuscript and made many improvements. Peter Kushner was of great assistance at a crucial time and I thank him for his labours. The M.Litt. in Reformation Studies class read an early version of the text and offered sharp and insightful comments in our discussion. I would like to thank Bett Tapscott, Andy Drummond, Adam Marks, Lisa Clifford, Taren Heinz, Melissa Arch, Tiffany Christiensen and Robert Jackson. My undergraduate class on the Northern Renaissance also weathered with good cheer having to read my chapters on Calvin. To them also I am grateful. Philip John dazzled me with his ability to make maps on the computer screen. To others who offered encouragement and support along the way, many thanks.

The final version of this book was completed just as I leave St Andrews after fourteen years for a new life with my family in the United States. Sitting in my office late on a Friday afternoon I cannot but think of the students and colleagues who have made those years a great pleasure. I have learned more from them than I could ever teach, and their generosity will remain with me. The St Andrews Reformation Studies Institute has been my intellectual home and it is a pleasure to acknowledge the enduring friendship of Andrew Pettegree. If I may be permitted to select one other name, Keith Brown proved a true friend at a bad moment, confirming Calvin's view of Romans 13. Others I would like to mention include Murray Leishman, whose wisdom inspired me more than he will know. And, with sadness, David Wright, whom I had the honour of knowing for over twenty years: for me and many others, he represented the ideal of the Christian scholar.

To my family I owe nothing short of everything. Charlotte asked all the best questions. Rona taught me the meaning of our vow 'in sickness and in health', and to her I dedicate this book with all my love.

St Andrews 2008

Calvin's Europe

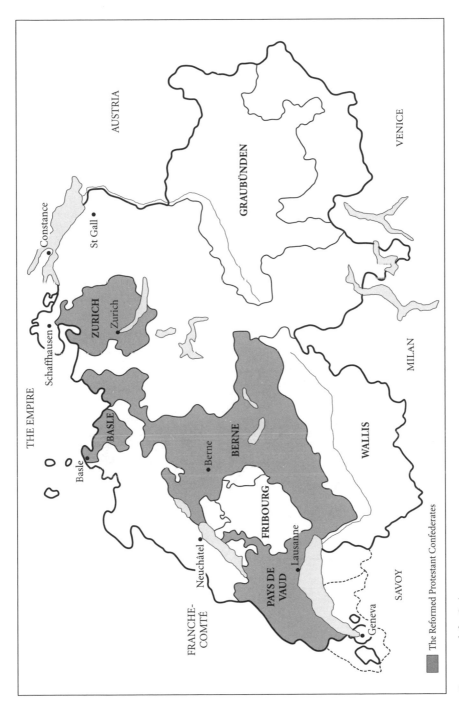

Geneva and the Swiss

THE EMPIRE

AUSTRIA

Constance •

St Gall •

Schaffhausen •

ZURICH
Zurich •

Basle •

BASLE

Berne •

BERNE

FRANCHE-
COMTÉ

Neuchâtel •

FRIBOURG

Lausanne •

PAYS DE
VAUD

Geneva •

SAVOY

WALLIS

MILAN

GRAUBÜNDEN

VENICE

The Reformed Protestant Confederates

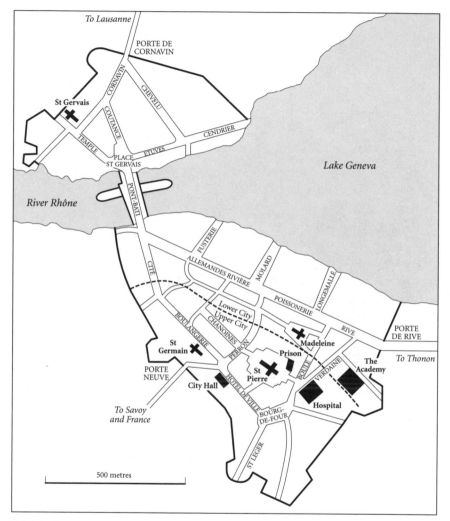

Calvin's Geneva

CHAPTER ONE

A French Youth

Ways of Speaking

JOHN CALVIN as a child does not come easily to the eye. Our imagination quickly runs to familiar representations of an ageing, bearded man stooped by years of hard labour and illness and to the stool on which he allegedly had to sit to preach in his declining years, or to nineteenth-century illustrations of the great prophet declaiming before the cowering faithful. Of the young boy growing up in the cathedral town of Noyon, sixty miles north of Paris, we know almost nothing. Expansive reflections on his youth form no part of Calvin's writing. Even the self-portrait offered in the preface to his psalms commentary, written later in life, passes almost in silence over his early years in Picardy. He offers only the single insight that his father had a change of heart. 'When I was as yet a very little boy, my father had destined me for the study of theology. But afterwards, when he considered that the legal profession commonly raised those who followed it to wealth, this prospect induced him suddenly to change his purpose.'[1] A solitary childhood memory also appears in a 1543 tract when Calvin recalled the manner in which the good people of Noyon venerated the relics of saints.

His written words do, however, contain revelations of the man. In the psalms preface of 1557 Calvin describes himself as being at once awkward, timid and bashful – qualities that his later opponents might be forgiven for failing to recognize. As with everything he wrote, however, context is essential. The preface is not autobiographical in any modern sense, but rather a carefully crafted account of his providential call to the ministry, utterly devoid of sentimentality. Providence is God's will, mysterious to humanity, that guides all things. It extends to specific events and actions, works through particular human characteristics and comforts men and women, who by faith see that the world is not random and chaotic, but in God's hands. For Calvin, it was God's providence that he had been chosen to serve in a special capacity. Yet within the lines of elegant Latin prose dwells something of the boy who became the man, and this takes us to the heart of Calvin's story. His great endeavour was to interpret the Bible to the world, and through scripture he saw his own life mapped out. In the Bible he found the man he was called to be: a prophet and apostle single-mindedly dedicated to one cause. His vocation, as described in his psalms preface, brought him face to face with the divine command and demanded unquestioning obedience, something he required both of himself and of others. He lived simultaneously in the world and before the face of God: judgement awaited, pressing upon Calvin the urgency of his calling and a sense of never having done enough. This was only intensified by his weaknesses. His body-destroying illnesses and volatile temperament were theologically interpreted and embraced within his sense of mission. This coexisting divine calling and human frailty formed his identity.

The Bible provided Calvin with the narrative of his life and it is possible to catch echoes of his lost childhood in the biblical characters about whom he wrote and preached so fulsomely. It would be too simplistic to draw direct autobiographical references from biblical reflections primarily theological in intention, yet the manner in which he spoke about childhood in the Bible does cast a refracted light on his own experiences. With his contemporaries, and much in contrast to our age, Calvin did not consider his childhood as psychologically formative: it was a brief and brutal preparation for adulthood associated primarily with ignorance, volatility and waywardness.[2] The view was common enough. The great Dutch humanist Desiderius Erasmus, to take one example, did not care for St Augustine's *Confessions*. He thought the church father talked too much about himself and discussed 'silly' and 'sordid' topics 'such as childhood, adolescence, his feelings of lust and such things.'[3] From the vantage point of a mature man who had come to see his life in providential terms, Calvin regarded childhood as something a young person traversed with the guidance of parents, teachers and masters. Without authority and discipline childish ways distort character, a perversion not easily remedied in later life.

Calvin read himself into scripture. In his account of his conversion written twenty-five years after the event, he compared himself with David, the shepherd boy called to be Israel's king.

> For although I follow David at a great distance, and come far short of equalling him, or rather, although in aspiring slowly and with great difficulty to attain to the many virtues in which he excelled, I still feel myself tarnished with the contrary vices. Yet, if I have anything in common with him, I have no hesitation in comparing myself with him. In reading the instances of his faith, patience, fervour, zeal and integrity, it has, as it ought, drawn from me unnumbered groans and sighs that I am so far from approaching them. It has, however, been of very great advantage to me to behold in him, as in a mirror, both the commencement of my calling and the continued course of my actions, so that I know more certainly that whatever that most illustrious king and prophet suffered was exhibited to me by God as an example for imitation.[4]

The image of the mirror, or speculum, recurs throughout Calvin's writings to suggest both likeness and difference. In Calvin's eyes, he and David were separated by a vast temporal and cultural gap, but, as humble men called by God to a special office, they were one. 'As he was taken from the sheepfold, and elevated to the rank of supreme authority, so God having taken me from my originally obscure and humble condition, reckoned me worthy of being invested with the honourable office of a preacher and minister of the Gospel.'[5]

In reading his own experience through the world of an ancient Israelite we are introduced to both a key aspect of Calvin's thought and a fundamental ambivalence in his character. The past, for Calvin and the other Protestant reformers, was to be reclaimed for the present. This was not to suggest the donning of Old Testament armour or Roman togas; it was the appropriation and application of what was good from earlier times to remedy the corruption and error of contemporary society. Thus Calvin found himself in the ancient figures of the Bible. Yet this was not unproblematic. A supreme confidence in his role as divinely appointed reformer of the whole Church, not simply of Geneva, sat alongside an uneasy, fretful sense of falling woefully short of that commission. Such was the man who rarely, if ever, changed his mind on a topic, yet continuously and restlessly reformulated and rewrote his thoughts in pursuit of greater clarity and insight.

Early Years

How then do we begin the story of this enigmatic figure? The sources on Calvin's youth are extremely sparse, forcing us to pick over the few known facts.[6] To open with his name, it was, like much of his life, a creation of his adult years. Jean Calvin was born Jean Cauvin and only assumed the Latinized Calvinus later in Basle, probably in imitation of the Roman proconsul named in Cicero (106–43 BCE), the great Roman statesman and orator. There was logic in this. Cicero was in many respects Calvin's guide to the classical world: it was through the Roman writer that he became familiar with much of ancient philosophy and literature, and we know from Theodore Beza's biography, written after Calvin's death, that he re-read Cicero every year. Name changing was a commonplace among humanists of the sixteenth century: Johannes Heusegen, literally house lamp, became Oecolampadius, the reformer of Basle, and Luther's colleague, Philip Schwarzerd, black earth, is better known as Melanchthon.

From his name we move to geography. Sixteenth-century Picardy comprised the lands of the Somme river basin north of Paris stretching towards the Low Countries, scene of the worst fighting of the First World War. The inhabitants spoke Picard, close to but distinct from French, and this dialect would have been John Calvin's native tongue. The Cauvin family was local to the Noyon region where his father was an industrious and ambitious man who had achieved bourgeois status in 1497, just over a decade before John's birth. Girard Cauvin, the son of a cooper, made a remarkable ascent up the social ladder through the patronage of the de Hangest family, the bishops of Noyon. Girard married Jeanne Le Franc, a devout daughter of a local innkeeper who died in 1515 when their son John was only six years old. Calvin's positive ruminations on the good fortune of those brought up in the faith may well contain a trace of boyhood reflection, for his mother encouraged her children in devotion, and his later claim that he was blinded by superstition was at the very least a back-handed compliment to the traditional piety in which he was nursed.[7]

There were plenty of children in the Cauvin family: John had one elder brother, Charles, who became a priest, though he ultimately turned his back on the Roman church, as well as two younger brothers, François and Antoine. François is thought to have died at an early age, while Antoine followed his brother to Geneva, where he became John's close confidant and business manager. Of the two sisters, very little is known: they were born to a second marriage and we know only the name of Marie, who likewise came to Geneva.[8]

Girard Cauvin held a series of significant and prominent local positions that bore testament to the effectiveness of his patronage connections: notary, procurator to the cathedral chapter, and member of the judiciary. He was closely linked to the workings of the church, though his relations with the clergy were hardly easy, and his character bespoke a man who never stepped away from a fight, a quality evidently passed on to his son. John benefited from the close relationship with the de Hangest family actively cultivated by his father, and at the age of twelve received his first ecclesiastical benefice – barrels of wheat from the revenue of La Gésine, one of the altars of the cathedral. It was a straightforward arrangement whereby Calvin received income from the church benefice without the inconvenience of having to perform any religious duty. As a means of supporting the education of a talented young boy there was nothing remarkable in this arrangement; the revenues of the church had long been in the clutches of families eager to expand their patronage networks.

Calvin owed his education to aristocratic patronage, and for this he had good reason to be grateful. However, relations with his social superiors remained deeply problematic for him all his life. In certain respects he was besotted with the nobility, utterly persuaded that they ruled as of right. At the same time, he despised their immorality, their world of religious and political compromises and their addiction to material comforts. It was a conflict between the divine order of society and the corrosive effects of sin, a tension he never resolved. With the support of the de Hangest family, he began his rudimentary studies at the Collège des Capettes in Noyon, whose pupils were recognizable by their short gowns. Here Calvin received his first instruction in Latin, an essential prerequisite for advancement in the world, whether in the church or the law.[9] Girard Cauvin well understood the importance of a good education to the further improvement of his family's standing, though there have been suggestions that the provision in Noyon was deficient. We know nothing of Calvin's days as pupil, but they were unlikely to have been pleasant. Schooling was a harsh world of rote learning and corporal punishment. Thomas More's *Utopia* of 1516 comments that English school masters would sooner beat their boys than teach them.[10]

The most widely accepted, or at least most repeated, narrative has Calvin leaving Noyon in 1523 for Paris in the company of several sons of the Montmor family. Theodore Beza, who wrote two biographies of Calvin after the reformer's death based on personal information, tells us that Calvin began his studies at the Collège de la Marche, where as an *auditeur*, one following a

course of study, he came under the direction of Maturin Cordier.[11] Although
the story is extremely patchy, attempts to deconstruct this version of events
have not proved persuasive.[12] What is not in doubt is that the young Calvin,
who his father, with the financial support of the de Hangest family, had sent
to Paris to study for the priesthood, was taught by Cordier. Later, in an affectionate dedication of his commentary on 1 Thessalonians, Calvin attributed
to providence his arrival at Cordier's feet.[13] He recalled the master's generosity
towards a young boy whose Latin was far from proficient, and that he willingly
and patiently condescended to teach the rudiments of the language, an act he
remembered as a 'singular kindness on the part of God'.[14] He had indeed been
most fortunate. Maturin Cordier represented the best of French humanist
pedagogy, committed to studies in the promotion of the Christian life and
with a particular genius for the education of the young.[15] His *A Little Book for
the Amendment of Corrupt Phrases in Our Speech* (Paris, 1530) offered a
succinct creed: 'There is a twofold reason for my undertaking this work: first,
so that every learned person might be drawn to the writing of something
better; and next, that youths may not only be stirred to speaking Latin, but
stimulated to the leading of a noble life. . . . For without piety what progress
is there in letters?'[16] The reciprocity of study and faith, so famously expressed
by Erasmus and inculcated in the young pupil in Paris, became Calvin's lifelong standard.

How unlikely it must have seemed in 1523 that the lives of this celebrated
humanist master and his young pupil would become so closely interwoven.
Labelled a 'luthérien' in 1534 Cordier was forced to flee Paris for Bordeaux
before travelling to Geneva to teach at the Collège de Rive, a position he was
required to relinquish in 1538 specifically on account of his close association
with the disgraced Calvin.[17] For four decades the two men remained in contact
and died in the same year, the master thirty years older than his former pupil.
It was not just Calvin who found inspiration in this remarkable figure: the
Savoyard Sebastian Castellio, whose initial friendship with Calvin putrefied
into raw enmity, likewise saw in Cordier the perfect mixture of humanist
education with biblical piety. Castellio named him his spiritual master.[18]

After initial studies at the Collège de la Marche, Calvin moved to the more
prestigious Collège de Montaigu at the end of 1523.[19] From its creation, the
University of Paris had been divided into four faculties (arts, medicine, law and
theology) with around forty colleges founded by patrons eager to enable young
men from their regions to study in the city.[20] All of these colleges were situated
in the Montagne Sainte-Geneviève in the Latin Quarter, whose residents had

long complained about the violent and debauched conduct of students.
Teaching took place through the colleges, but the higher faculties of theology,
law and medicine retained their pre-eminence. The university consisted of
four nations (France, Picardy, Normandy and Germany) with the French
subdivided into five provinces (Bourges, Paris, Reims, Sens and Tours).[21] Each
college had a distinct character owing to its head, or rector, men of influence
who shaped education in the late-medieval period. When Calvin arrived at
the Collège de Montaigu in the mid-1520s he entered a prestigious institution, radically reformed over the previous two decades, whose students were
predominantly intended for the church, which, as far as we know, was the
young man's path. Montaigu's two hundred students were divided into the
'domestiques' or 'galoches', who endured a brutal regime wherein they had to
work for their keep, the stipendiary students and the 'cameristes'. It was to the
last group that the talented boy from Noyon belonged, with his provincial
patronage which enabled him to pay for board and lodgings.

Under the rectorship of Noël Beda in the early years of the century
Montaigu had emerged as a centre of conservative scholarship and religion.[22]
Beda raised the Collège to become one of the elite institutions of the university, and its rigour was widely admired, if not always by its students. Among
those who passed through its doors were Erasmus and the writer François
Rabelais, while during his stay Calvin possibly coincided with the Spaniard
Ignatius Loyola, later founder of the Jesuits. Erasmus, never one for the
discomforts of life, left a scathing account of his experience. 'In the middle of
winter, they were fed a little bit of bread and made to drink from the well
water which was dangerously spoiled, when it had not been frozen by the
morning cold. I knew many people who, even today, are not able to recover
from the illnesses they contracted at Montaigu. . . . I will not talk about the
cruelty with which they whipped the scholars, even when they had done
nothing.'[23]

The Montaigu of Rabelais, Calvin and Loyola in the 1520s was presided
over by Pierre Tempête, infamous for his cruelty and rabid insistence upon an
austere monastic regime. Students were to rise at four in the morning and
begin their lessons an hour later. At seven mass was heard, followed by a
meagre breakfast of bread. From eight till midday the major part of the
instruction in the elements of the arts curriculum took place. Following
another meal the students passed the afternoon honing their debating skills in
public disputations under the watchful eyes of their masters. An evening
repast was followed by further study and prayers, and finally bed at nine. It

may have been brutal, but it instilled in Calvin a disciplined pattern of life and work he would maintain until his death. Unless prevented by illness, the mature Calvin rose daily around four and his long work day was punctuated by prayer and simple meals.

The students at Montaigu had a reputation for submissiveness, less a virtue than a shrewd recognition that their masters controlled the levers of religious patronage. As most of the students were being prepared for service in the church, good behaviour, diligence and the approbation of Tempête marked the path to a secure future. These young men were cultivated in the spirit of Beda to become defenders of religious orthodoxy against heresy, and to serve as obedient servants of the church. It is inviting to speculate on the extent to which Calvin's later ambivalence towards the patronage system was rooted in the authoritarian atmosphere of Montaigu. Certainly, he did not encounter at Montaigu the evangelical currents coursing through the streets and homes of Paris in the 1520s, but they were not far away.

Exactly what Calvin studied at Montaigu has led to much speculation, but it has remained just that: speculation. Attempts have been made to connect him to a range of theological lines of thought such as nominalism and late-medieval Augustinism.[24] It has been suggested that he studied Thomas Aquinas, Duns Scotus, Gregory of Rimini and other luminaries of medieval theology, but again nothing can be established with certainty. It is not even known whether he studied theology in Paris at all. It appears most likely that during his years at Montaigu he followed a course of studies in arts in which he was instructed in the traditional curriculum of the trivium (grammar, logic and rhetoric) and the quadrivium (arithmetic, music, geometry, astronomy). This would have served as preparation for the higher study of theology, as his father originally intended – a path he was, however, soon to abandon.

The France of Calvin's Youth

It is tempting for a biographer to fill gaps in a life with background context and suggest tendentious connections. Yet if we are to understand the formation of Calvin's character, some knowledge of the intense, exciting yet perilous world of Renaissance France is essential. While we possess precious few details about his life in these years, we know that he was profoundly affected by the whirlwind of events he witnessed as a student. The French religious world into which he was born was marked by the bewildering contrasts found throughout late-medieval Western Europe. The Hundred Years' War (1337–1453) had left a scarred landscape across France of ruined monastic houses and parish churches that even a half-century had barely healed. Clerical education was often miserable, the higher offices of the church frequently held by unqualified scions of noble families, and the religious orders were in disarray. The church was beset by endless jurisdictional conflicts between bishops, cathedral chapters, monastic houses, the universities and the Parlements. The Parlements were legal bodies which had emerged out of the Middle Ages to administer laws and propose edicts and, consequently, frequently found themselves in conflict with the monarchy. The largest and most significant was the Parlement of Paris, whose jurisdiction covered much of northern France. Things were so bad in 1499 that the University of Paris went on strike. At the same time, however, genuine and powerful voices for reform could be heard. King Charles VIII sponsored synods during the 1490s that examined spiritual, doctrinal, institutional, legal and fiscal problems. His hopes of restoring the French church, however, fell victim to his political ambitions, and following the French invasion of Italy in 1494 reform plans vanished into the smoke of artillery fire.

The endemic problem within the late-medieval French church was authority. Paralyzing conflicts over the right to make appointments to offices went to the highest level of relations between the king and the papacy. In 1438 the Pragmatic Sanction of Bourges had assured considerable independence from Rome for the French church: most papal reservations were abolished, appeals to Rome were forbidden before all legal processes in France were exhausted, and the election of bishops, abbots and priors was restored to chapters. The relative independence of the French church, known as the Gallican liberties, also heightened the tension between the king and the institutions of the church within his own lands.

In 1516 Francis I strengthened his hand with the Concordat of Bologna by which Pope Leo X granted the French crown significantly greater control over the church. A storm broke as the Parlement of Paris, fearful that the king would trample under foot the liberties of the Pragmatic Sanction, dragged its feet for two years before registering the Concordat.[25] After the king had forced the Parlement into line in 1518, the university rose in revolt only to be brutally crushed and warned, in no uncertain terms, that further meddling in the affairs of state would lead to loss of privileges.[26] The defenders of the Gallican church had good reason to worry. The king possessed the right of nomination to the 114 episcopal and archiepiscopal seats of France, as well as to eight hundred abbeys: papal approval was a mere formality.

The king's relationship to the church dominated the intellectual world of France, embracing political theories of the Renaissance, the reform of the legal system and humanist-inspired religious ideas. Monarchical power had its strongest voices in Claude de Seyssel and Guillaume Budé. Seyssel's *Monarchy of France* (1519), based on long years of royal service, formed a comprehensive study of government in its social, political and economic dimensions.[27] Seyssel argued for the sacred nature of the French monarchy and closely linked Gallican liberties with royal authority, making the French king the defender of the Christian faith and the Sorbonne the pre-eminent theological body. For Budé, as for his friend Desiderius Erasmus, the humanist studies of literature, history and language were not mere private pursuits of the elite; far more than that, they were the very means by which society could be made sacred. He laid out a new path by which France would embrace the glorious legal tradition of Rome. His work inspired and enthralled a new generation which flocked to the legal faculties, including the young John Calvin; it was the most exciting intellectual development of the age – a new vision for France. In 1513, Budé presented to the young Francis I a manuscript entitled *De l'institution du Prince*, in which he laid out a programme for the Renaissance prince.[28] Here he put forward the case that humanist studies formed an essential foundation of the monarch's authority and, in a manner echoed later in Calvin's Seneca commentary, Budé argued against institutional restraints on the king's authority. Such bonds were not necessary, he continued optimistically, as the humanist arts would teach Francis to be a naturally just and wise ruler. In other words, the king was not simply to be a patron, but a student, in order to become the new Solomon.

In this endeavour Francis proved a willing pupil.[29] Humanism as it had emerged from the Italian Renaissance embraced a passion for ancient litera-ture, the eloquence of rhetoric and the writing of elegant, classical Latin.[30] The new learning flourished in France, though largely outside the halls of the universities. From the start of his reign the king sought to found a royal college dedicated to humanist studies, making Paris the undisputed centre of learning, ruled over by a true Renaissance monarch.[31] In 1517 Budé undertook to tempt Erasmus, Europe's leading scholar, to Paris with generous words. 'What a distinction! How it will redound to the high standing of scholars as a whole, if learning like yours recommends you to the greatest and most illustrious of monarchs and he seeks you out and summons you to a land afar off!'[32] Erasmus did not bite, rightly anxious of the proximity of his enemies at the theological faculty in Paris, the Sorbonne. The issue of the humanist college was further complicated by the fierce reaction against evangelical ideas in Paris during the 1520s, but Budé pressed on and from 1522 led a vigorous campaign that resulted in the establishment of the royal lectureships in 1530.

The Birth of the Evangelical Movement

Institutional troubles were only one aspect of the religious world of late-medieval France. In common with England and the German lands, devotional activities of every conceivable sort flourished.[33] The fifteenth century was the great age of preachers who moved through the cities and towns, not only encouraging the people to reform their lives but also providing a good deal of entertainment. Large numbers of the faithful went on pilgrimages either to local shrines or to great centres such as Saint-Michel. In church communities increasing control over the affairs of the parish was exerted by a laity eager to play an enhanced role in procuring its salvation, a development little opposed by the lower clergy. The Eucharist was the most powerful symbol of all. Although most people took communion only once a year, its sacramental and ritual force was evident in every church.[34]

France was deeply affected by what is known as the Northern Renaissance, where the reverence for ancient culture flowed into movements for religious renewal. Erasmus, with his belief in the harmony of pagan learning with Christian piety, was the greatest and most celebrated exponent. His *Adages* and Greek New Testament represented all that was exhilarating and fresh, and from Poland to England young scholars were inspired to embrace classical learning in the service of church and society.

The growing role of the laity in late-medieval religion led to a lucrative market for French vernacular devotional and instructional works.[35] Most notable in circulation were a translation of the Bible by Jean de Rély (1495), frequently reprinted in the early sixteenth century, and a 1507 gloss on the letters of Paul intended for the reader with no Latin. In addition, literate Christians had access to works such as the *Exposition of the Sermon Delivered by Our Lord on the Mount* (1515) by François Regnault, friend of Erasmus. Jean Gerson (1363–1429), perhaps the greatest French religious voice of the fifteenth century, remained a favourite, and his *Opus Tripartitum*, an instructional work for poor clergy and laity, continued to be printed through the 1520s and early 1530s.[36]

In 1518 the Luther controversy arrived in France.[37] The Wittenberg professor had defied the papacy with his call for reform. The writings of the

German were formally condemned by Rome and by theologians in Louvain in the Spanish Netherlands and Cologne in Germany in 1519, but in France itself the response was slower, and the Sorbonne did not act until 1521. By that time Luther's works had been circulating for several years in the kingdom.[38] The Basle printer Johann Froben reported to Luther that six hundred copies of his books had been sent to France and Spain and that they had been well received, even by some members of the theological faculty.[39] These works, however, were in Latin, and their impact should not be overemphasized. There are hints that writings by Luther and Melanchthon were translated into French before 1521, but the evidence for this has been lost.[40] The impact of these prophetic voices of reform was significantly enhanced, however, by the gloomy atmosphere in France. In the early 1520s harvests failed, war raged, plague took a grim toll, and both the Parlement and the Sorbonne feared social unrest.[41] The infiltration of Lutheran ideas, in the eyes of horrified Catholic leaders, was closely associated with the woes of the kingdom, yet another sign of divine disfavour.

Events in France, however, did not ape the German reformation. Indeed, it is easy to overplay Luther's role; he was not the lead actor, as the tardiness of the Sorbonne to condemn him demonstrated. He was foreign, and many of his ideas set in the German context were of little relevance in France. Luther's more polemical texts, such as *On the Babylonian Captivity of the Christian Church* or *Address to the Christian Nobility of the German Nation* and his attacks on the papacy, were not printed in France, where the subject lacked urgency. In contrast, there was clear preference for his more devotional and edifying writings.[42] His works were often printed together with those of Erasmus, and the two men, much to their mutual mortification, were linked as proponents of a scripture-based Christianity. Consequently, the Luther known in France was quite different from his persona in Germany, where he was a national hero.[43]

The greater and more immediate threat, as far as the theology faculty was concerned, was posed by Jacques Lefèvre d'Etaples, a native Frenchman with many admirers.[44] A native of Picardy like Calvin, Lefèvre had taught philosophy in Paris at the Collège du Cardinal-Lemoine from 1490 to 1507 and travelled to Italy to study classical Greek literature and Neoplatonic philosophy. In Paris, he was the pre-eminent scholar of Aristotle, possessing good, but not flawless, Greek.[45] From 1507 he lived in the Saint-Germain-des-Prés Abbey in Paris, where his former pupil Guillaume Briçonnet was abbot, devoting himself to the editing of texts, a task he regarded as his vocation. His *Psalterium quintuplex* (five Latin versions of the psalms), issued in 1509 and revised in 1513, established Lefèvre's reputation across Europe; it was carefully read and annotated by two young men later to become reformers, Martin Luther and Huldrych Zwingli.[46] Lefèvre also wrote a commentary on the Pauline epistles in which he articulated a distinctly spiritualist tendency which downplayed the role of sacraments and the institutional church. In the second edition he challenged Erasmus' edition of the New Testament, which had appeared in 1516, criticizing the Dutchman on a series of points of interpretation. A celebrated dispute broke out between the two men, the implications of which went far beyond their studies.[47] Lefèvre represented France and its intellectual achievements, and his argument with Erasmus was embraced by many with patriotic fervour.

It was Lefèvre, not Luther, who shaped French evangelical thought in the 1520s, and the German reformer's writings were read through the lens of the French humanist. Lefèvre's importance lay not only in his call for the renewal of spirituality and his translations of scripture into French; he was an iconic figure – a symbol of French humanist achievement and the possibility of church reform. His was an Olympian status which neither Erasmus nor Luther could achieve, and it made Lefèvre all the more dangerous in the eyes of his opponents. Luther himself had been an admirer of the Frenchman's work on Paul, though not without reservations, believing that Lefèvre had not fully understood the doctrine of justification.[48] Lefèvre, for his part, read the works of the German and Swiss reformers with approval, though without any inclination to leave the Catholic church.[49] By the mid-1520s there were clear lines of contact between the followers of Lefèvre in France and reformers in the empire, a vast collection of territorial principalities, imperial cities, and ecclesiastical states that extended from the Baltic to the Swiss lands.

Led by Noël Beda, Sorbonne opposition to the evangelicals gathered pace.[50] In 1523 the theological faculty met 103 times, far more often than usual, to condemn heretical ideas in the writings of Luther, Erasmus, Melanchthon, Caroli and Lefèvre.[51] The Sorbonne took upon itself a new role in French religious politics; whereas previously it had been the defender of orthodox doctrine, increasingly it became an inquisition, not hesitating to attack prominent figures. In August 1523 Beda led the faculty to condemn all editions of scripture in Greek, Hebrew and French, and by April the following year discussion of Lefèvre's work was forbidden. Beda was not satisfied, and in the autumn a forceful attempt to have Erasmus' writings condemned was nearly successful.[52] In what would prove one of its worst decisions, the Sorbonne proscribed translations of the Bible into French; this would later provide the evangelicals with an open door through which to send a flood of vernacular Bibles into the country. The king was put in a difficult position, torn between his love of humanist scholarship and his commitment to preserve his kingdom from the taint of heresy. Francis was loath to accept Beda's conclusion that humanism was the Trojan horse of heresy, yet he, like many others in France, was shocked to the core by the manner in which separate churches had emerged from the German and Swiss reformations and by the social and political turmoil caused by the Peasants' War of 1525 in Germany, where radical religious ideas played a key role. The situation was further complicated by the king's beloved sister, Marguerite of Navarre, who was closely linked to a group of reform-minded figures, known as the Circle of Meaux.[53]

Reform and the Meaux Circle

With its stunning gothic cathedral, built between the twelfth and sixteenth centuries, Meaux lies twenty-five miles north-east of Paris. Its diocese and bishop occupied an important place in the French medieval church, and from 1516 the incumbent was Guillaume Briçonnet, who belonged to precisely the type of aristocratic family promoted by Francis I.[54] His high standing was reflected in his involvement in the negotiations with Leo X leading to the Concordat of Bologna in 1516, the year he was appointed to the diocese of Meaux. Unlike many of his contemporary bishops, however, Briçonnet held strong and sincere religious convictions. His reforms emphasized preaching and the reading of scripture, noble goals very much in the spirit of endless late-medieval reform legislation; the difference was that Briçonnet was intent on their implementation.[55] His primary interest was, however, in the restoration of spirituality and morality, not the introduction of Luther's teachings, and in 1523 he forbade priests in his diocese from possessing books by the German reformer. The closeness of his reform programme to currents entering France from the empire, however, aroused the ire of the Sorbonne.

Upon arriving in Meaux Briçonnet undertook a series of reforms aimed at improving standards among the clergy, and it was in this cause that he invited several humanist-minded reformers to his diocese. Lefèvre arrived in Meaux in 1521, following difficulties in Paris, and joined a group that included the Hebraist François Vatable, Gérard Roussel, the court preacher Michel d'Arande, the Sorbonne doctor Martial Masurier and Guillaume Farel. Farel, whose parents had at one time intended him for military service, had come to Briçonnet's attention through Lefèvre. The Meaux Circle, as it became known, was not a formal institution with records so much as a spiritual fraternity of personal contacts and correspondents. Dedicated to the study of the Bible, this diverse group of figures drew inspiration from Lefèvre's work on the Pauline Epistles, and without question the venerable scholar's French translation of the New Testament was its greatest success. Between 1523 and 1525 it was printed four times in Paris, once in Anvers and once in Basle, and across France over the following decade. Lefèvre followed his New Testament with a translation of the psalms in 1524 and the Old Testament in 1528, opening the gates to a torrent of scriptural publications followed by works of rudimentary religious instruction. Another member of the Meaux Circle led the way: Guillaume Farel prepared an exposition of the Lord's Prayer and Creed first printed in 1524 and then revised and printed in Paris the following year.[56] Much of the circle's effort was devoted to preaching to the laity, and its ideal was Christ-centred, straightforward exposition of scripture. As early as 1523 cracks began to appear in the plaster as some members of the circle grew more radical and departed to be replaced by men such as Matthieu Saunier, who would die at the stake in 1525, and the Paris doctor Pierre Caroli, who later made endless trouble for Farel and Calvin. Farel, influenced by the theology of the Swiss reformer Huldrych Zwingli, was moving in a different direction. The voices of French religious reform were growing discordant.

A royal connection preserved this circle of evangelical churchmen. Marguerite of Navarre was a devout and talented woman who shared her brother's love of learning, but her interests ran more to religion. Deeply attracted to ideas of Lefèvre, she became involved with the Meaux Circle from 1521, inviting Michel d'Arande to court to preach, and arranging for the distribution of Lefèvre's Bible translations and Briçonnet's pastoral letters.[57] Marguerite acknowledged that she and these men were 'united in the same spirit and same faith'.[58]

The crushing French defeat at the hands of the Spanish at Pavia in 1525 left Francis I imprisoned in Madrid, and in Paris the regency of his mother, Louise of Savoy, was hostile to Meaux. The opponents of the Navarrists (as the circle around Margarerite was known) were not slow to exploit the opportunity; the defeat at Pavia was seen as divine punishment for the toleration of false religion and the Parlement of Paris demanded that tribunals be set up to smoke out heretics. Louise was entirely sympathetic, and with papal support the Parlement was granted control of heresy cases. From 1526 the persecution of suspected heretics intensified: books were censored, printers and booksellers threatened, and evangelical literature publicly burned. Leading members of the Meaux Circle were to be prosecuted for heresy. Francis, from prison in Madrid, attempted to intervene on behalf of the humanists, but to no avail. Many of the Navarrists, including Lefèvre, Roussel, Caroli, Farel and d'Arande, fled to Strasbourg, then part of the empire, where they were received hospitably.[59]

With his return to France in 1526, however, Francis I continued to support evangelical writers, much to the consternation of their opponents. The Meaux Circle was gone, but Marguerite remained a crucial patron: Briçonnet became royal tutor, Roussel a personal chaplain and d'Arande a bishop. But not everything remained as before. The former allies divided sharply between moderate voices for reform within the Church and those, such as Farel, drawn towards the more radical Swiss line of reform which abandoned any hope for reform within the Roman church. The difference between these two parties formed the religious topography of France in Calvin's formative years: the majority, who believed that conformity with established powers offered the best hope of transforming the church, and a radical minority, which had turned its back on the Roman church. For the latter there was no place in the kingdom, and they were forced into exile. Farel and others moved to the French-speaking lands of the Swiss Confederation from where they would launch a notorious strike in 1534.

The 1520s were torrid times as the evangelical cause fought for its life in France, but we need to keep a sense of perspective. The evangelists' publications amounted to only a small proportion of what was printed in France at that time, roughly 80 of the 2,500 works produced in the period 1521–30.[60] Nevertheless, a small number of publications could generate a great deal of fear, particularly as the authorities had no idea how many within the kingdom were sympathetic to the reformers. In March 1521, before the writings of Luther and Melanchthon had been condemned, the Parlement declared that no religious books could be printed without prior examination by the faculty of theology. In truth, the evangelicals' best defence was the inability of the Parlement and the faculty to enforce such draconian regulations.[61] Further, the Parlement of Paris possessed only limited authority; similar edicts would have to be issued from the provincial parlements, and Lyon, for example, with its proud tradition of civic independence, was unlikely to accept such a decree from the capital.[62]

Printers played an unsung role in these early years of the reform movement, though it is not always easy to determine their motives. Many acted from deep religious convictions and risked all to produce evangelical literature for their countrymen. For others, religious sentiments combined easily with profit margins. The market for popular Reformation authors was great, and there was money to be made. Mostly the printers formed smallish circles of friends and acquaintances, yet with their extensive web of foreign contacts they were able to ensure a constant flow of literature into France which passed under the radar of the censors. Basle and Strasbourg were important bases for the importation of books and pamphlets in French.[63] Such publications circulated in France as the authorities struggled to find an effective response.

We cannot attach the adolescent Calvin to any of these movements in the 1520s and we know nothing of his religious disposition. On the great events that took place he has left no commentary, but even the college walls would not have shielded him from the vicissitudes in the capital. And in his own life an important change had taken place. He left Paris for Orléans intending to study law.

CHAPTER TWO

Among the Princes of Law

CALVIN'S SHIFT from theology to law in the late 1520s has long confounded historians, largely because he has left almost no clues as to why and when it took place.[1] His biographers Beza and Nicolas Colladon provide a range of explanations, possibly drawn from personal knowledge: that Calvin changed course out of reverence for his father (Beza); that he moved away from theology out of contempt for its corrupt nature (Colladon); and, finally, that both Calvin and his father changed their minds (Beza, second version).[2] The best-known story, and from Calvin's own hand, is that his father opted for a career in the law for his son on the grounds that it was more lucrative. It is a brutal assessment of paternal motives, with little corroborating evidence, that no doubt speaks of Calvin's complex relationship with his father. There is no record of a confrontation, and Calvin certainly played the dutiful son when his father lay dying, returning home at the end. It remains, however, one of the many mistier aspects of Calvin's life. For a talented and ambitious young man the study of law was a natural path, and there is no evidence that he did anything other than pursue it eagerly. Yet, in his retelling of the story many years later in 1557, he attributes ambition to his father, not himself. Sustained by more than his memories, Calvin crafted an account that exonerated him from the sin of ambition, against which he had been repeatedly forced to defend himself.

Equally mysterious is the figure of Pierre-Robert Olivétan (Olivetanus), whom Beza suggests played a key role in Calvin's religious formulation. Related by blood – they were cousins – and both from Noyon, the two men were in Paris and Orléans together, though Pierre-Robert studied classical and biblical languages. The nature of their relationship eludes easy conclusions, for although Olivetanus was attached to the theology of the Swiss reformer Huldrych Zwingli by the mid-1530s, we cannot assume this to be the case when he was with Calvin a few years earlier.[3] It remains an attractive possibility, though, that Calvin's shift to biblical humanism was brought about by a member of his own family, but that is conjecture.

More certain is Calvin's arrival in early 1528 in Orléans, the ancient city named for the Roman Emperor Marcus Aurelius 80 miles south of Paris. The law faculty of the thirteenth-century university, one of the oldest outside Italy, was among the most distinguished in northern Europe. The magnetic force for Calvin and his friends was the great Pierre de l'Estoile, long recognized as the outstanding French jurist of his age.[4] A man of the church, having entered a religious house following the death of his wife, L'Estoile held the position of vicar-general of the diocese of Orléans. In this towering figure, Calvin was exposed to the complex interrelationship of legal studies, the church and politics. De l'Estoile was no solitary inhabitant of an ivory tower. As vicar-general he participated in the campaigns against heresy launched by the king and the Sorbonne: scholarship, teaching and persecution were without distinction of purpose. Deeply wedded to tradition, he had no sympathy for the evangelical cause, and, in common with many of his generation, held church reform to mean the rooting out of abuses, not the overturning of authority. Whatever Calvin's religious views were at this point, and we do not know, the hostility of his teacher to the religious innovations of his age did not in any way diminish his respect for the man he would call 'the Prince of French lawyers'.

Orléans offered Calvin a great deal intellectually and personally. In addition to the opportunity to study under a leading mind, he cultivated close friendships with fellow law students François Daniel, François de Connan and Nicolas Duchemin, as well as the German Melchior Wolmar, a brilliant scholar a dozen years Calvin's senior and, it seems, his first teacher of Greek.[5] This circle of intimates would play significant roles in Calvin's later life, though with the exception of Wolmar none would embrace the Reformation. Calvin was invited into the home of Daniel and shared accommodation with Duchemin. We can only wonder about their discussions, but without doubt they frequently ranged from the topics of de l'Estoile's lectures to the teachings of Erasmus and Lefèvre on the Bible and the perilous state of religion in Francis I's kingdom.

Calvin probably left Orléans in the spring of 1529 for Bourges, where the flamboyant Italian Andrea Alciati had arrived to teach law at the university.

Bourges in those years had become a haven for reformist thought under the patronage of Marguerite of Navarre. Wolmar, Daniel and Duchemin all later joined Calvin in the city while storm clouds gathered in Paris as the Sorbonne turned on the royal lecturers of the Collège Royal (Budé, Nicolas Cop, Pierre Danès and François Vatable), the spiritual disciples of Lefèvre.

Calvin's legal studies cast in relief the central intellectual and spiritual questions of the French Renaissance, as witnessed in the different approaches advocated by his rival French and Italian teachers. Both were exponents of humanist methods, but in quite different ways. De l'Estoile remained deeply wedded to the medieval tradition of legal commentary. Rejecting the Renaissance emphasis on rhetoric and historical analysis, he favoured a method in which the sixth-century body of Roman law, known as the *Corpus iuris civilis*, was interpreted according to genus and species.[6] This meant that material was gathered together under specific headings, or topics, in a manner in which little attention was given to its historical development.

Alciati, whom Calvin encountered in Bourges, though only briefly, offered a different view not only of how ancient texts should be read, but also of the relationship of the past to the present. A professional jurist and humanist who had studied in Pavia and Bologna, Alciati was a vital transalpine link between the Italian and French intellectual worlds.[7] Unlike de l'Estoile and his careful mining of texts for crucial terms, he embraced a more bravado approach based on conjecture and intuition.[8] This shocked many of his opponents, who regarded him as something of a dilettante picking and choosing his way through ancient texts. Alciati, however, believed himself to be doing something rather different. Like de l'Estoile, he regarded the *Corpus iuris civilis* as a coherent body of work, and argued that it was the interpreter's task to reveal the connectedness of passages. At the same time, he rejected de l'Estoile's faith in an underlying stratum of logical meaning. Rather, words and passages were to be examined stylistically (rhetorically) and with regard to particular circumstances (historically) in order to discern particular meanings. That this approach might reveal contradictions did not disturb him. He believed that this method of interpretation enabled the scholar to distil 'proper' interpretations from the mass of evidence.

The differences between Alciati and de l'Estoile went beyond the lecture hall when the Italian savagely attacked the Frenchman in print. At this point, the intellectual exchange between the two scholars became personal for Calvin. His friend Nicolas Duchemin wrote his *Antapologia adversus Aurelii Albucii* as a defence of de l'Estoile and invited Calvin to contribute a preface.

The text, probably first drafted in 1529, though not published till 1531, was a robust expression of fidelity to the methods espoused by de l'Estoile. Calvin took care of the arrangements for the production of the work by Gérard Morrhy, a minor Paris printer, and his preface, signed and dated 6 March 1531, provides us with a rare opportunity to locate him precisely. His contribution took the form of a letter to his fellow student François de Connan in which he sought to act as a mediator between the two sides in the dispute, thus curiously putting himself at odds with Duchemin's intention of defending de l'Estoile.[9] This perversity in undermining the text is our first glimpse of Calvin's intellectual independence. The preface demonstrates his excellent command of Latin prose and familiarity with classical references.[10] More significantly, it reveals an unwillingness to submit to the intellectual agenda of another.

Calvin might well have found Alciati the more attractive figure, given that the Italian represented the best of humanist legal scholarship in the tradition of Budé and that his emphasis on the historical and contextual in reading texts became central to Calvin's later work. Yet this was not the case. In common with many of his fellow students, Calvin was offended by Alciati's contempt for France and French culture, and the preface opens with an enthusiastic endorsement of de l'Estoile's learning and character. The great man's encyclopaedic knowledge of Roman law had impressed the young Calvin in Orléans – it was a form of learning he would emulate in committing to memory most of scripture and an extraordinary amount of the church fathers. Whether Calvin really disliked Alciati or not cannot be satisfactorily established in the sources, and the issue is in any event not important. De l'Estoile's significance for Calvin went beyond the mere scholarly: he represented the Gallic church and its proud tradition of independence from Rome. Calvin the humanist was also Calvin the Frenchman.

There were also other reasons for the preface. In the spring of 1531, Calvin, now 'Maistre Jean Cauvin, licentié en lois', had no clear direction, though possible career paths lay open in the law, the church and scholarship. We have no evidence whatsoever that he intended to enter the church, so the choice was most likely between jurist and scholar. For these professions he needed patrons, but they were in short supply, especially for a provincial student of no reputation.

The period of legal studies belongs, for the historian, to the lost years of Calvin's life, and we are left only with fragments, including Beza's portrait of the young student. The preface to Duchemin's work reveals the range of

Calvin's learning – classical and legal references abound – and Beza draws the reader's attention to his extraordinary appetite for knowledge and intellectual energy:

> He [Calvin] worked hard at his university studies and there are still trust-worthy men alive today who were on intimate terms with him at Orléans and who can testify that he often stayed up till midnight to study and ate hardly any supper in his eagerness for his work. Each morning when he woke, he would stay in bed for a few moments while he recalled to mind all that he had studied the previous day and mulled it over, so to speak.[11]

Beza adds that Calvin's regime of study prepared him for his 'profound scholarship in the study of Holy Scripture, and helped him to develop the remarkable powers of memory which were so evident in his later life'. The cost of these long hours of study was lasting damage to his health.

Calvin's rigorous legal training left its imprint on every aspect of his life. It sharpened his mind to interpret texts and form precise arguments based on humanist methods; it provided him with a thorough grasp of subjects, ranging from marriage and property to crime. He was taught to frame legislation, write constitutions and offer legal opinions, all of which would loom large in his Genevan career. But the legacy was also intellectual. It was from the law that he would draw some of his most fundamental theological concepts, such as the Holy Spirit as 'witness', the nature of 'justification', God as 'legislator' and 'judge', and Christ as the 'perpetual advocate'.[12] The philological and historical methods drawn from both de l'Estoile and Alciati would become the foundations of his biblical commentaries as he revolutionized the art of interpreting scripture.

Seneca

Shortly after completing the preface to Duchemin's work, Calvin travelled to Noyon to tend to his dying father. During his stay in his native city in the summer of 1531 he worked on a commentary on Seneca's *De clementia* which he had probably started before his departure from Bourges. While still a law student Calvin expressed his ambition to enter the lists of French humanism by taking on the great Erasmus on his home ground: he sought to improve upon the Dutchman's 1529 edition of Seneca's *De clementia*. The dedication of Calvin's commentary to Claude de Hangest, Abbot of Saint-Eloi, offers an illuminating portrait of the young man undertaking an audacious project while his father lay close to death. The choice of patron made perfect sense; the de Hangest family had long supported the Cauvins and had financed John's early education in Paris. The abbot was a nobleman about the same age as Calvin and the family was prominent in Noyon; successive generations had served as bishops.[13] This time, however, the relationship proved more complex as the young author, eager to publish his first work, quickly saw that the patronage of de Hangest was insufficient to see the commentary through the press. Calvin was forced to sell off part of his patrimony and to obtain a loan from Nicolas Duchemin. The book was eventually printed in Paris in early 1532, but the stress, and humiliation, of the situation had an unpleasant physical effect: Calvin, not for the last time in his life, was laid low by severe diarrhoea.[14]

The dedicatory letter of the Seneca commentary reflects a conflicted mind. Hardly mentioning Claude de Hangest, Calvin avoided the traditional paean of praise for a patron's learning and virtue.[15] The warmest he could manage was to laud de Hangest's 'lively and generous disposition' and a 'memory well stocked' – hardly florid words in the tradition of Renaissance writers, who generally fell over themselves to win the hearts and purses of potential bene-factors. In contrast, Calvin offered a form of inverted praise, full of distaste for flattery and spiced with an evident sense of intellectual superiority. Rather than concentrating on his patron, he wrote of himself and Seneca, reflecting on his own situation and defending his decision to write. 'There are those who publish through arrogance with little to say,' he claimed, but as for himself, he was 'an ordinary person from the ranks of the people, endowed with moderate, nay rather a modest learning, and having nothing in me which could excite any future hopes of celebrity. In fact, it was precisely this consciousness of my obscurity, which had induced me so far to abstain from publishing anything.'[16] Not only did Calvin rather perversely deny the patron his due right in receiving the work, he seemed very close to cutting the ground from under his own feet as author. This is not false modesty, a trait Calvin never mastered, but it did reflect a troubled attitude towards ambition and the pursuit of glory in the humanist sphere.[17] Although the sources are silent, it is tempting to believe that his reading of Paul, whom he would later cite on matters of ambition, was already having some effect.[18]

The choice of Seneca as a subject was significant and instructive. The Roman Stoic philosopher and statesman (4 BCE–65 CE) was an adviser to the Emperor Nero, and his work on clemency, written late in life, was a favourite of medieval and Renaissance authors. Seneca was central to humanist discourses on good government, and Calvin was fully aware that Erasmus had recently completed two commentaries on *De clementia*. Although Calvin did suggest that his readers would find some corrections to the Dutchman's text, the argument that this was some sort of point scoring with the most pre-eminent humanist in Europe does not fully explain his intentions. Calvin knew perfectly well that this first venture into print would not turn the world on its head – he was a nobody. Nevertheless, he made a patriotic appeal by praising Budé as the greatest humanist of his day and placing Erasmus second.[19] The commentary was intended to demonstrate to a learned French audience Calvin's legal, philological and philosophical skills. But the young scholar was also working to make sense of his education, to formulate his own understanding of the relationship between classical culture and contemporary society, to find a way forward. It was the beginning point of a long intellectual journey.

Seneca's short treatise is divided into two books in the form of advice to the young Emperor Nero, who had ruled for only three years. It is a series of reflections on the nature of power and justice and how they are best employed by the prince seeking not to become a tyrant. In true Stoic fashion, Seneca advised Nero to stand above the passions that rule the lives of lesser men, for the prince is subject to no laws and must, consequently, govern himself. Measured liberality (*liberalitas*) was essential in bestowing honours and punishments, while punishment must never be an act of revenge but rather medicine for the offending individual and community. Freedom from the passions brings wisdom that enables the ruler to do what is properly just. Clemency is a virtue that belongs to princes, for they alone can temper the full rigour of the law with a mercy stemming from their understanding of what is best in each case. Seneca urged Nero to practise clemency to make his people love him. Tyrants, in contrast, must forever fear their enemies and can never rely on the support of those they coerce to serve them. Cruelty does not belong to the office of the prince, while clemency, as the source of peace, makes the ruler 'like the gods'.

What did Calvin make of this text? In truth, he made a great deal on various fronts. In terms of scholarship, it was a golden opportunity to demonstrate the learning acquired both as a student and as a diligent reader of classical and Christian texts. His commentary overflows with etymological and grammatical notes in which he set out his stall as an interpreter. He elucidated approximately fifty rhetorical terms and sought to demonstrate how Seneca's style was profoundly shaped by the author's rhetorical intentions. This is most clearly seen in the discussion of 'accommodation', the manner in which Seneca adapted his message to his audience. In *De clementia*, as Calvin noted, the Roman orator addressed an emperor not known for either his wisdom or the practice of virtue. To overcome this rather considerable hurdle while avoiding angering Nero, Seneca, according to Calvin, resorted to flattery in order that the emperor might see himself in the model of the good prince. Flattery gives way to instruction as the guise of praise and compliments enabled Seneca to advance his philosophical positions. The idea that the teacher or preacher must accommodate the needs and disposition of his audience remained Calvin's lifelong conviction.

The technical notes are accompanied by a large body of historical, philosophical and literary commentary. Calvin's love of history is immediately apparent in the attention to context he lavishes on events mentioned in *De clementia*, as well as in his lengthy and full descriptions of Roman institutions, law and culture. Although Calvin also made considerable use of Livy, Tacitus and Plutarch, his primary source was the second-century Roman historian Suetonius (69–122?) with his pithy and dramatic accounts of the first eleven emperors in his *Lives of the Caesars*, crafted in a lucid and sharp style which would certainly have appealed to Calvin, especially as this was the very issue on which he most severely criticized Seneca. In philosophical matters Calvin's own study of Aristotle, particularly the *Ethics*, is evident throughout, as is his knowledge of other schools of ancient philosophy, though much of this was probably mediated through his reading of Cicero and Pliny the Elder.

Throughout the commentary Calvin sprinkled his text with proverbial wisdom drawn from ancient writers, often to humorous effect. At one point when he wished to ridicule the superstitious nature of Roman religion and its reliance on auguries, he quoted Cato's observation that priests charged with cutting open animals to divine the gods' will must hardly have been able to keep from laughing when they met one another the street. In addition to the ancient sources he also made considerable use of contemporary works. Of Erasmus' writings he must have known a considerable amount. Not only was he entirely familiar with the Dutchman's own editions of Seneca, but the *Adages* formed a central part of his reading. We might conjecture whether the vast array of classical literature to which reference is made in the commentary speaks for the depth of knowledge of this twenty-year-old. Doubtless Calvin was a voracious reader who threw himself into the study of the classics, but much of what he used came from readily available source collections. In addition to Erasmus' *Adages*, he was able, for example, to draw material from

Philippus Beroaldus the Elder's commentaries on Suetonius, Apuleius and Cicero. He also made extensive use of Gratian's *Decretum*, with its collection of sources, which he would have known well from his legal studies. There was no shame in this common practice of Renaissance writers.[20] Calvin was also almost entirely dependent on Latin material as he had not yet learned Greek to a very high standard.[21]

Calvin was favourably, though not uncritically, disposed towards Seneca. In the preface he focused directly on the Roman statesman's reputation and character, describing him as the 'best of authors' who had been unjustly attacked and mocked. Quintilian (c. 35–100), the orator and legal writer, had defamed Seneca on account of personal enmities, yet even he recognized Seneca's talent. What Calvin found attractive in Seneca was his 'vast erudition and signal eloquence' and his skill with 'elegant and florid' language, which 'bears the stamp of a moderate writer, such as becomes a philosopher'.[22] Seneca was to be ranked only behind Cicero, but was by no means beyond criticism. Calvin was particularly irritated by the Roman's tendency to set out the order of an argument and then manifestly fail to prosecute it; such intellectual and literary chaos offended his sense of precision and order. In later years, anyone who dared have his text read by Calvin risked being scolded for wordy prose and poor structure.

The manner in which Calvin wrote the commentary is significant. It follows the text of Seneca's *De clementia* line by line in an attempt to explicate the mind of the author. Even when highly critical of the loose manner of argumentation, Calvin was adamant that the commentator was obliged to follow the flow of a text. This clearly foreshadows the approach to biblical exegesis outlined in his famous preface to his Romans commentary written in 1539. The commentator must not impose his own categories on a literary work, but must respect its integrity. When it came to interpretation it was a different matter. Calvin felt quite at liberty to rephrase and restructure Seneca's arguments in order to expound. This could, and did, enable him to make Seneca say something quite different from the original text, a practice Calvin would later repeat with Paul when he offered summaries and rewordings of the Apostle's arguments.

Calvin's legal training pervades the commentary, and his concern with the Roman legal concept of equity (*aequitas*) put him in line with the major humanist jurists of his day, above all his esteemed Budé.[23] The eminent scholar's legacy to the French legal culture was the search for a moral and philosophical basis by which law could be practically applied. In reading

Seneca Calvin was pursuing that goal as a disciple of Budé.[24] The young scholar's legal mind was also very much at work in his treatment of Seneca's three uses of the law: as punishment to improve the character of the offender; to make an example of the person for the community; and to remove criminals in order to protect the community. The wicked should fear a prince while the good love him, and Calvin marshalled a vast array of support from ancient poets, philosophers and historians as his witnesses. This was the proper use of law, and its application was possible, as the example of Emperor Augustus' clemency illustrated. Calvin regarded the threefold use of the law as a cornerstone of the Roman legal system that should be applied in his own day. And this is precisely what Calvin did when he set out the terms of church discipline in Geneva.[25]

Behind such dextrous and subtle textual work lay an ambivalent attitude towards Roman culture in which admiration for its institutions and thought was shaded by revulsion at its tyranny and corruption. The Romans embodied both the possibilities and flaws of humanity: Calvin was suitably awed by their achievements, and together with his generation saw Roman law as the highest articulation of human reason. Yet he referred to the Roman empire as 'a great robbery to which those peoples subjugated by war paid tributes, while those who preferred to make a treaty paid dearly for that ambitious alliance, which was not far removed from slavery'.[26] The horrors and brutality of the Romans are energetically catalogued in his treatment of the emperors Tiberius and Caligula, and Calvin sneered at the pretensions of Augustus' divinity. Roman religion was dismissed as little more than the superstitions of an arrogant and rapacious people. Yet in their legal system and institutions as properly conceived Calvin saw the presence of a natural law by which justice, clemency and good governance were possible. He never suggested that Roman rule was deficient on account of the absence of Christian revelation. But, as Nero himself adequately exemplified, the stench of corruption was pervasive. Calvin emphasized the place of natural law, the order of law embedded in creation that makes all human laws possible. This was the foundation of Roman governance and its greatest glory. Calvin would later argue in his *Institutes* that all laws must seek to establish equity, and associated equity with natural law and the Ten Commandments.

In reading the commentary we cannot but be struck by the seriousness with which Calvin took the Stoic philosophy of Seneca. He found much that was congenial, and following his conversion sought to Christianize those concepts, and continued to read classical philosophy through the lens of scripture.[27]

Seneca described clemency as 'a necessary conviction not only among those of us who regard man as a social animal, begotten for the common good, but also for those who give man over to pleasure, whose words and deeds all look to their own advantage'.[28] Calvin was attracted to this Stoic ideal of community and its rejection of virtue as merely individualistic, responding 'that clemency is a sort of bond of human society and kinship. It is axiomatic that men have begotten for the sake of their fellows to share one another's toil, to take counsel together, to share themselves and their possessions, insofar as it is for the public good.'[29] He provided references to Plato, Aristotle, Cicero and other works by Seneca to reinforce his point. He did not directly connect this concept of human sociability with natural law, which establishes the norms of behaviour, but he would do so in 1536 in the *Institutes*, reflecting his belief that the manner of speaking of human community that he drew from the Stoics was not incompatible with Christianity.[30]

A more explicit example of Calvin's study of the harmony between classical and Christian ideas can be seen in the attention he pays to Seneca's reference to clemency and the household. Seneca was primarily concerned with the theme of clemency as practised by rulers and spoke of how 'every house that clemency enters she will render peaceful and happy, but in the palace she is more wonderful in that she is rarer'.[31] Calvin took this sentence in a different direction by remarking that:

> clemency dwells indeed in every private house; it dwells – if you will – in poor huts and rustic cottages; when the father of the family conducts himself with moderation toward wife, children, and servants, and forgives, overlooks, is kind and invites rather than compels them to do their task. On this account Peter in his canonical epistle does not wish masters to be ill-tempered and hard on servants.

Not only is this one of the few places where Calvin harmonized Seneca's words with scripture, he did so by deliberately reorienting the subject to address clemency in the common household. Clemency, rooted in Calvin's understanding of Roman law, is the proper foundation of domestic relations.

The enduring legacy of Calvin's legal training on his theology was enormous. His positive account of the law, by which believers are taught the will of God, his attachment to order and discipline in the church, and his emphasis on the majesty of God all flow from his training in the law.[32] In particular his treatment of accommodation, by which principles are adapted to specific circumstances, so central to his understanding of scripture and biblical interpretation, drew upon the debate within humanist legal circles on the concept of equity.[33] Calvin the lawyer and theologian was profoundly concerned with how particular laws in the changing circumstances of human life could adequately reflect the unchanging law of God.

The Love of Friends

The intended audience for his Seneca commentary was the generation to which Calvin himself belonged: young, university-trained men impassioned by the world of French humanists and on their way to becoming jurists. All his life Calvin would define friendship in terms of a commitment to a common cause; it was within that framework he was able to express fraternity and intimacy. His models were classical and contemporary: Cicero's treatise on friendship was a standard work among Renaissance readers, as was Erasmus' contribution to the subject. Calvin's teacher of law, Alciati, had printed a book on emblems in which four chapters were dedicated to the ideal of friendship. Friendship, these authors agreed, grew from Aristotle's belief that it forms the basis of community. The concept was not the loose term of today; it belonged to the discipline of law and formed an integral part of Calvin's studies. Friendship was a legal concept, and what exists between friends was a contract of reciprocity.[34] It defined a series of obligations that in many ways rejected the self in favour of formal structures. It gave little place to the intimate and personal. Beyond its legal manifestations, friendship was understood as the foundation of the scholarly life and community. Following the classical model, the activities of reading, writing and collecting books were essential aspects of the scholarly existence.[35] It was a difficult life, requiring an austere commitment to learning, limited to those who possessed the requisite training. Such intimate relations were not simply among students and scholars, who lived as equals, but extended to the more hierarchical relations between masters and pupils. Friendship in its academic and personal forms became a defining influence on John Calvin.

In accordance with the principles of classical and humanist friendship, Calvin expected much: his friends should promote his work and use it in their teaching, and he was anxiously solicitous about sales and reception. His anxiety was made evident to François Daniel. 'Do write as soon as you can,' he told his friend,

> and let me know with what favour or coldness they [the copies of the Seneca commentary] have been received, and try also to induce Landrin

to lecture on them. I send one copy for yourself. Will you take charge of the other five, to be forwarded to Bourges for Le Roy, Pigney, Sucquet, Brosse and Baratier? If Sucquet can accept it for the purpose of lecturing, his help will be of no small service to me.[36]

In the years of his legal studies Calvin's friends provided him with a stability absent in both himself and his family. He never found friendship easy, as we shall see in his long relationship with Guillaume Farel, but he relished it greatly. Friendship provoked his most contradictory impulses. Towards those closest to him he could be fierce and intemperate, yet this was often followed by a peculiar form of abject contrition without admission of fault. At heart, friendship was difficult for him because he struggled with the idea that he was the equal of others. From our earliest written sources it is clear that he maintained a sense of intellectual superiority to those around him. The Seneca commentary was itself a symbol of his self-confidence, and its dedication hardly concealed any swallowing of pride. The preface to Duchemin's little work and the commentary present us with a young man of precocious talent, a strikingly independent mind and a restless yearning to free himself from the demands of patronage.

There were important lessons in Seneca beyond the political and legal. Calvin was dependent upon a minor patron whose parsimony he deeply resented and he allowed this anger to be expressed in the faint praise of his dedication, but Seneca proved a wise old teacher, and Calvin drew from him the Stoic emphasis upon the need to free oneself from the passions and from the praise of others to live a life of virtue.[37] That would drive his search for the inner peace he sought, a tranquil conscience. Such a life could enable those of lower birth to rise in the world. Ambition, when grounded in self-serving obsequiousness to others, was morally indefensible. However, an ambitious author of lower birth could rise in the world through the cultivation of virtue. The commentary bears witness to Calvin's character as his father was dying. Through Seneca he was searching for Stoic virtues of self-reliance and self-dependence. His intellectual growth was not matched by the reception afforded his commentary. Despite his own efforts, and those of his friends, it was simply lost in the vast number of books printed in Paris that year. In short, it made no impression. The deafening silence from the French intellectual world that greeted the Seneca commentary was wounding, and no doubt it came as a jolt to his pride, but Calvin had his eye on the prize, and that was Paris.

CHAPTER THREE

'At Last Delivered':
Conversion and Flight

Paris

FOR AN aspirational French humanist, Paris was everything. And in March 1531 Calvin returned to the city in the hope of studying under the lecturers of the Collège Royal. He also had the task of seeing through the press Duchemin's *Antapologia*, complete with his own preface. Perhaps he hoped to meet the patriarch of the Collège, Guillaume Budé, whom Calvin would praise in his Seneca commentary. In Bourges and Orléans he had been in the presence of greatness in the figures of de l'Estoile and Alciati, but Calvin wanted more – to dwell among the Olympian figures of French humanism.

Then came the news of his father's impending death and Calvin rushed to Noyon. After a series of quarrels, Girard Cauvin had been excommunicated by the cathedral chapter, and he died on 26 May 1531 without the sacraments of the Church. John's brother Charles had to negotiate for a posthumous absolution in order that their father could be buried in consecrated ground. Calvin's reaction to the death was curiously muted. Writing to Duchemin, who was worried about the delay in his book's publication, he evinced little grief or emotion, all the more perplexing given an effusive expression of warmth towards his friend.[1] What accounts for this contrast? His relationship with his father was complex, though not cold. It is entirely possible that Calvin's emotional bonds lay more with the friends with whom he lived, studied and travelled than with a family he had hardly seen. We cannot dismiss the influence of the Stoic philosophy of Seneca with which he was engaged; the letter may speak to a stylized role of impassivity as a means of dealing with his loss. What is certainly misleading is any suggestion that he was unaffected by death and grief. The raw emotions that poured forth later at the loss of his infant son and wife, as well as at the death of close friends, counter any sense of a Calvin hewn from stone. It is more likely that in 1531 he was masking feelings and emotions which had not yet found articulation. Only after his conversion and in his biblical commentaries, in the stories of the Old and New Testaments, and particularly in the psalms, did he find an emotional vocabulary inaccessible to a young man of twenty-two.

Following the death of his father Calvin returned once more to Paris, finding various places to stay before taking up residence in the Collège de Fortet in the Latin Quarter. He became an 'auditeur', following the royal lecturers of the Collège Royal, which was less an institution than a group of learned individuals surrounded by students. He deepened his knowledge of Greek and perhaps studied Hebrew.[2] This was the pure oxygen of humanist studies, though the atmosphere was fraught with peril. In 1530 the Sorbonne had condemned the principle that biblical languages were essential to the study of scripture. It was not the theological faculty, however, that brought Calvin's studies in Paris to a conclusion: plague descended on the city in the autumn, forcing the cancellation of all teaching and a general flight to safety, for those able to flee. We catch only brief glimpses of Calvin in the crowd. The Seneca commentary was completed in February 1532 and printed in Paris the following April.

Calvin returned to Orléans to continue his legal studies before vanishing once more from the records for almost a year and a half. The destruction of the archives in Orléans during the Second World War has thrown a cloak over these months, leaving us with few details of his activities or whereabouts. It was a time for being with his friends, including François Daniel, Nicolas Duchemin and François de Connan. Daniel was somewhat older than Calvin and de Connan came from a prominent family in Orléans. Of all these young men, it was Daniel, whose family he had known well, to whom Calvin was closest.[3]

In 1533 François Daniel encouraged Calvin to find a patron by applying for the position of vicar-general to a bishop.[4] It was a natural course for a young man with legal training, and Calvin would have been well qualified for the position. We know nothing of his response, but it was unlikely to have been enthusiastic as there is no indication that he desired anything other than a literary career. Nevertheless, the Daniel family, whether from affection or duty, looked out for the young Calvin. By the autumn of 1533 he was back in Paris at the request of the family and involved in the negotiations between Canon Jean Cop and the Abbess of Aug concerning when one of the Daniel sisters should make her religious vows. The Daniels had taken Calvin among them, though they were not the only family with which he was forging bonds in Orléans. He had also grown close to the Cop family, and the canon's uncle, Nicolas, was rector of the University of Paris.

Conversion

In the early 1530s Calvin would have had every reason to be optimistic. The humanists seemed to be prevailing against the Sorbonne and he enjoyed the material support of affluent and prominent families who could open doors to a profitable career. During the autumn of 1533 everything changed. He had, in his later words, remained 'obstinately addicted to the superstitions of the papacy', but:

> God by a sudden conversion subdued and brought my mind to a teach-able frame, which was more hardened in such matters than might have been expected from one at my early period of life. Having thus received some taste and knowledge of true godliness I was immediately inflamed with so intense a desire to make progress therein, that although I did not altogether leave off other studies, I yet pursued them with less ardour.[5]

Calvin has left us two accounts of his conversion and they differ in signifi-cant ways.[6] In 1539, writing to Cardinal Sadoleto, he stressed that he had been brought up a Christian, and that his conversion was essentially a shift of allegiance from the Church of Rome to the Word of God. He speaks of it in terms of gradual transition spurred forward by his fear of divine judgement and a laden conscience.[7] The conversion is portrayed as a rejection of false worship, or idolatry, and the growing discovery of scripture and the true worship of God. His enduring regard for the Church had kept him from leaving the religion of his youth, but he found that its authority, by which his conscience was being bound, was fraudulent and that 'the world was plunged into ignorance and sloth, as in a deep sleep, that the pope had risen to such an eminence, certainly not appointed head of the church by the Word of God, nor ordained by a legitimate act of the church, but of his own accord self-selected'.[8] Torn by an innate faithfulness to the Church and a conscience that reminded him daily of the false religion he continued to profess, Calvin was cast into despair.

> Being exceedingly alarmed at the misery into which I had fallen, and much more at that which threatened me in view of eternal death, I, duty bound, made it my first business to betake myself to your way, condemning my past life, not without groans and tears. And now, O Lord, what remains to a wretch like me, but instead of defence, earnestly to supplicate you not to judge that fearful abandonment of your Word according to its deserts, from which in your wondrous goodness you have at last delivered me.[9]

In language similar to that of Martin Luther, Calvin spoke of the spiritual and psychological anguish of breaking with the old faith, a tormented conscience and fear of God's judgement. This is a complex, human picture in which he recalled the pressure to conform and accept the authority of the church, which only drove him to a greater sense of alienation. There is no Road to Damascus moment, no flash of light; rather it is the story of a young man whose spiritual life was increasingly in conflict with the world around him. This is an early expression of Calvin as a stranger in a foreign land.

Almost twenty years later, Calvin offered a second account of his conversion in the preface to the psalms commentary (1557). Gone is the sense of protracted inner turmoil, to be replaced by a 'sudden conversion' with its clear parallels with the Apostle Paul.[10] No longer the anguished, despairing wretch, Calvin presents himself as the reluctant servant of God, shy and nervous, sought out by others for his teaching, intentionally evoking images of Moses, David, Jeremiah and Paul. His readership was not meant to miss the connection. The 1557 preface to the psalms commentary was written by a man who regarded himself as a prophet of the Church.

The two accounts are not antithetical, revealing some inconsistency in Calvin's memory, but rather two different ways of expressing the same reality, and this gives us reason to pause and consider what he meant by conversion. From his earliest Christian writings the young Frenchman described the Christian life with metaphors of journeying and pilgrimage. The imagery was as old as the ancient books of the Hebrew Bible, but Calvin's brilliance lay in his ability to infuse old traditions with new life. Conversion, he believed, was the beginning point of a journey, not its conclusion. Whether speaking in terms of mental anguish or of sudden conversion he sought to explain how God had acted to change his life and put him on a new course, to send him out in a different direction. Both accounts are suffused with theology. In saying that he had been brought up in the Church, Calvin wanted to indicate that his was not a conversion to the Christian life from nothing. The focus was elsewhere, on his new life of service to the Church and his status as a prophet. Similarly, in describing his human weaknesses and his likeness to the young David, Calvin sought to ensure that God and God alone remained the principal character in the account.

Out of Calvin's conversion narratives emerges his view of the Christian life and of his calling. Fear is the means by which God calls people from torpor to self-reflection; that reflection reveals a person's sinfulness and idolatry. Fear plays an important part in Calvin's theology, it was something he knew well from his years in France, an emotion he could describe vividly.[11] The tormented conscience, aware of its betrayal of God, seeks comfort only found in the promises of God revealed in scripture. Those promises require more than intellectual assent – they demand a radical change of life to conformity with Christ. To a certain extent Calvin allowed his personal conversion to stand as a model for others, not because he regarded himself as exemplary in any virtuous way, but as a means of demonstrating the power of God to work through individuals. The analogy extended only so far, for Calvin was clear that he was called to a special office. He was a prophet whose conversion was not a private affair but an act of the Church; he was to teach the true fear of God and piety. His conversion was the creation of a leader.

Return to Paris and First Flight

But what did Calvin convert to? There was no Protestant church in France. He did not immediately leave the Catholic church. Part of the problem in answering this question arises from the difficulty that we have only sporadic sightings of Calvin in this period. We know that he was in Noyon at the end of August 1533 to attend a meeting of the cathedral chapter, and that, faced with an outbreak of plague, it was decided to hold a procession.[12] Calvin's response is unknown, and beyond this there are no footprints in the sand. Most likely he had moved in the direction of a Lefèvrian evangelicalism.

At the time of his conversion, following the establishment of the Collège Royal by Francis I, the French kingdom was more divided than ever over religion.[13] Francis continued to assert his authority against both the Sorbonne and the Paris Parlement.[14] The Navarrists around Marguerite, although sympathetic to much of Luther's writings, looked in horror at the events unfolding in the German empire and grew desperate to avoid schism. They were not prepared to abandon the Catholic church, which, despite its manifold errors, they firmly held to be the true Body of Christ; their hope was for internal reform. In Lent 1533 and 1534 Gérard Roussel, former disciple of Lefèvre and now almoner in Marguerite's court, delivered a series of sermons before crowds of up to five thousand.[15] The degree of royal support enjoyed by this group became evident in 1533 when Noël Beda was banished from Paris after the Sorbonne unwisely censured Roussel's preaching.[16] His sermons were the starting point of the turbulent events of 1533 in Paris.[17] Among that crowd of five thousand was John Calvin.

The hand of politics rested heavily on the matter. For all his love of Renaissance literature and culture, and his fury with the Sorbonnists at their condemnation of Erasmus, the king did not share his sister's religious disposition. Francis I supported neither the evangelicals nor the Sorbonne, which had resisted the Concordat of Bologna with its concentration of power over the church in royal hands. His actions were instead largely determined by his ongoing war against Emperor Charles V. Charles had been elected Holy Roman emperor in 1519 over Francis, continuing the dynastic ascendancy of the Habsburgs in the empire that was to end only in 1806. To undermine his hated Habsburg rival Francis supported the Schmalkaldic League of Protestant German princes and cities, formed in 1531 to defend the German reformation against anticipated attack by the emperor. Francis' dealing with the League was a clear case of the enemy of my enemy being my friend. The persecution of religious reformers would not have advanced that strategy. His tolerance of evangelical activity in France, however, should not be confused with support. He had been named 'Most Christian Prince' by the pope, and in Francis' eyes this meant the defence of his kingdom against heresy.

A zephyr of humanist and evangelical ideas blew through Paris during the early years of the 1530s, and it was felt by Calvin. The year 1532 brought the publication of François Rabelais' *Pantagruel,* under a pseudonym, in which the doctors of the Sorbonne were mocked. In a long and newsy letter from October 1533, his conversion year, Calvin recounts to Daniel Lambert the events surrounding the performance of a scandalous play by students that led officials to launch an inquiry.[18] He moves to the disastrous story of the theological faculty's condemnation of a work entitled *The Mirror of the Sinful Soul,* a volume of devotional verse, published in Alençon in 1531 and in Paris two years later, which turned out to be by none other than Marguerite of Navarre herself, who promptly complained to her brother, the king. This calamitous act on the part of the theological faculty was a clear contravention of a decree passed by the Parlement forbidding the censuring of books, and the theologians were in hot water. The other faculties quickly dissociated themselves with the event and an investigation was undertaken by the rector of the university. Humiliated, the theological faculty was forced to retreat. Calvin's account is cool and dispassionate, giving no sense of participation in the events; rather he was an observer, a journalist – neither anyone's client nor the disciple of any particular teacher.

So what was Calvin doing in Paris? The conversion account mentions that he continued to study, and we must assume that during the summer and autumn of 1533 he was reading the church fathers and contemporary writers while following the lectures of the Collège Royal. We also know that he was lecturing on Seneca's *De clementia* in Paris.[19] Whatever the state of his Christian convictions at this moment, he was clearly committed to the study and teaching of the classics.

Martin Luther was certainly among the authors he was reading. From the early 1520s Luther's works had been circulating in France both in Latin and in translation. We have no direct evidence of what Calvin read of the German reformer, but his familiarity with Luther's ideas was revealed in the famous, or infamous, inaugural address held by the new rector of the university, Nicolas Cop, in the church of the Mathurins on All Saints' Day 1533. Before the gathered body of the university Cop announced his theme as 'Christian Philosophy', but what his audience heard was an Erasmian account of scripture with unmistakably Lutheran overtones, particularly on Law and Gospel: the first part of the address was taken from Erasmus' *Paraclesis*, the preface to his Latin translation of the Bible of 1516, while Martin Luther's interpretation of Matthew 5:3 was cited at length from a Latin translation made by Martin Bucer.[20] The Law, Cop held, 'is contained in precepts, it threatens, it burdens, it promises no good will. The Gospel acts without threats, it does not drive one on by precepts, but rather teaches us about the supreme good will of God towards us.'[21] The representatives of the theological faculty present immediately smelled a rat. Cop was a physician and they doubted his ability to conjure such words; the hunt was under way to find the ghost writer. Scholarly opinion has remained divided over whether Calvin was the man they sought, but recent research suggests that he was indeed involved in preparing the text.[22] Certainly Beza's biography leaves no doubt that Calvin was the author.[23] The issue is not easily resolved: on the one hand there is a manuscript of the text in Calvin's hand, though it may be a later copy; on the other, Calvin's subsequent interpretation of the crucial biblical passage, Matthew 5:3, differs significantly from the interpretation in Cop's address, which, as we have noted, came from Luther.[24] Whatever the case, we can be sure that Calvin was in sympathy and probably knew of his friend's intentions, even if he did not write the address itself. The backlash was swift: Cop fled Paris for the Swiss city of Basle, and Roussel was arrested. Calvin's own rapid departure from Paris is the most persuasive evidence for the degree he felt himself to be implicated.

The Generosity of Friends

His safe haven took the form of the country home of his good friend Louis du Tillet, priest in Claix, whose distinguished family owned a considerable residence near Angoulême in the south-west of France.[25] The du Tillet brothers, of whom there were five, including two named Jean, were to be found in high offices in Paris, where they held positions at court and in the Parlement. According to a late-sixteenth-century source, Calvin acted as a tutor to the family while living in Angoulême. Not only was he able to visit once more this close friend from his student days, but he was in the vicinity of those reform-minded churchmen gathered in Nérac around Marguerite of Navarre, including Jacques Lefèvre, the ageing doyen of French evangelical thought, who had retired to Nérac following the attacks on the humanists led by Noël Beda. Calvin was given an opportunity to visit the old man, which he seized, but their exchange is lost. Beza has left an account: 'This good old man . . . was delighted with young Calvin, and predicted that he would prove a distinguished instrument in restoring the kingdom of heaven in France.'[26] Beza may have heard this from Calvin himself, but the reformer never referred again to the meeting. Lefèvre, who had suffered much for his beliefs, had found safety in the south from persecution. Calvin, in contrast, was only beginning to learn what it meant to act on what he professed. Whatever happened in this encounter, his months in the south of France were filled with study as du Tillet and Angoulême offered rich libraries to use at leisure and in peace. Calvin pored over editions of the early church fathers, which he would soon be able to quote from memory.[27]

In early 1534 Calvin wrote an undated letter to Daniel that opens a window on these months. Describing his situation, he remarked that he was 'getting on well' despite the 'constitutional weakness and infirmity of which you are aware'. He most appreciated the peace and quiet offered after his flight from

Paris, although he was not certain whether his present circumstances were better described as 'exile' or 'retirement'. He spoke to Daniel of his need to be content with life in Angoulême and to commit himself to study. This letter offers the first use of the providential language that would pervade his thought and a revealing glimpse of his expectations. 'When I promised myself an easy tranquil life then what I least expected was at hand, and on the contrary, when it appeared to me that my situation might not be an agreeable one, a quiet nest was built for me beyond expectation, and this is the doing of the Lord.'[28]

There were many unresolved ambiguities in Calvin's life. What, in this relatively tranquil world away from the maelstrom of Paris, was his religion? He was residing with a friend who was a priest of the Catholic church, though he undoubtedly shared many of Calvin's reformist views. There were no Protestant churches, so did Calvin continue to attend mass? He may well have practised a form of dissembling in which he continued to observe the outward rites of a church whose teachings he had already rejected – a practice he would viciously demonize after he left France. There is evidence that he did attempt to balance his beliefs with some degree of conformity. It comes from an account written by the polemical Catholic jurist Florimond de Raemond later in the century in his popular history of the origins of heresy in France.[29] He wrote:

> Calvin stayed for several years in the city of Angoulême, still wearing the mask of a Catholic, appearing at church, but as little as possible. He was used by the chapter to give Latin sermons as was the custom when the synod assembled for the Supper. He did this two or three times in the Church of St Peter. During his stay in Angoulême he did not preach, pray, or worship in any way contrary to the Catholic custom.[30]

The source is hostile, but it corroborates statements by Beza and Colladon that Calvin was engaged in some form of teaching. It is clear that he was well regarded in the region for his learning and he was employing it in the service of the faith, even if that meant concealing heterodox beliefs.

Calvin's overtly evangelical views probably took shape during the winter and spring of 1534 and there are tantalizing traces that link him with known reformers in Paris while he was still in the south of France,[31] making all the more plausible the long-held belief that he had begun writing his *Institutes* while staying with du Tillet.[32] Even if the evidence is partial it is certainly possible that by the spring/early summer of 1534 Calvin's mind had fundamentally shifted, though he was not yet prepared to declare his hand. His experience of dissembling in Angoulême may well have nurtured his later uncompromising belief that the true Church is only served by a complete and open break with the false.

At the end of April 1534 Calvin made one more journey to Noyon with a particular purpose. He had decided to give up the church livings which had supported him and his education since the age of twelve. He gave notice to the canons of Noyon cathedral that he would now, at the age of twenty-five, renounce the benefices. The income from the chapel de la Gésine was sold for a small sum and he gave to a friend the benefice of the parish of Pont-l'Evêque. What lay behind this move? Age was one consideration: at twenty-five he was now legally an adult and the issue of a career was more pressing than ever. That, however, was perhaps only incidental. More persuasive is the argument that during the spring of 1534 Calvin was moving beyond mere Lefèvrian sympathies towards turning his back on the Catholic church. He had a circle of wealthy friends who could support him, and with whom he was sharing his religious ideas, and with his legal training the prospects of a career were good.

Following Calvin's conversion, he had embraced a Lefèvrian form of evangelical Christianity that kept him within the bounds of the Catholic church, but perhaps only formally. We have little knowledge of what took place during the autumn and spring of 1533–4, and he never chose to throw any light on this key period in his life. Reduced to speculation, its seems most probable that he came to the conclusion that his beliefs were irreconcilable with the Catholic church, and that he practised a form of dissembling, an experience that led him later to the repudiation of this form of conduct as unChristian.

The Placards Affair

The Placards Affair was a defining moment of Calvin's early career, though he did not play a direct role. In the dead of night of 17 October 1534 tracts (placards) denouncing the sacrifice of the mass as an abomination were posted across Paris including, most audaciously, at the door of the king's bedchamber.[33] The texts themselves were crude, but the reaction was swift and brutal. Over the next weeks several hundred supporters of the reform movement were rounded up as the king feared a swelling, yet hardly visible, movement of sedition. Books were seized as a wave of persecution was unleashed, leading to nine executions. When the placards appeared again on 6 January 1535 the response was even more violent: eleven executions in ten months, together with banishments and the confiscation of goods. A list of seventy-three 'Lutherans' was drawn up, among whom were three printers, two bookbinders and a bookseller.[34] Francis I's response revealed the extent of his loyalty to the Catholic church. The persecution lasted until the summer of 1535 when, with the Edict of Coucy, Francis freed all except those identified as 'sacramentarians' – as the followers of Huldrych Zwingli were known on account of their supposed rejection of Christ's presence in the Lord's Supper. It was nothing more than a sop to appease the Protestant German princes of the Schmalkaldic League.

Although the deed had been spectacular, the placards played brilliantly into the hands of the opponents of reform. The views they expressed, largely derived from the theology of Zwingli, hardly represented the vast majority of French evangelicals, and Marguerite was quick to dissociate herself from the affair.[35] The importance of the occasion lay elsewhere. The Sorbonne had been handed a public relations coup: all advocates of the evangelical faith could be easily tarred with sedition. On 21 January 1535 Paris was cleansed of heresy by a spectacular procession led by the king's court, the university, religious orders and the guilds. The Catholic monarch and church reasserted themselves in all their splendour. The most precious relics of the Parisian churches were carried through the streets with the Bishop of Paris himself bearing the Holy Eucharist. Directly behind the bishop was the penitent Francis I, bare headed, dressed in black and carrying one lit candle.[36] He urged all Parisians and Frenchmen to denounce heretics; burnings followed soon after.

There was panic that the kingdom was under attack from an enemy outside its borders, for the placards had not been printed in Paris or even France, but in Neuchâtel in the Swiss Confederation. They were, however, the work of a Frenchman, Antoine Marcourt, who was preaching in Geneva, and they had appeared simultaneously in the cities of Paris, Rouen, Orléans, Blois and Tours.[37] The role of the laity in this affair was crucial, for although the clergy largely remained loyal to the Catholic church, it was among merchants and artisans that the evangelical polemic found a receptive audience. Travelling merchants became the disseminators of subversive ideas, which severely handicapped royal officials as it was impossible to search every person entering the cities on business. The only real limitation on the production of these works was the small number of printers willing or able to produce such literature.

The Placards Affair cast into high relief the extent to which religious reform in France had two very different faces. The circle around Marguerite of Navarre, men such as Gérard Roussel, continued to espouse an Erasmian ideal of reform from within the institution of the church. Fiercely opposed to this were those who rejected the Catholic church and its hierarchy and saw those who remained within it as traitors to the Gospel. The most prominent figure in this later group was Guillaume Farel, once a member of the Meaux Circle but now living in exile in the Swiss Confederation. Farel, Marcourt and others had been radicalized by the persecution and oppression of the 1520s and early 1530s.

Calvin did not belong to either of these groups, but aware that his religious views put him in danger he left Paris once more for Orléans. Significantly, he chose to flee Paris after the first Placards Affair when the reaction was not particularly fierce. Even in Orléans he knew he was not safe, and the prospect of exile lay before him. He had never been out of France and knew no other spoken language except Latin. To leave France was to cut himself off from family and friends.

At the end of 1534 Calvin and his good friend Louis du Tillet made their way out of France using assumed names – in Calvin's case Martinus Lucianus – to cover their tracks. Travelling across Alsace they arrived in Strasbourg where Calvin had already made contact with Wolfgang Capito and Martin Bucer, the reformers in Strasbourg and leading figures of the southern German reformation. But on this occasion Strasbourg was not their final destination; Calvin was not looking to become a reformer or to head a church. He sought another place like Angoulême, where he could continue his studies and writing. That desire led him south along the Rhine into the Swiss Confederation and the city of Basle.

'We Afterwards Pass into the Land of Promise': The Pilgrim

Exile had been the fate of the prophets and of David fleeing Saul; it was now Calvin's lot. From his conversion experience he had undergone a spiritual journey which led to the gradual break with the Catholic church. There was no defining or dramatic moment; it took place in study, conversation and prayer – all of which remain hidden from the eyes of historians. Exile was an act of obedience to God, a separation from a false church and a declaration of faith. The role of the prophet was as an outsider, and to respond to God's call in his conversion Calvin had had to leave France.

While in Orléans he had begun writing a work which mapped his spiritual journey on the eve of his departure from France. Ultimately entitled the

Psychopannychia, meaning soul sleep, and printed in 1542 in Strasbourg, Calvin's text circulated among friends and colleagues in manuscript. The initial response had not been encouraging, and at some point he sent the text to Wolfgang Capito in Strasbourg, who shared the view that it should not be published.[38] Not only did Capito find Calvin's handwriting illegible, but the subject matter and tone were uncongenial.[39] Calvin's strident prose, reflective of the polarizing religious world of France, was not welcome in Strasbourg and Basle, where delicate balances between opposing parties had to be maintained. Calvin brought the text with him to Basle and there he wrote a new preface in response to critical replies, but there is no suggestion that he fundamentally altered the argument.[40] Even in its redacted form, which is all we have, the *Psychopannychia* offers the first detailed insight into Calvin's thought as he emerged from the shadows of French evangelicalism.

It is difficult not to share the bewilderment of Calvin's contemporaries over his choice of topic. Why would a young man, in danger of persecution for his beliefs, put quill to paper on the subject of the immortality of the soul? Without doubt, the question was significant, even fashionable, and had occupied theologians and philosophers of the fifteenth and early sixteenth centuries.[41] Even more curiously, Calvin claimed to be attacking the teachings of 'Anabaptists', who taught the false doctrine that the soul goes to sleep at the moment of physical death. In truth, neither the doctrine of the immortality of the soul nor the Anabaptists were his primary concern. He had in mind someone else from his Paris days: the medical student Michael Servetus and his Italian circle in Paris.[42] Michael Servetus was a Spanish humanist, theologian and medical doctor who had travelled through Europe during the 1520s and 1530s spreading a mixture of brilliant and heretical ideas. Infamously, he was to meet his death in Calvin's Geneva in 1553, causing a Europe-wide scandal.[43] Calvin and Servetus certainly already knew one another and in 1534 the Frenchman left Saintonge, where he was staying with du Tillet, to meet the Spaniard in the rue Saint-Antoine in Paris. Servetus failed to keep the appointment, as Calvin would point out to him twenty years later in Geneva. Beza argues that Calvin put himself at considerable risk in agreeing to meet the heretic, explaining that he had hoped to silence the man.[44] It is possible that the *Psychopannychia* was written to achieve what could not be done in person. Whatever the case, Servetus and the doctrine of soul sleep formed only part of the picture. Before leaving his homeland, Calvin had written in this work a moving defence of the fidelity of the evangelicals to scripture.

In this meditation on the Bible Calvin set out a theme that he would continue to develop throughout his life – the Christian life as a pilgrimage through the world towards eternity. Drawing on his own experience, though never referring to himself, he offered comfort to those who suffered for their faith in God's Word by holding before the reader the examples of great figures of the Bible, such as Job and Abraham. Death was not a peculiar or morbid topic: it is the moment for which all women and men of faith must prepare themselves, a joyful release from the pain and suffering of this world. The overwhelming sense of the *Psychopannychia* is of a God who is the source of all goodness and in whom there is certainty. The death of the soul is not physical but abandonment by God in which 'the mind retains its power of perception, yet evil concupiscence is, as it were, a kind of mental stupefaction'.[45] Death takes two forms: the separation of body and soul, which is the fate of all humans, and an alienation from God wherein the person dwells in an 'abyss' and 'confusion'. Those who perceive God's presence must endure pain and anxiety, for they live in fear of divine judgement.

Calvin asked his readers to imagine how Adam must have felt when God called, 'Adam, where are you?' Job, for Calvin, was an everyperson, perhaps even John Calvin himself, representing that moment for the Christian when the only reality is the anger of God. If Job was Calvin's model of the suffering man in the *Psychopannychia*, however, it was in Abraham that he saw the man of faith.

> The Apostle speaks of Abraham and his posterity who dwelt in a foreign land among strangers not only as exiles, but as sojourners, scarcely sheltering their bodies by living in poor huts in obedience to the command of God given to Abraham, that he should leave his land and his kindred. God had promised them what he had not yet exhibited. Therefore they trusted the promises afar off, and died in the firm belief that the promises of God would one day be fulfilled. In accordance with this belief, they confessed that they had no fixed abode on the earth, and that beyond the earth there was a country for which they longed, viz., heaven.[46]

For the patriarchs of the Old Testament, the promises of God may have been a distant light, but for Christians the Kingdom of God has, in part, already been achieved. It exists within each individual, growing as that person develops in 'perfection'.[47] 'For those who in a manner have the Kingdom of God within them and reign with God, begin to be in the Kingdom of God; and the gates of hell cannot prevail against them.'[48] It is 'hidden with Christ', perceived only by those who live in faith. This perception of the Kingdom of God is an essential part of the state of 'expectation' which must be matched by action: the Christian must conform to the life of Christ by taming the senses and shaping them through 'mortification' and 'purification'.[49]

Death befalls every Christian, but it is not the end of the road. This state of rest in Abraham's Bosom after death, though comforting, is not the final stage in the progression of the soul. 'Our blessedness is always in progress up to that day which shall conclude and terminate all progress, and that thus the glory of the elect, and complete consumption of hope, look forward to that day for their fulfilment. For it is admitted by all, that perfection of blessedness or glory nowhere exists except in perfect union of God.'[50]

In an elaborate expansion on Paul's words to the Corinthians (1 Corinthians 10:1–5), Calvin uses the Israelite exodus to exemplify the spiritual journey of the Christian.

So that we may be permitted to say that in baptism our pharaoh is drowned, our old man is crucified, our members are mortified, we are buried with Christ, and removed from the captivity of the devil and the power of death, but removed only into the desert, a land arid and poor, unless the Lord rain manna from heaven, and cause water to gush forth from the rock. For our soul, like that land without water, is in want of all things, till he, by the grace of his spirit, rain upon it. We afterwards pass into the land of promise, under the guidance of Joshua, the son of Nun, into a land with milk and honey; that is the grace of God frees us from the body of death by our Lord Jesus Christ, not with sweat and blood, since the flesh is then most repugnant, and exerts its utmost force in warring against the spirit. After we take up our residence in the land, we feed abundantly. White robes and rest are given us. But Jerusalem, the capital and seat of the kingdom, has not yet been erected; nor yet does Solomon, the Prince of Peace, hold the sceptre and rule over all. The souls of the saints, therefore, which have escaped the hands of the enemy, are after death in peace. They are amply supplied with all things, for it is said of them 'they shall go from abundance to abundance'. But when the heavenly Jerusalem shall have risen up in its glory, and Christ, the true Solomon, the Prince of Peace, shall be seated aloft on his tribunal, the true Israelites will reign with their king.[51]

The passage is as beautiful as anything Calvin would write later in life. Calvin the exile was also Calvin the pilgrim, and from Erasmus and Lefèvre he had learned to read Paul's letters in terms of a spiritual journey.[52] Paul was not only Calvin's guide, but the Frenchman had clearly acquired the Apostle's accent. The *Psychopannychia* demonstrates the extent to which Calvin had made the language of scripture his own; it had become the voice of his personal journey towards God. The text is suffused with images of exile; yet at the same time it points repeatedly to a God who draws the pilgrim forward, providing sustenance and hope. The work throws light on the meaning of Calvin's conversion. It was a transformation to a life in which one's eyes were on God alone, a journey of obedience marked by suffering and anxiety. This was for Calvin a wrenching of his inner and outward self, for as he was discovering the richness of an inward journey led by God's certain promises, he was physically leaving the land which was home and the object of his affections. He was heading both towards and away from Jerusalem.

The year 1534 is perhaps the most intriguing of Calvin's life. Some things we know for certain, but much remains shrouded in mist. What happened to the man who went to the south following the Cop address and before leaving his homeland at the end of 1534? We know he studied, preached and moved among friends and family sympathetic to the evangelical cause, but his path was largely that of a loner. He was on a spiritual journey that led him away from the Catholic church to a vision of something else. But what was his goal? There is good reason to accept the long-held belief that while in the south of France Calvin had begun to construct his distinctive theological system, that he had at least drafted his *Institutes* before he arrived in Basle at the end of 1534 or beginning of 1535.[53] The last two parts of the *Institutes* argue most heavily in favour of this possibility, for here Calvin offered a vigorous defence of the evangelicals persecuted in the wake of the Placards Affair.

CHAPTER FOUR

Exile in a Hidden Corner

The City of Erasmus

CALVIN'S JOURNEY to Basle was fraught with the hazards of sixteenth-century travel. 'Near Metz he was plundered by a servant,' Beza reported, 'who saddled one of the strongest horses and fled with so much speed that he could not be apprehended, after he had perfidiously robbed his masters of all things necessary for their journey, and reduced them to great difficulties. The other servant, however, lent them ten crowns, which enabled them to proceed with considerable inconvenience to Strasbourg, and thence to Basle.'[1] In the psalms preface, Calvin speaks of his departure from France less dramatically as a flight from undesired notoriety to an Arcadia where he might pursue literary studies. Calvin may still have hoped for a career as a humanist scholar, but his point was to contrast personal desire with God's providential plan. 'In short, while my one great object was to live in seclusion without being known, God so led me about through different turnings and changes that he never permitted me to rest in any place, until, in spite of my natural disposition, he brought me forth to public notice.'[2] Providence, Calvin saw from the vantage point of 1557, had led him to Basle to become famous, but in God's service.

For a young man eager to pursue a literary career there were good reasons to choose Basle. The city was anything but the 'obscure corner' described by Calvin.[3] With its strong links to France and the evangelical cause in the kingdom, many French nobles sought protection in the Swiss city on the Rhine after the Placards Affair. Among the numerous French refugees who found themselves in a city where they were more tolerated than welcomed was Nicolas Cop, the former rector, upon whom the Sorbonne had exacted revenge and driven into exile. Calvin was thus reunited with a family friend who must have been a reassuring face in a strange world where the young Frenchman did not speak the language.

Basle may have offered the French refugees relative safety, but it was hardly a walled garden isolated from the tumults of the period. The city had embraced the Reformation only in 1529, and unresolved tensions abounded.[4] Religious change owed less to the leading preachers than to the agitation, even violence, of the artisans and hand-workers. The ruling patrician class had kept a cool distance from both Zwingli and Zurich, who represented a fierce Swiss patriotism for which they had little taste. Unlike the other major Swiss cities of Zurich and Berne, Basle saw itself as close to the Holy Roman Empire, and it remained a free imperial city, meaning that its loyalty was to the emperor and that it was entitled to representation at imperial diets. Despite the theological kinship of Zwingli with Johannes Oecolampadius, the principal reformer of Basle, the differences between the two cities had been all too apparent in the reluctance of the Baslers to support Zurich in the Second Kappel War of 1531 in which the Catholic Swiss Confederates routed Reformed Zurich.[5] The war ended disastrously in October with Zwingli's violent death in a botched campaign; Oecolampadius died soon after, of natural causes, though Catholic opponents falsely suggested it was suicide. For all the internal Protestant rancour, however, from the point of view of the Catholic Swiss Confederates Basle was a full member of the heretical Protestant alliance and in the peace settlement after Kappel punitive financial damages were imposed on the city. This hit Basle where it hurt most. By far the wealthiest Swiss Confederate, the city frequently acted as banker to the other Confederates. It did not take the Basle patricians and merchants long to divine that the bellicose religious politics of Zwingli and Zurich were bad for business.

Basle was also the city of the ageing Erasmus, though he took little part in public affairs and certainly did not embrace the new religion.[6] Most of those close to him, such as the Amerbach family, did adhere to the Reformed faith, but on their own terms.[7] Their religious inclinations were a fluid amalgam of evangelical and humanist principles, generally more in sympathy with the ideas of Martin Bucer than their own church leader, Oswald Myconius – whom Erasmus once described as 'homo ineptus'. The Basle church leadership was divided without any clear sense of theological direction. Myconius was a weak and vacillating man who had once been an enthusiastic supporter of Zwingli – to the extent of writing a hagiographical poem in honour of the dead reformer. In sharp contrast was Andreas Bodenstein von Karlstadt, Luther's old nemesis, now resident in Basle, whose theology had a more radical hue.[8] In between were distinguished figures such as Simon Grynaeus and Sebastian Münster, humanist scholars of Greek and Hebrew. As Calvin arrived in the city, the Basle church and civic authorities were in the midst of a bitter dispute over the university, which had been closed since 1529.[9] The principal issue was whether the newly reopened university should offer degrees. A seemingly arcane point, but for the reformers the medieval universities and their traditions had been the great enemy, and degrees smacked of a return to hated Roman practices.

A major attraction of Basle for Calvin was its printing industry, which enjoyed a well-deserved reputation for the production of scholarly, luxuriant and mostly Latin works.[10] The figure of Erasmus loomed large. The 1513 edition of his *Adages*, one of the great masterpieces of the northern Renaissance, appeared from the Basle presses in a handsome new roman type created especially for the work. The result was visually stunning, consolidating the relationship between Europe's leading humanist and the city, and elevating Basle to the front rank of print centres. Basle printers became renowned for their technical and artistic prowess expressed through the reproduction of elegant woodcuts and the use of different typefaces to effect a general 'harmony and simplicity' of presentation.[11] Basle was most closely associated with the printing of Bibles, which had been produced in the city before the Reformation. It was also known for its critical editions, and Erasmus' presence set the standard. He had come to Basle to oversee the edition of Jerome (1516) printed by Johann Froben, who soon became a close friend. Over the ensuing fifty years Basle presses also produced an impressive series of critical editions of the church fathers, such as Augustine, Chrysostom and Origen, all of which had been edited by the great Dutch humanist.

For a brief period in the 1520s Basle had been a centre of French evangelical printing, though this had petered out by the end of the decade. Early pamphlets by Guillaume Farel were printed by Andreas Cratander in 1524, who during the 1520s also produced several of the biblical commentaries of Jacques Lefèvre d'Etaples. Various people Calvin came to know in Basle had played decisive roles in the printing of evangelical literature sent to France. His hosts, Conrad Resch and his wife Katarina Klein, were a good example. Through Resch Calvin was introduced to a group of scholar–printers deeply

committed to the evangelical cause, including Balthasar Lasius, Thomas
Platter, Robert Winter and Johannes Oporinus.[12] Late in his life Platter
wrote one of the most extraordinary autobiographical works of the sixteenth
century, describing his journey from poverty in Wallis (now south-western
Switzerland) to the centres of the reform movement in Zurich and Basle.[13] He
was an early supporter of Zwingli and eventually married one of Oswald
Myconius' maids. In Basle he came under the patronage of Johannes Oporinus,
for whom he worked until he could find employment as a teacher of Greek in
the school. Eventually, Platter, Oporinus and Lasius were able to set up a print
shop. Platter's son Felix also kept a diary in which he recounted an episode
from his childhood when he and his father had met John Calvin as he was
passing through Basle lands in 1541 on his way to Geneva from Strasbourg.
According to Felix, the young boy had to wait while Calvin and his father
chatted about the *Institutes* over sugar wine at a local inn.[14]

The luminary among the group, without doubt, was Johannes Oporinus, a
native of Basle and formerly assistant to the printer Froben.[15] Oporinus was
not simply a technician or businessman, though he was both; he was also a
scholar whose knowledge of ancient languages surely impressed the young
Calvin. His careful copyediting of texts had enabled him to master both Greek
and Latin, and shortly after Calvin's departure from Basle Oporinus became
professor of Greek at the university.

Thirty years after Calvin's arrival, the Reformed theologian Peter Ramus
lodged in the Resch home in Basle with the aged widow Katarina, who remembered the young French exile of 1535. Her recollections to Ramus differ somewhat from Calvin's account in his psalms preface, where he emphasizes the
loneliness and solitude of his 'hidden' existence. Katarina recalled the
numerous French students and refugees with whom Calvin had contact, above
all Nicolas Cop and Louis du Tillet, with whom he had arrived in Basle from
France.[16] Indeed, far from shutting himself away, Calvin seems to have cultivated relations within the French- and German-speaking circles, including two
students from the Dauphiné, Gaspard Carmel and Claude Chanisien, who had
matriculated at the university in the autumn of 1535 and who became close
friends. Calvin also came to know Claude de Féray, with whom he would later
work closely in Strasbourg. Among other notables was Pierre Viret, who was
briefly in the city in November 1535 and met Calvin. More ominous encounters featured the future enemies Pierre Toussaint and Pierre Caroli; when
Caroli arrived in Basle he was already railing against Guillaume Farel, whom
he claimed had attempted to murder him in Geneva.[17]

The lynchpin of the Basle intellectual world was Simon Grynaeus, who had returned from the Lutheran university in Tübingen in the summer of 1535 to take up residence in the Collegium, where he gathered together a circle of French students.[18] Calvin was introduced to Grynaeus by Antoine Morelet du Museau, a dazzling figure from a distinguished French family related by marriage to the Briçonnets. Antoine had been close to Erasmus and Budé, as well as to the leading Swiss reformers, and had been a royal secretary in Paris before coming to Basle shortly before the Placards Affair.[19] There were numerous royal agents in Basle posing as evangelicals but Morelet was not one of them. He was sincere in his beliefs, though he returned to the king's service as a diplomat and continued in that role until his death in Basle in 1552. The life of an exile was perilous in the extreme, particularly for the prominent. Not only might they be forced to forsake worldly goods in leaving France, but danger abounded on every side. It was not uncommon for French noblemen to be attacked or kidnapped outside the walls of Basle. A horse-ride in the country could be fatal. The danger was not only from local brigands, but from agents of the crown.[20]

Alongside Grynaeus, the leading humanist scholar in Basle was the Hebraist Sebastian Münster, who just prior to Calvin's arrival had completed a translation of the Old Testament into Latin.[21] A diffident man, Münster was a true humanist in the spirit of Erasmus who believed in using philology to establish the best possible text. He also made extensive use of medieval Jewish sources, a deeply controversial step that earned him a reputation among some as a 'Judaizer'. Luther admired Münster for his translations but criticized him for his friendliness to Jewish scholarship, while the Catholic theologian Johannes Eck referred to him as 'Rabbi Münster'. Calvin was drawn to this mild-mannered scholar and they remained in correspondence till Münster's death from the plague in 1552. It is possible that Calvin studied Hebrew with Münster, as Colladon suggested in his life of Calvin, but the evidence is not conclusive.[22] Calvin's closeness to Münster was demonstrated by his fidelity to the annotations made by the master in his Latin translation of the Hebrew Bible. Also, there was a familial bond, for Calvin's cousin Olivetanus had attended Münster's lectures on Genesis in 1531. During his stay in Basle, Calvin probably heard Münster at the university, but as a visitor, not a student.[23]

The one person whom Calvin never met was Erasmus, who had returned to Basle in 1535 a very ill man. We have no idea whether Erasmus knew anything of Calvin, but the Dutchman's closest friends in the city warmed to the young

Frenchman. Bonifacius Amerbach was a well-known jurist who had also studied under Alciati. A magnificent scholar and a man of expansive views, he believed in the study of legal texts through a rigorous philological and grammatical approach, the very tradition that had shaped Calvin.[24] His theology was Erasmian, but heavily influenced by Martin Bucer. He rejected the Zwinglianism of the Basle reformers in favour of a stronger sense of spiritual presence in the sacrament. Calvin must have found such a like-minded and sympathetic figure congenial company.

The flow of exiles and merchants in and out of Basle brought disturbing news of the desperate situation in France. Trumped-up charges of sedition had been used by Catholics to turn the king against the supporters of the evangelical faith. It was this traducing of his brethren, according to Calvin, that led him to write the *Institutes* and confront the persecutions in his letter of dedication to Francis I. In Basle he was engrossed in following events in his homeland, but the culture of the city in which he had found refuge left its mark. Basle was his first experience of an officially Protestant state. Even though the Reformed church in the city was divided and its polity still fluid, Calvin saw for the first time the workings of a Protestant magistracy; he worshipped in churches in which the new liturgies were followed, though he would not have understood the language. The university, where he followed courses without matriculating, was not a match for Paris, Orléans or Bourges, but it was his first exposure to a Protestant institution of higher education. All in all, it was entirely different from anything he would have seen or known in France.

The Broken Body

From Basle Calvin had an unobstructed view of the fight tearing apart the Protestant world of the German-speaking lands. This was the dispute over the Lord's Supper. From the early years of the Reformation Martin Luther and Huldrych Zwingli had profoundly and acrimoniously parted ways in their teaching over what took place in the sacrament.[25] To reduce a complex matter to a few words, the disputed point was whether and how Christ is present in the bread and wine. Both sides loudly and clearly rejected the medieval doctrine of transubstantiation central to the mass, in which the elements truly become the body and blood of Christ. Yet, for Luther and his followers Christ is nevertheless truly present. Zwingli, in contrast, emphasized that Christ was not physically present, but that the elect had union with him through faith. Although the battle lines formed between Wittenberg and Zurich, many reformers held views which fell between the principal antagonists. What made the debate so damaging was not only the theological division, which was bad enough, but the fact that without agreement on the sacrament there was no possibility of any form of union between the German and Swiss Protestants, and this severely hamstrung the Reformation.

The greatest casualty was the unity of the Protestant princes and cities against the Catholic emperor. Efforts at reconciliation were made, most notably by Philip of Hesse, who in 1529 managed to bring Luther and Zwingli together in Marburg. The attempt failed. The acrimony was theological and personal. When Zwingli was killed on 11 October 1531 Luther snorted with contempt. The enmity between Wittenberg and Zurich which came to dominate Calvin's life is difficult to understand when the arguments seem so abstract, but its importance cannot be overstated. Fundamentally, the two sides held irreconcilable doctrines of the Eucharist, the very symbol of Christian unity. At heart was the presence of Christ in the sacrament, and Calvin's pursuit of church unity hinged on finding a resolution to this intractable debate.

The Protestant curtain was torn and all efforts to mend it appeared doomed to failure. The man who most actively pursued this seemingly hopeless cause was Martin Bucer, the reformer of Strasbourg. Initially closer to Zwingli than to Luther, Bucer spent much of the early 1530s trying to pull together the southern German cities into a unified theological front.[26] Luther blew hot and cold on the idea of reconciliation with the Swiss, preferring their complete capitulation. Philip Melanchthon, the distinguished professor and theologian in Wittenberg, in contrast, was more flexible and politic. Bucer and Wolfgang Capito travelled hundreds of miles and wrote document after document in search of peace. For them, unlike for Luther and Heinrich Bullinger, Zwingli's successor as head of the Zurich church, the debate over the meaning of 'this is my body' was a battle over words which could be resolved by calm heads.

There was, however, a great deal at stake, as the newly formed Schmalkaldic League of Protestant princes and cities, set up as a defence against the emperor, desperately required theological unity.[27] After a meeting in Kassel at the end of 1534 Bucer largely accepted Luther's position on the sacraments. This paved the way for the southern German cities and principalities to enter the League. The theological formulation which took place at the conference in Wittenberg in May 1536 brought compromise on both sides, but the resulting Wittenberg Concord, as it was known, was largely Lutheran in character.[28] The concord was essentially drafted by Philip Melanchthon and imposed on Bucer, whose response was characteristically prolix, but ultimately positive.

For their part, the Reformed Swiss likewise sought theological unity following the catastrophe of Kappel in 1531. In January 1536 the leading theologians gathered in Basle to draft a statement in Latin of their theological positions.[29] The principal force was Heinrich Bullinger, who later recalled having met the young John Calvin at this time. Bucer and Capito attended the session and initially hoped that it might serve as the basis for negotiations with the Lutherans. Even Luther himself was not entirely put off by the Swiss document, which became known as the First Helvetic Confession. However, when the Swiss declared themselves against the Wittenberg Concord the game was over and old hostilities renewed. For the Swiss, the First Helvetic Confession was a crucial stage of theological reconstruction after Zwingli's death, and it confirmed the supremacy of Heinrich Bullinger as their leading churchman. However, their refusal to accept the Wittenberg Concord placed them outside the Schmalkaldic League and beyond the pale of the German reformation. They lost their influence over the southern German cities and lands, and Martin Bucer emerged as the principal theological and ecclesiastical voice of Protestantism in the region.

Calvin was learning his first lessons in the self-destructive nature of disunity within the Reformation. The divisions between the Lutherans and the Zwinglians would haunt him over the next two decades as he tried to break the impasse. Like Bucer, Calvin came to believe that reconciliation was possible if the parties really wanted it. Martin Bucer, in his relentless pursuit of unity, became Calvin's model churchman, and the greatest influence on his formation as a minister and teacher.

A New Author

In many respects Calvin obtained in Basle exactly what he sought, a place to write and study. The fruits of his labours were extraordinary, revealing an astonishing capacity for work. In addition to the revision to his *Psychopannychia*, which he had brought from France, Calvin had completed his *Institutes of the Christian Religion* by the autumn of 1535, and would bitterly complain about the slowness of Oporinus in producing the work, which did not appear until spring the following year. Even if he had already begun the text while with du

Tillet in France, its polished and elegant form strongly suggests many hours of later endeavour. The literary achievements of his stay in Basle in part reflect the intellectual currents to which Calvin was exposed. In the dedication of his Romans commentary to Simon Grynaeus he recounted the fraternal manner in which the two men had discussed the Bible and its interpretation. There were many opportunities for such conversations with a range of remarkable figures. But circumstances and contacts alone do not explain the result. The Basle period saw the appearance of works of astonishing depth, elegance and intellectual penetration. A young man who had never formally studied theology presented to the world writings that dazzled his contemporaries. A brilliant writer had emerged.

When Calvin arrived in Basle at the end of 1534 he made contact with his cousin Pierre-Robert Olivétan (Olivetanus), whom he had probably not seen since his Paris days. Olivétan's edition of the Bible in French (known as the Serrières Bible) had been paid for by the Waldensians, a religious group that thrived in the Dauphiné and Piedmont regions and had been evangelized by Protestant reformers, and it was ready for printing at the beginning of June. Calvin was asked to provide two prefaces, in Latin and French, to the New Testament.[30] It is not known whether he worked on the translation itself, but Olivétan has left us a sense of the complexities. 'It is as difficult to render Hebrew and Greek eloquences into French as to teach the gentle lark to sing the song of the raucous crow.'[31] Indeed, when Calvin came to revise the text of Olivétan's Bible over ten years later in 1546 he argued that the language was 'crude' and full of mistakes, though he was careful not to criticize his cousin.[32] The French language was in a rapid state of transition; it was a time of extraordinary creativity, with new forms being created as works were printed. Calvin would play a lead role in that story.

The Latin preface, addressed to 'All Emperors, Kings, Princes, and Peoples of the Kingdom of Christ', is less remarkable, containing many stock reflections on the nature of the Bible and the difficulties of translation.[33] Calvin attacked Catholic theologians and defended evangelical printers against charges that they had attempted to remain anonymous by not putting their names to their works, a practice frequently used by Pierre de Vingle, who had produced the famous Placards of 1534. He also addressed the question of whether the Bible should be translated into the vernacular. Citing the examples of the church fathers Augustine, Jerome and Chrysostom, Calvin held that there was a long and honourable tradition of making scripture available to the 'simple people'. There was nothing radical in this point, found in

virtually all Protestant vernacular translations of the period, including the
Zurich German Bible of 1531.[34]

The French preface, however, entitled 'Letter to those who love Jesus Christ
and his Gospel' and placed at the head of the New Testament, was work of a
different order. It was a song of praise to the glory of God and creation. The
preface is strikingly close to the first edition of the *Institutes*, particularly with
its concern for true piety. Humanity, Calvin writes, was created in the image of
God, yet in exercising its free will it chose sin.[35] Nevertheless, while humankind
may have rejected God, God has not turned against creation, which abounds
with signs of the divine presence, a principal theme of the *Institutes*.[36] Taking
his cue from Paul ('Since what may be known about God is plain to them,
because God has made it plain to them' – Romans 1:19), Calvin offers an
evocative description of how even the dumb creatures of the world praise
God's work. God's revelation in the universe leads humans on the right path in
searching for God, but that revelation, following Paul, is to be found within
humans themselves.[37]

There is no disharmony between God's revelation and the order of creation.
God called a people, the Israelites, to be the chosen people, but they were not
faithful to God's law, preferring idolatry to true worship. To reconcile the
gentiles and Jews, God made a second alliance through Jesus Christ, the
second Adam. Christ was the fulfilment of the promise given to Abraham, and
the ceremonial laws of the Old Testament a foreshadowing of the goodness of
the Son of God. Christ is the Messiah, and the Old and New Testaments unite
in their testimony to that truth, and that he will come again in the fullness of
time. With his arrival Christ had concluded a new, eternal covenant sealed by
his death on the cross. What makes all of this real is faith. It is faith that opens
one's eyes to the signs of God's goodness and governance in the world.

Read together with the *Psychopannychia*, the preface to the Bible shows the
depth of Calvin's grasp of theology and of his biblical piety. But most remarkable is the intimate nature of Calvin's God, dwelling through Christ in the great
figures of the Old Testament. The preface was an exquisite hymn to the divinity
and humanity of Jesus Christ, filled with references to the Gospels and the
Pauline letters. Calvin cited various church fathers, including a misplaced reference to Tertullian. How had he absorbed so much? There have been suggestions
of various possible models for the work, and while he would have had a great
deal of Protestant literature available to him in Basle, there is no obvious
exemplar.[38] The preface was the product of an original mind. Calvin developed
the understanding of God first revealed in the *Psychopannychia*. God is not

distant, but present in the world with the faithful. In this respect, Calvin had moved away from the teaching of the Stoic philosophers who held that God was a distant, remote figure, in favour of the divinity he found in scripture. God accompanies those who journey through the world, not from afar, but through the indwelling of the Spirit. This may offer us the clearest hint of the nature of Calvin's conversion: an intimate and comforting sense of the nearness of God. Home, for the exile, is not a location, but union with God.

'Not One Seditious Word': The *Institutes* of 1536

The preface to the Olivétan Bible closes with an appeal to kings and bishops to commit themselves to the education of the faithful. This spirit guided and informed Calvin's greatest achievement of the Basle period, the *Institutes of the Christian Religion*. As its dedicatory preface to Francis I reveals, the *Institutes* was intended both as an apology for the Reformed faith in France and as a tool of instruction in the essentials of true piety. Structured in six chapters, treating the Law, the Creed, the Lord's Prayer and the two sacraments of the Lord's Supper and Baptism, the text possessed the traditional form of a catechism, which meant that it followed the key learned elements of the faith. In this, as has long been recognized, Calvin drew from Luther's *Small Catechism* of 1522 and *Large Catechism* of 1529.

From his contacts in Basle Calvin was alarmed to hear of a ruse employed by the opponents of reform in France to justify persecution of evangelicals: 'Certain wicked and lying pamphlets were circulated, stating that none were treated with such cruelty but Anabaptists and seditious persons, who by their perverse ravings and false opinions were overthrowing not only religion but also all civil order.'[39] Outraged by the suggestion that the evangelicals were either Anabaptists or seditious, Calvin sought 'to prove that these reports were false and calumnious, and thus to vindicate my brethren, whose death was precious in the sight of the Lord; and next, that as the same cruelties might very soon after be exercised against many unhappy individuals, foreign nations might be touched with at least some compassion towards them and solicitude for them'.[40] Twenty years later, he reflected on what he had intended. 'It appeared to me that unless I opposed them to the utmost of my ability, my silence could not be vindicated from the charge of cowardice and treachery. This was the consideration which induced me to publish my *Institutes of the Christian Religion*.'[41]

The term 'institute' (*institutio*) was a significant choice and requires some explanation. It had been used by the Roman writers Quintilian and Lactantius, and more recently by Erasmus and Luther, who employed it in his *Larger Catechism* of 1529. It is important that we do not confuse the 1536 edition with later versions of the *Institutes*; the book which appeared in Basle was not designed as a comprehensive treatment of the Christian religion. The *Institutio* was fundamentally a practical book of instruction, like a catechism.[42] It was also never intended to be Calvin's final word. Almost as soon as he finished, he began the process of revision and expansion that would culminate in the final 1559 edition. The work changed shape, but in key respects retained its essential character: Calvin wanted to find the clearest possible means of making the articles of faith comprehensible.[43]

The dedicatory letter to Francis I was reprinted in all subsequent editions of the *Institutes* till its final version in 1559, twelve years after the king's death. Calvin revised it, particularly in 1539, though the tone remained largely the same – a description of the circumstances which had led him to write the work, an appeal for his persecuted brethren, and a defence of the Reformed faith against Catholic attacks. Calvin the humanist and lawyer found his voice in this beautifully crafted piece of prose in which arguments are formulated with precision of language and thought. Deeply respectful of the monarchy, he was unwilling to offend and never suggested that Francis was responsible for events in the kingdom. 'I perceived that the fury of certain wicked persons prevailed so far in your realm that there is no place in it for sound doctrine.'[44] For himself, his role was 'to instruct . . . that you may learn the nature of the doctrine against which these madmen burn with rage who today disturb your realm with sword and fire'. Calvin had become Seneca, and Francis was his Nero. He pleaded with the king to cease the persecutions of the evangelicals, again without assignation of guilt. Similarly, he did not wish to suggest that he wrote from any sense of personal gain.

> Do not think that I am here preparing my own personal defence, thereby to return safely to my native land. Even though I regard my country with as much natural affection as becomes me, as things now stand I do not much regret being excluded. Rather, I embrace the common cause of all believers, that of Christ himself – a cause completely torn and trampled in your kingdom today, lying, as it were, utterly forlorn, more through the tyranny of certain Pharisees than with your approval.[45]

Calvin defended the evangelicals against charges that their religion was new, doubtful and uncertain. The appearance of innovation, he argued, arises from the depredations of the Catholic church, for the Gospel has been long buried under the charade of false practices. As for the demand that the evangelicals confirm their faith with miracles, 'we may also fitly remember that Satan has his miracles, which, though they are deceitful tricks rather than authentic acts, are of such sort as to mislead the simple-minded and untutored'.[46] Calvin struck repeatedly at the central accusation of the Catholic polemicists that the evangelical faith was a new weapon which had slashed the Church's artery, its traditions. Like all other reformers, Calvin understood fully that he had to be able to answer the question of authority and tradition. Against expectation, the fathers of the early Church, he assured Francis, were by no means a sure foundation for the teachings, practices and laws of the Roman church. Quite the contrary; their biblical doctrines were those taught by the evangelicals. Similarly, the Catholic use of 'custom' was invalid. Just because a practice had become a custom in the church did not grant it divine sanction. In one of his most effective passages Calvin opined,

> now, then, let our adversaries throw at us as many examples as they wish, both of past and present ages. If we hallow the Lord of Hosts, we shall not be greatly afraid. Even though many ages may have agreed in like impiety, the Lord is strong to wreak vengeance, even to the third and fourth generation. Even though the whole world may conspire in the same wickedness, he has taught us by experience what is the end of those who sin with the multitude.[47]

The true Church is not the visible institution with its corrupt hierarchy; it exists where the preaching and hearing of God's Word and the lawful administration of the sacraments are found. This Church, according to Calvin, can at times be invisible, hence its apparent disappearance from history, but it is never entirely lost. God knows the chosen: 'let us therefore leave to him the fact that he sometimes removes from men's sight the external notion of his Church'.

In response to the charge faced by all the reformers, from Wittenberg to Zurich, that their doctrines were the source of social and political tumult, Calvin offered the standard reply. Quoting 1 Kings 18, he wrote, 'Elijah taught us what we ought to reply to such charges; it is not we who either spread errors abroad or incite tumults; but it is they who contend against God's power.' He wished to relieve Francis of any impression that evangelicals were to be confused with Anabaptists, the true agents of Satan and disseminators of unrest. Those who truly profess Christ follow his Gospel and are utterly loyal to the monarch. Calvin concluded with a wonderful piece of inversion.

> We are unjustly charged, too, with intentions, of a sort as we have never even given the least suspicion. We are, I suppose, contriving the overthrow of kingdoms – we, from whom not one seditious word was ever heard; we, whose life when we lived under you was always acknowledged to be quiet and simple; we, who do not cease to pray for the full prosperity of your-self and your kingdom, although we are now fugitives from home! We are, I suppose, wildly chasing after wanton vices! Even though in our moral actions many things are blameworthy, nothing deserves such reproach as this.

The dedication is a brilliant legal defence of the evangelicals in France, a torrid denunciation of papistry and a vision of the Church. The *Institutes* was not written as devotional literature; it was for the people of the Church. True faith exists within the structures of the Church and must have order and form, for humanity is weak and sinful. God calls that Church to reject idolatry and embrace true worship. The letter of dedication unites Calvin's legal and biblical worlds. The trained lawyer and the self-taught theologian were coming together. At the very moment he was making the case for true religion, he was setting out the legal framework of the Church.

The influence of Luther on Calvin's 1536 *Institutes* is unmistakable, though by no means slavish. The work opens with Calvin's famous line: 'Nearly the whole of sacred doctrine consists in these two parts: knowledge of God and of ourselves.' He had found his own voice in expressing the primacy of faith, which he writes 'is nothing else than a firm conviction of mind whereby we determine with ourselves that God's truth is so certain, that it is incapable of not accomplishing what it has pledged to do by his holy Word [Romans 10:11]'.[48] He strongly asserted the role of Christ as the one true mediator and robustly defended the doctrine of the Trinity against those who argued that such language is not to be found in the Bible. 'Christ, the true son, has been given to us as our brother by Him [God the Father] in order that what belongs to Him by nature may become ours by benefit of adoption, provided we embrace with sure faith this great blessing.'[49] Speaking of the sacraments, Calvin displayed the influence of Zwingli, though again not uncritically. Criticizing both the Roman doctrine of the mass and those who have weakened the role of the sacraments, he subtly navigates through the treacherous waters of Reformation thought to present a distinctive position that was more than mere compromise. Faith and sacraments are inextricably bound together, neither subordinated to the other. This was an argument he would expand and develop over the ensuing decades.

In the final part of the *Institutes*, Calvin treats themes that would become the hallmarks of his life as a reformer: the freedom of a Christian, the Church and political authority. Once more echoing Luther, the freedom of the Christian is the freedom to obey God without compulsion. It is directed towards the service of God, but without injury to others and without being shackled to human traditions. The crucial distinction lies in the difference between those things essential to faith and those not. To confuse the two is to imperil Christian liberty. The Church must not bind the consciences of the faithful with human laws; its role is to ensure the true and orderly worship of God, the preservation of the community of the faithful and the promotion of concord through the wise use of human ordinances. Temporal rulers are charged by God with the maintenance of the state, and in carrying out this duty they have divine sanction. They must avoid tyranny and excessive leniency. Equity, the theme of the Seneca commentary, figures prominently in Calvin's discussion. The positive laws of the state must be shaped by a sense of proportion and appropriateness: rulers must use wise discernment in applying judgement and punishment. The people, Christians included, require the firm hand of civil government. The world is a mixture of the godly and ungodly, and the magistrates rule over both without distinction. As servants of God, the magistrates must be obeyed by all, including Christians, and Calvin offers no grounds for political resistance.

Although Calvin fundamentally altered the structure of his *Institutes* in 1539, not least as a result of his intensive study of the church fathers, his understanding of what it meant to be a theologian was in place in Basle. God has spoken to humanity in scripture, opened a relationship in which women and men should know and worship God – a worship not confined to religious services, but which embraces every aspect of human existence. The Word of God animates all human faculties; it consecrates them to the service of God. The theologian, versed in the tools of rhetoric, interprets the Word and brings it into the public sphere. Those who hear are not just taught, but are moved to live the Christian life characterized by love and sacrifice. This was the rhetorical element of the *Institutes*. Calvin sought not only to teach, but to persuade people of the truth. He rejected theology as a speculative science; it is an utterly practical art by which Christians are taught how to live. To do this required that they had to be persuaded to change.

Calvin fundamentally disagreed with the great medieval Dominican Thomas Aquinas on the nature of theology. The *Institutes* was intended as a guide to scripture for those who felt God's grace, to strengthen them in that sure knowledge of salvation promised by God. In short, it was to encourage true piety and devotion. How this beautifully crafted expression and interpretation of God's loving power appeared from the hand of a twenty-five-year-old exile who had never formally studied theology cannot be adequately explained by historical circumstances. The *Institutes* succeeded just as the Seneca commentary had failed: it was an immediate publishing success and drew praise from across the Protestant world. The *Institutes* marked a sea change in Calvin's sense of self: in the *Psychopannychia* he had come to speak in the language of scripture, above all Paul. Now he presented himself as a doctor of the Church. He was instructing the faithful as a learned interpreter of the Word.

CHAPTER FIVE

Violent Reformations and Tumult

Court Intrigue

TOWARDS THE end of Calvin's stay in Basle a mysterious episode occurred. Suddenly in March 1536, he and Louis du Tillet travelled into Italian lands to visit the court at Ferrara of Renée of France, daughter of King Louis XII (1498–1515). The details of the journey have remained unclear, though it seems that Calvin had been invited following the publication of his *Institutes*. Physically deformed, for which she was mercilessly mocked, and married to a philandering husband, Renée was a woman of remarkable character to whom Calvin developed a sincere and lasting attachment.[1] Deeply committed to the evangelical faith, she made her court a refuge for French religious refugees while attempting to preserve relations with the papacy. Like her cousin Marguerite of Angoulême, Renée was in an impossible situation: suspected of heresy by Catholics and criticized by the reformers for not leaving the Roman church, she sought to remain true to her religious principles while preserving her royal position. In Ferrara, Calvin enjoyed good relations with the duchess and her entourage, and all went well until Good Friday, when after a protest against the veneration of the cross in the chapel it became evident that numerous evangelicals were living at the court under her protection. In fact, she was harbouring men who had been involved in the Placards Affair of 1534. This led to a bitter fight between Renée and her husband, who was implacably opposed to the evangelical faith. The men were arrested – it has even been suggested that Calvin was one of them. Renée appealed to her cousin Francis I, who granted a pardon. Amid the commotion Calvin and du Tillet fled and returned to Basle.

Ferrara exposed Calvin to the murky world of noble court culture, where religious convictions often conflicted with political and cultural demands. Even those of profound biblical faith, like Renée, had to mask their beliefs to avoid detection and persecution. In Ferrara Calvin experienced once more the nebulous culture of dissembling, one he had known in France and fled. Yet he also saw how a woman of the highest rank could act to protect the evangelical movement, as Marguerite had done in France. He was drawn to the pious French noblewomen, sensing in them both a spiritual bond as well as access to their less devout but politically decisive husbands.

A Prophetic Encounter

The Edict of Coucy of July 1535 permitted exiles to return to France on condition they renounced their heresy within six months.[2] The following year Calvin made use of this opening to travel to his homeland to conclude family business, though without intention of recanting. He could hardly have known it would be his last visit to his native land. Back from Italy, he continued on to Paris to bring his brother Antoine back to live with him in Basle. He also instructed his brothers to sell the remaining family lands in Noyon. The return to Basle was complicated by the resumption of war between Charles V and Francis I. The normal route through Strasbourg and along the Rhine was blocked by hostile armies, so, together with Antoine and their sister Marie, he diverted through Geneva.

The plan was to overnight in the city on Lake Léman before returning to Basle, where Calvin had pressing writing commitments. He had not informed anyone of his arrival and took an assumed name. Louis du Tillet, however, got word of his close friend's presence and excitedly informed Guillaume Farel, who lost no time in tracking down his fellow Frenchman. What transpired next has become legend.

> Farel, who burned with an extraordinary zeal to advance the Gospel, immediately strained every nerve to detain me. And after having learned that my heart was set on devoting myself to private studies, for which I wished to keep myself free from other pursuits, and finding that he gained nothing by entreaties, he proceeded to utter a threat that God would curse my retirement, and the tranquillity of the studies which I

sought, if I should withdraw and refuse to give assistance, when the necessity was so urgent. I was so struck with fear by this threat that I desisted from the journey which I had undertaken, but mindful of my natural bashfulness and timidity, I would not bring myself under any obligation to discharge any particular office.[3]

Who was this man who loomed up before the bashful and timid Calvin to threaten him with eternal damnation if he did not commit himself to the service of the Church? Guillaume Farel was an incendiary, prophetic and highly divisive figure who had led the Reformation in the French-speaking lands of the Swiss Confederation and carried the movement to Geneva.[4] The dramatic encounter with Calvin was entirely in keeping with a character whose ministry was straight from the Old Testament. In the course of his preaching campaigns churches were damaged, priests publicly mocked and the people warned of God's fury at their idolatry. He was a man of confrontation, and where others saw a fiery demon, Calvin perceived in Farel the hand of God.

Violent Reformers and Reluctant People: The Pays de Vaud

Calvin's arrival in Geneva makes sense only against the background of the Reformation of the French-speaking lands in what is today western Switzerland. From 1528 Farel had been engaged by the Bernese to spread the Reformed faith in the French territories under their control. This he did with alacrity, but not entirely successfully. His inflammatory sermons were badly received and he was forced to move from one community to another, often with haste. His greatest triumph came in the city of Neuchâtel in the autumn of 1530, following a campaign of preaching in which he poured forth his invective against the mass and the priests.[5] He used tactics and language made infamous with the Placards Affair of 1534: in 1530 he posted placards in Neuchâtel denouncing those who celebrated the mass as 'villains, murderers, thieves, renouncers of Jesus Christ and seducers of the people'.[6] The assault on the mass was the focus of Farel's campaign; churches were to be purged of idolatrous worship. It was a message that had come from Zurich and which he and his band proclaimed from pulpits and in the streets with impassioned rhetoric.

In the autumn of 1530 a frenzied crowd carried Farel into the cathedral in Neuchâtel where he denounced the abomination of images. Stirred by his castigations, the crowd turned on the saints, altars and vestments in a fury of destruction. The force of crowd violence pushed the Reformation to a vote, and by a slim majority the new faith carried the day. Farel had made Neuchâtel the first French-speaking city of the Reformation and a vital base for the propagation of the movement in neighbouring France. He was accompanied by his former student Pierre Viret, a native Vaudois from Orbe. Their campaign was significantly bolstered by the arrival in Neuchâtel of the printer Pierre de Vingle, who produced the tracts written by Antoine Marcourt in the Placards Affair. Using Vingle's press, Farel, Viret and Marcourt printed venomous literature pillorying the mass and the Catholic priesthood. It was from Neuchâtel that Farel went to Geneva, where from 1532 he was decisive in turning the city towards the Reformation.

Farel's activities enjoyed the protection of Berne and its considerable military force. The Bernese encouraged his campaign of violence by turning a blind eye to destructive and illegal acts. In addition to printing abusive attacks on priests, Farel and his fellow ministers engaged in covert acts of iconoclasm in which Catholic churches were attacked, often in the dead of night, and images desecrated. Violence took many forms: hatred in print, excoriating sermons and physical damage to churches. This conflict was a world away from the orderly reformations in the German-speaking lands of the Swiss Confederation. In the French-speaking lands it was pitched battle between a small but fanatical number of reformers and a resolutely Catholic population utterly resistant to their charms.

In 1536 everything changed when Bernese troops marched westward across the Pays de Vaud to the walls of Geneva, taking by force the lands which had belonged to the Duke of Savoy. Lausanne, the cathedral city on Lake Léman, became an administrative outpost of the Bernese, while Geneva was permitted autonomy, though dependent on Berne politically and militarily. The easy success of the campaign, which was virtually unopposed, masked a deeper problem. The people of the Pays de Vaud may have had no love for their Savoyard overlords, but they were faithful Catholics with no interest in Berne's Reformed faith.[7] At first, the Bernese were content that their new French-speaking subjects should retain their old religion, but this proved untenable, and the process of Reformation was begun by force.

From the perspective of the reformers in Berne, the situation in the Vaud was dismal: only twelve of the 154 parishes in the region showed any trace of evangelical activity.[8] The imposition of the Reformed faith began in the summer of 1536, shortly after Calvin's arrival in Geneva. To provide a sense of legitimacy, the Bernese magistrates employed a tactic often used in the Swiss reformation: they summoned a disputation to allow both sides to fight it out. It was to be held in

Lausanne in October and ten points of Reformed teaching provided the basis of the debate. This was not an open exchange of views: the outcome was already determined as the Bernese authorities intended to persuade the reluctant Vaudois to accept the new faith.[9] Pierre Viret, supported by Farel, Pierre Caroli and Antoine Marcourt, led the Reformed side and spoke to seven of the propositions.[10] Their opposition, in this case the cathedral chapter, was given the chance to respond before the floor was opened to interventions. Catholic representation, however, both numerically and intellectually, was feeble.

Notable was the contribution made by the twenty-seven-year-old John Calvin, who cited Tertullian in the debate on the Lord's Supper.[11] Scholars have heralded this moment as demonstrating Calvin's intellect and ability to turn a debate. He did score, but only when his team already held an invincible lead. Viret and Farel had carried the day and the outcome was not in doubt.[12] Calvin's intervention is, nevertheless, interesting, for in quoting the church fathers from memory, though not entirely accurately, he demonstrated the directions in which his studies were taking him. His formidable powers of recall, evident at this early point, became a hallmark of his career, much to the vexation of hapless opponents. In Lausanne, however, he was very much a team player. The foregone conclusion was declared: the mass was to be abolished in the Vaud and by 19 October a first reformation edict required the removal of altars, images and liturgical instruments. Religious objections, however, did not blind the eye to the value of these goods and many were sold to neighbouring Catholic parishes, while others were brought to Berne.[13] Only those items that could not be transported were destroyed. As everywhere else in Europe, the Reformation in the Vaud had its profiteers.

If ever Calvin needed to be taught a lesson about the implications of a semi-Reformed church full of people who conformed to religious practices in which they did not believe, the Vaud provided it. The Bernese were left in the awkward position of governing a region that had adopted the Reformation in name alone. The Reformed party was a tiny faction facing a hostile population determined to maintain its Catholic faith. Only a handful of the two hundred priests took up the offer to become Reformed ministers, though almost all continued to live in their parishes and draw the livings. The priests-turned-ministers had absolutely no interest in fostering the new faith, yet were not willing to choose exile over the financial security of remaining in office. As a result, they practised an inverse form of the dissembling that had already become evident in France. Their hopes, clearly, lay in the eventual restoration of the Catholic faith through either the proposed Council at Mantua or the

Duke of Savoy. Until then, they were prepared to engage in a level of outward conformity that, in the eyes of many, did not compromise their religious beliefs. The centre of opposition to Bernese rule was Lausanne, where the mass continued to be celebrated with little fear of retribution. It was a strange limbo in which ministers continued to dress as priests and the people retained their rosaries and statues of the saints. Few laypeople came to the Lord's Supper or brought their children to the Reformed church for baptism, and there was little that resembled evangelical preaching. Instead, Catholic prayers were often said in the Reformed churches outside the regular hours of worship.[14]

A City Reformation: Geneva

Geneva was in a peculiar situation during these events of the early 1530s. A foreign clerical leadership, gathered around the bishop and aligned to the House of Savoy, had dominated the political and economic life of the city until the mid-1520s. The magistrates, determined to wrest their independence from Savoy, needed to overcome the power of the church with its extensive landholdings and income. This led to the defining conflict between spiritual and temporal authority during the 1520s and 1530s. By 1527 Savoyard authority in Geneva had been broken, but the question of the church and its loyalties was far from resolved. The largely Savoyard clergy were viewed by many as hostile foreign agents working against the new republic and its liberties.[15] In the period leading up to 1535 the magistrates began a systematic confiscation of the church's sources of revenue. It was at this point that through the preaching of Farel and others evangelical ideas began to be heard in the city, winning supporters among Genevans and creating a tense religious atmosphere.

Although Geneva broke from its bishop in 1536, it was not an independent city.[16] In addition, the revolution which had swept the new order to power required a root-and-branch restructuring of every aspect of government, including religion, education, the judicial system, the chancery and defence. French replaced Latin as the language of Geneva's official records.

Geneva was a middling urban community of approximately 12,000 inhabitants, most of whom lived within walls rebuilt during the 1530s. Divided into the 'lower' and 'upper' city, it grew ever more crowded following the dismantling of its extramural suburbs where many of the more prosperous citizens had previously lived. The lower part of the city housed many of the merchants, craftsmen and inns, contained three large public squares, and was served by the church of the Madeleine.[17] Heading towards the upper city one passed the Hôpital, the poor house of Geneva, before arriving at the former cathedral of Saint-Pierre and the city hall. It was in the cloister house near Saint-Pierre that the Consistory and Company of Pastors met during Calvin's time. Geneva is divided by the River Rhône, and in the sixteenth century it was traversed by a great wooden bridge lined with shops, houses and mills with the church of Saint-Gervais, the second most important in Geneva, on one side. Three main roads brought merchants and travellers into the city demonstrating the key directions in which Geneva looked: Lyon and the south; Paris and Dijon; and Lausanne and the Swiss lands. Lake Léman provided the people with fresh water, fish and a travel route. In contrast to Basle, Zurich and Berne, Geneva had a very small rural hinterland, meaning, among other things, that it was unable to recruit much of an army when threatened. Geneva's military vulnerability, particularly with hostile Savoy and France as neighbours, only deepened its reliance on Berne.

The most important institution of the Genevan government was the Small Council, which consisted of twenty members and was presided over by four syndics (civil magistrates) who formed an executive.[18] The Small Council made the most important decisions for the city, and after the Reformation controlled the church, hiring and firing ministers and working with the Consistory. Next was the Council of Two Hundred, which consisted of representatives from the neighbourhoods of the city who voted on measures presented by the Small Council. The largest body in Geneva was its General Assembly, which included all heads of households and met four times a year. Its role was to approve or reject legislation from the Two Hundred. All in all, the political structures of Geneva mirrored those of most middling European cities of the sixteenth century. In most respects there was nothing remarkable about the city: its life revolved around trade; it had to worry about its larger neighbours; and the magistrates struggled to maintain social order by limiting drinking and violence, controlling prostitution and dealing with the poor and destitute.

But the factionalism tearing at the fabric of the city was calamitous. Guillaume Farel had arrived in Geneva in June 1532 and immediately aligned himself with a group of evangelical supporters and with the political faction known as the Eidguenots, or 'Les Enfants', which had led the struggle for Genevan independence and favoured closer ties with the Swiss Confederation. Employing the confrontational manner for which he had developed such a reputation in the Vaud, Farel demanded the abolition of the mass and the establishment of Gospel preaching. This brought him into direct confrontation with the bishop's vicar-general. The support afforded by the victorious

Eidguenots enabled the evangelicals to make headway and the first official evangelical worship service in Geneva was held on Good Friday 1533.

In January 1534 a disputation was held between Farel and the Dominican Guy Furbity. The result in favour of evangelical preaching was backed by the Bernese, eager both to undermine the bishop and to spread their religion. The hapless bishop was left without support and by October 1534 was easily deposed by a Genevan council determined to complete the appropriation of ecclesiastical authority and revenues. This did not indicate, by any means, that the Reformation had been established, for it was not until May 1535 that the mass was abolished, and only in the spring of 1536 was the new faith adopted by edict.

Certainly not all within the city were won over to the new religion, and traditional Catholicism remained strong. As in the Vaud, Farel divided communities with his aggressive methods. From 1535 we have the following graphic account by Jeanne de Jussie from the Convent of Sainte Claire in Geneva in her *Short Chronicle*.

> On the feast of the Madeleine [22 July], when the bells were ringing solemnly for mass in her church and the whole parish and other good Christians in the town were gathered there to hear the holy mass in great piety, that miserable preacher Farel brought his whole congregation. They came in their ordinary clothing to the church of the blessed Madeleine to obstruct her feast, and when they got inside they closed the church and stood at the door and forced people to hear that sermon. This greatly distressed and troubled everyone, the women cried out loudly and the men made such a ruckus that they left the church despite their plans. All divine service was stopped. But after those dogs left, the Christian people came back to the church, and the priest said the mass even more solemnly than ever and in great piety. Those dogs did the same thing at vespers, and they took possession of that holy church and preached there everyday afterward, and then in the church of Saint-Gervais. They did the same thing at the Dominican monastery on the Feast of their father Saint Dominic, and they obstructed divine services in all the churches.[19]

Building the Reformation

Why did Calvin decide to stay in this city torn by faction and lacking both a university and major intellectual figures? On the surface, Basle was a much more natural perch. For all his ferocity, Farel could not have compelled Calvin to stay – he had no hold over him. We must take Calvin at his word, that he felt the hand of providence; God wanted him to remain in Geneva. But he was there as a teacher, not a preacher. In September 1536 he began delivering a series of lectures on scripture to a small group gathered in the cathedral of Saint-Pierre. His material rewards for this endeavour were paltry as the Genevan council was loath to pay for his services; in early 1537 he complained that he had seen little of his promised salary. A year later, he was at the Latin school offering daily lectures on the New Testament. The continued reluctance of the magistrates, who referred to him as 'that Frenchman', was further evinced by the fact that his lectures were held outside the city. It was to the Pauline letters, most likely Romans, that Calvin turned in September 1536 when he began his course of lectures. His Basle printer and friend Johannes Oporinus wrote in March 1537, 'I understand that you are commenting on the Epistles of St Paul to the praise and benefit of us all. Thus I ask you not to hesitate in ensuring that we might be able to convey to others what you have commented on and annotated for your people.'[20]

Calvin edged slowly towards the pastorate and it was probably in the spring of 1537 that he began to preach, though he was never ordained. We know little about his activities during his first stay in Geneva, though it has been reckoned that he eventually preached regularly on Sundays as well as during the week.[21]

Under Farel's leadership meetings known as the Congrégations were instituted in Geneva from 1536 onwards.[22] Modelled on the so-called *Prophezei* in Zurich, these were gatherings of ministers, and some laity, to hear scripture read and expounded. More than mere instruction, they brought together learning and worship.[23] But this required educated men trained in the ancient languages, possible in Zurich, but in the mid-1530s not in Geneva, apart from Calvin and Farel. Nevertheless, the concept of a public discussion of the Bible was quickly established as central to the life of the Reformed community in Geneva. A council note from 1538 reads: 'Regarding the congregation [it is decided] that it shall not take place in Saint Pierre, but at Calvin's [place] or at [the school of] Rive, (there where one wishes) and to ring the bell as customary.'[24]

In January 1537 the Genevan preachers presented the council with their *Articles Concerning the Organization of the Church*, outlining the implementation of regular celebration of the Lord's Supper, excommunication, the instruction of youth through the catechism, singing in worship, and the replacement of the Roman marriage laws. The Lord's Supper was to be celebrated every Sunday, defended by excommunication against unworthy participation. Although Calvin himself had little experience in drafting church legislation, Farel was a veteran. He had produced some of the earliest evangelical liturgical works of liturgy in the French language. His *Summaire* of 1529 was the first statement of evangelical faith in French, and his *Manière et fasson* the first French liturgy for the Lord's Supper, Baptism, preaching and worship. While it has generally been assumed that Calvin was the author of the 1537 *Articles* on account of striking similarities to his 1536 *Institutes*, it is quite possible that it was the more experienced Farel.[25]

This point is significant because it reveals contrasting perspectives in the two men. The *Articles* uses the terms 'pure' and 'purity', which for Farel meant preserving the people from the contamination of the papist religion. Calvin, however, employed the language of 'purity' in his early writings to refer more closely to an inner spiritual quality.[26] Farel's language was more harshly polemical and specifically directed against the Catholic clergy as the perpetrators of false religion and ignorance, drawing, no doubt, on his preaching campaigns in the Vaud. Calvin's writing has a more theological hue as he attempted to capture the Pauline sense of the Christian life. Already in Geneva the differences between the two men were becoming apparent. Farel was the oppositional prophet, while Calvin tended towards the building of the Church.

The *Articles* appeared in conjunction with a series of other texts intended to serve as the foundation of the new church. The *Confession of Faith* of 1536 was very much Calvin's work, largely drawn from the *Institutes*. In turn, the *Confession* formed the basis for the *Catechism or Instruction of the Christian Religion of the Church of Geneva* (1537), by which the laity were to be taught the essentials of the faith. The *Catechism* was laid out in the form of *loci communes* (common places) following the order established in the *Confession*.[27] Together, the *Confession* and *Catechism* were presented as the standard of orthodoxy in newly reformed Geneva.

The Stench of Heresy: The Caroli Affair

As Calvin was beginning to settle into his work in Geneva a dispute arose with implications far beyond those he could have imagined. The triumph of Farel, Viret and Calvin at the Disputation of Lausanne in 1536 was quickly soured by a decision by the Bernese council to appoint Pierre Caroli chief preacher in Lausanne over Viret. Born in 1480, Caroli had, like Farel, belonged to the Meaux Circle around Briçonnet, and during the persecutions of the early 1530s had spent periods of time in Geneva and Basle, where he seemed to have adopted the Reformed religion. A complex and temperamental man, throughout his life Caroli wavered between Catholicism and the Reformed religion, all the time maintaining a consistent inability to work with others. Following his appointment in Lausanne his relationship with Pierre Viret became venomous. At issue was Caroli's distinctly unReformed teaching that it was acceptable for Christians to pray for the dead.[28] Viret, in line with reformers across Swiss and German lands, categorically rejected this position. In response, Caroli accused Viret, Farel and Calvin of Arianism, an ancient heresy that Jesus Christ as the Son of God was not equal with, but subordinate to, the Father. The evidence for this charge was Calvin's apparently limited reference to the Trinity in his *Institutes*. It was a serious accusation that impugned the Trinitarian teaching of the reformers in French-speaking lands. Calvin cited the recent Genevan *Confession* as evidence to the contrary, but Caroli dismissed his defence. His intention to sow disquiet in the minds of the major Swiss reformers about what was happening in the Vaud was well calculated. Calvin and Farel saw the danger and hurried to Berne bearing long letters seeking to persuade the magistrates and church leaders that a synod was needed to resolve the conflict.

In February 1537 Calvin wrote to Kaspar Megander, chief theologian in Berne and close friend of Heinrich Bullinger, describing Caroli as an 'ambitious man' – a term of derision – who sought celebrity by promoting a 'new' doctrine. Calvin lampooned Caroli as a buffoon playing to the gallery. Worse was the disgraceful manner in which Caroli had waited until Viret's visit to Geneva before making his accusations. Such a man could only be 'immoral' and 'irrational', in contrast to the Genevan reformers, who were worthy of the greatest respect. When, according to Calvin, he, Farel and Viret sought to reason with Caroli, the man had flown into a rage, described as the 'rabid fury of the little ass'. The letter was an effective piece of character assassination, an art Calvin had learned well. Megander was not to miss the point. 'You can hardly believe how sorely the foundations which have hitherto been laid have been affected by this one blow, while in the meantime the unskilled are told that we are not agreed among ourselves upon the doctrine of religion. Nor can there be any doubt that more serious consequences will presently follow unless we apply the needed remedy.'[29] Demonstrating a remarkable insensitivity to the nature of the Bernese church, which was under the firm control of the council, Calvin told Megander not to wait for the magistrates to act, but to take matters into his own hands. Helpfully providing a list of measures to be undertaken, he concluded, 'do, by your piety and prudence, see that you are not wanting in a matter of such great importance and arrange at once for the meeting before Easter'.[30] The utter improbability of a Bernese minister proceeding in such a manner is never acknowledged in the letter.

As Calvin had calculated, Megander proved the crucial point of contact with the other Swiss churches. To Heinrich Bullinger Megander wrote that 'we hold several of the Frenchmen in the newly conquered territory under suspicion that they do not have proper understanding of Christ and Trinity. For this reason Calvin has come to Berne and asked that a synod be summoned urgently. That has been denied him till after Easter'.[31] On 14 May, at a meeting in Lausanne, the Geneva ministers gave a full account of their Trinitarian theology and were vindicated. Caroli, in contrast, was dismissed from his post. This was not, however, the end of the matter as the disgraced yet unbowed minister refused to acknowledge before the Bernese magistrates the orthodoxy of Farel, Calvin and Viret. However, he lost his nerve and, no longer certain of support in Berne, fled the city by night, leaving the three Genevan ministers in the clear.

Megander proved a good ally, defending the Genevans in Berne and writing to Bullinger of the 'pious men'. Nevertheless the Caroli controversy reveals a dimension often overlooked – the cultural gap between the German- and French-speaking worlds.[32] In March Megander complained to Bullinger: 'see how much we have to deal with these superstitious or, better said, seditious French'. The 'French' in question were not Calvin and Viret, but the inhabitants of the Vaud, whom Megander, like most of the other German-speaking reformers, regarded with contempt as half-Reformed and foreign. The Bernese attitude of superiority towards the Vaudois and Geneva was the lens through which they viewed Calvin and Farel. Language was a formidable barrier that only served to heighten suspicion.

Vindication in Berne did not bring problems to an end, and controversy dogged Calvin and Farel throughout the summer of 1537. Rumours were abroad, as far as Strasbourg, that the Genevan ministers held unorthodox views on central doctrinal points. In sheer exasperation Calvin wrote to Simon Grynaeus that 'to sum up the whole, this affair has been most maliciously, as well as artfully, cooked up by certain individuals in order to stir up an evil report, and to encourage a bad opinion of us through all countries. And although this man of straw [Caroli] has not so far been able to succeed in his vain endeavour, it is certain that he has greatly irritated'.[33] The suspicion over their teaching lingered like an unpleasant odour: the Bernese council demanded satisfaction, and Calvin and Farel were summoned to explain themselves. No civil authority wanted to be associated with heresy, and the Bernese were determined that the theology of their church would be adopted in Geneva. The strain of events took its toll: Calvin reported to Viret that Farel was 'more exhausted with greater anxiety than I would have thought possible for one with such an iron constitution'.[34]

What Calvin had quickly grasped was the extent to which his position in Geneva was dependent on the other Swiss churches, and that he needed to establish lines of communication. The unmoved mover was Heinrich Bullinger, and Calvin recognized the need to bring the Zurich reformer on side. The exchange with Megander had saved the day, but a more direct route to Zurich was required. Calvin tried various approaches, including contacting Oswald Myconius, head of the Basle church, who informed Bullinger that he had been asked by Calvin to forward both the Genevan *Confession* and the letter addressed to Grynaeus.[35] Two weeks later Bullinger replied that he had read both and found nothing wanting, though, typically, he expressed some trepidation about the state of affairs among the French-speaking ministers and how this controversy might damage the wider Protestant church.[36] He claimed, tactfully rather than truthfully, not to be well informed about the Caroli affair. Quite clearly, preoccupied with problems at home, Bullinger did not want to be drawn into the mess. Calvin was informed of Bullinger's favourable verdict and at the end of the summer penned a letter on behalf of the Genevan church to the ministers of Zurich in which he once more defended their conduct against Caroli.[37] The letter reveals the issues as Calvin saw them: the theology of the Genevans had been impugned, and the Genevans were believed to have dealt too severely with Caroli. With ample appeal to the church fathers, Calvin offered his defence and expressed the hope for greater co-operation between the two churches.

The problem for Calvin was that Geneva was dependent on Berne, and Berne was in the midst of a vicious internecine battle over its theological direction. Calvin's arrival in Berne in September 1537 could not have come at a more sensitive moment. The Caroli affair, crucial as it was to Calvin, took a back seat to a much more serious crisis. Although the Bernese Disputation of 1528 had established the reformation along Zwinglian lines, the influence of Martin Bucer in the city had grown considerably since 1531, in particular through his work to draw the Bernese church towards the Wittenberg Concord, which he regarded as the basis of Protestant union.[38] The leader of the Berne church, Kaspar Megander, was a loyal defender of Zwingli's theology, and for much of 1537 the city was torn apart by the bitter conflicts between Bucer and Megander, which only came to a conclusion early in 1538 when Megander was dismissed.

For Calvin Megander's dismissal was a sobering lesson in the power of magistrates over the church. However, the events in Berne brought renewed contact with Martin Bucer, who took an active interest in the young Frenchman's career. Bucer encouraged the Genevans to draw up a statement of faith on the Lord's Supper, the centre of the dispute in Berne, and was well pleased with their efforts. At the same time, Bucer, Capito and Myconius defended Calvin, Farel and Viret in a small quarrel in which the Genevans were attacked for their use of the term 'Jehova'.[39] Bullinger, in contrast, was incensed by what he regarded as Bucer's meddling in Berne, and relations between the two men plunged into mutual distrust. Fortunately, the head of the Zurich church did not associate Calvin and Farel with Bucer and on 1 November 1537 sent a friendly reply assuring them that he had never believed the accusations made against them.[40]

We learn something of Calvin's character in this heady period from two epistolary exchanges with older mentor figures. In neither case did Calvin fare well, demonstrating arrogance and misjudgement arising from impatience. In early 1538, following the deposition of Megander in Berne, Calvin fired off a letter to Martin Bucer rebuking him for his role in the affair.[41] Among his numerous accusations he charged Bucer with moving too close to Luther on the issue of the sacraments. He was furious about the degree to which the magistrates had been permitted to intervene in the theological debate in Berne. The letter reveals an intemperate Calvin, perhaps someone who had spent too much time with Farel. Bucer eventually replied, but we know of this only from an account written twenty years later by Calvin.[42] Bucer's response was moderate yet firm; he conceded no ground and argued that what he had done had been out of love. The effect was devastating. After reading Bucer's reply, according to Calvin, he was dumbstruck and humiliated by his over-weening pride, crashing to despair on account of his 'impatientia' – he could not sleep and was agitated for three days. Calvin's fragile disposition was clearly exposed. He had had the gall to admonish an experienced man of the church and had been taught a lesson in humility and generosity of spirit.

There was more to come. Peter Kuntz had replaced Megander as the head of the church in Berne and Calvin made no attempt to conceal his contempt for the man. On 4 March 1438, Simon Grynaeus wrote to Calvin contrasting the favourable manner in which Kuntz had spoken of Calvin and Farel with the young Frenchman's description of Kuntz as an ignorant peasant. While agreeing that Kuntz was perhaps a little uncouth, Grynaeus slapped Calvin down for his arrogance.

> When I consider his intentions, the man's faith, however uneducated he
> may be, his zeal for the Church, then I cannot reject this brother. Should

we not take account of the man's nature, the area from which he has his origins, his tribe, his birth place in the middle of the Alps? Certainly, if you compare him with yourself, with your upbringing in the middle of France, surrounded from your earliest youth by highly educated people, you will quickly realize why he offends you in the mere encounter.[43]

For a man sensitive about his own origins, the humbleness of which he later emphasized in the psalms preface, this rebuke from the gentle-natured Grynaeus was a harsh blow. Grynaeus had the measure of the man he had befriended in Basle – an admirable intellectual power bedevilled by arrogance and even snobbishness. There was no doubt that Calvin was intellectually superior to those in Berne, and even to Farel himself, but was the church to pay a price for this? This would remain an open question for the rest of his life.

'Detestable Sacrileges': The Polemicist

Calvin's first major writing following his *Institutes* was a series of public letters published in January 1537 under the title *Epistolae duae* in Basle. The difference from his earlier work could not have been more dramatic. The *Institutes* had won widespread praise for their theological clarity and vision, but what followed in the letters was raw polemical invective. They had first circulated privately among Calvin's contacts during the autumn of 1536, causing considerable unease. Wolfgang Capito, who had been so cautious about the *Psychopannychia*, wrote to Calvin warning him not to publish anything before consulting others. His concern was understandable: the *Epistolae* was a coruscating attack on the Catholic church and, more significantly, on those who remained within it while professing evangelical beliefs. What makes the letters all the more astonishing is that they are addressed to two men Calvin had once held in high regard: his friend Nicolas Duchemin and Gérard Roussel, whose Lenten sermons in Paris had once stirred him.

Written either in Ferrara or possibly after his arrival in Geneva, the letters were an expression of Calvin's desire to demonstrate the necessity of breaking with the Roman church.[44] The first letter to Calvin's friend Duchemin is a reply to a request for religious guidance. The answer must have stunned him.

The Roman church is that Egypt where so many monsters, idols and idolatries are found, and where detestable sacrileges, pollutions and filthiness swarm. There is only one way to escape pollution. That way is to resist its beginnings and never contemplate it, for if we allow ourselves to contemplate it we have already passed over its boundaries. True piety engenders true confession.[45]

Calvin could not be clearer. Christians cannot remain within the Catholic church.

Those who give or receive by the very act approve and consent to the detestable evil. The vulgar and common excuse that it is necessary to appease the rage of the priests, and that this can be done with a piece of money great or small, is like the argument of one who throws a morsel of meat into the mouth of a dangerous beast.[46]

The invective against priests as murderers echoed the literature of Farel and Marcourt distributed in the Vaud in the early 1530s, and without doubt their influence on Calvin was considerable. Still a young and impressionable man, Calvin had adopted the confrontational voice of Farel, who had encouraged his younger colleague to write polemically against the Catholic church.

If the response to Duchemin was a harsh warning, it paled in comparison to Calvin's letter to Gérard Roussel. A former member of the Meaux Circle and preacher at the court of Marguerite of Navarre, Roussel had become a bishop, and this revolted Calvin. The letter could not have been more personal. Roussel was addressed as a 'former friend' and denounced as a murderer, fraud and traitor. Calvin systematically demolished the argument that reform can be achieved from within the Catholic church; the holding of its offices was utterly incompatible with the Gospel. Roussel had shown himself not to be a Christian.[47]

Calvin's two letters were written as he was involved in the publication of the records of the Lausanne Disputation, and together they formed an assault on what he regarded as the unacceptable face of French evangelicalism. He had come to share Farel's assessment of the Navarrists, those around Queen Marguerite, as a spent force from which nothing could be expected. They had traded the faith for high office in the church, and this was beneath contempt.

Confrontation and Defeat

The civic elections of February 1537 in Geneva were won by the party led by Michel Sept, leader of the Eidguenot faction and supporter of the reformers, though it was suggested at the time that the vote had been fixed by organized violence in the city.[48] Opposition to the result was vocal and protests against the loss of liberty were heard. A major decision facing the new council was whether to accept Farel's and Calvin's insistence that all citizens swear an oath of allegiance to the new faith as laid out in the *Confession*. The Small Council accepted the ministers' demand, with the rider that excommunication was not to be used against those who refused to take the oath. The magistrates wished to retain the power to banish those who refused to co-operate. There was considerable resistance among the Genevans to being forced to take an oath imposed by French clergy – had not their struggle for liberation been against the Savoyard-dominated church? The merchants were most vocal in their opposition, though many of the leading families were similarly hostile.[49] It was beyond the power of the council to enforce banishment, particularly on members of Geneva's most prominent families. The Bernese were also opposed, as excommunication was not the prerogative of their church, and they had no desire to see it introduced in Geneva.[50] When Calvin and Farel appeared before the council in January 1538 to demand the right to refuse communion to those whom they regarded as upsetting the unity of the Church, they were summarily told that they were not to withhold the bread and wine from anyone. Their position was also imperilled by the weakness of Sept's party, which was leaking support, and in the elections of February 1538, against expectations, it lost. Calvin wrote gloomily to Bullinger, 'We have not been able to ensure that the faithful and holy exercise of ecclesiastical excommunication is rescued from the oblivion into which it has fallen, and that the city, which in proportion to its size is very populous, is divided into parishes, as is made necessary by the complicated administration of the church.'[51]

After the elections of 1538 returned a new council much less favourable to Calvin and Farel, the debate shifted from the oath to the use of Bernese liturgical rites.[52] These included unleavened bread, cups made of stone, and the celebration of Christmas, New Year, the Annunciation and Ascension. The very fact that such things could bring about conflict tells us about the breakdown of government in the city. At the root of the problem was the deep distrust that many in Geneva felt towards Berne, and Calvin had emerged as their representative. The letter to Bucer can be partially explained in that light. The departure of Megander from Berne was, for Calvin, the loss of an ally and a strengthening of those in that city who despised him. Calvin had interpreted Bucer's actions as playing directly, though unintentionally, into the hands of the Bernese magistrates. What offended Calvin most was Berne's habit of foisting ministers on the Genevan church who were not only untrained but 'worthy of the gallows'.[53]

Calvin and Farel were closely associated with those in Geneva who sought to liberate the city from Berne's influence. In March 1538 six supporters of Farel on the council put forward a plan whereby Geneva would move away from Berne by allying itself more closely with France.[54] Although the council was in principle open to this suggestion, as the matter was further investigated, all six men were removed from office. In a sermon on the same day Calvin openly denounced a 'council of the devil' and as a result both he and Farel were forbidden to interfere in political matters. Calvin's polemic was no longer limited to the page. When he arrived in Geneva he had little experience of preaching; by 1538 he was confident enough to denounce rulers from the pulpit.

The argument over the liturgical rites was doomed to end badly. Berne was determined to enforce its authority in Geneva, and Calvin and Farel were equally adamant that the affairs of the church should not be determined by civil magistrates. The two men were in a losing position as the new regime in Geneva was prepared to accept the Bernese position. Summoned to a synod in Lausanne, Calvin and Farel were told that participation was contingent on acceptance of Berne's demands.[55] By this point the two men hardly represented their church, and when they returned to Geneva they were forbidden to use the cathedral of Saint-Pierre. They were now to gather either in Calvin's house or in the school.

In Berne it was Calvin, not Farel, who was identified as the chief troublemaker, and when the magistrates wrote to Geneva they listed their names in that order. Berne wanted peace, but on its terms. The factions in Geneva were urged to reconcile, though the introduction of the Bernese liturgical rites was non-negotiable. Calvin and Farel argued that this was a matter for the wider Swiss church. Easter communion was approaching and arrangements had to be made in Geneva for the celebration of the Lord's Supper. The Genevan magistrates, looking to Berne to support their precarious position, insisted that the Bernese rites be used. Calvin and Farel raised the stakes by declaring they would not use the rites and would refuse communion to the whole city. From this point events proceeded at speed: their close colleague Elie Couraud, a blind minister, was forbidden to preach, an order he ignored when on 20 April he entered the pulpit. Calvin and Farel made good their threat and refused to administer communion, while some of Farel's supporters became violent.[56] Couraud was imprisoned and Calvin and Farel made sure that no one would take their place at the communion table. One minister, Henri de la Mare, told the council that he had been forbidden by the two Frenchmen from preaching and celebrating the Lord's Supper on punishment of excommunication.[57] The conflict between the two parties was past the point of resolution. The three governing bodies in Geneva all affirmed that the Bernese rites were to be adopted. Calvin and Farel were deprived of their offices and ordered to leave the city within three days. Knowing that their hours in Geneva were numbered, and without waiting for the judgement of the magistrates, the two men departed for Zurich.

CHAPTER SIX

Discovering the Church

Unwanted Troublemakers

EN ROUTE to Zurich, Calvin and Farel broke their journey in Berne where they made a deposition in which they unreservedly blamed the Genevan council for their expulsion.[1] The two men emphatically denied having opposed the Bernese liturgical rites and claimed that the celebration of the Lord's Supper had become impossible on account of the mounting chaos. They claimed there had been a conspiracy against them, and they cited rumours circulating in France that Genevan merchants would resume business only once the two reformers had been driven out.[2] When the Bernese forwarded the deposition to Geneva they heard a very different story. Outraged at the manner in which they had been traduced by Calvin, the Genevans insisted that he and Farel had adamantly refused to use the Bernese rites despite several admonitions.[3] Calvin's ham-fisted attempt to win over the Bernese by offering a tailored account of events failed badly. The Bernese feared that the whole catastrophe might result in the reinstatement of Catholicism in Geneva and looked for a means of restoring peace.

In Zurich things did not go much better. A synod of the leading Swiss churchmen met from 28 April till 4 May 1538, but not until 2 May was the issue of Geneva raised, introduced by Martin Bucer.[4] The atmosphere was tense, reflecting crumbling relations between Bullinger and Bucer. It is difficult to imagine how the two men could even have sat in the same room, given the open contempt of the former for the latter. The principal talking points covered not Geneva, but the internal warfare among the leading clergy in Berne and the continuing dispute with Luther over the Lord's Supper. When the matter of Geneva was finally addressed Calvin and Farel found to their horror that they were presented not as victims, but as the problem.[5] In the eyes of the reformers, they had committed the grievous error of bringing discord to the church. The suspicion that Calvin and Farel had, through their conduct, imperilled the newly Reformed church in Geneva ensured a frosty reception in Zurich. The two men resolutely declared themselves prepared to accept criticism, but they could hardly have believed their ears when they were admonished to conduct themselves with 'the greatest discretion'. The formulation probably came from the lips of Bullinger, who on the day of the synod wrote of Calvin and Farel that 'their zeal is perhaps too great. And yet they are pious, learned men, and in my opinion one should forgive them a great deal.'[6] The excess of zeal on the part of Calvin and Farel was one point on which the reformers could agree: Grynaeus, Capito and Bucer all expressed the view that the two men had acted rashly and precipitously.[7] Other, harsher voices accused Calvin and Farel of introducing a 'new papacy' in Geneva. Although the leading reformers rejected this view, they must have had little idea of what to make of Calvin. Farel, with his uncompromising, confrontational manner, was well known, but Calvin less so. Only Grynaeus had spent much time with Calvin during his stay in Basle, and he, as we have seen, was well aware of the Frenchman's volatility.

A few weeks after the synod in Zurich Calvin wrote to Bullinger from Berne complaining bitterly about the hostility of the Bernese ministers, who, in his words, had not honoured the decision taken to support him.[8] Calvin hoped that the Swiss Reformed churches, and Bullinger in particular, would side with him and Farel, but it was not to be. Sensing a lost cause, he changed tone and reflected, 'now, therefore, we start upon our journey which it may please the Lord to prosper, for as we look to Him in our proceedings so we commit the success to His wise disposal'.[9]

Calvin and Farel left Berne for Basle at the end of May 1538, arriving in the city 'rain soaked and completely worn out'. A letter to Pierre Viret describes how they were almost swept away by the swollen currents of the Rhine. Over the summer of 1538 Calvin moved between Basle and Strasbourg, writing a series of letters reiterating his innocence in the Genevan debacle. From Strasbourg, he reported to du Tillet that the synod in Zurich had unambiguously supported him and Farel 'to shut the spiteful mouths of the malignant'.[10] He added that it was his intention to return to Basle to wait 'to understand what the Lord would have me do'. Once more striking a providential chord, he claimed that he did not fault the Strasbourgers for not taking him in, as they had sufficient cares on their hands, and suggested that he could survive on the money left to him and from the sale of his books in Geneva. Despite the brave face, however, Calvin did not attempt to conceal from du Tillet the degree to which he had been traumatized by what had transpired.

> Above all, however, on looking back and considering the perplexities which surrounded me from the first time I went there [Geneva], there is nothing I dread more than returning to the charge from which I have been set free. For though when first I took it up I could discern the calling of God which held me fast and by which I consoled myself, now, on the contrary, I am in fear that I would tempt him if I were to resume so great a burden, which I have already felt to be insupportable.[11]

His confidence in his calling had been seriously shaken and he drifted without clear sense of direction or purpose. Failure on this scale was unknown to him, and even the continuous references to God's providence in the correspondence could not wholly mask a wounded, and very human, pride.

While Calvin moved between Strasbourg and Basle, Farel was called to minister to the church in Neuchâtel at the end of July 1538, and departed Basle without taking leave of his colleague. Calvin remained extremely anxious about the degree to which he and Farel continued to be slandered in Geneva. He pondered his next move. To Farel he confided, perhaps advised by Grynaeus, that he wanted to avoid open conflict, reflecting that there was something to be said for simply being 'out of the way'.[12] He sensed that Bucer wanted him in Strasbourg, but felt disinclined to go. The ever shifting balance in his relationship with Farel is evident from Calvin's injunction to 'determine nothing about me without first of all giving me previous warning'.[13] He sent Farel several letters he had received from Bucer, including one in which the Strasbourg reformer suggested that the two men be separated, as they were a bad influence on each other. It was a view shared by a number of the Protestant leaders, most of whom felt that Calvin had been poorly advised by the headstrong Farel. The point was made more emphatically in a second letter of August 1538 in which Calvin told Farel that the Strasbourgers were more eager than ever that he (Calvin) should come to them. However, 'they will allow you [Farel], indeed, quietly to go forward in the work of the Lord, but will not suffer us to labour together'.[14]

The same letter lays bare Calvin's emotional paralysis in the months following the expulsion. From Basle he related the unhappy story of Farel's nephew, who had been been struck down by plague. Although informed of the young man's dire predicament, Calvin explained that he had been unable to act on account of severe headaches. Everything possible, he added, was done for the dying boy, who was visited by Grynaeus and then by himself once the headaches abated. Calvin offered a self-conscious and rather artificial account of his own pastoral role. In his final hours the nephew passed in and out of consciousness as Calvin offered 'spiritual rather than bodily comfort'. He had taken up the death watch when it became evident to others that he 'did not fear the danger'. When the young man woke he asked Calvin to pray with him, as he had heard the reformer speak about prayer, and then he died. Calvin's letter continued at some length on the subjects of the boy's material possessions and the expenses of the funeral. Anyone familiar with the consolation letters of Martin Luther might wonder at the cool, clinical tone of this strikingly self-regarding letter, reminiscent of his missive to Duchemin following the death of his own father. The manner in which Calvin placed order above compassion or grief is telling. His overarching concern to convey to Farel that he had acted well in ministering permits a glimpse of his troubled state. Not only was Calvin yet to find his pastoral voice, but he was mentally and physically shattered, disorientated and without emotional articulation.

Pastor, Teacher, Colleague

Three years in Strasbourg changed Calvin.[15] Verging on thirty, he could already claim an eventful life as an exile and as the author of a major theological work. He certainly enjoyed a reputation, if not entirely one he might have sought. Nevertheless, if providence, as he would have understood it, had not led him to Strasbourg in the summer of 1538 he could well have become yet another forgotten figure of the sixteenth century. Nothing he had achieved at this point would have guaranteed posthumous fame, and like so many other reformers of his generation he might have disappeared into the trough of the wave. One man, above all others, is responsible for that not happening. By the mid-1530s Martin Bucer was the most significant reformer of the south-west empire, and when Calvin arrived in Strasbourg he encountered a man at the height of his powers. Bucer had successfully steered the major German imperial cities of the south away from Swiss Zwinglianism towards Luther in the form of the Wittenberg Concord, thus facilitating their entry into the Schmalkaldic League.[16] It was a remarkable achievement.

As a relatively secure bastion of the Protestant church, Strasbourg offered Calvin the opportunity to study and write, as had Basle, but the circumstances were changed.[17] In 1535 he had arrived in Basle an anonymous refugee, one of hundreds. Three-and-a-half years later in Strasbourg he was a well-known author and a leader, if expelled, of a church. The purely scholarly had given way to the bruising world of church life. Calvin was bowed, but not beaten, and his stay in Strasbourg involved a long and profound meditation on the nature of the Christian calling and ministry under the tutelage of Bucer and his colleagues, Wolfgang Capito and Johannes Sturm. Calvin was put in charge of a congregation and invited to teach in the Strasbourg Academy.

In fact, Calvin was not really needed in Strasbourg. Bucer took him under his wing to teach him how to be a pastor, but his purpose was ultimately missionary: Calvin was to return to Geneva and resume his work. Bucer possessed a clearer sense of Calvin's future than did the young Frenchman. In September 1538 Calvin began preaching in the church of Saint-Nicolas-des-Ondes and then at the chapel of the Penitents of Sainte-Magdelène, undertaking the organization of the first French parish and using Bucer's Strasbourg liturgy with its singing of the psalms, an aspect of worship he had introduced in Geneva.[18] Now he was also able to implement the church discipline he had proposed in Geneva: in the French church, admission to communion was only for those who presented themselves to the ministers for examination. The question of discipline in Strasbourg was deeply divisive as Bucer struggled for the institution of a rigorous system independent of the magistrates in which the church would have a free hand in the use of excommunication.[19] Although he failed, and discipline remained in the grip of the magistrates, the experience taught Calvin much about the delicate balances to be maintained in dealing with temporal authorities.

At Sturm's Academy Calvin taught biblical exegesis, beginning with the Gospel of John and Paul's first letter to the Corinthians. The combination of teaching, preaching, writing and pastoral care was doubtless exhausting, but it was the routine familiar to all sixteenth-century reformers. Melanchthon in Wittenberg, Bullinger in Zurich and Bucer himself in Strasbourg knew nothing other than long days of labour and service that began with early-morning worship and ended with writing and reading texts and letters by candlelight. It was how they had been educated from boyhood, and many had monastic backgrounds. The extraordinary discipline and single-mindedness of the reformers becomes apparent only when we stop to consider how much they achieved. Calvin had been from youth highly disciplined, but in Strasbourg he learned what it meant to work in a church.

On 29 July 1539 he received the citizenship of Strasbourg. His financial situation, troubling at first, was improved by a regular salary from the city council.

But his greatest gain was a group of friends who looked after him. For a young, single reformer the obvious next step was to marry, and his friends took up the matchmaking game. Like all the reformers, Calvin strongly advocated clerical marriage, though he did not himself struggle greatly with sexual temptation. There is no evidence that he sought a wife before 1539. He hardly presented himself as an ideal modern husband. 'I have never married, and I do not know whether I ever will. If I do, it will be in order to be freer from many daily troubles, and thus freer for the Lord. Lack of sexual continence would not be the reason I would point to for marrying. No one can charge me with that.'[20] Nevertheless, the indefatigable Martin Bucer was determined to reform all aspects of Calvin's life and he sought an appropriate woman for him. His choice was not to Calvin's liking, and the Frenchman got cold feet. Farel took up where Bucer had failed and by May another woman was in prospect. Calvin revealed that he was growing irritated with the pressure on him to marry. 'I am not one of those insane kind of lovers, who, once smitten by the first glance of a fine figure, cherishes even the faults of his lover. The only beauty that seduces me is of one who is chaste, not too fastidious, modest, thrifty, patient, and hopefully she will be attentive to my health.'[21] Needless to say, the woman vanished.

The matter rested till early the following year when a wealthy woman with a considerable dowry was offered to Calvin. He was not interested in her money and quite reasonably felt there to be little point in marrying someone who did not speak French. Taking matters into his own hands, he asked his brother Antoine to find another more suitable candidate. When he did, Calvin wrote excitedly to Farel about the favourable prospects of marriage, but once more there was disappointment, and Calvin was left with the wealthy, and extremely eager, family. The problem with these prospective in-laws was that they were all too likeable. 'The relatives of that young lady of high rank are so determined that I take her to myself. I could not think of ever doing this unless the Lord has altogether demented me. But it is unpleasant to refuse, especially in the case of such persons who overwhelm me altogether with their kindness. Most earnestly I desire to be delivered out of this difficulty.'[22] Such were not Calvin's usual opponents.

This string of embarrassing failures left Calvin in no mood to look for a wife. However, by the summer of 1540 he had encountered a woman with whom he genuinely fell in love. He married Idelette de Bure, the widow of an Anabaptist and mother of two children, and in August 1540 Farel travelled to Strasbourg to bless the union. It is extraordinary that we know almost nothing of the event or the woman. Calvin does not mention his marriage in the autobiographical psalms preface and nothing is to be found in his surviving correspondence. He may have claimed in advance that his wife had to be a pious servant, but in reality he cherished Idelette. He reported to Farel that after the marriage he and his new wife enjoyed a brief but happy honeymoon that was cut short by plague – a truly early-modern experience – and that when they were separated Idelette was 'in my thoughts day and night'.[23]

One comment in Beza's biography has not served Calvin well, and that was the suggestion that he and Idelette had a sexless marriage, adhering to chastity. The intention behind the remark is not clear. Calvin was aware that during his life he was derided by his opponents as cold and asexual. In his own defence he pointed out that 'God has given me a son. But God has taken away my little boy.'[24] There seems no good reason to believe that Calvin and Idelette did not enjoy normal marital relations. In addition to a son, they may well have had several daughters, but sadly none of the children survived. In his sermons and biblical commentaries Calvin has nothing but positive remarks for the healthy sex lives of wives and husbands.

The Master: Martin Bucer

At first glance, Martin Bucer and John Calvin cut very different figures.[25] In 1538 Bucer was a veteran of the Reformation whose achievements owed as much to his patience and fortitude as they did to his theological acumen. His efforts in establishing the reformation in Strasbourg and in seeking peace between the warring Protestant churches had come at considerable personal cost, all too often pilloried by both sides for his flexibility – or his lack of principles, as it was portrayed by his detractors. Calvin, eighteen years his junior, was a volatile firebrand who oscillated between overweening self-confidence and crippling self-doubt. Yet Bucer saw in him the possibility of greatness.

Bucer's cumulative influence on Calvin during these years forms a central part of our story.[26] Above and beyond the opportunities afforded by refuge, a congregation and a teaching post, the Strasbourg years witnessed a discernible broadening and deepening of Calvin's theology, and for this he owed much to Martin Bucer. In particular, he believed Bucer to be the best of the Protestant commentators on scripture, and often paid homage to his teacher. 'Endowed, as indeed he is, with a singularly acute and remarkably clear judgement, there is at the same time no one who is more religiously desirous to keep with the simplicity of the Word of God, and less given to hunt after the niceties of interpretation that are foreign to it . . .'[27]

Calvin's debt went further and became evident after his subsequent return to Geneva, where his fourfold office of ministry, the liturgy and church discipline bore the mark of Bucer's teaching. He embraced Bucer's understanding of the early church as a model for the organization of the church in the sixteenth century. While in Strasbourg he began work on a French edition of the homilies of John Chrysostom (349–c. 407), for which he wrote a Latin preface praising the Greek church father as a model of scholarship and piety.[28] The text, probably written as Calvin was preparing his commentary on Romans, throws light on his intensive discussions with Bucer on the proper interpretation of the Bible and the authority of the ancient church.

Bucer put himself out for Calvin in every respect: he provided accommodation in his own home, introduced him to his circle of friends, and finally found a house with a shared garden where they might easily meet and converse.[29] Calvin's Strasbourg letters contain numerous references to evenings spent deep in conversation with Bucer's circle, which he came to refer to as 'we'. Latin was their shared language, though occasionally, and to Calvin's intense irritation, the group would speak German, leaving him entirely in the dark. Even in this idyll and with a man he admired as much as Bucer, Calvin's relationships were never straightforward. By the time he returned to Geneva he would describe his relationship to his teacher in terms of father and son, and expressed his willingness to submit himself to the Strasbourg reformer's authority.[30] But as with all sons and fathers there was conflict and wilful declarations of independence. Calvin warmly praised Bucer's work in seeking reconciliation among the Protestants, but there were personal rankles which did not reflect well on the Frenchman. Calvin could not, for example, abide Bucer's irritating habit of alternating effusive praise with criticism. 'I would rather that he had been more sparing of praise, and at the same time have abstained from any charge against us that he might not have this vantage-ground from which he may flatter himself that he has won the victory.'[31] Calvin's waspishness indicated his extreme sensitivity to any criticism, perceived or real. His instinct was to see criticism of himself as a moral or intellectual shortcoming in others.

Yet, for all that, Bucer remained foremost in Calvin's affections.[32] Although we have no access to their conversations in their shared garden, we know that Calvin's relationship with Bucer was different. Farel was a loveable, if frustrating, uncle; Bullinger was the close cousin; Melanchthon the good school-friend; Beza the son. Bucer was truly the father figure. When he died in England in 1551, exiled from Strasbourg, Calvin was deeply affected, and it was Farel who was able to catch the right tone. 'I have received pious Bucer's last letter. What a heart! What a man has gone! We must rejoice in our sorrow that a man so fond of us has journeyed to God. I have no doubt that after his journey he commended us to God. How rightly he thought of you and how justly he loved you!'[33]

Return of an Enemy

Strasbourg may have been some sort of paradise, but there was certainly trouble. In 1539 the reviled Pierre Caroli returned to Swiss lands seeking reconciliation. In Neuchâtel Farel had reportedly embraced him and declared their enmity at an end. Calvin was incandescent with rage, declaring that he would never accept Caroli's hand without a full retraction of the accusations he had made. Bucer, Capito and Sturm attempted to mediate and Calvin described the occasion to Farel in one of his most extraordinarily bitter letters.[34] At various points in the missive he accused his Strasbourg colleagues, as well as Farel, of working behind his back. Despite Bucer's request that he enter into discussion, he refused to do so on the grounds that he did not accept Caroli's sincerity, believing his remarks to be sophistry concealing malice. When Calvin met with Bucer and Sturm he lost his temper spectacularly.

> There I sinned grievously in not being able to keep within bounds, for bile had taken possession of my mind to the extent that I poured out bitterness on all sides. There was certainly some cause for indignation, if only moderation had been observed in expressing it. I complained that they had presented these articles to me for the purpose of exonerating Caroli, and that it was their opinion that these articles were good. While I was unheard, and judgement had already been pronounced, they required me to subscribe [to the articles], which if I refused would turn them into my adversaries.

Calvin stormed out of the room.

> Bucer followed, and when he had soothed me by his gentle words he brought me back to the company. I said that I wished to consider the matter more fully before making any more distinct reply. When I got home I was seized with an extraordinary paroxysm, nor did I find any other solace than in sighs and tears, and I was the more deeply afflicted because you [Farel] had occasioned those evils for me. Again and again

they reminded me of your leniency, who had mercifully embraced Caroli upon the spot, saying that I was too headstrong and could not be moved one inch from my judgement. Bucer, indeed, has tried every mode of representation that he might soothe my mind on the subject. Meanwhile, he invidiously uses your example against me.

He concluded harshly: 'because I am aware that you are quite accustomed to my rudeness, I will make no excuse for treating you so uncivilly'.

Calvin's loss of control was complete and his embarrassment evident. Yet the description is revealing: that his conduct was unbecoming of a Christian, he freely admitted, but there was no suggestion that he was wrong. This was his personal struggle – between his passions, over which he could lose control, and his intellect, of which he entertained few doubts. Bucer provided the tempering influence of which Farel was wholly incapable; he recognized, as Calvin did, that the Frenchman needed to be anchored in the bonds of friendship. Foreshadowing debates and disputes to come, Calvin's mind frequently turned disagreement into conspiracy against him. As he grew in his sense of prophetic calling he increasingly saw dissent as disloyalty, and as something deeply personal. However, one of his greatest strengths in his later career was an acute awareness that despite remarkable confidence in his calling and intellect he remained dangerously prone to moments of poor judgement on account of anger.

The *Institutes* of 1539

It was not long before Calvin began revising his 1536 *Institutes*. His friend, the scholar and printer Johannes Oporinus, had urged him to do so on the basis of the notable success of the work. But Calvin's mind was developing and the 1536 text no longer adequately expressed his understanding of Christian theology, nor was it expounded in the manner in which he wished to present it. Richard Muller has demonstrated that Calvin's catechisms of 1537–8 marked the crucial point of development between the first two editions of the *Institutes*. Here Calvin introduced topics not found in the 1536 *Institutes*: the universal fact of religion, the distinction between true and false religion, free choice, election and predestination, church offices, human traditions, excommunication and the civil magistracy.[35] He also changed the title of the work from *Of the Christian Religion, an Institution* to *An Institution of the Christian Religion*. This was not mere semantics. The new title reflected Calvin's distinction between the different disciplines of theology, biblical commentary and catechism. The 1536 *Institutes* was largely catechetical in nature. In 1539 it had been reworked as a book of instruction, largely for ministers.[36] Calvin made the point clearly.

> It has been my purpose in this labour to prepare and instruct candidates in sacred theology for the reading of the divine Word, in order that they may be able both to have easy access to it and to advance in it without stumbling. For I believe I have so embraced the sum of religion in all its parts, and have arranged it in such an order, that if anyone rightly grasps it, it will not be difficult for him to determine what he ought especially to seek in Scripture, and to what end he ought to relate its contents. If, after this road has, as it were, been paved, I shall publish any detailed expositions of Scripture, I shall always condense them, because I shall have no need to undertake long doctrinal disputations, or to wander about in the basic topics.[37]

The *Institutes* was now envisaged as a guide to the whole of the Christian religion constructed through the collection of 'common places' (in Latin *loci communes*) such as 'predestination' or 'grace'. The greatest influence on this restructuring came from Philip Melanchthon, whose 1521 and 1536 *Loci communes* played a major role in shaping Calvin's thought.[38] The order of the theological topics was also heavily shaped by Paul's letter to the Romans, regarded by Melanchthon as the theological heart of scripture. Following Melanchthon, Calvin looked to Romans for the proper order of Christian doctrine. The importance of the epistle was already evident in his 1535 *Letter to All Those Who Love Jesus Christ*, written for the Olivétan Bible.[39] It was no accident that as he completed his revision of the *Institutes* he turned in 1539 to write a commentary on Romans.

A Lost Friendship

Questions surrounding his ministry and the failure in Geneva weighed heavily on Calvin. What had gone wrong? In the eyes of the Swiss reformers, and indeed of Martin Bucer, his uncompromising conduct had created needless discord. To declare the absolute demands of the Gospel was imperative, on that there was no disagreement, but the seasoned reformers also understood something further that Calvin had yet to grasp: building a church required flexibility and patience. One had to work with magistrates who had other priorities, as well as with colleagues with different perspectives and weaker dispositions.

During his time in Strasbourg Calvin exchanged a series of letters with Louis du Tillet, who had provided refuge in his home after the Placards Affair and who had initially shared his religious views. The friendship had deep roots: they had left France together for Basle. Du Tillet's decision to join Calvin in flight from France, abandoning his office and church livings, had put his distinguished family in a difficult and dangerous position. Yet in exile things had changed. Du Tillet had excitedly discovered Calvin in Geneva in 1536 and summoned Farel, but by early 1538 he saw things very differently. For some unknown reason, du Tillet left Geneva for Strasbourg and ultimately France, returning both to his native land and to the Roman church.[40] The infighting and Calvin's handling of church affairs had evidently persuaded him that the Reformation was a serious mistake.

Du Tillet's letters to Calvin in Strasbourg are a damning indictment of his friend's character.

> I am disposed to think that all the things which have happened to you have been brought about and pursued by the evil disposition of persons who have more care about the aims and ends of this world than consideration of what is of God. But what I beseech you to take in good part is that you have to consider for your part whether the Lord has not meant to warn you to consider whether there has been anything in you to reprove in your administration, and to humble you in His sight, and that by this means the great gifts and graces by which our Lord has furnished you may be employed to His glory. . . .[41]

It got worse. On 7 September 1538 du Tillet wrote, 'I doubt that you have had your vocation from God, having been called there only by men . . . who have driven you away from there, just as they received you by their sole authority.'[42] The accusation struck deeply; from the time of his Seneca commentary, Calvin had wrestled with ambition and remained acutely sensitive to suggestions that his calling might be confused with a desire for worldly gain. He had played the same game, never hesitating to blacken the names of his opponents such as Caroli by impugning their motives with ambition. Now he was made to feel the blade of his own sword.

In reply, more than three months later, Calvin did not attempt to conceal his hurt. 'True enough, so far as our enemies are concerned, I have with good reason always maintained my innocence . . . but I have never failed to declare, either in public or in private, that we must accept that calamity as a singularly remarkable chastisement of our ignorance as well as of our other vices.'[43] He rejected du Tillet's argument that his call was not legitimate, for 'it is quite clear to my own satisfaction'. But he added revealingly, 'you do well to admonish me not to confide too much in one's own understanding, for I know my range to be such that I cannot presume even so little upon myself without exceeding'.[44] He was aware, he admitted, of his 'insufficiency' for the job in Geneva and confessed that there was a great risk that ambition might become the driving force. 'I know well enough that foolish ambition might hoodwink me so as to deflect the straightforwardness of my judgement.' This was as close as Calvin was ever prepared to sail in admitting his errors.

Notably, he defended his office in prophetic terms. He preached because God had appointed him to do so, and should he cease God would seek him out as God had done with Jonah in sending him to the city of Nineveh. Jonah was an image Calvin invoked to suggest that his vocation ran counter to personal inclinations or normal desires for material comfort. He was entirely persuaded that 'the will of God has otherwise disposed', and that this had been recognized by men of good judgement. In a stinging rebuke he labelled Louis' refusal to acknowledge his calling an 'injustice to the truth of God'.

Du Tillet returned to Paris and publicly abjured his Protestant beliefs. Although we know of no further contact between him and Calvin, Louis' brother Jean travelled to Geneva, where he had a frank discussion with the reformer about Louis.[45] Despite all that had happened, Calvin was willing, as far as possible, to remain cordial, but this proved virtually impossible. The du Tillet family was seriously embarrassed by Louis' connection with Calvin and there was no possibility of further contact. Du Tillet had concluded his correspondence with an offer of money to help out his old friend, but it was politely declined.

'My Bounden Duty': Letters to Geneva

Calvin may have been expelled from Geneva, but he did not turn his back on the city, with which he remained in surprisingly close contact during his Strasbourg years. He stated in his first letter to the Genevans, 'I have been unable to refrain from writing to you to assure you of the affection with which I ever regard you, and my remembrance of you in the Lord, as it is my bounden duty.'[46] Although he repeatedly protested that he would never return, his correspondence reveals a profound concern for what was taking place in the city. Following his and Farel's expulsion, they had been replaced by local ministers of little distinction. Within the city, the atmosphere was thick with intrigue and violence as Geneva became embroiled with Berne over the renewal of the treaty of 1536.[47] Negotiations made little headway, bogged down in Geneva's factional politics. The endless disputes between the main factions boiled over in the spring of 1540 when a riot broke out against those whom many Genevans believed were prepared to sell out the city to Berne. During the summer and autumn more unrest and arrests followed as the Articulant faction was defeated by the Guillermins. Relations between Berne and Geneva were completely poisoned and war was avoided only when the Genevans turned to their old enemy the Savoyards for aid.

Shortly after his arrival in Strasbourg Calvin wrote to the Genevan church offering both advice and a defence of his actions. Paraphrasing Paul to the divided churches at Corinth he told his brethren that their warfare was spiritual, to be fought by spiritual means. They were to be 'guided solely by your zeal for the service of God, moderated by His Spirit according to the rule of His Word'.[48] Calvin admitted that he and Farel, whom he did not name, had been punished by the Lord that they might recognize 'our ignorance, our impudence, and those infirmities which, for my part, I feel in myself, and have no difficulty in confessing before the church of the Lord'. In a second letter written in the summer of 1539, the degree to which Calvin had begun to speak with Paul's voice is even more striking. Listen to the opening address: 'Nothing, most beloved brethren, has caused me greater sorrow since those disturbances which so sadly scattered and almost entirely overthrew your church than your struggles and contentions with those ministers who succeeded us.'[49] The words could have come from the New Testament.

Resolving the chaos in the Genevan church, according to Calvin, required the restoration of the Christian ministry. 'For He [God] not only commands us to be willingly obedient with fear and trembling to the Word while it is proclaimed to us, but He also commands that ministers of the Word be treated with honour and reverence, for they are dressed as His ambassadors, whom He would have us acknowledge as His angels and messengers.'[50] In case the Genevans might not remember Calvin and Farel as angels, he informed them that his change of situation had enabled him to present his argument in a different light: 'as long as we were among you, we did not try very much to impress on you the dignity of our ministry, so that we might avoid all grounds of suspicion. Now, however, that we have been placed beyond the reach of danger I speak my mind more freely.' The Genevans must do two things: follow the instructions of the clergy, the servants of God, who had in view the preservation of the Church; and secondly ensure that only honest men with a true vocation were made ministers. Calvin concluded with an admonition and warning: if the Genevans wished to remain in Christian bond with him they must accept his teaching on the ministry. Failure to do so would condemn them to eternal bickering.

Letter to Sadoleto

As Calvin was writing to the Genevan church and completing his commentary on Romans, he entered into a public exchange of letters with Jacopo Sadoleto, a remarkable figure of the Catholic church. Learned and reform-minded, the cardinal belonged to that generation of senior churchmen who believed that the problems of the Reformation could be resolved by negotiations between Catholics and Protestants. A man of great piety and a diligent bishop, Sadoleto was the author of a commentary on the Letter to the Romans which was regarded in Rome as too favourable to Protestant views and was subsequently banned. During the chaos in Geneva Sadoleto wrote to the city attempting to entice it into returning to the Catholic fold. The arrival of his letter on 26 March 1539 marked the third occasion on which he had sought contact with the Protestants: in 1537 he had written to Philip Melanchthon but had received no reply; the following year his letter to the Strasbourg magistrate Jakob Sturm resulted in a fiery polemical response.

Whatever had encouraged the cardinal to write, when Sadoleto's letter was received in Geneva the council decided to forward it to Berne, where the leading ministers declared themselves insufficient to the task, and the search was launched for a suitable respondent. Curiously, Peter Kuntz suggested his erstwhile adversary John Calvin. The Bernese magistrates, not unexpectedly, had reservations, but consented on the condition that Calvin made no mention of Berne in his reply. Calvin reported to Farel: '[Simon] Sulzer has brought the letter of Sadoleto. I was not very much interested in writing a reply to it, but our friends have at length compelled me. At the present moment I am entirely occupied with it. It will be six days' work.'[51] His response was printed in September 1539 together with Sadoleto's letter. In January 1540 a French translation appeared in Geneva from the press of Michel du Bois, with the permission of the council.

The Genevans, Sadoleto had written, had been deluded by 'vain philosophy' and had strayed from the call of the Lord transmitted by the Church, the sole mediator of Christ.[52] He rejected the Protestant teaching of salvation by faith alone and repeatedly emphasized the role of the institutional church, which the reformers had insidiously deceived the faithful into leaving. The arguments were hardly original, but they were compelling: the historical continuity of the Catholic church set against the 'newness' of the reform movement echoed Johannes Eck's words to Luther in 1519 at the Leipzig Disputation. More unexpected was Sadoleto's lengthy treatment of the Last Judgement. The cardinal set up a courtroom trial before the Almighty with the contrasting fates of two figures, one who had remained within the Church and one who had fallen into the new errors. The first, of course, provided an entirely satisfactory account and confessed that 'though new men had come with the Scripture in their mouths and hands, who attempted to stir some novelties, to pull down what was ancient, to argue against the Church, to snatch and wrest from us the obedience which we all yielded to it, I was still desirous to adhere firmly to that which had been delivered to me by my parents, and observed from antiquity'.[53] The heretic, in contrast, was driven by hatred of the clergy, envy of their positions and bitterness at not having been rewarded for his studies. In frustration and anger the man sought to tear apart the fabric of the Church and denounce established forms of authority.[54] Sadoleto ended with a question: 'I ask you, my Genevan brethren, whom I long to have of one mind with me in Christ, and in the Church of Christ, what judgement do you think will be passed on these two men and their associates and followers?'

Calvin's reply was considerably longer than the original letter. He neither refuted Sadoleto's arguments point by point nor followed the structure of the cardinal's epistle, but took aim at what he regarded as its most execrable contentions. The suggestion that the reformers were pedlars of false doctrine, avaricious, quarrelsome and dishonest was for Calvin deeply personal and brought forth a stunningly frank assessment of his own talents.

I am unwilling to speak of myself, but since you do not permit me to remain wholly silent, I will say what I can consistent with modesty. Had I wished to consult my own interest, I would never have left your party. I will not, indeed, boast that there the road of preferment had been easy for me. I never desired it, and I could never bring my mind to catch at it, although I know more than a few of my own age who have crept up to some eminence – among whom some I might have equalled, and others surpassed. This only will I be contented to say: it would not have been difficult for me to reach the summit of my wishes: the enjoyment of literary ease with something of a free and honourable station. Therefore, I have no fear that anyone not possessed of shameless effrontery will object to me that out of the kingdom of the Pope I sought for any personal advantage that which was not there ready to my hand.[55]

Calvin was convinced that he could have had a successful career in France. He was in no doubt about his prospects, but he would not pay the price – dissembling his faith in order to receive material rewards. He was not prepared to take the low road of Duchemin, Roussel and du Tillet, as he perceived it.

Calvin addressed what he saw as the heart of Sadoleto's case – the nature of the true Church. He seized on the cardinal's argument that those who put their faith in Christ do so for their salvation. Christianity, he countered, is not about individual salvation but about the glory of God. The Church is not grounded in institutional authority but on the reading of scripture by which individuals, though they can err, are guaranteed the path to salvation.[56] The letter to Sadoleto exposes Calvin's evolving thought on the Church. Against the cardinal he spoke in terms of individuals reading scripture under the guidance of the Holy Spirit; the influence of his Strasbourg years, his pastoral work and the religious colloquies of the early 1540s, however, would lead him to develop a fuller vision of the Church as an institutional body. This would appear in his reworking of the *Institutes* in 1543.

Calvin inverted Sadoleto's courtroom drama, presenting the defence before God's tribunal of the person who had embraced the Reformed faith. This was the story of his own conversion. In elegant, moving prose he describes the religious world of his youth, a world in which he knew of a salvation that was denied him.

> I had indeed learned to worship you as my God, but as the true method of worshipping was entirely unknown to me, I stumbled at the very threshold. I believed, as I had been taught, that I was redeemed by the death of your Son from liability to eternal death, but the redemption I thought of was one whose virtue could never reach me. I anticipated a future resurrection, but hated to think of it, as being almost too dreadful.[57]

Calvin's journey was away from the uncertainty of his youth, and in this was perhaps his greatest legacy: he taught a generation that to know salvation was to be certain that it was freely offered. If there was one thing a person could be certain of, it was God's promises.

Compromise and Disappointment: The Religious Colloquies, 1540–1

In Strasbourg Calvin found himself quickly drawn into the heady world of imperial religious politics as soldiers rubbed shoulders with diplomats and churchmen on the roads traversing the German lands. Bucer, according to Calvin's letter to Farel, dragged him along to the Leipzig Disputation of January 1539 and then to the imperial diet in Frankfurt six weeks later. In those years the unity of the Church seemed to be in the hands of a few men, of whom Bucer was one.[58] And Calvin became a student of his mentor's actions, carefully studying his reports from the meetings of the Protestant leaders and theologians. Two months later Calvin was in Frankfurt for the meeting of the Schmalkaldic League, where he made personal contact with Philip Melanchthon, having intentionally sought him out. He had sent Melanchthon twelve articles on the Eucharist as a possible basis for unity talks between the Lutherans and the Swiss. Melanchthon read the articles with approval, but counselled against publication.[59] The German was cooler about Calvin's ideas on excommunication, which he regarded as impractical.[60] Contact with Melanchthon encouraged Calvin to believe that Protestant unity was achievable, and he reported enthusiastically to Farel that he detected a willingness among the Germans to talk with the Swiss.[61] Perhaps under the influence of Farel and Bullinger, Calvin's attitude towards German Lutheranism had previously been largely negative, but his tune was changing. 'Consider whether we are not being unjust to such people when we accuse them at our leisure, while they do not suffer themselves to be pushed away from the true way by any danger or terror.'[62]

Calvin's change of heart may well have come about when the Strasbourg printer Crato Mylius returned from Wittenberg in 1539 with letters in which Luther greeted Calvin and indicated he had read the Sadoleto letter. 'If we were not overwhelmed we must truly be made of stone. I am overwhelmed!' Calvin declared.[63] The fully understandable response was part of a discernible shift in Calvin's attitudes towards the German reformation. From his perch in Strasbourg, and under the influence of Bucer and Melanchthon, whom he had now met, Calvin was becoming receptive to the Lutheran world. In the Wittenberg Concord, so hated by the Swiss, Calvin found an acceptable expression of his views. In 1540 he signed Melanchthon's Variata of the Augsburg Confession, a revision to the original Lutheran text of 1530.

Calvin was writing, teaching and serving the French church in Strasbourg, but he continued to follow imperial events. He attended the first religious colloquy at Hagenau in summer 1540, though not in an official capacity. The religious colloquies of 1540–1 were intended to find some way of uniting the Catholics and Protestants, though they seemed doomed to failure from the start. Nevertheless they were attended by the leading princes and electors of the empire and lengthy negotiations were held to find formulas of agreement. A principal point of discussion was the nature of the Church, and the Protestants found themselves forced to consider carefully their understanding of what constituted the visible Body of Christ. Calvin was in the midst of the leading theologians of the German church debating the central questions of doctrine. His immediate interests, however, were the establishment of Protestant unity and to win German support for the evangelicals in France. On both counts he was disappointed. The Swiss did not come to Hagenau and Bucer showed little interest in France. Everywhere the prospect of war was discussed, though almost no detectable progress was made in negotiations between the Protestants and Catholics. It was agreed to meet again in the autumn.

When the sides met again in Worms later in 1540 Calvin was assigned to the party of the Duke of Lüneburg, along with Johannes Sturm. Calvin's placement with a Lutheran prince, and alongside a distinguished theologian, demonstrated that he was not regarded as a 'sacramentarian' (Zwinglian) and that his reputation was strong. He spoke on several occasions during debates on justification and scriptural interpretation, but it was in the discussion of the mass that he made his most significant contribution, outlining an argument already found in his 1539 *Institutes*, full of confident references to the church fathers.[64] Justification is God's act of making humanity righteous. For the reformers this was by no means dependent on human effort, but entirely resulting from God's merciful grace. Before leaving for Worms, Calvin had engaged in a disputation in Strasbourg with the dean of Passau cathedral, Ruprecht Mosheim, on the subject of justification. According to Johannes Sturm, Calvin demonstrated his sharp wit in the debate and had won the admiration of the Strasbourg magistrate Jakob Sturm.[65] When Calvin demolished Mosheim once more at Worms Melanchthon was duly impressed.

It was while Calvin was scoring triumphs at Worms and enjoying the company of Melanchthon that Geneva began to make overtures to him about a possible return to the city. During October and November a series of letters was addressed to the Strasbourg council asking for Calvin's release from his duties. It must have gratified the Frenchman greatly when Bucer, Capito and Johannes Sturm replied to Geneva from Worms that Calvin and Farel were 'really exceptional and extraordinary organs of Christ'.[66] The thought of leaving centre stage where he moved among the leading figures of the German reformation to return to the scene of his humiliation in faction-ridden Geneva could hardly have appealed. Yet all was not entirely well at Worms. Melanchthon and Calvin grew distinctly uneasy with the atmosphere, which had the rancid odour of compromise, particularly given Bucer's flexibility towards reform-minded Catholics. Both men were of the opinion, shared by many of the Catholic representatives, that the discussions of church union were nothing more than an elaborate, and probably insincere, charade. They had made the point in print: Calvin in his *Epistolae duae* and Melanchthon in his *On the Authority of the Church*.[67] Calvin wanted Protestant union and aid for France, not accommodation with the Roman church. On this point he parted ways with Bucer. Both men were passionately committed to church unity, but what that meant for each of them differed radically. Bucer believed that through negotiation and compromise it would be possible to win the reform-minded over to the Gospel. This very idea was noxious to Calvin, and by the time he left Worms, disillusioned with the wordplay, he was beginning to turn his back on the Strasbourg approach. Perhaps it was also time to leave the city which had offered him so much. For all the fine words that had passed between the reformers some bitter truths were emerging. Calvin vented his spleen while still at the colloquy in his only known piece of verse.[68] The long poem, entitled *Epinicion*, was written for New Year 1541, and with its martial imagery formed a frightening expression of his hatred of the Roman church, upon which Christ wreaks vengeance.

> The voice is Christ's sword and the lance is the mouth's breath,
> So once the voice is raised it can level the enemy.
> This sword, here, there, more than twenty years
> He brandishes, the robust advocate, not without killing, in hand.
> Satan, prince and pope of a church-robbing army, eluded
> Them, until today the sword-stroke has been delayed.
> But now he fights, experienced and shrewd, at last
> Each wounded man groaning with an unfamiliar wound.
> Next it's the pope's henchmen stunned and dazed
> He hangs them, the mob shudders from its very souls.[69]

The vision was apocalyptic. In transforming the ancient tradition of presenting new Roman consuls with edifying poems in the New Year, Calvin conjured a bloodbath in which the enemies of Christ are slaughtered.

On account of his knowledge of French, Calvin was present at the colloquy at Regensburg in January 1541 as a representative of the Strasbourg council. The experience did little to lift his spirits and he remained cynical about Catholic intentions. He did not believe in any of the theological formulations and was revolted by the willingness of Protestants to surrender key doctrines in the name of spurious union. Protracted negotiations between the French and the German Protestants went nowhere.[70] Philip of Hesse, leader of the anti-Habsburg forces, rejected dealings with Francis I, but his own position as a Protestant leader was badly compromised by a bigamous marriage. He was completely dependent on Charles V's benevolence, and the scandal emasculated the Reformation cause. Calvin sensed that the weak and vacillating German princes, as he saw them, were too scared of Charles and of war to be of any use in forming an alliance with Francis I that might serve French evangelicals. Wearying of the talk and absence of results, and aware from Farel of the dire situation in France, where fresh persecutions had broken out, Calvin began to ponder a return to Geneva.

CHAPTER SEVEN

'Lucid Brevity' for the Sake of the Church: Romans

THE RELIGIOUS colloquies of 1540–1 yielded precious little in terms of Protestant unity or support for the French evangelicals. Calvin, however, had emerged from the disappointment a much enhanced figure who stood among the front rank of Protestantism. It was a remarkable transition from the dark days of 1538 following his expulsion from Geneva when few had wanted to know him. Although recognition must have brought a degree of satisfaction, Calvin remained deeply anxious about the divided house that was the Reformation. In 1540, the year of the Hagenau and Worms colloquies, he published a work that radically transformed Protestant theology: his commentary on Paul's epistle to the Romans.

Paul's letter to the Christians of Rome, written some time in the middle of the first century, was his theological masterpiece addressing justification, salvation and the nature of God. In the sixteenth century the epistle had drawn extraordinary interest: Erasmus, Lefèvre and Luther had famously engaged with Paul; in 1515 the young professor Martin Luther held his lectures on Romans in Wittenberg. Between 1529 and 1542 alone over fourteen different commentaries appeared from Catholic and Protestant writers.[1] Melanchthon, Bucer and Bullinger had addressed the text in different forms, and for Calvin it was the logical point of departure.

What astonishes the reader of Calvin's commentary is his fresh approach to the Bible, his theological vision, his engagement with tradition and his understanding of the Bible as the basis for a vision of a unified church. This was a seminal moment in his life, bearing the fruit of his pastoral and scholarly work in Strasbourg as well as his engagement with the wider Protestant dialogue on the Church and its sacraments. He sought to demonstrate how one could draw on the tradition of biblical interpretation to speak of the ills of one's day. He presented hope for a Protestant world in which difference did not mean enmity. And this vision included a very particular role for Calvin himself.

The Bible

In the 1539 *Institutes* Calvin remarked that 'who even of slight intelligence does not understand that God is accustomed to prattle, as it were, with us, like nurses with babies? Such forms of speaking do not so much give a crystal-clear picture of what God is like as accommodate the knowledge of him to our slender capacity.'[2] Scripture is God's means of speaking to humanity, and the interpreter's task is to explain the various media by which God communicates – instruction, admonition, pastoral comfort, polemic.[3] To achieve this, Calvin believed, following Erasmus and Melanchthon, a scholar required the tools of humanist rhetoric by which he could explain faith. All the reformers distinguished between the Bible and the Word of God, or Gospel. Scripture *contains* 'perfect doctrine', which is God's revelation, but it is not itself the Gospel.[4] The purpose of the Bible is as an instrument of the Holy Spirit to reconcile humanity to God through Jesus Christ in the community of the church.[5]

The Fellowship of the Word

Calvin's dedication of his Romans commentary to his friend and mentor Simon Grynaeus was a self-conscious declaration of his membership of the international Protestant fraternity. As he was writing the commentary he was only beginning his engagement with imperial religious politics, but his familiarity with the Swiss and German reformations was considerable. To Cardinal Sadoleto he had insisted that the reformers stood as one on the key doctrinal issues of the Reformation. At the same time, the dedication is an audacious and brilliant declaration of intellectual independence. Having witnessed at first hand the divisions among the Protestants, Calvin offered a distinctive perspective as a basis for unity. For the Catholics, there was nothing to be said, as he fully endorsed Melanchthon's repudiation of reconciliation with the Roman church. For the Protestants, however, he wished to make a very different point: there was room for differences of theology and method as long as it was among those whose primary commitment was to the Word of God. This was his application of the concept of friendship to church unity. The churches were not to be identical, but bound together by common cause and reciprocal obligations. Calvin's legal and humanist backgrounds emerged in full force in expressing his view of the Reformation.

Written only a month previously, Calvin's letter to Sadoleto forms the crucial context for the dedication of the Romans commentary. In the letter, Calvin had robustly denied that either tradition or institutional continuity formed the basis of the true Church, which as the body of Christ constitutes the unity of believers strewn across the world. In the dedication he set out to define a very different understanding of the true Church in its diverse localities. He speaks first of the 'ancient commentators, whose godliness, learning, sanctity, and age have secured them such great authority that we should not despise anything which they have produced'.[6] He then turns to what he terms the most significant modern commentators, Melanchthon, Bucer and Bullinger, all of whom he praises. The point is clear – a line exists from the ancient authorities to contemporary reformers. Each of the three men is lauded for his achievement: Melanchthon for his learning, Bullinger for his ease of expression and Bucer as the precise and diligent interpreter of scripture. The rhetorical message is unmistakable: whatever else divided them, the most significant centres of Protestantism (Wittenberg, Zurich and Strasbourg) stand united in their fidelity to the Word of God and true Christian scholarship.[7]

Having established his framework, Calvin suggests he will do something rather different from his colleagues for the sake of the 'common good of the Church'.[8] In other words, he wished to contribute to the debate about Romans among the leading reformers. He reminds Grynaeus that they had agreed on the virtue of 'lucid brevity' (*brevitas*) and offers this as his guiding principle. This brings him to what is unsatisfactory in the methods of his colleagues. Melanchthon's use of common places, or *loci*, so influential for Calvin's 1539 *Institutes*, is not, in his view, appropriate to biblical commentary because such groupings of theological topics can lead to the neglect of parts of scripture. This was a violation of the humanist principle of reading the whole text. Bucer is praised for the profundity of his thought, but not for his prolixity. As Calvin remarks, the man never knew when to stop – a reflection shared, and not infrequently articulated, by others, including Bullinger, who on one occasion admitted that he could only bear to skim through Bucer's lengthy letters. Of Bullinger himself, Calvin claims that his work is rightly praised, but offers no direct criticism – a significant silence. At the point at which he wrote the

Romans commentary his relations with Zurich were not sufficiently strong to withstand criticism, and he was hoping to reconcile the Zwinglians and Lutherans.

In contrast to Melanchthon, he would treat the *whole* of Paul's epistle, but concisely, so as to avoid Bucer's wordiness. To elaborate, he made a series of points concerning the role of the interpreter, the purpose of interpretation and the needs of the audience. The commentator requires humility, and this in two respects. the recognition that God's generous gift of grace alone makes the Word accessible, and an acknowledgement that full wisdom is not granted to any one person. God's Word must be received in the context of community, for humans are social beings, as Calvin had noted in his Seneca commentary. God's gifts are distributed unequally, requiring Christians to work together and to recognize in others what they lack in themselves.

Humility, however, must not be confused with diffidence, and Calvin made no effort to mask his confidence in his ambitious plan to treat Paul's letter verse by verse from start to finish. This was the proper task of the interpreter, to follow the text exactly as it was written in order to elucidate the mind of the author. The commentator should not introduce extraneous themes or topics but concentrate on lucid and brief explanations of the texts.[9] To achieve this requires a high standard of education with competence in biblical languages, history and the humanist arts. The commentator should have a mastery not only of biblical sources, but also of profane ones, for they too can shed light on God's Word. To this end, he must understand the ancient world that produced these texts so that they can be properly understood in their historical and literary contexts.

And what of his role? Calvin's comments in the dedication throw light on how he saw himself among the reformers. 'These writers', he says of his fellow reformers, 'frequently vary from one another, and this fact creates much difficulty for simple-minded readers. Therefore, I should not regret having undertaken this task if, by pointing to the best interpretations, I relieve them of the trouble of forming a judgement.'[10] Calvin located himself as the mediator between the parties, a man whose new voice and method offered a means of resolving differences. The dedication is an expression simultaneously of Protestant unity and of his own distinctive place within the churches of the Reformation.

Embracing the Tradition

The model set up by Calvin in his dedication of a conversation between the reformers extended to his treatment of the church fathers, who were central to his attempt to understand Paul's writings.[11] 'Hence the tradition of the fathers must be examined; and it is a mark of prudent discretion to observe what they contain, and whence they proceed. If we discover that they have no other tendency than to the pure worship of God, we may embrace them; but if they draw us away from the pure and simple worship of God, if they infect true and sincere religion by their own mixtures, we must utterly reject them.'[12]

They were humans, they disagreed with one another, and could get it wrong. Indeed Calvin felt no compunction about rejecting their views. In the biblical commentaries Augustine and Chrysostom not infrequently are declared to be dead wrong. Nevertheless, for Calvin, as for the other Protestant reformers, the church fathers were so highly regarded that they were constantly quoted and referenced. In his writings he rarely named any contemporary authors, even those from whom he borrowed heavily, such as Bucer or Melanchthon. Likewise, the medieval scholastics, although certainly present in his arguments, almost never appear by name. Early-modern authors, including Calvin, did not footnote sources; they felt no obligation to state from where they took an argument or against whom they were speaking. Contemporary writers did not merit such attention, and, besides, the learned public reading the text would usually be able to identify the source. With the church fathers, however, it was an entirely different matter. They were both named and quoted as a mark of respect.

Calvin's use of the church fathers was grounded in the firm belief that the consensus of their views supported his theology. He did not, however, simply trawl through their works seeking evidence for his own position; he read them carefully and widely and was guided by their views. They were, in his words, witnesses from a 'primitive and purer Church', though everything they said had to be subjected to the rule of scripture.[13] The fathers belonged to a period that Calvin regarded as the 'golden age' of the Church, approximately the first five centuries after the death of Christ, a time when there was general consensus about doctrine and when the Church had not yet been disfigured by the papacy. He did not invoke them as authorities – Paul was the authority – but they were the great commentators of the Church and their wisdom throws much light on scripture.

Calvin's relationship with the medieval tradition is more difficult because it is all but invisible to the untrained eye. He offers little assistance, as he almost never acknowledged his scholastic sources. Yet it has been long recognized that he was a diligent student of medieval authors.[14] One does not have to read long before finding one of his barbed remarks about the scholastics, but his target was often the masters of theology at the Sorbonne, and not the distinguished teachers of the medieval church.[15] The relationship was inevitably more complex: he read the scholastic authors and appropriated their methods and arguments explicitly and implicitly. They became part of his theological framework and influenced the direction of his thought.

From 1540 onwards, as he wrote his biblical commentaries Calvin unceasingly studied the church fathers and the medieval doctors, and this was reflected in his writings. He saw himself engaged in a sustained conversation with ancient and contemporary interpreters, none of whom was infallible. It was a conversation in the service of the Church, guided by the Spirit and grounded in the Word of God.

Commenting on the Word

Biblical commentary was, in Calvin's eyes, distinct but not separate from other forms of religious literature, such as a theological treatises, sermons, devotional writings and polemic. His intention was to prepare something useful, to reform Christian teaching in conformity with the best interpretation of scripture.[16] The systematic organization of theological topics is a different genre, belonging to the *Institutes*, yet his theology developed through the intensive study of scripture. Calvin insisted that the *Institutes* were an introduction to scripture to be read by ministers alongside his commentaries. There was a symbiotic relationship between the *Institutes* and the commentaries in that both served the purpose of elucidating scripture, but from different perspectives. Commenting on scripture was different from theology. The former is necessarily a little freer, reflecting the lack of uniformity in the Bible. Calvin accepted that there was more liberality in scriptural teaching than in teaching theology.[17] As one developed so did the other, and this revealed a certain circularity to Calvin's system: to be able to interpret scripture properly one already had to be versed in doctrine and scripture. The faithful, for example, could only understand what the preacher explained to them from the Bible if they had already been instructed by the catechism. Calvin, like the other reformers, understood that scripture could not stand without a framework of interpretation. And that framework ultimately supported his theological conclusions. This was precisely how it worked in Reformed, Lutheran and Catholic churches of the sixteenth century.

In his dedication to Grynaeus, Calvin praised the breadth and depth of Melanchthon's learning, referring to his command of the classical and biblical languages as well as to his knowledge of dialectic and rhetoric. Beginning with his Romans commentary of 1522 Melanchthon had opened a new path for biblical commentary in which rhetoric played a central part.[18] This was followed in 1530 by a clear statement that the doctrine of justification by faith was the essential doctrine in Romans. Although Calvin departed from Melanchthon's method of interpretation, he fully shared his conclusion that the epistle was the theological heart of the Bible.[19] He made extensive use of the rhetorical and dialectical tools set out by Melanchthon in his 1529–30 commentaries, and although it cannot be proved directly, it is highly likely that he wrote his commentary with Melanchthon's works open in front of him. At the same time Calvin showed himself to be in agreement on many points with Bullinger's 1533 and Bucer's 1536 commentaries on Romans. His dedication draws attention to the different ways in which the commentators conceived of the relationship between the interpretation of individual verses and the argument of the whole letter. Melanchthon, according to Calvin, referenced everything to the principal message of the letter, justification by faith alone. Bullinger, Bucer and Calvin, on the whole, gave more attention to the contours of individual passages.[20]

Imitating Paul

Calvin loved Paul, whom he regarded as the supreme teacher and pastor, the very model of Christian conduct. From his earliest writings he continually invoked the Apostle as his authority and guide in understanding scripture and making the message of the Gospel relevant to daily life. In Geneva and Strasbourg he had taught and preached on the Pauline letters. Yet Calvin's Paul was never one dimensional. He could appear in different forms depending on the message intended: the educated Jew well versed in the Law; the rhetorician addressing the Greeks and Romans in classical terms; the towering figure of authority; the patient pastor, full of love and humility. For Calvin, Paul was extraordinarily adaptable. His special gifts included the ability to 'be all things to all men'. But Paul was also intensely human and, consequently, fallible. Calvin never deified the Apostle: he was a human person who demonstrated how the fruits of the Gospel could be realized in this life. Paul could, and should, be imitated. While Calvin insisted that one should imitate Christ, this had its limitations in that humans cannot be God. Paul, in contrast, was a human model.

For Calvin there was a deeply personal resonance. Paul was not just an example of the Christian life, he was his personal teacher and mentor. It was in Paul that Calvin found his true patron. But it was not simply a case of superior and subordinate. Calvin's relationship to Paul was shaped by the Renaissance understanding of imitation and emulation, and in this respect he owed much to Budé and Erasmus. For Renaissance humanists, imitation was not akin to our modern sense of 'copying'. From Petrarch to Milton it occupied a prominent and recognizable position in historical, literary and theological works.[21] Although existing in a myriad of forms, imitation was widely understood as a transformative process by which a person became the model. In other words, through intensive study, prayer and conduct Calvin sought to become Paul. This was by no means straightforward and possessed many levels of complexity, as any reader of the commentaries quickly discerns. The imitation of which Calvin spoke derived from both his reading of Erasmus and his humanist legal studies under Alciati, and was closely linked to his view of the Church. For Calvin, following Erasmus and the French humanists, imitation was shaped by historical and cultural difference. One could not pretend that Paul, living in the first century, might be transformed into a sixteenth-century Frenchman. Likewise, the churches of the Reformation might view the Apostolic church as their model, but they could not replicate it. A proper understanding of the relationship of the present to the past rested on sensitivity to historical difference.

Imitation was closely linked to the role of the commentator, who, according to Calvin, was to occupy the mind of the author. This is precisely what Calvin sought to do with Paul by embracing his forms of argumentation, expression and vocabulary, but according to the essential humanist principle of decorum, which were part of Renaissance rhetoric. One speaks with decorum when, in Erasmus' words, 'our speech suits the people and conditions of the present'.[22] Calvin strove to be Paul in full knowledge that he was not Paul – they were separated by fifteen hundred years. Nevertheless, through his absolute confidence in his ability to interpret Paul, Calvin was certain that he could be the voice of the Apostle in his own age. In so doing he adopted another aspect of Renaissance imitation, and that was dissimulation. He never openly acknowledged his imitation of Paul: it was implicit, particularly in the biblical commentaries and correspondence, but never directly stated. He saw himself, again in the Erasmian spirit, as understanding the historical distance between himself and Paul, and seeking, therefore, to accommodate Paul to the world of the sixteenth century. He did the same thing for the prophets of the Old Testament, saying, for example, of Jeremiah, 'and if Jeremiah himself were now alive on earth, he would add, if I am not deceived, his recommendation;

for he would acknowledge that his prophecies have been explained by me not less honestly than reverently; and further, that they have been usefully accommodated to present circumstances.'[23]

The extraordinary association with Paul is borne out throughout the commentaries. Here from Philippians:

> But it is asked, how is it possible that one who really is superior to others can suppose those to be above him whom he knows to be far beneath him? I answer that this wholly depends on the right estimate of God's gifts and our own infirmities. For however anyone may have outstanding endowments, he should consider that they have not been given to him that he might be self-complacent, that he might exalt himself or even venerate himself. Let him instead work at correcting and detecting his faults, and he will have great material for humility. In others, on the other hand, he will regard with honour whatever they have of excellence, and will in love bury their faults. Whoever grasps this rule, will have no difficulty in preferring others before himself. Therefore it is possible that a pious man, even though aware that he is superior, may still hold others in greater esteem.[24]

In speaking here about Paul, Calvin offered an astonishingly revealing portrait of himself: his assurance of his own talents, his struggle for humility and the complexities of his relationships with others. In working on Romans he not only inhabited the mind of the author, but assumed his voice. The Paul of the Romans commentary is Calvin himself.

We find other means by which Calvin appropriated Paul's voice. One does not have to read far before encountering paraphrases or rephrasings of Paul's words. He frequently pauses to tell the reader that 'what Paul means is . . .'. At other moments he clarifies a point he feels Paul has not sufficiently articulated. This was a known classical device by which an author speaks with the voice of another, and Calvin employed this technique repeatedly in his commentary in order that he might speak with apostolic authority.

Calvin's God

God's creation, in Paul's words, reveals 'his invisible qualities – his eternal power and divine nature'.[25] Yet, on account of the blindness of sin, humanity fails to see 'what has been made plain to it'. The failure is inexcusable, for men and women know God without giving thanks and prefer their own wisdom to

God's glory. Calvin takes this passage and reflects how 'man was formed to be a spectator of this created world and he was endowed with eyes for the purpose of his being led to God himself, the Author of the world, by contemplating so magnificent an image'.[26] So where does that leave humanity? Accused by the created world in which it lives, yet unable to find the seemingly invisible and inscrutable God who will pronounce judgement, it contrives to form its own ideas about that God. Paul speaks of God's abandonment of humanity to its carnal lusts and preference for the created over the spiritual. Nevertheless, Calvin responded that 'Paul's object was to teach us where salvation is to be found.'[27] The first lesson is that humans in no way merit salvation. All delusions of goodness vanish in the face of Paul's citing of the prophet Habakkuk: 'The righteous will live by faith.' This, for Calvin, is the very essence of the letter to the Romans; righteousness 'is the groundwork of our salvation, [and] is revealed in the Gospel: hence the Gospel is said to be the power of God unto salvation'. Calvin interpreted Paul's use of the term 'righteousness' to mean both God's free remission of sins and the grace of regeneration, which is the ability of the Christian to grow in faith over the course of life.[28] 'When at first we taste the Gospel, we indeed see God's smiling countenance turned towards us, but at a distance: the more the knowledge of true religion grows in us, by coming as it were nearer, we behold God's favour more clearly and more familiarly.' The righteousness of God launches the Christian on a lifelong journey towards the creator.

If, in Paul's words, human unrighteousness serves to reveal God's righteousness, does human wickedness form an effective barrier to God's will? Calvin joined with the Apostle in an emphatic 'No!' For 'the Lord, in spite of the lies of men, which are a hindrance to his truth, will still find a way for it where there is no way, that he may emerge victorious by correcting in his elect the inborn unbelief of our nature'.[29] Calvin's description of God finding a way towards lost humanity forms an attractive parallel with his earlier description of the Christian journeying towards God. In both cases God reaches out and draws the chosen forward. The divine hand is extended in Christ, and Paul's description of the Son of God as the 'sacrifice of atonement' (Romans 3:25) succinctly captured, for Calvin, the distinction between God's love of humanity and God's revulsion at its sinfulness: 'God does not hate in us his own workmanship, that is, the fact he has created us as living beings; but he hates our uncleanness, which has extinguished the light of his image. When the washing of Christ has removed this, he loves and embraces us as his own pure workmanship.'[30]

The Righteous Man: Abraham

Calvin, following Paul, described Abraham as 'the mirror and pattern of right-eousness'. As a mirror – a favourite Calvin metaphor – Abraham's calling and his obedient response are not mere historical facts, but a vibrant image of how Christians are to live. The whole story of Abraham is suffused with signifi-cance for the contemporary reader. Notice, Calvin remarked, how Moses pays no attention to what other people thought of Abraham, or even of what he thought himself. This was very much Calvin's ideal, but not one he could meet. Only the details of the relationship between God and Abraham are worthy of mention. Even this great figure of the Old Testament brought nothing to his partnership with God; his response to the call grew from the righteousness imputed to him. Just as God initiated Abraham's journey, so must it be for Christians.

It was God's calling that cleansed Abraham of his sins, and Calvin drew attention to the chronological precedence of the call over his circumcision. God's favour is not bound to any external ritual. It is the indwelling of the spirit – Calvin employed Paul's language of the 'circumcision of the heart'. Yet, while humans cannot cause God to grant the grace that brings them to life, neither are they to remain passive. Receiving means responding.

Let us also remember that we are all in the same condition as Abraham. Our circumstances are all in opposition to the promises of God: He promises us immortality; we are surrounded by mortality and corrup-tion. He declares that he counts us just; yet we are covered with sins. He testifies that he is propitious and kind to us; yet outward signs threaten his wrath. What then are we to do? We must close our eyes, disregard ourselves and all things connected with us, that nothing may hinder or prevent us from believing that God is true.[31]

The stories of the Bible unite past and present in an unbroken continuum: we see in the men and women of the Bible our own lives. Scripture contains both the story of humanity *and* humanity itself; the whole palate of human emotions, from joy to grief, kindness to cruelty, is amply displayed. But the story of Abraham is not about the person of Abraham – it is not his human qualities that should catch our eye. 'Paul maintains therefore', Calvin commented, 'that the record of Abraham's life was not written for its own sake alone. It does not refer to the individual calling of one particular person, but is a description of the way to obtain righteousness, which is one and unchanging among all believers.'[32] The great figures of the Church are great only insofar as God has chosen to act through them. This was Calvin's view of the prophetic office he held.

'Jacob I Have Loved, Esau I Have Hated'

How are the faithful distinguished from the reprobate if no person, not even Abraham, merits salvation? If all are guilty, what separates believer from non-believer, and why, in fact, does one believe and another not? Such questions shaped Calvin's interpretation of Romans 9, where Paul movingly speaks of his love of the Jews, of whom he says, 'theirs are the patriarchs and from them is traced the human ancestry of Christ, who is God over all'. But not all are Abraham's children, for it is not natural descent that makes them the chosen ones of God. What emerges is the distinction between God's covenant made with the Israelites and election, by which only those whom God has chosen will be saved. That the two are not the same thing is illustrated most dramatically in the story of Isaac's two sons, Esau and Jacob, borne in old age by Rebekah. God chose Jacob, the younger, declaring, 'Jacob I have loved, Esau I have hated.' This is the doctrine of election. God's choice was made before the twins were born; it was not on account of any good or bad on their part that the decision was made. Calvin noted that, although both sons were initiated into the covenant by circumcision, God's grace was not equally distributed. It is a particularly striking example, Calvin argued, because they came from the same mother and were twins, so in natural terms there was little to divide them. With regard to God's grace, however, the difference could not be greater. Jacob is separated from Esau by God's election, which is 'gratuitous, and in no way depending on men, so that in the salvation of the godly nothing higher must be sought than the goodness of God, and nothing higher in the perdition of the reprobate than his just severity'.

Calvin's reading of Paul permitted him to find the doctrine of election clearly presented.

> Paul's first proposition therefore, is as follows: 'As the blessing of the covenant separates the people of Israel from all other nations, so also the election of God makes a distinction between the men in that nation, while he predestines some to salvation, and others to eternal condemnation.' The second proposition is, 'There is no basis for this election other than the goodness of God alone, and also his mercy since the fall of Adam,

which embraces those whom he pleases, without any regard whatever to their works.' The third is, 'The Lord in his unmerited election is free and exempt from the necessity of bestowing equally the same grace on all. Rather, he passes by those whom he wills, and chooses whom he wills.'[33]

The human mind cannot comprehend God's election, and nor was it ever intended to do so.

> The predestination of God is indeed in reality a labyrinth from which the mind of man can by no means extricate itself. So unreasonable is the curiosity of man, however, that the more perilous the examination of a subject is, the more boldly he proceeds, so that when predestination is discussed he cannot restrain himself within due limits, thus he immediately through his rashness plunges himself, as it were, into the depth of the sea.

This inability to understand God's election makes Paul's questions all the more urgent: 'What then shall we say?', and 'Is God unjust?' he writes (Romans 9:14). Calvin argued for the necessity of knowing God, but that knowledge suddenly hit a brick wall. To know God is essential to salvation, yet in overreaching a person engages in vain and damaging curiosity. A proper balance is required, and for Calvin this consisted in accepting what has been revealed in scripture. 'Let this then be our sacred rule, to seek to know nothing concerning it [predestination] except what scripture teaches us: when the Lord closes his holy mouth, let us also stop the way that we may not go farther. But as we are men, to whom foolish questions naturally occur, let us hear from Paul how they are to be met.' What *can* be known is that God does choose the faithful, that without election there is no salvation, that human merit has nothing to do with election, and that God never abandons those who are called.

The most common charge made by the numerous opponents of Calvin's teaching on predestination was that the logical conclusion of his argument was to make God the author of evil. This rendered Paul's question whether God is unjust of particular significance. The Apostle illustrates his point with the story from Exodus of God's hardening of Pharaoh's heart. 'I raised you up for this very purpose, that I might display my power in you, and that my name might be proclaimed in all the earth' (Romans 9:17). Can humans be held responsible if God causes hearts to turn to stone? Calvin replied emphatically that Pharaoh's mood swings cannot be interpreted in terms of mere human emotions. Pharaoh was a tool in the hands of a God who not only knew in advance what the Egyptian ruler would do, but caused it to happen. Nowhere is Calvin's vision of an omnipotent God more dramatically presented.

> If we wish to understand Paul's meaning, we must examine almost every word. There are vessels prepared for destruction, that is, appointed and destined for destruction. There are also vessels of wrath made and formed for the purpose of being proofs of the vengeance and displeasure of God. If the Lord bears patiently with them for a time by not destroying them at the first opportunity, but postponing the judgement prepared for them, this is in order to set forth the decisions of his severity that others may be terrified by such dreadful examples. It is also to make known his power to which he makes them submit in many ways, and also that this may make the extent of his mercy toward the elect better known and shine with greater clarity. Is there anything reprehensible in this dispensation? Finally, it is so the greatness of his mercy towards the elect may be more fully known and more brightly shine forth.[34]

The Law, Jews and Gentiles

The question of the Law – the Ten Commandments – and its meaning looms large in the Romans commentary. Calvin drew the analogy of a widow.

> The Law was our husband, under whose yoke we were held until it became dead to us: After the death of the Law Christ took us to himself, that is, he freed us from the Law and took us to himself. Being, therefore, united to Christ who has been raised from the dead, we ought to cleave to him alone. And as the life of Christ is eternal after the resurrection, so hereafter we shall never be divorced from him.[35]

There is nothing evil in the Law itself, but it reveals the extent of evil, as no person is able to meet its standard of perfection.

Calvin was highly sensitive to Paul's pain in discussing the plight of the Jews. He spoke of the Apostle's love for his people and his concern for their salvation.[36] Calvin went so far as to say that the Jews rejected God out of ignorance, not maliciousness, believing that by crucifying Christ they were acting in accordance with the Law – a failure to recognize that their Law leads to Christ. Moses was a preacher of the Gospel, and his calling was to instruct the people in repentance and faith by example. He was to lead God's people to Christ, the end of the Law. However, because Christ remained behind a veil, not evident to the Israelites, Moses had to teach a form of works righteousness (that salvation can be achieved by human endeavour) through observance of the precepts of the Law. This works righteousness was, strictly speaking, in opposition to Christ, but that was not Calvin's main argument. Rather, although Christ was the end, he could only be dimly seen, therefore God's righteousness had to be fulfilled in another way, a way from which the Israelites ultimately departed through their lack of faith.

When Calvin discussed Paul's lament for the Jews and his willingness to die for their salvation, he was clear that the Jews should be honoured on account of the station granted them by God. He meant by this that the gifts of God and not the people themselves were to be honoured. Christians should not denigrate the Jews, but neither should the Jews themselves be flattered into thinking that all is well without accepting Christ. God was never unfaithful to the people of the covenant, and that the Jews were the chosen people should not be forgotten. God's own son came from the Jews, and this was the highest honour for the people, but such distinctions, according to Calvin, are as nothing when separated from piety.

Calvin saw Paul's preaching to the gentiles as confirmation both of the Apostle's calling and of the opening of salvation. Preaching is the principal, though not the sole, means by which God has chosen to make the Word available to humanity. Without that Word there can be no true knowledge of God. It does not, however, follow that preaching automatically brings about faith. Calvin rejected any notion of universal salvation, for preaching bears fruit only among those chosen by God to be saved. Calvin would have encountered few Jews before his arrival in Strasbourg. His writing on Paul and the Jews in Romans certainly reflected another new experience in the city.

'A Taste of his Goodness': Christian Living

Paul teaches that the Christian life 'is pleasing and acceptable to God when we devote ourselves to purity and holiness'. Calvin did not limit this life to a rejection of pleasures or abstinence; it is more positively spoken of as a renewal of both the body and mind. The two cannot be separated as if the Christian exists as some sort of disembodied spirit. The taming of the body and the cultivation of the mind belong together in the pursuit of a life of 'purity' and 'wisdom'. The holy men and women of both Testaments of the Bible provide the necessary examples of the good life, which is not a brainless existence of subservience, but is filled with a wisdom that rejects the thinking of the world. This path of wisdom requires one to tread between two evils: ignorance and excessive curiosity. The wise person possesses discernment, a crucial word for Calvin, and knows both what is appropriate and the boundaries beyond which it is forbidden to pass.

The world is a place of conflict, but not without order. All humans are bound by natural law – the order of law embedded in God's creation – which provides them with ideas of justice and good government. God has placed rulers, both Christian and non-Christian, to uphold the order of the world. The basis of their authority is natural law, which is not to be confused with biblical laws. Therefore, rulers who are not Christians and states whose laws are not grounded in scripture are, according to Calvin, entirely legitimate and worthy of obedience from the faithful. When Paul speaks of 'the debt of love', Calvin summarized these words to articulate his own view that love and the cultivation of community are at the root of Christian obedience to the state. 'It is as though he had said, "When I request you to obey rulers, I require only what all believers ought to perform by the law of love. If you wish the good to prosper (and not to wish this is inhuman), you ought to strive to make the laws and judgements prevail, in order that the people may be obedient to the defenders of the laws, for these men enable us to enjoy peace." '[37]

The Christian lives not for his or her self, for 'nothing does more to hinder or delay our service of other people than the excessive self-concern which leads us to neglect them, and to follow our own plans and desires'.[38] Selfishness must be replaced by a readiness to accommodate, a willingness to do whatever is necessary for another according to the scriptures, by which 'we make progress in piety and holiness of life'. This touched on the nature of salvation, which Calvin continued to develop in his writings. Salvation is not about individuals, but about the community of the Church, and in the Romans commentary Calvin, drawing on his Strasbourg experiences, began to think more clearly about the way in which the body of the faithful must work together. Paul's statement that 'everything was written to teach us that through endurance and the encouragement of the scriptures we might have hope' offered Calvin the place to reflect upon the themes of consolation, patience and hope. He defined patience as meekness 'by which we willingly submit to God, while a taste of his goodness and fatherly love renders all things sweet to us. This patience cherishes and sustains unceasing hope in us'.[39]

In every aspect of the Christian life there are bonds of mutuality which define the relationship between the faithful as well as the duty of the Christian to sacrifice self for another.[40] It is this duty of love that has for God an 'acceptable odour'. Likewise, Calvin sees in Paul's anticipation of his reception among the Romans a humbling lesson in the reciprocity of the Christian life. Paul recognizes that he must establish the nature of his office and set out why the Romans should take his words seriously. Yet in return he expects to be received with kindness. Kindness and communication, Calvin commented, form the bonds of faith and the mutual regard for the unity of the body. But what is most striking is a reflection on the Apostle's character that must have resonated strongly with Calvin. 'Paul's remarkable forbearance is seen clearly in the fact that he did not cease to work for those who might not, he felt, be prepared to welcome him. We must imitate this attitude, so that we do not cease to do good to those from whom we are quite uncertain whether we shall receive thanks.'[41]

The theme of unity runs through Paul's salutations at the end of the epistle as he mentions persons according to their faith and works. Calvin saw in Phoebe, Prisca, Aquila and others the model Christian community. Nevertheless, they too offer the opportunity for reflections that have little to do with Paul's text. Paul commends Phoebe, the bearer of the letter, to the Roman community, requesting them 'to receive her in the Lord in a manner worthy of the saints, and give her any help she may require from you, for she has been a great help to many people, including me' (Romans 16:2). Calvin began by recognizing the task performed by Phoebe in bringing the letter, remarking that all who perform offices of the church should be properly honoured. Further, her kindness and concern described by the Apostle require that she be well treated by others, to whom she has set an example.

Not only was Paul Calvin's ideal minister, but the Romans themselves were the ideal congregation. They show themselves to be 'obedient and teachable' as well as kind in their hospitality. Yet their virtue makes them vulnerable to the ways of the world. Although simplicity is to be admired in a person, Calvin found in Paul's admonition 'be wise about what is good, and innocent about what is evil' (Romans 16:19) the necessary caution to the Christian community to exercise 'wisdom' and 'discernment' so as not to be misled by fraudulent teachers. Simplicity is not ignorance; it is the absence of evil. It is found in the practice of wisdom and justice by those who have a disposition that turns from evil to demonstrate caution in all things.

The relationship between Paul and the Romans formed for Calvin a model of the church, an example he was seeking to emulate. The Romans commentary is full of theological significance that falls outside our brief, but its importance for Calvin's life cannot be overlooked. It was a text of extraordinary symbolic value embodying his growing views of community in different senses. There was the community of the reformers in which he placed himself in the dedication. Calvin was now part of the fraternity of international reformers committed to the whole Church. In the letter he laid out his understanding of the life of the Christian within the Church, centred on the doctrine of justification by faith alone. Finally, he set out the model of the minister and leader in the person of Paul, who had guided him through his conversion and whom he now acknowledged as his patron. The commentary marked Calvin's emergence in many ways, but most significantly with an identity drawn from the Apostle.

CHAPTER EIGHT

Building Christ's Church

'I Will Not Disappoint Your Expectation': Return

THE EXPULSION of Calvin and Farel in 1538 had not brought about the peace desired by their opponents, and for three years Geneva remained in turmoil. Calvin's former teacher, Mathurin Cordier, and Antoine Saunier, the rector, joined with the wealthy Genevan Ami Perrin to foster opposition to the magistrates and ministers appointed to replace the deposed Frenchmen. The result was further trouble as Cordier and Saunier were likewise expelled. Nevertheless, factionalism did not loosen its grip on Geneva's throat, and Berne's hopes to stamp its authority on its fractious client were frustrated. From Strasbourg Calvin had continued to advise and his presence was felt in Geneva, whose rulers grew to realize that the best hope of resolution lay with his recall.

Calvin's friends Pierre Viret and Guillaume Farel led the campaign for his return. Viret even ventured to suggest that Geneva would be good for Calvin's fragile constitution: 'I read the passage in your letter, not without a smile,' came the reply, 'in which you show so much concern for my health, and recommend Geneva on that ground.' A volcanic response followed. 'But it would be far preferable to perish for eternity than be tormented in that place. If you wish me well, my dear Viret, do not mention the subject!'[1] In January 1541 Viret arrived in Geneva from Lausanne on loan for six months to preach in the city. He was extremely well received and did much to moderate the situation, but he found Geneva exhausting and continued to press for Calvin's return. Farel, with whom Calvin had remained in close contact, was characteristically inexhaustible, once more threatening him with divine punishment. The time for such prophetic thundering, however, had passed, and Calvin did not cower. Instead, he grew impatient with Farel's ignorance of the pressing issues of the wider Reformation.[2] The role played by Martin Bucer was also complicated: originally he had not intended that Calvin would remain in Strasbourg, yet with the years he had come to appreciate the Frenchman's superb mind and debating skills as well as his head for politics and grew decidedly less eager to lose an important ally.

The question of Calvin's return was tangled, and his protestations to Viret do not tell the whole story. He had never washed his hands of Geneva and we know that he retained material possessions in the city. But during the heady days of his participation in the religious colloquies in the empire in 1540 he was too engrossed in international affairs to accept any overtures from Geneva. However, as he witnessed, with growing revulsion, the willingness of Protestant princes and reformers to compromise with Catholics his mood changed. Still, he needed to be certain that a return to the scene of his greatest humiliation was a good idea. There was no possibility of simply resuming where he had left off when he and Farel had ridden out of Geneva in April 1538.

Matters began to shift when the major Swiss churches became involved. Zurich and Basle wrote to Strasbourg arguing that the only way to restore peace in Geneva was by releasing Calvin and allowing him to return.[3] Calvin was deeply moved by Bullinger's active interest. Their relationship had not enjoyed good times, particularly after Calvin had so closely associated himself with Strasbourg and signed Melanchthon's Variata in 1540. But the Frenchman understood perfectly well the political realities, and without the support of the leader of the Swiss Reformed churches his position in Geneva would be untenable. Nevertheless, Calvin's expression of gratitude to Zurich was, as ever, tempered by his determination to remain his own man. Writing to the Zurich church from Regensburg in May 1541, he presented himself as one badly wronged, the faithful servant of the Church whom events had ultimately vindicated.[4] The letter resounds with self-confidence. Not just the Genevans, but the Swiss churches after his exile had erred in their assumption that he was a troublemaker. He portrayed himself as a quasi-martyr made to suffer for his decision to remain and face the persecution. There would be no triumphal entry into Geneva, and he needed allies. He addressed them with supplicatory language. 'I rejoice that you [the Zurich ministers] have formed such an opinion of me with respectful regard to yourselves that there is scarcely anything you may not venture to promise yourselves. You may certainly do so, for I will not disappoint your expectation.'

Having decided to return to Geneva, Calvin did not rush. During the summer of 1541 he kept putting off the inquiries of Farel and Viret by speaking of unfinished business in Strasbourg. By the start of September a mounted escort led by Ami Perrin arrived to accompany Calvin. Strasbourg wrote to Geneva requesting that the Frenchman return once he had completed his work in restoring the church, to which the Genevans replied that they hoped to retain Calvin this time.[5] He travelled through Basle, Zurich, Berne, Solothurn and, finally, Neuchâtel, where Farel had once more got himself into trouble.

It took Calvin about two weeks to reach Geneva, and when he arrived he wanted no formal reception. He had left Idelette behind in Strasbourg, so the Genevan magistrates sent horses and a carriage to fetch her and their household goods. By the end of September 1541 Calvin was back, this time a married man. The council made generous provision: he was given a house in the rue des Chanoines near the cathedral of Saint-Pierre and an income of five hundred florins, which made him better paid than most of the magistrates. Part of his income was paid in the form of wheat, wine, fur and cloth. The generosity of the council carried the expectation that Calvin's income was not private and that he would maintain a household in Geneva in which students, churchmen, political figures and distinguished guests would be received and entertained. The reformer's house, as in Zurich or Wittenberg, was an extension of the church.

Calvin's return to Geneva in 1541 belonged to the changing world of the urban reformations in German and Swiss lands. In the early days of the 1520s everything had seemed possible, including the establishment of godly communities based on harmonious relations between rulers and churchmen. The dream proved a delusion, and men such as Calvin and Bullinger faced a new reality. The preaching of the Gospel frequently and loudly clashed with the desire of magistrates to preserve order, forge alliances and foster economic prosperity. Calvin's task was to create a church order that would satisfy divergent expectations. The reformers' doctrine of the church was but one element; the realities confronting implementation of reforms required angry compromises alongside a canny sense of what could be achieved. The new Protestant churches, whether Lutheran or Zwinglian, faced the daunting prospect of appeasing their political masters, dealing with rapidly changing populations and negotiating relationships with established popular and religious practices.

When Calvin re-entered Geneva on 13 September 1541 it was neither as a prodigal son nor as a sulking Achilles reluctantly summoned from his tent. The decision to recall him to Geneva had been entirely pragmatic, and not unanimous. The city desperately needed quality clergy. Calvin had been able to strike a deal whereby his return was contingent upon the establishment of discipline, and with the *Ecclesiastical Ordinances* he secured the authority to restore a church in a state of meltdown. Such authority, however, by no means indicated personal domination. During the 1540s he faced strong and effective opposition as he attempted to chart a course through the choppy waters of Genevan factionalism. But whatever doubts he may have entertained about returning, once in Geneva he was resolved to erect a godly community, even if the means were brutal. Over the next ten years he ruthlessly prosecuted the incompetent and obstinate, who were not allowed to impede the progress of reform. In this his personality loomed large: he neither forgave nor forgot those he held responsible for the humiliation of 1538. No longer the naive neophyte once frightened by Farel into staying, Calvin was now a man who had trodden the stage of Reformation politics at the highest level; his perspective extended far beyond the walls of the city to France and the empire.

Calvin had been recalled by a council firmly in the hands of the Guillermin faction after its triumph over the Articulants. For any faction, loss of political power and exile had serious material and economic consequences, and many Articulants had suffered the appropriation of their property by the victors.[6] A central plank of Guillermin policy was independence from Berne, though the powerful Swiss Confederate retained control over Geneva's foreign relations and offered the only viable Protestant military protection. Not for the first or last time, the city of Berne and its lands became a haven for opponents of the prevailing regime in Geneva. But this was only the beginning of the troubles: threatened by Savoy and Berne, Geneva had virtually no means of defending itself, and, with its coffers empty, the city had to go cap in hand to Basle.

Disaster had another face – plague. Death swept across the Swiss Confederation in 1542 claiming many prominent reformers, including Calvin's friend and mentor Simon Grynaeus, to whom he had so fondly dedicated the Romans commentary. The outbreak of the plague in Geneva probably owed something to the passage of ten thousand French troops through Genevan lands in 1542; twelve months later the city was firmly in its grip.[7] The magistrates responded: the plague hospital was prepared and spies were sent to Nyon in the Vaud to watch for those intentionally spreading disease.[8] The ministers were asked by the council to provide a person to tend plague victims, a dangerous job rewarded with almost certain death. Both Calvin and Sebastian Castellio volunteered, but neither was accepted. Unsurprisingly, none of the ministers was eager for the position and for this they were rebuked by the council, which declared that all were to serve in the plague hospital except John Calvin, who was vital to the church.[9]

Reeling under this succession of blows, the Genevan magistrates were desperate for stability. To end the internecine warfare, from 1543 many of the Articulants were invited to return. Loans from Basle eased the financial crisis and negotiations were undertaken with Berne to settle outstanding territorial disputes. Basle, the traditional peace broker in the Confederation, played its role, and under its guidance the Genevans and Bernese reached an agreement which brought both financial and political security.[10] Calvin was regarded by the magistrates, if reluctantly by some, as their best hope for the spiritual life of the city.

'Mingled Many Hypocrites'

Study and writing, pastoral service and the religious colloquies had focused Calvin's mind on the Christian Church. 'For we have said that Holy Scripture speaks of the Church in two ways,' he wrote in the *Institutes*.

> Sometimes by the term 'Church' it means that which is actually in God's presence, into which no persons are received but those who are children of God by grace of adoption and true members of Christ by sanctification of the Holy Spirit. Often, however, the name 'Church' designates the whole multitude of men spread over the earth who profess to worship one God and Christ. In this Church are mingled many hypocrites who have nothing of Christ but the name and outward appearance.[11]

The vision was clear: the Church in this world is a mixture of the elect and the damned, who are separated only at death. Therefore, until the Day of Judgement the Church must labour to preserve its worship from idolatry and contamination.[12] To achieve this, it must have institutions, laws and discipline.

Calvin never doubted that the lineage of the Genevan church extended back to the Apostolic age following Christ's crucifixion. Guided by the Holy Spirit, the Church has a long history, and despite numerous lapses into error God never permits it to be wholly lost. The Church does not, however, have a fixed appearance and its external organization and forms of worship have radically changed over the centuries. Calvin never viewed this as a problem. Although committed to the institutional church, he was largely indifferent to precise forms of organization and practice as long as they were grounded in scripture. For example, he had no objection to the term 'bishop', which he included in the first draft of the *Ordinances*, though he was also not much bothered when it was removed. He saw no serious distinction between bishop and minister, except that the former held an organizational position for the purpose of maintaining order. Sixteenth-century Geneva could legitimately look to the Apostolic church as its model without having to copy the conditions of the first century. As with his relationship with Paul, Calvin believed that proper imitation involved the recognition of historical change, and he was too good a reformer and lawyer to believe that the New Testament provided a legislative basis for church government. There was no pretence that the structures set up by the *Ecclasiastical Ordinances* of 1541 were found in the early church; Calvin was more concerned to demonstrate that they embodied its spirit.[13] It was a practice in line with other Protestant reformers that involved a selective reading of the past.[14]

The Foundations

Within the remarkably brief period of two months Calvin succeeded in having the framework of a new church order drawn up and passed by the Genevan council. A committee had been appointed, but the result was very much Calvin's vision, along with a series of amendments from the magistrates.[15] A draft was debated by the Small Council on 27 September and by 20 November had been approved by the General Council – the new church now existed, at least on paper. Long gone was the abrasive approach taken by Farel and Calvin during their first stay in Geneva, when they had attempted to force their terms on the magistrates. The *Ecclesiastical Ordinances* of the autumn of 1541 expressed Calvin's understanding of the church as developed in the 1539 *Institutes*, in his commentary on Romans, and in his experiences of working as a minister in Strasbourg. The *Institutes* provided the historical and theological justification for the practices set out in the *Ordinances*. Calvin's legal mind was also very much in evidence.

What was proposed was a decidedly mixed form of government in which ministers and laity were bound together under mutual responsibility for building the godly society. Church and government were linked but separate entities, with the laity responsible for the election and correction of ministers, who in turn were to teach the Word of God and oversee the Christian life of the community. The role of the bishop was to be filled by two institutions: the Company of Pastors and the Consistory. The presiding officer of the Company was a moderator, while that of the Consistory was one of the four syndics. Calvin held the position of moderator in Geneva from 1541 until shortly before his death in 1564.[16] The *Ordinances* also established one of his cherished principles: the restoration of parishes, structures deemed essential for the maintenance of discipline and pastoral care.[17] To Calvin's great satisfaction, in 1541 the Genevan council created parishes in which every person was to be baptized, receive the Lord's Supper and learn the catechism. He had sought this during his first stay and failed.

The *Ordinances*, catechism and liturgy introduced in 1541–2 formed the bulwark of the Reformed church in Geneva, with the catechism establishing the standard of orthodoxy. Together they built on changes introduced from 1536, when virtually all traditional forms of worship and devotion were abolished, including the large network of confraternities. Even time was recalibrated: the calendar was reformed after 1536 with the removal of all saints' days and festivals; only Sunday was to be observed. The Genevan authorities expected the people to work six days a week and rest on the Sabbath. Following the Bernese pattern, and despite Calvin's opposition, the festivals of Ascension, Incarnation, Circumcision and Christmas continued to be marked until 1545, when the council accepted his recommendation that they be abrogated.[18] Christmas remained a sticking point and was only abolished in 1550 with a decree that forbade any holy days apart from Sunday. Christmas 1550 was a working day for the council, representing the elision of secular and sacred time in Geneva.[19]

The seeds of conflict were planted as soon as Calvin returned. With the *Ordinances* he crafted a particular view of the Church, but one not entirely shared by the magistrates. He envisaged a clearer separation of the church from the authority of the magistrates than the Genevan rulers were prepared to accept. The debate echoed Bucer's experiences in Strasbourg in the 1530s. On the issue of disputes over doctrine, for example, Calvin's text had originally proposed that contested points should be resolved by ministers, who could then call in the elders. The council insisted that the amended version read that the elders were appointed by the magistrates. Calvin's visceral distaste for any involvement by theologically untrained politicians in matters of doctrine was not to prevail. The additional paragraph concerning the Consistory brought the point home.

All this must be done in such a way that the ministers have no civil jurisdiction nor use anything but the spiritual sword of the Word of God as
St Paul commands them; nor is the authority of the consistory to
diminish in any way that of the magistrate or ordinary justice. The civil
power must remain unimpaired. In cases where, in future, there may be
a need to impose punishments or constrain individuals, then the ministers and the consistory, having heard the case and used such admonitions
and exhortations as are appropriate, should report the whole matter to
the council which, in turn, will judge and sentence according to the needs
of the case.

The Consistory, a mixed body of clerical and lay officials, was to oversee the
morality of the people, and in contrast to similar bodies in the Swiss Reformed
churches it possessed the right of excommunication. Yet the *Ordinances* make
it very clear that the ministers were entirely subject to the rule of the magistrates. They were paid officials of Geneva, and it was to the council they owed
allegiance.

The *Ordinances* determined four orders of ministry: pastors, doctors,
deacons and elders. The pastors 'are sometimes named in the Bible as over-
seers, elders and ministers. Their work is to proclaim the Word of God, to
teach, admonish, exhort and reprove publicly and privately, to administer the
sacraments and, with the elders or their deputies, to issue fraternal warnings.'
Doctors were entrusted with the teaching of the Christian faith in Geneva.
The 1541 *Ordinances* anticipated the creation of educational facilities that
would serve the training of ministers, although as this did not come about
until the transfer of the Lausanne Academy to Geneva in 1559, the position of
doctors within the Genevan church was initially rather opaque. Elders were
chosen from among the council, and their responsibility lay in the supervision
of Christian morals in Geneva. They were to be men of good standing and
their selection was to be discussed with the ministers before being submitted
to the General Council for approval. As we shall see, these men tended to
come from the less influential circles of Genevan politics, though they were to
form part of Calvin's core supporters during the 1540s. Finally, there were the
deacons, who were to care for the poor and distribute alms, though, as amendments to the *Ordinances* illustrate, there was concern to avoid confusion of
roles with existing institutions within the city, principally the hospital.

In addition to the four orders of ministry, the *Ordinances* made provision for
the two sacraments, Baptism and the Lord's Supper. Baptism of infants was

required and all names duly registered. The Lord's Supper was to be celebrated four times annually. The Lateran Council of 1215 had made it a minimum requirement that every Christian confess and receive communion at least once a year, although Calvin favoured much more frequent communion reflecting its centrality to worship. But in recognition of its infrequency in the late-medieval church, four times a year (Christmas, Easter, Pentecost and the first Sunday in September) was seen as a reasonable compromise.

The Company of Pastors

The Company of Pastors existed to oversee the doctrine and fellowship of the Genevan church and met every Friday, possibly at seven or nine in the morning after worship.[20] The Genevan church was divided into urban and rural parishes, the latter covering the relatively small expanse of territory outside the walls that fell under the council's authority. All the urban ministers were expected to attend, the rural pastors when they could. Meetings commenced with the Congrégation, open to the public, where a minister would lecture on a biblical passage. At the end of the session a minister or layperson could respond to the teaching. Calvin dominated these gatherings. Even when he was not the appointed teacher, his responses often took the form of lectures.[21] Yet, although his role was extremely influential, it is evident that a wide range of minsters was involved, allowing the meetings of the Congrégation to represent the Genevan ideal of collective study of the scripture and recognition of the distribution of the gifts among the church.[22]

After the Congrégation had concluded, the Company prosecuted the rest of its business in private: correspondence was discussed, ministers admonished and candidates for the ministry examined and interviewed. Ministers not deemed ready for service in the city were allocated to rural parishes. It was the council, however, which held the right of appointment, acting on the recommendation of the Company. Calvin dominated the Company, holding the position of moderator, and stamping his personality on the institution by dealing with the ministers. Although reasonably forgiving of ignorance, from the start he made it clear that he would brook no discord. He was adamant that the church must speak with one voice and would use his devastating combination of articulacy and memory to quash dissidents harshly, which was a source of considerable resentment.[23] To his opponents he seemed severe and unrelenting, but among most of his colleagues he commanded respect, particularly as the majority had been appointed by him. In his role as moderator he became the public face of the Company, frequently appearing before the Small Council on a range of church and legal matters. He did so not purely in an advisory capacity, but often to defend his own actions.

'They are Rude and Self-Conceited, Have No Zeal, and Less Learning': The Clergy

Calvin's first major hurdle in Geneva was the clergy, many of whom were woefully inadequate to fulfil the roles envisaged in the *Ordinances*. During the period 1541–6 he oversaw a radical transformation of the ministry in which mostly local Genevans were replaced by well-educated Frenchmen closely connected to the French reformer. This was not the first time Geneva had witnessed such dramatic change. Before the Reformation the city and its rural territories had been home to more than four hundred priests, monks and other religious – 160 had been associated with the cathedral of Saint-Pierre alone. With the introduction of the Reformation the Catholic clergy were removed, leaving many rural parishes with no minister and the city with as few as two.[24] This situation contrasted sharply with the German-speaking Reformed churches of Zurich, Basle and Berne, where most of the Catholic clergy were perfectly happy to turn themselves into Protestant ministers.[25]

Calvin had an extremely high view of ministry – upon which the Church depended – and his crucial biblical text was Ephesians 4:11–12: 'It was he who gave some to be apostles, some to be prophets, some to be evangelists, and some to be pastors and teachers, to prepare God's people for works of service, so that the body of Christ might be built up.' He spoke of 'true and faithful' ministers as those who have a legitimate call, carry out their duties and preach the Word of God.[26] Paul was the supreme example. A minister must live the Christian life he preaches, be prepared to suffer, to learn, to be admonished, not to dominate but to serve.[27] The *Ecclesiastical Ordinances* set out what sort of person the minister should be: sound in doctrine and of holy life. Further, the Company of Pastors was to look for candidates 'fit to teach', possessing the ability to communicate.[28]

What Calvin outlined in the *Ordinances* was a hope, not an observation. As he pointed out to Oswald Myconius, head of the church in Basle, Geneva was not overly blessed with talent:

Our colleagues are rather a hindrance than a help to us: they are rude and self-conceited, have no zeal, and less learning. But, worst of all, I cannot trust them, even though I very much wish that I could, for in many respects they demonstrate their opposition to us, and give little indication of a sincere and trustworthy disposition. I bear with them, however, or rather I humour them with the utmost leniency, a course from which I shall not depart even on account of their bad conduct. But, in the long run, the sore needs a severer remedy. I shall do my utmost to avoid disturbing the peace of the church with our quarrels by every means I can think of. For I dread the factions that always arise from the quarrels of ministers. On my first arrival I might have driven them away had I wished to, and that is also even now in my power. I shall never, however, repent the degree of moderation that I have observed, for no one can justly complain that I have been too severe.[29]

This combination of generosity and veiled threats proved its value over the following years. Calvin was sympathetic to the plight of the men and their families attempting to serve the church. Although he himself was well paid, his situation was not typical: many ministers, in particular in the rural parishes, were virtually destitute. He regularly interceded with the council for increased financial and material support for colleagues. Further, he was extremely concerned by how often they were worked to the point of exhaustion by the demands of their communities. Such daily labours became extraordinarily dangerous once the plague hit the city in 1543.

Concern could, however, cut both ways. Calvin also used his authority against those he had rejected. Most notable was Henri de la Mare, a minister whom he had known during his first stay in Geneva. The roots of the hostility probably dated to de la Mare's refusal to leave Geneva with him and Farel in 1538. When Calvin returned in 1541, de la Mare was in his sights. Over the next five years he waged an unrelenting campaign, never missing an opportunity to make the man's life a misery.[30] Despite de la Mare's resistance, he was moved from a parish in the city to the countryside. He was excluded from additional financial support offered to other ministers and his workload increased. His parish church was in such a ruinous condition, with no pulpit, that people were staying away, yet Calvin obstinately refused any aid. His house was missing a wall. De la Mare's offence in the eyes of Calvin and his supporters lay in his association with open critics of the reformer's teachings. Matters came to a head in 1546 when Pierre Ameaux, a citizen of Geneva, was publicly humiliated for opposing Calvin's teaching on predestination. The council had proposed a fine, but Calvin and his colleagues insisted on something more degrading: Ameaux was forced to walk through the city dressed only in a shirt and carrying a torch. De la Mare for his part was imprisoned and ultimately dismissed once it became clear that the ministers in the city would never accept the reconciliation sought by the council. Calvin's return was not without some settling of old scores.

The dire assessment of the ministers offered in Calvin's letter to Myconius was not, however, completely wide of the mark. Several of the ministers left the city on account of their support for the Articulant party, or were forcibly expelled, creating a highly volatile situation in which the Genevan church had little continuity. Others faced allegations ranging from refusal to serve in the plague hospital to adultery. Neglect of duty was a frequent charge heard by the Company of Pastors, though Calvin and Viret, for practical reasons, were reluctant simply to dismiss the miscreants. But some cases proved beyond the pale.[31] The minister Simon Moreau was accused of having fornicated with two women at the plague hospital in 1545 – an accusation frequently made against those working in such institutions – and was arrested before being banished from Geneva.[32] The chronic shortage of men able to serve in parishes required a plan deployed in the other Swiss churches whereby ministers were moved from one parish to another.[33] Admittedly a hasty remedy with little guarantee of success, the tactic proved expedient for harassed church leaders with few options.

Calvin did what he could. He reported to Farel that at least some of the ministers possessed a modicum of learning and that their sermons were not entirely dreadful, though not infrequently they bewildered their congregations.[34] He hoped they could be trained to speak better. He noted that the ministers appointed after Viret's departure in 1541 were not entirely dismal, and that the best possessed at least some education and could be helped. Even the best of them, however, were 'nothing' compared to his beloved Viret, he lamented, and by no means so popular. To compensate, he himself was forced to preach more often than he felt able.

The first significant shift took place in 1546 with the arrival of new ministers to replace those who had been forced from the city. These men were of an entirely different calibre and stock – educated Frenchmen close to Calvin and eager to support his vision of reform.[35] Like the ministers they replaced, the new men were French speakers, but that is where the comparison ended. Nicolas des Gallars, Reymond Chauvet, François Bourgoing and Michel Cop were well-educated men who had already served the French evangelical cause in different capacities. They commanded respect and their experience led to the transformation of the Genevan church. Des Gallars and Bourgoing were of aristocratic birth, while Cop was the nephew of the Paris rector whom Calvin had known well. These men were further distinguished as published authors of religious tracts.[36] For the rural parishes, men of humbler status were appointed, but they too were Frenchmen and much more congenial to the cause. Calvin had turned the ministry of Geneva into a powerful group of like-minded men. How had this been achieved? Through the Consistory and the Company he had worked closely with Genevan magistrates who took the state of their church very seriously and was able to provide well-educated replacements for the ministers who had performed so poorly. And here was a formula that would serve Calvin well throughout his time in the city: extremely hard work on his part combined with the disorganization and failings of his opponents.

This new generation brought about a marked change in the position of ministers in Geneva. In the first five years following Calvin's return the common complaint was about the impoverished state of the clergy, but the new ministers were men of means not dependent on the meagre pastoral salaries, and fully capable of involvement in the economic life of the city. Naturally this heralded problems. These men were not closely connected to the leading Genevan families and their wealth distinguished them clearly from their less affluent parishioners, fuelling resentment. A number of the ministers who had been expelled or forced to resign, in contrast, were members of, or had married into, Genevan families with whom they retained contact after their departure. When they left the city and its rural parishes, they tended to slip across the border into churches in the Bernese lands where they could continue to voice opposition with impunity.[37]

The Consistory

The Company of Pastors governed the clergy of Geneva; the Consistory oversaw the laity. Calvin had made the founding of a consistory a condition of his return and it was created by the council in November 1541, assembling for the first time a month later. The Consistory met every Thursday, and additionally on Tuesdays before communion.[38] Sessions were presided over by a syndic as this was a secular–church body, and twelve elders from the two councils attended along with all urban ministers. The elders had particular responsibility to watch over the residents of their neighbourhood and resolve disputes; when unable to settle a matter they were to bring the parties before the Consistory. The ministers were likewise to watch over the lives of their parishioners, a role that hardly endeared them to the people.

Those who appeared before the Consistory were interrogated, sometimes individually, before a course of action was determined. Most frequently the Consistory would admonish or reprimand, quoting passages from the Bible. Such verbal censures could have a powerful effect.[39] It had, however, other options at its disposal, including reparation, the ban and referral to the Small Council. The ban meant forbidding participation in the Lord's Supper. There were serious consequences for a banned person as he or she would be unable to take part in godparenting or marry. Excommunication was a different matter. To be excommunicated was to be prevented from entering the church and might even entail banishment from the city. It was rarely used before 1555, and even after Calvin's victory few people were excommunicated.

Punishment was intended to bring about reconciliation with the community. Even a decision to ban from the Lord's Table envisaged the return of a penitent sinner. Most dramatic, and humiliating, was a practice by which the penitent was forced to get down on his or her knees before the congregation to make a confession of sin.[40] Finally, the Consistory could send a malefactor before the Small Council, which might mete out more draconian punishments such as banishment or even the death penalty. As with all early-modern disciplinary bodies, there was a degree of self-interest: the fees of the members of the council were paid by the fines collected.[41] There was a division of authority between the Consistory and the council, though that line was often difficult to discern. The Consistory was essentially a court in Geneva, but as the ministers who sat on it were mostly French, it was the object of much Genevan resentment of foreigners in their city.[42]

In the 1543 *Institutes* Calvin carefully developed his understanding of how the church should exercise discipline. Judicial means should be employed to enable it to effect its spiritual government.[43] This was no vision of moral perfectionism or separation from society. For Calvin, God's Church on earth included all people, the faithful and the reprobate. The business of the Church was not to sort out who was who, but to maintain its witness and worship until Christ's return. This was to be undertaken in a spirit of love and moderation, marked by humility. Christians do not achieve perfection in this world; they struggle along the path needing both encouragement and correction. Towards sinners Calvin counselled patience and gentleness, arguing that 'it is not our task to erase from the number of the elect those who have been expelled from the church, or to despair as if they were already lost. It is lawful to regard them as estranged from the church, and thus from Christ – but only for such time as they remain separated.'[44]

Work on the Genevan Consistory has yielded an extraordinarily complex picture of religious beliefs and practices in the city. In its first two years alone the Consistory heard 639 cases concerning 1,105 people from all walks of life.[45] Most of these cases in the early years concerned the religious practices of Genevans, and equal attention was given to men and women. Indeed women were more often questioned about their attendance at sermons and whether they recited the correct prayers. Most of these women were either mothers or widows, suggesting that the Consistory recognized the central role played by women in religious education in the household. To reform the family, the mother was the lynchpin.

It was not a particular distinction to serve on the Consistory as a lay elder. Many who did so belonged to the Articulant party and had a background in the civil courts, a legal expertise which formed a bond with Calvin. In the years after 1546 an effective alliance evolved as these elders became supporters of the Frenchman.[46] Given Calvin's earlier attachment to the Guillermin party, this arrangement might surprise us, but such was the fluidity and volatility of the situation in Geneva that party allegiances were not cast in stone. The elders of the Consistory in the formative period of the 1540s clearly came under the influence of the ministers, and perhaps most notably of Calvin himself. They were politically less significant men whose rise was closely linked to the success of Calvin and his small group of followers.

Worship

It took several years before the orders of worship laid out in the *Ordinances* were brought into effect.[47] Calvin was mindful of the overworked ministers and firmly opposed a decree by the council in 1549 that they should preach every day. The council had a high view of preaching, believing in its power to resolve communal problems and instil order, and offered to pay for additional ministers.[48] Genevans were required to attend services on Sunday and Wednesday, which was regarded as a day of prayer. Services were intended to last one hour, though they frequently ran for much longer, largely on account of the sermon. Genevans could also attend either the Congrégation or the lectures in theology that were intended for the students, where Calvin figured prominently. The *Ordinances* give a false impression of the frequency of services in the 1540s when the new order was in its infancy. Likewise, the rural areas, with their dilapidated churches and distance from the city, had nothing like the provision of pastoral care available to urban dwellers.

There was considerable concern about attendance at services and the magistrates worked to ensure men and women went to church. In common with communities across Europe, the people came up with innumerable reasons for their absence, citing work, family demands and illness. The Consistory, not unreasonably, was concerned that reluctance to attend church was a manifestation of latent or concealed Catholic sympathies in the city and its rural hinterland. The Reformation gave Protestant leaders a quick lesson in the limitations of official decrees and new forms of worship in supplanting long-held beliefs and practices. The standard response was to demonize these recalcitrant elements as 'superstition' or 'idolatry' in the hope of making a clean break, but change was slow. During Calvin's time in Geneva he encountered a people who held hybrid religious beliefs derived from the new and old faiths, as well as from lore and popular tradition. As Calvin himself well understood, change would come about only through long-term education; as generations passed away, so too would memories of older practices. Nevertheless, the evidence suggests that during the 1540s sermons were well attended and most Genevans were not inclined to stay at home.[49] Indeed, there were many complaints about churches being over-crowded, a problem exacerbated by the influx of French refugees.

The reform of worship in Geneva took shape in 1542 with the *Form of Prayers and Ecclesiastical Songs* and the *Catechism*. Calvin's liturgy was drawn almost entirely from Bucer's in Strasbourg. Women and men were separated. They worshipped without kneeling, which was associated with the veneration of the elements of the mass. They sang the psalms in unison, an act of worship that came to define Genevan and later French Protestant spirituality. Unlike Zurich, though in common with Strasbourg and Basle, music was integral to worship in Geneva, a passage into the world of the sacred, and to this end cantors were appointed to the churches of Saint-Pierre and Saint-Gervais. Calvin planned to teach children to sing the psalms as a means of reaching their parents.[50]

While Calvin was in Strasbourg, the transformation of the physical space of worship in Geneva had begun. A stone pulpit was placed in La Madeleine along with benches and new stained glass which bore the arms of the city.[51] Likewise, the rood screen in Saint-Pierre, which divided the chancel from the nave, was removed. During the years 1543–7 extensive renovations of the churches continued as the seven medieval parishes were reduced to three: Saint-Gervais,

La Madeleine and Saint-Pierre. These urban churches, along with the rural parish churches, were redesigned. The churches were often already in serious need of structural repair. The roof of La Madeleine, for example, was leaking, and in 1543 services were suspended for fear that it would collapse. Similarly, in 1549 there was concern that the belfry of Saint-Pierre might tumble down.[52] A shortage of bells was also a major problem, for not only did bells summon the faithful to church, they were also the principal means by which time was measured in the city, determining, for example, market hours. Calvin actively engaged in efforts to improve the fabric of the Genevan churches, and in 1546 his intervention provided the impetus for changes to Saint-Gervais: a new pulpit was installed, gravestones removed, the walls whitewashed, choir stalls transformed for use by civic authorities, and the chapels cleared to accommodate benches for the people. In 1543 Saint-Pierre had a new pulpit built in the body of the church as the walls were whitewashed, covering all remaining images. During 1546–7 the choir stalls were moved into the body of the cathedral as seating for members of the council during sermons.[53] Between 1545 and 1547 La Madeleine was also fully restored and refurnished, so that by 1548 the main churches in Geneva were largely in sound structural shape and adapted for Protestant worship. The precise nature of this polity would not be lost on anyone who gazed at the new stained-glass windows in which the coat of arms of the city rulers was set.

Adults in Geneva in the 1540s would have had memories of a very different world of worship. Although it had been common to receive the Eucharist once a year, generally at Easter, in the medieval church the symbolic power of the Body of Christ was compelling. During the celebration of the mass the people would have heard the bells, smelt the candles and incense, and responded to the familiar chants of the priests. When the host was elevated at the moment of consecration, the presence of Christ himself was declared. The churches were filled with art, their walls painted with scenes from the Bible and the lives of saints, and side altars would have been used for intercessory masses. Preachers, many of whom were itinerant, arrived in the city to deliver sermons during Lent. It was a religion that engaged the senses.

The whitewashed churches of the Reformed churches offered an arresting contrast. 'When I consider to what purpose the churches are dedicated and ordained,' Calvin wrote, 'it appears to me a thing unseemly to their sanctity to display any other images than those which God has consecrated with his Word, and which bear his true imprinted mark. I mean the Baptism and the Holy Communion of the Lord, together with the ceremonies.'[54] The simplicity of the churches was designed to concentrate the eye and mind of worshippers on the service. The whitewashed walls rejected any material mediation of the divine and emphasized its immanence. Churches were closed outside times of worship to prevent them from becoming places of superstitious activity.[55]

Calvin's plans for the arrangement of the churches, in which the equality of believers was stressed, can be viewed as the local embodiment of the true Church with no distinctions between men and women, master and servant.[56] But at the same time there were distinctions within the community: women and small children sat on the lowest benches directly in front of the pulpit while men sat behind on the higher ones. During the 1540s there was a gradual reorganization of the worship space whereby levels of authority within the city were recognized by place. Also, areas were created for those required to attend sermons as penance for their actions. The emergence of these distinctions demonstrated new ways in which the congregation was under the surveillance of the magistrates and ministers. Worship in the church demonstrated the dual reality of the Church visible and invisible.

'The Preachers Do Nothing But Insult Us'

The pulpit was the principal point of contact between John Calvin and the people of Geneva. As he preached almost every day of the week for about an hour, his voice would have been extremely familiar. Martin Luther had spoken of preaching the Word of God as warfare: it would not bring peace so much as stir up the devil and outrage the ungodly. Calvin had few illusions about the task facing him. Shortly after his arrival in Geneva he reported to Farel that 'the sermons at least are well attended; the hearers are decent and well behaved enough. But there is much yet that requires correction, both in the under-standing and in the affections, and unless it is treated gradually there is some danger that it may yet break out into the most virulent sore.'[57] This early observation touched on the complexity of the issue. Sermons were more than mere tongue-lashings intended to flay a recalcitrant people. They were to instruct, edify and correct, and to do so they had to be both rooted in the Word of God and delivered in an appropriate manner. Preaching was the cornerstone of church building, but it had to take place within the wider context of worship and the cultivation of private and public godliness. The preacher, Calvin believed, was required to address the real and pressing concerns of the community whether or not the people wished to hear them. Not to do so amounted to neglect of the apostolic duty. It was, to a certain extent, a conversation between the preacher and the congregation in which the message of the Bible was situated in the life of the community. But often that conversation could turn into an argument.

In preaching the minister was to teach the people the Word of God, but they were not merely learning; the Word had to embrace their heart and move them. Through the spoken word Christ is present in the community. As Thomas J. Davis has put it: 'Preaching spans the gap between the "then" nature of the events of the Gospels and the "now" nature of redemption.'[58] Union with Christ was Calvin's central theme.[59] The Christian has communion with the Body of Christ: scripture, the sacraments and preaching both point the faithful to that body and truly offer it.[60]

The anger and resistance engendered by the preaching of Calvin and the French ministers during the 1540s require a sense of context. What took place in Geneva was not unique for the Protestant Reformation. As we have seen in the Vaud, preaching was an incendiary device of reform, and control of the pulpits was the crucial battle of the early Reformation. Across the Lutheran lands of the empire, the imperial cities of the south-west and the Swiss Confederation, every successful Protestant reformation had to deal with the question of preaching. In an oral culture preaching was by far the most effective form of communication; churches were gathering points of the communities; and ministers had the ears, if not always the hearts, of the people. This could stir both devotion and dissent.

During the 1540s there is ample evidence that many Genevans hated what they were hearing from the pulpits. In 1547, in the wake of a marital dispute between Ami Perrin and his wife a note was left in the pulpit threatening the ministers with death if they did not remain silent about the matter. Such threats are hardly surprising in a society in which violence was a common recourse to settle disputes. In a volatile urban community the words of Calvin and his fellow ministers were often inflammatory, all the more so as they did not hesitate to name names in denouncing moral turpitude. Calvin's situation was no doubt dangerous and frightening, but such was the lot of early-modern preachers. Violence against clergy, whether verbal or physical, was by no means infrequent in late-medieval and sixteenth-century Europe.

Senator Pierre Tissot was arrested in 1545 for causing a riot after Calvin allegedly declared that seven to eight hundred of the 'enfants' in the city should be hanged. The term 'enfant' referred to those Genevans who had overthrown the prince bishop as well to those who belonged to the party opposed to Calvin. In 1546 another commotion leading to arrests took place after Calvin apparently described the Genevans as 'brute beasts'. This theme was repeated in 1549 when he changed metaphors to liken the Genevans to dogs chasing bitches in heat. On two occasions he was forced to explain his preaching before the magistrates and was cautioned. In particular he was warned not to inveigh against the rulers of Geneva. Calvin was not alone among the Company of Pastors in being disciplined for preaching: Cop, Chauvet and Louis Treppereaux all fell foul of the Genevans.

The process of communication in sermons was not straightforward, as anyone knows who has given a public talk. What is said or intended is not necessarily what is heard. The members of the Consistory were generally left to adjudicate on the basis of the evidence of witnesses, many of whom could not remember what was proclaimed in the sermons or even who had preached. And although the French spoken by refugees and ministers was not that far removed from the Genevan dialect, language was a complicating factor. People took offence at sermons, particularly given the ministers' habit of naming and shaming individuals as a means of warning the people. Richard Aemons, from Normandy, remarked that 'the preachers do nothing but insult us'.[61] Calvin, in contrast, expected much of his audience, and the doctrinal level of his sermons was high, reflecting his belief that God was speaking through the mouths of men.

The image of waging war against the immoral 'Libertines' of Geneva, cultivated by Calvin himself and perpetuated in subsequent accounts, distorts the reality and complexity of early-modern religious cultures. The Word of God with its absolute demands clashed with the profane and worldly interests of urban communities reliant on trade and commerce, and seeking political and military survival. It was an argument to be found in every community of Reformation Europe. In Geneva, the situation was amplified by the force of John Calvin's character and the depth of political and social factionalism.

Turmoil

From 1546 the two major ecclesiastical institutions of Calvin's Geneva achieved a new level of stability. The Company of Pastors consisted of well-educated, experienced preachers who shared a commitment to the reform of the church. The Consistory likewise found its feet. All, however, was not well. In an act of civic harmony the Articulant party was permitted to return to Geneva in 1544 following the deaths of the principal leaders of the Guillermins.[62] Factionalism raised its ugly head once more as a new party formed around Ami Perrin.

The foundations of Calvin's church were quickly tested in the years following 1546 by a series of conflicts that underscored the fragility of Genevan society and its new order. Dancing at the wedding of the daughter of Antoine Lect, a prominent citizen, brought more acrimony. When the matter was examined, the participants denied any wrongdoing, a response that seems to have sent Calvin into an apoplexy of anger. He thundered from the pulpit against dancing and the 'shocking' conduct of the Genevans. He recounted his rage to Farel.

> After your departure the dances caused us more trouble than I had supposed. All those present were summoned to the Consistory, with the two exceptions of Corna and Perrin, [where they] shamelessly lied to God and us. I was incensed, as the vileness of the thing demanded, and I strongly inveighed against the contempt of God in that they thought nothing of making a mockery of the sacred admonitions we had used. They persisted in their contumacy. When I was finally informed of their state of ease, I could do nothing but call God to witness that they would pay the penalty for such perfidy. I at the same time announced my resolution to uncover the truth even though it should be at the cost of my own life lest they should imagine that any advantage should come of lying.[63]

Calvin related his role in forcing a confession, telling the family that a separate city should be built for them as they would never be able to avoid God's laws in Geneva. He emphasized the moderation of his own conduct in the interrogation and praised as exemplary the presiding syndic. The defence of the Lect family, that visiting Bernese guests had suggested that dancing was acceptable, was roundly rejected. The case was not only significant for Calvin because of his own role in denouncing from the pulpit the conduct of the family. More importantly, it drew him into conflict with Ami Perrin, who was close to the Lects and had been reprimanded by the Consistory. The seeds of his later showdown with Perrin were germinating.

A more immediately threatening incident arose in the summer of 1546 when a play by Abel Poupin, entitled *Acts of the Apostles*, was performed in Geneva. Calvin had approved the text, but his views were not shared by Michel Cop. Once again, Calvin described to Farel what happened.

> At dawn, Michel, instead of preaching, inveighed against the actors. But so vehement was the second invective that a gang of people made straight for

me with loud shouts, threats and what not. And had I not by a strong effort restrained the fury of some of them, they would have come to blows. I endeavoured in the second debate to appease their anger, acting moderately, for I judged that he had acted imprudently in having at such an unseasonable time chosen such a theme for preaching. But his extravagance was the more displeasing as I could not approve of what he had said.[64]

Calvin's account of what transpired next is revealing. According to him, the crowd shouted that their quarrel was not with Calvin, but with Cop. The council declared that all were to retire to their houses, but the streets remained full of demonstrators. When a meeting was held the next day, the perpetrators of the violence, according to the letter, announced that they would have killed Cop had they not so reverenced Calvin. The Senate, Calvin wrote, was on his side, but had acted timorously and failed to comprehend the implications of the matter. The play was performed while Cop was admonished by both the Small Council and by Calvin himself. Calvin's emphasis on the personal danger he had faced and his moderation in placating the crowd, while no doubt genuine, was part of a recurring rhetorical pattern in which he drew attention to his self-sacrifice on behalf of the church. He might not be in danger of being martyred, as his fellow countrymen and women were, but he too suffered for the truth.

Further incidents followed as relations between Genevans and the French ministers disintegrated. Later in 1546 Calvin related a 'humorous' story to Farel.

The wife of Froment lately came to this place. She pronounced through all the shops, and at almost all the cross-roads, against long garments. When she knew that I was aware of it, she excused herself by alleging that she had said with a smile that we were either unbecomingly clothed, to the great detriment of the Church, or that you taught what was erroneous, when you said that false prophets could be distinguished by their long vestments. When I was rebutting so stale an accusation she began to ascribe to the Holy Spirit what she had said against us. What is the meaning, she asked, of that passage of the Gospel, 'They will come to you in long garments?' I replied that I did not know where that sentence was to be found, unless, perhaps, it might occur in the gospel of the Manichaeans. The passage in Luke 20:45 is as follows: 'Beware of the Scribes, who desire to walk in long robes' but not 'They will come to you' etc., which she had taken from Matthew 7:15. Feeling that she was closely pressed, she complained of our tyranny because there was not a general licence to prattle about everything. I dealt with the woman as I should have done.[65]

Although the fiesty woman was unwise to attempt to best Calvin in quoting scripture, she did manage to gall him by being warmly received by others on account of her abuse of the ministers. Such hybrid views drawn from scripture and the street were more representative of Genevans than Calvin would accept, but daily encounters with the people in the market squares and narrow passages found expression in the timbre of Calvin's sermons and shaped his sense of the possibilities and limitations of Christ's church on earth.

Of all the confrontations, by far the most significant was the trial for treason of Ami Perrin and Laurent Meigret in 1547.[66] Meigret, who had once served as valet to Francis I, was closely connected to Calvin and France and was an enemy of Berne, which was eager to be rid of him out of Geneva. He was arrested on a long list of charges. Ami Perrin, in turn, stood accused of plotting with the French against the magistrates that he might govern Geneva in the name of Francis I. The two men, languishing in prison, became the rallying figures for bitterly opposed factions. Lavish dinners were held in their cells by supporters as the city once more descended into tribal warfare. Perrin was released in November 1546 but banished from the city, while Meigret was declared a French spy. Calvin made a dramatic appearance before the Council of Two Hundred on behalf of Meigret. Ultimately, Perrin was restored to the Small Council and Meigret was freed. A fragile peace was restored, but the city was as divided as ever.

Despite his extraordinary success in reforming the ministry and building institutions in Geneva during the 1540s, Calvin did not dominate the city as he would after 1555. He was without doubt a towering presence, whose theological, pastoral and legal brilliance distinguished him from all around him, but officially he was a minister and did not hold any political office. It must be remembered that he was not a citizen of Geneva and was therefore excluded from voting in civic elections. He constantly battled powerful enemies within the city who might well have won had they been better organized. His position as a Frenchman made him vulnerable and despised by many, but the case can be overdrawn. From the pulpit he had all of Geneva as an audience, and they certainly heard him.

CHAPTER NINE

Calvin's World

WHAT WOULD it have been like to have known John Calvin? One picture emerges from his letters and sixteenth-century biographers: serious, though not without a sense of humour, intense and deeply spiritual. Discipline was not simply for the church; discipline was his way of life. Calvin believed that he lived each day in the presence of God and that every activity, great and small, was consecrated to the Lord, to whom he would have to give account. He rose around four in the morning to begin the day with prayers with Idelette and their servants. Prayer punctuated the day, at meals and again before retiring. Work itself was a form of prayer as he laboured to penetrate the mysteries of scripture by reading, translating and writing. From 1543 until his death he lived in a house in the rue des Chanoines which had a bedroom, a living/dining area, and a study where he had his books and papers.

By his own admission, Calvin could be shy and awkward around other people, and he certainly had no facility for small talk or gossip. Time was to be sanctified by service in its various forms, and from his student days he developed a fearsome capacity for work. The price was his health. In 1541 he was already suffering from punishing migraines and serious stomach and bowel disorders. He was highly conscious of possessing a brilliant mind in a failing body, and the disparity between the two was a recurring metaphor in his writing. His crumbling body exemplified the distinction of flesh from spirit. The demands on his time were unrelenting, and once back in Geneva he became increasingly reliant on an entourage of family, friends and disciples. Idelette, invisible to us, kept the house and welcomed visitors; Antoine, his brother, was close, and often attended to his business affairs. Secretaries were employed as Calvin, not infrequently from his bed, dictated letters and tracts in Latin and French, which he would then read and correct. The demands he placed upon these assistants is evident from a letter to Bullinger of 1554 when he blamed his tardiness in replying on one of his secretaries, who although worthy and until recently a servant of the French king, was 'too much taken up with a young bride who had come from France to give his undivided attention to my business'.[1]

Much has been made of the anxious Calvin, though the temptation to put him on the psychiatrist's couch reflects modern obsessions. There is, however, no doubt that he suffered from formidable worries, and possessed a volatile temperament. When the manuscript of his commentary on 2 Corinthians went missing while being transported to Frankfurt he suffered a mental collapse and his immediate reaction was to swear off writing. Fortunately, the text was found and a personal crisis averted, but Calvin was not playacting; agitation about events, about the thoughts and actions of others and about his own perceived inadequacies was a constant and unwelcome companion. What he saw as the perfidy and unreliable conduct of others dogged him daily. It is a difficult circle to square: Calvin the supremely talented and confident voice of the church and the haunted, often bedevilled, individual. He was ferociously defensive of his reputation and few things could rouse his ire more rapidly than the suggestion that his name was in bad odour or that he was being traduced by an opponent. Perceived slights and insults cut deeply and were frequently recounted in letters to intimates. The anxieties of endless conflict and labour are projected onto his portrait of Paul in 2 Corinthians.

> But although Paul was involved in these struggles almost continuously, it is probable that at that time he was harder pressed than usual. For certainly Christ's servants hardly ever have respite from fears and Paul was seldom free from outward struggles, but because he was at this time being more violently pressed, he speaks of his struggles and fears in the plural meaning that he has had to fight in many different ways against many different enemies and at the same time has had many different fears.[2]

In his prophetic and apostolic role as church leader Calvin possessed a power for battle absent from the more private man. From the pulpit, before the Consistory and Council, and from the printing press, issued forth a single-minded determination to have the last word and to be proved right. This was not simply for the sake of ego: he was absolutely certain that he was right. On the public stage he spoke with a confidence and power which evoked both admiration and fear; served by his astonishing memory and intellect he could illuminate the faithful and excoriate his opponents. Calvin never doubted the special nature of his calling or his position within the Genevan and wider Protestant churches, but there is a continuous sense that he was not doing enough. So much more could have been attempted to further the Gospel. There was a relentless urgency to Calvin as though he knew his time was brief.

His model was Paul: ceaseless devotion to the Church shaped by love. The publication of the Consistory records has allowed us a more nuanced view of Calvin's manner.[3] His inclinations were to find peaceful and just solutions and avoid scandal, and he demonstrated real concern for the plight of women and children. The intention, whether in denouncing, admonishing or counselling, was to apply the appropriate medicine. This, however, had its limitations. Opponents fell into an entirely different ontological category, and to such Calvin revealed how harsh he could be. His response to those he regarded as a threat was to seek total victory and their humiliation. He could explain this in terms of divine justice, but, in the case of a man like Sebastian Castellio, it was unvarnished vindictiveness.

Strong of mind and weak of body Calvin had an enhanced sense of the precariousness of the world. At any moment this life could end and one would face the justice of God; this formed the basis of a striking meditation in the *Institutes*.

> Embark upon a ship, you are one step away from death. Mount a horse, if your foot slips, your life is imperilled. Go through the city streets, you are subject to as many dangers as there are tiles on the roofs. If there is a weapon in your hand, or your friend's, harm awaits. All the fierce animals you see are armed for your destruction. But if you try to shut yourself up in a walled garden, seemingly delightful, there a serpent lies hidden. Your house, continually in danger of fire, threatens in the daytime to impoverish you, at night even to collapse upon you. . . . I pass over poisonings, ambushes, robberies, open violence, which in part besiege us at home, in part dog us abroad. Amid these tribulations must not man be more miserable, since, but half alive in life, he weakly draws his anxious and languid breath, as if he had a sword perpetually hanging over his neck.[4]

This was not Calvin the arch-killjoy. His views were commonplaces of proverbial wisdom of the sixteenth century, replete with black humour to describe the grimness of existence. From Franche-Comté came the expression 'when you've made a good soup, the devil comes and shits in it'.[5]

The enduring image of Calvin as an unyielding, moralistic and stone-faced tyrant who rejected all the pleasures of life has been his opponents' greatest victory. The iconography of the Frenchman has hardly helped matters, above all, the Reformation monument in Geneva, which casts him to look like some forgotten figure of Middle Earth. His sermons reveal a man whose attitudes towards material things were far more interesting and textured than his reputation suggests.[6] The fruits of the world, according to Calvin, are not simply for subsistence, but rather to be enjoyed: good wine, good food, conversation, friendship, the pleasures of children and of marital relations. He was fond of wine and, indeed, when the nobleman Jacques de Bourgogne was preparing to come to Geneva Calvin purchased a barrel of fine wine for him in anticipation of his arrival.[7] The drinking of a glass of wine was, for him, associated with the most pleasurable things of life – laughing with friends, sharing a meal with intimates, music and art. Naturally, he preached against gross consumption of worldly goods and immodesty; his own sense of style, however, allowed him to admire clean lines and simplicity. He liked what was tasteful. In his correspondence he could let drop a line that indicated an eye for beautiful buildings and a well-dressed woman. His painted portraits reveal his modest yet evident elegance – a good-quality cloak or gown with fur collar, nothing ostentatious or extravagant.[8] The fine things of life point to a gracious God. Through the eyes of faith the elect enjoy these things not as momentary pleasures but as the revelation of God's love. The Christian life is not just about suffering, though there was enough of that in the sixteenth century. The wonders of creation and the joys of life, when viewed through the lens of faith, sustain and nourish the pilgrim along the journey.[9]

Scholar at Work

Calvin worked fast and efficiently. His handwriting was concise, and the speed with which he wrote is evident from the numerous abbreviations he made on the page.[10] His letters suggest that it was not his habit to work late into the night, and he went to bed early. When he read books he underlined passages and scribbled notes in the margins to serve his memory. Although that memory was remarkable, he, like most scholars of his age, frequently erred in recalling a text or reference, though this did not much bother him. In common with much of the northern European scholarly world, he relied on agents to purchase books, and for this the annual Frankfurt book fair was the most important event of the year. In addition, the reformers frequently exchanged texts, often before they were completed. Bullinger and Calvin, for example, increasingly sent one another their writings with requests for critical appraisal. Calvin possessed a growing personal library that ultimately passed to the Academy after its founding in 1559.

Calvin loved to write and took delight in crafting elegant prose. His Latin was largely Ciceronian in style and wonderfully clear. For students of sixteenth-century history and theology, reading Calvin's Latin can offer welcome relief. For the most part he wrote in sentences distinguished by brevity and lucidity, but on occasion, as if to remind the reader of what he was capable, long intricately woven sentences appear, full of contrasting images. To read Calvin is to be in the hands of a master of language. He obtained considerable aesthetic and intellectual pleasure from piecing together his prose; language was one of God's great gifts.[11]

It was not just elegant, humanist Latin that engaged Calvin. He also threw himself into the vernacular, and sought ways of bringing the expressions and cadence of common speech into his sermons. Examination of his sermons on Genesis reveals an extraordinary familiarity with the colloquial and even the scatological. He was not nearly as bawdy as his notorious contemporary Rabelais, whose characters are forever defecating, but he was capable of such expressions as 'to piss in the holy water cup'.[12] Like Luther with his first translation of the Bible into German, he understood that the Reformation stood or fell on the ability of the reformers to speak to the people in their own language.

Calvin handwrote much of his work, but he relied on his secretaries for considerable aid. These included Nicolas des Gallars, with whom he developed a very close relationship and whom he sent to sort out the French church in London. With others it did not go well. François Bauduin, later a bitter opponent and the source of a hostile biography of him, became a secretary in 1547 and seemed a great prospect.[13] After they fell out in the 1560s Calvin accused Bauduin of having stolen some of his correspondence, writing, 'Bauduin, whom I once loved, I nourished that viper, that plague in my house.'[14] Bauduin did not give ground, calling Calvin the 'Jupiter of Lake Léman' who hurls thunderbolts at all who dare disagree with him. A much better relationship existed with François Hotman who, like des Gallars and most of Calvin's circle, had emerged from the law faculties of France, Calvin's natural recruiting ground. He wrote to Calvin in 1548: 'Since the day I found true religion I have loved no one, even my own father, more than you. Nothing could be more important or fortunate in my life than to find a way of living near you. . . . If I had twenty crowns or more, I would willingly spend the winter.'[15] Calvin took up the offer and Hotman came to Geneva to work as his secretary and literary assistant.

Calvin's rapidly expanding body of written work served the Genevan economy well by fostering its printing industry. He had worked with various printers in Basle and Strasbourg before returning to Geneva and had learned much about the business. Even in Geneva he retained close contact with Wendelin Rihel in Strasbourg, who had produced his 1539 *Institutes*, the reply to Sadoleto, the Romans commentary and the commentary on 1 Corinthians.[16] Calvin sent the Latin biblical commentaries written during the 1540s to Strasbourg, where Rihel had the expertise and means that allowed him to produce such sophisticated works. In Geneva the situation was quite different. The city was not a major centre of printing and Calvin was forced to work with Jean Girard, a man skilled in modern techniques but lacking the necessary resources. He entrusted Girard with his polemical treatises in French, which were relatively straightforward to produce.[17] The relationship, however, did not go well. Calvin's extraordinary output and determination that his work should reach French readers proved too much for Girard, who owned only one press. Girard also worked for Farel and Viret, who were on better terms with him, and not infrequently Viret had to intercede to resolve Calvin's disputes with his Geneva printer. Calvin's frustration boiled over in a 1547 letter to Farel.

> Your work is not being printed and I do not know whether this is due to Girard's laziness, to the chaos that reigns in his print shop, or to his thoughtlessness in taking on too many works at once. I have already spoken to him about this more than once, and he has made solemn promises regarding this matter. . . . The same is true of the *Institutes*, which should have been finished before this month, and which is not yet ready. I wanted to let you know briefly what is happening, so that you might know that I have not been negligent. Girard does not react much to my pleas, and simply assures me that he will be working on it.[18]

Calvin anxiously followed the distribution and sales of his works, and his daily contact with Girard must have heightened the mounting tension between the two men, which ultimately led to a parting of ways in the 1550s when other printers came to Geneva.

The Triumvirate

During the turbulent decade of the 1540s Pierre Viret and Guillaume Farel, in Lausanne and Neuchâtel respectively, were Calvin's brothers-in-arms. Viret and Farel had known each other from the earliest days of the Reformation in the Pays de Vaud. Together these three men formed an effective alliance that linked the three cities in the common cause of defending Calvin's theology and evangelizing France. It was a powerful network held together by deep friendships that weathered many storms through their mutual trust and loyalty to Calvin. For there was no doubt that Calvin was the dominant figure; Viret and Farel were friends, but as such he regarded it as their duty to act as his agents. To be friends with Calvin was to be permitted to work on his behalf.

Farel and Viret had come to know Calvin during the heady days of the Lausanne Disputation and the first period in Geneva. Farel was the elder figure, born twenty years before Calvin and Viret, but age meant little. Relations were not static. Over the 1540s Calvin increasingly saw Viret as his intimate, the man to whom he could pour out his thoughts and feelings. His letters to Farel remained full of personal reflections and information, but he grew more and more exasperated by the older man's inflexible and irascible conduct. The experience of 1536–8 had revealed Farel as a passionate though limited propagator of the Gospel, a man who in a changing world remained wedded to the oppositional culture of the Reformation of the 1530s. Although Calvin would never say so directly, there was little doubt that he held his friend largely responsible for the debacle of the first Geneva stay. Martin Bucer, along with the other Swiss reformers, had wisely discerned that the talented young Calvin needed to be separated from Farel, whom he pointedly did not invite to Strasbourg.

Calvin had no sooner arrived back in Geneva than he faced a controversy in Neuchâtel caused by Farel when he censured from the pulpit a prominent woman whose conduct he regarded as scandalous; this had roused the ire of her family, who demanded his immediate expulsion. The Bernese authorities were forced to intervene. Viret was dispatched by Calvin to the city with a letter supporting Farel, but when he arrived he found the situation far more complex than previously imagined. Neuchâtel was a principality under the authority of Berne, which held right of judgement in the case. As a minister in Lausanne, Viret was a Bernese subject, so the letter from Calvin and Geneva carried little weight. The Bernese officials, far from taking the approach favoured by Calvin, who supported the right of ministers to preach against scandal from the pulpit, took the view that unless the inhabitants of Neuchâtel sorted out this dispute Farel would have to go. By December Farel felt able to report to Calvin and Viret that the matter had been resolved and the dignity of the ministry preserved.[19]

It was a minor episode in the great scheme of events, but it brought home to Calvin how much he would have to restrain Farel if he was to build a network to support the French evangelicals. Geneva could not stand alone. Neuchâtel, Lausanne and Berne had, somehow, to be held together. In September 1541, days after his arrival in Geneva, Calvin grabbed his quill to warn Farel about his conduct. It was firm rebuke.

> When you have Satan to combat, and you fight under Christ's banner he who puts on your armour and draws you into the battle will give you the victory. But since a good cause requires also a good instrument, take care that you do not permit yourself to think that nothing is lacking on your part that good men might reasonably expect of you. We do not exhort you to keep a good and pure conscience, as to which we entertain no doubt whatever. We only earnestly desire that insofar as your duty permits you will accommodate yourself more to the people. There are, as you know, two kinds of popularity: the one, when we seek favour from motives of ambition and the desire of pleasing; the other, when, by fairness and moderation, we gain their esteem so as to make them teachable by us. You must forgive us if we deal rather freely with you. With reference to this particular point, we perceive that you do not give satisfaction to some good men. Even if there was nothing else to complain of, you err to this extent, that you do not satisfy those to whom the Lord has made you a debtor. You are aware how much we love and revere you. This very affection, truly, this respect impels us to a more exact and strict censoriousness because we desire earnestly that in those remarkable endowments which the Lord has conferred upon you, no spot or blemish may be found for the malevolent to find fault with, or even to carp at.[20]

'We' referred to himself and Viret, who Calvin admitted had advised him in writing the letter. This practice of consultation continued through the 1540s as Calvin frequently allowed his letters and texts to be read by Viret, whose role was often to moderate the language.

As with all deep friendships there were different faces. Alongside the brutal recriminations in private correspondence was unflinching loyalty to Farel in public. Calvin never ceased to describe him as a faithful servant of God. To Bucer, for example, he could give a more measured account.

> Farel was so indignant as to threaten de Watteville [the Bernese official] that the Lord would exercise severe judgement on a person who had inflicted such a heavy blow upon the church and the sacred office of the ministry. Consequently [de Watteville], who was not sympathetic to Farel, became his enemy. Truly it would have been better for Farel to have controlled himself, so that without dissembling what he felt, he had treated the man with greater mildness and more sensitivity in expressing his feelings.[21]

With Viret, however, Calvin felt no compunction about sharing his realistic assessment of Farel.

> I may therefore say of Farel what Cicero said of Cato [the Younger, 95–46 BCE], 'that he acts indeed with good judgement, but in counsel does not always show the best.' The cause of this is chiefly that, being carried away by the vehemence of his zeal, he does not always discern what is expedient, and either does not foresee dangers, or despises them; and there is to be added the evil that he cannot bear with patience those who do not comply with his wishes.[22]

The comparison was telling. Cato, the implacable foe of Roman corruption and moral turpitude, was stubborn, inflexible and of unimpeachable character. He used every possible device within his power to thwart the Roman triumvirate and was rewarded with their wrath. Renaissance literature remembered him fondly, but Calvin's reference had a sharper edge: the inability to make some accommodation in a fallen world leads only to failure and destruction.

Calvin's complex relationship with Farel extended to his role as literary editor. In 1549 Farel sent him a manuscript for his opinion. Calvin clearly did not think much of it, but sought to avoid undue offence.

> I am afraid that the involved style and tedious discussion will obscure the light truly contained therein. I know with delight that nothing other than excellence is expected of you. I do not flatter. Your book seems to me to deserve a place among works of that rank, but because readers today are so fastidious and do not possess great acuteness, I believe the language

needs to be crafted so as to attract them by fluency of expression. . . . This is my candid judgement.[23]

Such criticism, direct or tempered, should not blind us to Calvin's enduring affection and respect for his old colleague. He delighted in Farel's company when Farel made one of his frequent journeys to Geneva and stayed in Calvin's home; nothing gave him greater pleasure than to sit together with Farel and Viret, presumably with a glass of wine, and discuss the matters of the day. They were firm friends who enjoyed each other's presence. But friendship was always within the larger context of the church, and Calvin would not permit sentiment to prevail over necessity. In many respects Farel represented the world Calvin was relinquishing as he became an international reformer. He needed men who could work with the changing political and religious situations. Farel was gradually sidelined, though not in Calvin's affections.

For his part, Farel demonstrated remarkable equanimity. He readily acknowledged Calvin as his superior, and his expression of love for his younger friend finds few parallels in letters of the Reformation. 'You may be able to lead one who is so old to better things. Those who are hard are able to be improved. I beg you not to begrudge me the needful attention, although you owe it rather to yourself. Though I yield to Bucer in all things, yet in love and affection for you and reverence I yield not at all.'[24]

Calvin was open with Farel about the frequency with which he consulted Viret, and often the two men spoke as one. In matters of theology and church politics the triumvirate forged during Calvin's early days in the Vaud increasingly became a double act. In contrast to the volcanic Farel, Pierre Viret was of mild temperament and did not relish conflict. A native of the Pays de Vaud, Viret spoke the local dialect and was a popular, well-respected preacher who communicated easily with the laity. He possessed a gift for translating the evangelical faith into the vernacular, aided by a sense of humour which tended towards satire. He had never felt comfortable with the iconoclasm of Farel's reformation; the destruction of the material fabric of churches was not his way of proceeding. He was what Calvin and Farel could never be, a man of the people. And Calvin quickly recognized that Viret's prudence and moderation marked him as his man for negotiations and peacemaking.

Upon his return to Geneva Calvin was fully aware of the precious asset he possessed in Viret and was anxious, even desperate, not to lose him. To Farel he repeatedly wrote that he could not bear the prospect of Viret leaving Geneva, for not only was there no one else he trusted, he was uncertain he could manage alone. Calvin had never faced the reality of leading a church on his own. Previously he had worked with Farel in Geneva and then with Bucer and Capito in Strasbourg. Without doubt he was shaken by the prospect of working alone in this foreign and hostile city. To Farel he opened his heart.

> Therefore, should Viret be taken away from me I shall be utterly ruined and this church will be past recovery. On this account it is only reasonable that you and others pardon me if I leave no stone unturned to prevent his being carried off from me. In the meantime we must look for supply to the church of Lausanne, according as shall be appointed by the godly brethren, and by your own advice. Only let Viret remain with me.[25]

Calvin wrote to everyone he could think of to have them petition the Bernese authorities to allow Viret to transfer from Lausanne to Geneva. To Oswald Myconius in the spring of 1542 his tone became even more urgent.

> There appears a brighter prospect for the future if Viret can be left here with me. On this account I am all the more desirous to express to you my most thankful acknowledgement, because you share with me my anxiety that the Bernese may not call him away; and I earnestly beseech, for the sake of Christ, that you would do your utmost to bring that about, for whenever the thought of his going away presents itself, I faint and lose courage entirely.[26]

He also petitioned the leading ministers in Berne arguing that peace had been established in Geneva only by Viret's mild and cooling manner and that he did not feel that he alone could continue the excellent work begun in the city.[27] Simon Sulzer, the Bucerian churchman, was sympathetic and attempted to assist, but the Bernese magistrates had other plans, and by July 1542 Viret was back in Lausanne.

Viret's stay in Geneva prior to Calvin's return was decisive in various ways. Without Viret's contribution to calming the situation in the city and restoring some faith in the church, it is unlikely that Calvin would or could have returned. Viret subsequently worked with Calvin in drafting the *Ecclesiastical Ordinances*, requesting a copy for his use when he returned to Lausanne. As the two men deepened their friendship during the months from September 1541 to the summer of 1542, Calvin recognized that in Viret he had a colleague who shared his ideas. Over the next years Viret became not only the leading reformer in the Vaud, but Calvin's closest ally.[28]

Calvin's experiences in Strasbourg and at the German religious colloquies impressed upon him the need for solidarity and the resolution of internal conflicts. The Swiss had to be brought out of their isolation and provincial squabbling. Geneva, continually threatened by Savoy and France, could not possibly exist as an island of Protestantism; it needed protection, and that was offered by Berne alone. Calvin's plan was to anchor Geneva in the Swiss Reformed churches, but on his terms. His vision of a unified Reformed church, however, put him in conflict with two key tenets of the Swiss churches: the role of the magistrates in controlling the church, and the Zwinglian inter-pretation of the Eucharist. During the 1540s these two issues led to a series of bruising battles in which Calvin depended heavily on Viret, not only as a supporter but also as his agent.

Confrontation was not long in coming. Ever since the dismissal of Kasper Megander in 1538 the Bernese church had been deeply divided between those who favoured the Zwinglian teaching on the Lord's Supper and those more in line with Bucer.[29] In August 1542 the Bernese council reaffirmed its adherence to the Zwinglian doctrine established in 1528 and summoned the French-speaking ministers of the Vaud to toe the line. Viret, bound by the realities of his situation in Lausanne, complied, infuriating Calvin, whose own position on the Eucharist was closer to Bucer than to Zurich. Calvin supported the Wittenberg Concord as the basis for Protestant unity, and regarded conces-sions to the Zwinglians as imperilling further discussions with the Lutherans. The decision in Berne that no 'new doctrines' were to be introduced was a direct threat to him, as he did not share their theology.

Calvin used Viret in Berne with little regard for the difficult position in which he was putting his friend. He saw himself in a battle to protect the liber-ties of the church against opponents in Geneva and Berne. And Viret, in his view, was not so much his partner in the struggle as a subaltern who was not to make compromises. Such pressure put Viret up against the wall, for not only did he have to deal with a messy situation in Lausanne, where division and opposition to reform still held sway, but he was required to travel back and forth to Berne to negotiate with magistrates deeply suspicious of both his actions and his connections with Calvin. In November 1542 Viret, acting under guidance from Calvin, wrote to the Bernese council on behalf of the French-speaking ministers protesting against the control exercised by the rulers over the ministry. For his efforts he was once more summoned to Berne for a dressing down. The Genevan-style discipline proposed for Lausanne was completely rejected and the ministers were left in no doubt to whom they owed obedience. Excommunication was a matter for the state.[30]

Sebastian Castellio

Calvin wanted to ensure that the church retained the right to admonish individuals, and he warned Viret not to be too gentle. Such advice might help us to understand one of the saddest and most unedifying episodes of Calvin's early years in Geneva. In 1542 he had invited Sebastian Castellio, whom he had known in Strasbourg, to come to Geneva and teach in the college.[31] After his arrival Castellio also took up preaching in Vandoeuvres. Already a scholar of considerable standing, he would easily have been the most educated person in Geneva alongside Calvin. In many ways, he seemed to be exactly what Calvin wanted, but the relationship quickly soured. Calvin related to Viret an encounter with Castellio concerning the latter's translation of scripture.

> The day before yesterday he came to me, asked whether I could agree that his edition of the New Testament should be published. I replied that there would be need of many corrections. He inquired the reason why. I pointed them out to him from those few chapters which he had already given me as a specimen. Thereupon he answered that he had been more careful in what remained. Then he asked me over again, what I thought as to the publication. I answered that it was not my wish to hinder the publication; but that I was ready, nevertheless, to perform the promise which I had made to Jean Girard that I would look it over and correct it if necessary. He refused this arrangement, but offered to come and read it to me if I would fix a time. I refused to do this and will not bind myself to certain hours, even if he were to offer me a hundred crowns. Moreover, I would be obliged to dispute for a couple of hours over some little insignificant word. And so he left me, dissatisfied as it appears. That you may understand how faithful an interpreter he is, in many ways he wishes to change and innovate, in most things he corrupts the meaning.[32]

Castellio was rector of the Collège de Rive and the principal teacher of the Genevan youth, no mere apprentice. As rector, he taught Latin and Greek as well as French, one of the few people in the city who possessed a mastery of the ancient languages. Yet in Calvin's account Castellio is mocked and derided, made to appear a second-rate scholar, with the suggestion that time spent with this learned man would be nothing more than a dispute over insignificant words. Calvin's animus towards Castellio was both rational and irrational. He despised the manner in which Castellio's prodigious learning had led him to question and doubt; this, for Calvin, was a betrayal of humanism, which was to serve true wisdom and knowledge. Less explicable was Calvin's distaste for a perceived rival. Castellio mattered because he was somebody, unlike many of the semi-literate ministers Calvin had to deal with in Geneva. Castellio had status, and that made him all the more dangerous.

From 1542 onwards Calvin and his supporters made life for Castellio in Geneva almost impossible.[33] After the terrible plague and starvation that afflicted Geneva in 1542–3, Castellio was forced to find other ways to survive, and the council decided to make him a preacher. The Company of Pastors, under Calvin's leadership, refused to ordain him because he disagreed with Calvin on several theological points of secondary importance; one concerned the nature of the Song of Songs. Salt was rubbed into the wound when Castellio was denied both a rise in pay and the right to defend himself publicly against Calvin's accusations. The last thing the church leadership wanted in its ranks was a doubter, and Castellio was not to be tolerated. The simmering conflict boiled over in the spring of 1544 when at a meeting of the Congrégation Castellio stood up after Calvin had finished and unleashed a tirade of criticism, primarily against the Genevan ministers who had not wanted to serve during the plague. By early 1545 Castellio had left Geneva and settled in Basle, which would soon emerge as a centre of opposition to Calvin and his teaching.

The Matchmaker

The severity with which Calvin treated Castellio stands in sharp relief to the concern and compassion he expressed towards Viret and his family. In February 1546 Calvin became aware that Viret's wife was dying. 'Would that I also could fly thither, that I might alleviate your sorrow, or at least bear a part of it!' And after her death in March he pleaded with Viret to come to Geneva where his friends could look after him.

Come, on this condition, that you disengage your mind not only from grief, but also from every annoyance. Do not fear that I will impose any burden upon you, for through my means you will be allowed to take whatever rest is agreeable to you. If anyone prove troublesome to you, I will interpose. The brethren make the same promise to you as I do. I will also be surety that the citizens do not interfere with your wishes.[34]

Calvin continued to be extremely solicitous about the health of his friend and by the summer of 1546 had embarked on finding a wife for Viret, even engaging the services of his friend Jacques de Falais in Strasbourg to act as matchmaker. 'You know that our brother Viret is about to marry. I am in as much anxiety about it as he is. We have plenty of wives here, both at Lausanne and at Orbe, but there has not yet appeared a single one with whom I should feel at all satisfied. While we have this matter in hand, I beseech you earnestly, if you have seen anyone in your quarter who appears likely to suit him, please let me know.'[35] Not only did he find the prospective bride, but he took control of affairs. Viret was getting formidable legal advice gratis.

The more we inquire the more numerous and the better are the testi-monies with which the young lady is honoured. Accordingly, I am now seeking to discover the mind of her father. As soon as we have reached any certainty, I will let you know. Meanwhile, make yourself ready. This match does not please [Ami] Perrin, because he wishes to force upon you the daughter of Rameau. That makes me the more solicitous about preparing the ground in good time, lest we are obstructed by having to make excuses. Today, as far as I can gather, he will enter upon the subject with me, for we are both invited by Corna to supper. I will gain time by a civil excuse. It would promote the matter if I, with your permission, should ask her. I have seen her twice: she is very modest with an exceedingly becoming counte-nance and person.[36]

Calvin derived great pleasure from finding Viret a wife; it was precisely the form of friendship he most readily assumed, taking control of the lives of those closest to him.

'I Have Been Bereaved of the Best Companion of My Life': Widowed

Farel and Viret, together with the reformer's entourage in Geneva, provided Calvin with a circle of friends with whom he could share ideas and a common commitment to the Gospel. From his student days Calvin had relied on such friends, and although he often opined about the burdens laid upon him, he never expressed a desire for solitude. Friendship and company were crucial, and he desired and sought the presence of others. The silent partner in this was his wife Idelette, of whom we know so little. She appears at odd moments in the letters, and always in a most affectionate light. Her role was as keeper of the house, and she entertained guests for him when he could not be there. She seems to have played a particular role in his relationship with Monsieur and Madame de Falais, as Calvin never failed to mention her by name in his greetings: in 1545 he wrote to the de Falaises that Idelette, who was sick in bed, asked to be remembered to them.[37] But she was also the love of John Calvin's life. He was deeply wounded in 1547 when, during the baptismal service for his infant son James, he admitted that Idelette, as an Anabaptist, had not married her previous husband in a ceremony sanctioned by the magistrates in Strasbourg.[38] A woman present remarked that Idelette was, therefore, a whore.

As Idelette became increasingly ill during 1547–8, attempts made to find a remedy included sending her away from Geneva to recuperate. In the summer of 1548 she went to Lausanne to stay with Pierre Viret and his wife. Calvin wrote that his one consolation in this was that Viret had undertaken the care so willingly.[39] When Idelette died in the spring of 1549 Calvin wrote to his two closest friends, Viret and Farel. Loss is revealing of character and Calvin was prepared to open himself, at least partially. 'And truly mine is no common source of grief,' he told Viret, 'I have been bereaved of the best companion of my life, of one who, had it been so ordered, would not only have been the willing sharer of my indigence, but even of my death.'[40] If it were not for his powerful self-control, he remarked, he would not have been able to bear the weight of the loss.

But what constituted a companion for Calvin? In the letter to Viret his next remark concerns how important Idelette was to his ministry. Even during her final illness she had not wanted to disturb him from his work. He related to Viret that he had promised to look after her children, but her response was most curious: 'My husband is not to be urged to instruct them in religious knowledge and in the fear of God. If they be pious, I am sure he will gladly be a father to them, but if not, they do not deserve that I should ask for anything on their behalf. This nobleness of mind will weigh more with me than a hundred recommendations.' Calvin found succour in Idelette's pious death in which she affirmed everything for which he stood, including the doctrine of predestination. Yet it cannot be overlooked that the letter remains largely focused on himself. Even in moments of extreme grief Calvin was not free from the need to vindicate his own conduct.

When Calvin wrote to Farel four days later the story had assumed a more formal structure. His wrenching grief permeates the letter, but the account is largely that of an ideal death. Idelette is presented as the model Christian who takes leave of the world in full faith. The scene is completed by the gathering around her of her husband, her family and the clergy. Most movingly Calvin speaks of the last prayers they said together after he had spoken to her of Christ and their married life together. In the days after the Viret letter his grief had found expression in the crafting of Idelette's death as a perfect expression of Reformed piety.

CHAPTER TEN

Healing Christ's Body

WHEN HE entered the gates of Geneva in 1541 Calvin saw himself as part of the wider European Reformation, a member of the Protestant fraternity, that cloud of witnesses of the living and the dead that included Luther, Melanchthon, Bucer, Bullinger, Zwingli and Oecolampadius. They stood united in their commitment to the Word of God. What remained to be achieved was to make that unity real among the Protestant churches. Calvin's audacious plans to spearhead the evangelizing of France from Geneva required the support of the Lutheran and Reformed churches. But his eye was not just on France. With the failure of the religious colloquies, Catholics and Protestants had parted ways; the divisions between them had proved insurmountable. To Calvin the whole endeavour had been a delusion. The path forward was to Protestant unity, and in this, he believed, his spiritual brother was Philip Melanchthon.

Like Bucer, Calvin saw the dispute between Luther and Zwingli as a disfigurement of God's reform of the Church, the human folly of preferring contention to conversation.[1] The bonds of Christian humanist friendship permitted differences of opinion and approach, a respectful disagreement, but had no place for rancour and recrimination – that only played into the hands of the devil and his minions. New leadership was needed to break the cycle of hatred. Yet Calvin's optimism that he might play a decisive role in bringing about Protestant unity concealed a misapprehension about the independence of his theology. He was to discover over the course of the 1540s that in the eyes of Lutherans and Zwinglians alike he was anything but neutral. He was drawn into partisan bickering, and the rewards for his efforts would prove a bitter harvest.

In Praise of Luther

Calvin's relations with the German Lutherans required a healthy measure of wishful thinking. Despite various hints from Melanchthon to the contrary, the Frenchman continued to assert that they were fundamentally in agreement. It was a pretence that could not long be sustained. The cracks in the plaster emerged in an exchange with a prominent Catholic theologian, the Dutchman Albertus Pighius, in the winter of 1542–3. The origins of this dispute are as interesting as the matter itself. Calvin's 1539 *Institutes* had come to the attention of Bernardus Cincius, the Catholic Bishop of L'Aquila, who passed the work along to Cardinal Cervini.[2] They shrewdly agreed that this volume was far more dangerous than any other 'Lutheran' work and required an effective response. The task was given to Pighius, who attacked the *Institutes* in print in the summer of 1542, drawing attention to the disagreement between Calvin and Melanchthon on free will. Pighius was the first significant Catholic writer to identify Calvin as a major opponent – a compliment to the Frenchman's arrival on the international stage. Calvin rushed to pen a reply in time for the 1543 Frankfurt book fair. In the meantime, Pighius died, causing Calvin to drop a proposed section on predestination, commenting later that he had not wanted 'to insult a dead dog'.[3] Calvin dedicated his *Bondage and Liberation of the Will* to Melanchthon and claimed the Wittenberg professor as a supporter, although he knew full well their differences on free will and predestination.[4] He believed that rhetorical measures could explain away the discrepancies, though Melanchthon was more cautious. In expressing his gratitude he worried that the Frenchman had erred in drawing attention to a point of controversy. It would have been better, he noted, if Calvin had confined himself to agreed Protestant doctrine and not disputed issues.[5]

Undeterred, Calvin pressed forward his fictive united front of Geneva and Wittenberg, and in 1546 he published a French translation of Melanchthon's 1543 *Loci communes* with a preface in which he once more stressed their theological agreement. This time, however, he did acknowledge that Melanchthon's approach differed from his own.[6] His purpose was to make the Wittenberg professor known to French readers as a godly teacher of the Church. This was to demonstrate that there was an agreed body of doctrine among the Protestant churches and that in addressing the French evangelicals Calvin spoke with the common voice of the wider Reformation. Melanchthon did not respond to the translation and, with no French, probably never read the text.

Calvin may have left the empire in 1541 disgusted by what he witnessed at the religious colloquies, but he kept a weather eye on German events, and by no means lost interest. The news was mixed. The imperial forces of Charles V were laying siege to the city of Metz, which had embraced the Reformation (Farel was among those who had been active there).

More encouraging was the situation in Cologne where the sixty-five-year-old archbishop and elector Hermann von Wied, described by Calvin as a 'miracle of zeal', had gathered a group of reform-minded humanists, including Martin Bucer and Philip Melanchthon, and the Catholic Johannes Gropper. In the summer of 1543, when Calvin was in Strasbourg, Bucer and Melanchthon co-wrote their *Christian and True Responsibility*, a defence against the accusations of the theological faculty at Cologne. The archbishop appended an introduction affirming that reform had to proceed from the Bible. Luther was brutal in his judgement: 'too long and full of much blethering, so I can detect that babbler Bucer'.[7] Nevertheless, the text was accepted and, remarkably, in the Catholic diocese of Cologne evangelical preaching was permitted, the Lord's Supper was celebrated according to a largely Protestant liturgy, monks forsook their monasteries, and priests married. It was a brief moment brought to an end by the emperor's soldiers. Martin Bucer witnessed the arrival of the imperial troops and within ten days he was forced to return to Strasbourg, his vision of reform gone.

The situation for German Protestants looked bleak. Charles V was determined to bring an end to his interminable wars with Francis I and demanded that the German princes fall in line.[8] Although the Schmalkaldic League was undefeated, it was badly divided and many of its members were heavily in debt. The League had done nothing to protect Archbishop von Wied, and when its leaders met the emperor at the Diet of Speyer in 1544 they were prepared to do his bidding. By 18 September Francis I had capitulated and the Peace of Crépy was signed. The Protestant princes faced the riddle of the sphinx: how were they to balance fidelity to religion with loyalty to the Catholic emperor?

As the triumphant emperor made his way to the imperial diet at Speyer, Calvin, engaged by Bucer, prepared on behalf of the Protestant reformers a defence of their doctrines and an appeal for a council of the church in the German lands. It was an opportunity that Calvin relished. What greater affirmation of his international position than a commission to speak for the whole reform movement? The result, *On the Necessity of Reforming the Church*, was Calvin at his best – clear, persuasive and biting. His theme was unity, not only of the Reformation, but of the Church. He painted an admiring portrait of Martin Luther, a man, he argued, raised up by God to restore true doctrine to a Church which had lost the way of salvation. Luther was a 'light' to a benighted people, his motives selfless, and his only concern reform of God's Church. 'When Luther at first appeared,' Calvin intoned,

> he merely touched with a gentle hand a few abuses of the grossest description, now grown intolerable. He did it with a modesty which indicated that he had more desire to see these abuses corrected than determination to correct them himself. His opponents immediately sounded to arms; and when the conflict became more and more inflamed, our enemies deemed it best to suppress the truth by cruelty and violence.[9]

Calvin regarded Luther as the prophet of the Reformation in whose footsteps others followed. But there were additional, more politic, dimensions. In 1544 Calvin still hoped for reconciliation with the Lutherans, and his praise of the great man went hand-in-hand with his courting of Melanchthon. He knew perfectly well that he was not going to change the mind of the Catholic emperor and such was not his intention. *On the Necessity* was intended as a statement of what united Protestants. On this he was clear: true worship of God and knowledge of salvation were the heart and soul of the Reformation, the justification for the assault on the idolatrous Roman church. *On the Necessity* drew together his thinking about the Church in the Romans commentary and the *Institutes* with his experiences at the colloquies. He had proved himself a shrewd observer, and he had few doubts about the dangers posed by the emperor and Rome. Charles had arrived in Speyer with the Protestant princes on their knees before him: everyone spoke of war and visions of the end. The Reformation was in grave danger.

'He is Not Only Food to Our Souls, but Drink Also'

Calvin's desire to unite the Protestant churches during the 1540s was haunted, and ultimately undone, by the ghost of Huldrych Zwingli. By the early 1540s relations between Zurich and Wittenberg had all but collapsed, and although Bullinger and Melanchthon maintained cordial relations, Luther had firmly turned his face against the Swiss.[10] Bullinger and his circle in Zurich doggedly defended the person and teaching of Zwingli, continuing to have his works printed as part of their robust maintenance of the orthodoxy of their church.

Bullinger maintained that he was open to further negotiations. In truth, however, he offered few if any concessions, and certainly nothing that was going to change the minds of the Lutherans. The ageing reformer in Wittenberg for his part was prepared to accept the Swiss only on condition of an abject renunciation of their errors. Martin Bucer, the zealous intermediary of the 1530s, was *persona non grata* in the extreme in Zurich. The only person who might now be able to exercise any influence was Calvin. But he faced the irreconcilable: his dependence on Heinrich Bullinger as the most influential of the Swiss reformers and his determination to keep the door open to the Lutherans in the empire.

A purchase on the problems of these years is possible only if we recognize the importance of the Lord's Supper to Calvin. The sacrament had been the dramatic moment of conflict in 1538, and when he returned to Geneva three years later he made its celebration the very heart of the community. The *Ecclesiastical Ordinances* declared that the Lord's Supper was to be celebrated four times a year, and when asked in the Geneva catechism why God had instituted the signs of bread and wine, the response was 'the Lord consulted our weakness, teaching us in a more familiar manner that he is not only food to our souls, but drink also, so that we are not to seek any part of spiritual life anywhere else than in him alone'.[11] It is the very means by which God strengthens the faith of the believer with outward signs so that he or she might grow in certainty of the Gospel promises. The bread and wine are not mere symbols: they raise the heart and spirit of the believer to a true knowledge of God.[12]

Gospel and sacrament, for Calvin, are the same but different, and cannot exist without one another. Humans, sensuous creatures that they are, require external forms as aids to faith, and this is what God has provided. Eating the bread and drinking the wine are not simply an act, but together with the Word of God spoken from the pulpit they form the means by which the Christian receives Christ. In the liturgy he wrote for the church in Strasbourg, and had printed in Geneva in 1545, Calvin set out the four things the people needed to know in order to receive communion: that they are sinful by nature and unworthy of the Kingdom of God; that Christ alone brings about remission of sin; that Christ gave himself in the sacrament of the Lord's Supper; that by participating in the Lord's Supper the people receive the benefits of Christ's sacrifice.[13] With this knowledge the faithful can be assured of both God's purpose and the remission of sins.

Along with the *Institutes*, Calvin's most significant statement on the sacraments from this period was his *Short Treatise on the Lord's Supper*, also written in Strasbourg and brought to Geneva to be printed. Calvin developed a theme evident in the Strasbourg liturgy – knowledge and assurance.[14] He was deeply sensitive to the psychological needs of the faithful. Because union with Christ is incomprehensible to the human mind, believers require assurance of its reality. To accommodate this human frailty, God makes use of earthly signs to represent divine truths. These signs have no power in themselves; it is the Spirit acting through them that makes them effective.

> Here, then, is the singular consolation which we derive from the Supper. It directs and leads us to the cross of Jesus Christ and to his resurrection, to certify that whatever iniquity there may be in us, the Lord nevertheless recognises and accepts us as righteous – whatever materials of death may be in us, he nevertheless gives us life – whatever misery may be in us, he nevertheless fills us with all felicity. Or to explain the matter more simply – as in ourselves we are devoid of all good, and have not one particle of what might help to procure salvation, the Supper is an attestation that, having been made partakers of the death and passion of Jesus Christ, we have every thing that is useful and salutary to us.[15]

Through the instruments of bread and wine God gives Christ to the people – to receive the symbols (bread and wine) is to receive what they signify (Christ).

The dynamic in Calvin's teaching is between knowledge and faith. Through preaching, catechising and schooling the people are taught the nature of God and salvation through Christ. They are instructed in the Christian life. This is the knowledge revealed in scripture and it is the duty of ministers to teach and of laity to learn. But Calvin did not mean mere head learning, as we might call it – facts about religion. In learning of God and Christ a person begins to hunger for that salvation. That is the work of faith, which opens eyes to the reality of sin and the goodness of God. Yet because humans, even the faithful, are weak and sinful, they need to be continually fed. This is the role of preaching and the Lord's Supper. Calvin continued to develop this line of thought in his 1543 edition of the *Institutes* in which he wrote more fully on the relationship between Word and sacrament. Both are forms of God's accommodation to humanity, but the Lord's Supper appeals to the human need for visible, sensible symbols. It works together with the other forms of grace, such as preaching, teaching, prayer and worship, but has a distinctive character. The Eucharist brings knowledge and assurance to those who have been justified by God's Word.[16] It allows Christians to grow in faith through the awareness that they have received the benefits of Christ's sacrifice.

Reluctant Allies

Without question Calvin had read the works of Zwingli and found much agreeable in them, but on the question of the Lord's Supper his inclinations led him towards Strasbourg and the Lutherans.[17] The Zwinglian influences detectable in the 1536 *Institutes* evaporated during Calvin's stay in Strasbourg between 1538 and 1541. During this time he spoke to Farel and Viret of how he found Luther's theology far preferable to Zwingli's.[18] Even Oecolampadius, the reformer of Basle, whom he rated highly as an interpreter of scripture, fell short in discerning the full meaning of the biblical text.[19] In truth, Calvin was moving towards his own distinctive position, which was critical of aspects of the other parties in the Eucharistic debate. Against the Roman church he joined in the Protestant chorus of denunciation of the mass as idolatry. Against the Zwinglians he argued that they had surrendered too much in their rejection of Christ's presence in the bread and wine. Finally, he had no sympathy for the Lutheran teaching of ubiquity whereby it was held that Christ is physically present through the Spirit.

Calvin's problem was to find a means of expressing how God acts through the Lord's Supper without suggesting that Christ is physically present in the sacrament. Also, he had to achieve this without alienating the Zwinglians and Lutherans.[20]

Calvin proceeded with caution, subtlety, even subterfuge. The 1 Corinthians commentary of 1545, written with an eye to German Lutherans, is an excellent example of the manner in which he could tacitly support one side without openly saying so. He was emphatic that the Zwinglian teaching on the Lord's Supper was wrong, but his approach to Luther's doctrine of the Lord's Supper was more nuanced, and his language carefully couched. The doctrine of ubiquity, for which he had no time, was not attributed to Luther or his supporters by name, but rather attacked as a false teaching of the medieval scholastics.[21] It was a brilliant rhetorical manoeuvre. At the same time, his insistence on the reality of Christ's presence was never referenced to any of Luther's writings, though a clear similarity is detectable.

Calvin understood that both theology and personality made the dispute between the Lutherans and the Zwinglians irresolvable if one attempted, as had Bucer previously, to convince either side of the other's good intentions. Luther's publication of his *Short Confession* on the Lord's Supper in September 1544 proved the proverbial straw that broke the camel's back. Not only had the old man bashed the Swiss once more, as was to be expected, but Melanchthon and Bucer also found themselves under attack. The situation in Wittenberg was reputed to be so dire that rumours spread abroad that Melanchthon might be driven out. Melanchthon himself sent up signals that his position was becoming untenable. 'I have written to you about our Pericles [Luther],' he wrote to Bucer, 'who has begun again to thunder most vehemently on the subject of the Lord's Supper, and has written a fierce attack, in which you and I are beaten black and blue. I am a quiet, peaceable bird, nor would I be unwilling to depart out of this prison-house, if our disturber shall constrain me.'[22]

Farel believed that Calvin could play a role in calming the Zurichers after this latest assault from Wittenberg, but Calvin himself was sceptical. 'Already I fear the sort of answer they may return. They will not fail to dwell on the marvellous patience with which they have endeavoured to assuage him [Luther]. For even Bullinger himself, when he was complaining to me in a letter some months ago about Luther's unkindness, highly commended his own forbearance and that of his friends.'[23] Calvin was aware, nevertheless, that the ageing and increasingly cantankerous Luther was a major part of the problem. 'For at present the danger arises not so much from them as from Luther.'

Calvin did intervene, however, and wrote to Bullinger in November urging restraint in response to Luther's *Short Confession*. 'I hear that Luther has at length broken forth in fierce invective, not so much against you as against the whole of us.'[24] Although he referred to the Zwinglians as 'innocent people', what followed was an extensive admonition to Bullinger to regard Luther's flawed greatness as a reformer of the Church.

I earnestly desire you to bear in mind in the first place how eminent a man Luther is, and the excellent endowments with which he is gifted, with what strength of mind and resolute constancy, with such great skill, and with what efficiency and power of doctrinal statement he has devoted his whole energy to overthrow the reign of Antichrist, and, at the same time, to spread far and wide the doctrine of salvation. Often have I declared that even if he were to call me a devil, I should still nonetheless hold him in such honour that I would acknowledge him as an illustrious servant of God. But while he is endowed with rare and excellent virtues, he labours at the same time under serious faults. Would that he worked to curb this restless, uneasy temperament which is so apt to boil over in every direction.

In acknowledging Luther's harsh and crude manner, Calvin offered cold comfort to Bullinger on the Lord's Supper. He refused to condemn Luther's teaching, confining himself to the issue of peace within the Church. Citing Paul, he admonished Bullinger to look to the greater unity of the Church. Calvin's evident sympathy with the Lutherans must have made uneasy reading in Zurich.

It was Philip Melanchthon whom Calvin believed to offer the best hope for a theological arrangement, and once more he pursued the connection. The result was bitter disappointment. In January 1545, barely six months after the appearance of Luther's incendiary work against the Swiss, Calvin sent two letters to Wittenberg accompanied by a text against those in France who were espousing evangelical views yet refusing to leave the Catholic church. In a letter to Melanchthon, Calvin passed over in silence the rumoured estrangement from Luther and said how important it was to him that his work be read with approval in Wittenberg. 'And although it may have been somewhat forward of me to set about this, yet, notwithstanding, I would request as a friend that you do not refuse to take the trouble of looking over them. So highly do I value your judgement, as indeed is proper, that to me it would be very disagreeable to undertake anything of which you are not likely to approve.'[25] Calvin insisted that friendship did not require agreement on every point and invited Melanchthon to be free with his criticism, a custom he shared with his friends – to some extent. A second letter, addressed to Luther, was quite different in tone. Calvin did not dare risk familiarity and indicated to Melanchthon rather nervously that he was well aware of Luther's volatile temper, and that he would rely on Melanchthon's discernment in choosing the means and timing for presenting his work to the great man.

The letter to Luther was an appeal for support. He wrote of the dire situation in France and related how he had been contacted by a friend in Paris, Antoine Fumée, who reported that many objected to Calvin's insistence on no compromise with Catholic practices. These Frenchmen had wanted Calvin to consult Wittenberg.

Now, therefore, much respected father in the Lord, I beseech you by Christ not to begrudge the trouble for their sake and mine. First, that at your leisure you cursorily peruse the letter written in their name and my little books, or that you request someone to take the trouble of reading [them] and report their contents to you. Secondly, that you give your opinion in a few words. Indeed, I am unwilling to bring you this trouble in the midst of so many weighty and various demands, but such is your sense of justice that you cannot imagine that I have done this unless being compelled by the necessity of the case. I therefore trust that you will pardon me.[26]

There was only silence. Melanchthon, aware that Luther had come to regard Calvin as one of the 'sacramentarians', or followers of the hated Zwingli, did not even show him the letter. Once so elated by Luther's positive assessment of his response to Sadoleto, Calvin had been rejected by his hero. The subtleties of his own theological positions were in danger of drowning in the fierce polemical torrent consuming Protestantism, and his hope of finding agreement with the Lutherans was frustrated. The course of church unity would have to take another path, one which led eastward to the Swiss cities.

The Struggle with Berne

For Calvin, the mid-1540s offered a brief respite. Geneva was relatively calm, the reforming of the church was proceeding, and relations with Berne, while never easy, were fairly tranquil. The year 1545 saw him occupied with writing his commentary on 1 Corinthians. Abroad, however, there was cause for concern. The eyes of the Protestant world were fixed upon the looming war between Charles V and the Schmalkaldic League. The fearful atmosphere had at least some effect in focusing the quarrelling churches on the issue of unity. Luther's death in 1546 was marked by all sides; even his adversaries recognized that the great prophet of the Reformation was gone. Bullinger wrote a moving letter of condolence to Melanchthon paying tribute to Luther, though insisting that he had treated the Swiss badly.[27]

Calvin's peace was shattered in 1548 when a vicious battle over the Lord's Supper broke out in Lausanne between Pierre Viret and André Zébédée, the new professor of theology and an ardent Zwinglian. In a work written in French and published in Geneva, Viret had attacked both the Zwinglian theology of the Eucharist and the role of the Bernese magistrates in church affairs.[28] Essentially Viret presented Calvin's views on the sacrament, reflecting the truth that he was acting as the Frenchman's agent in Bernese lands.

Viret was summoned to Berne in April 1548 to explain himself, but by the time he arrived he discovered the situation had changed. The church leadership had undergone a reshuffle and Simon Sulzer, along with several other ministers sympathetic to Bucer's teaching, found themselves leaving the city.

In Sulzer's case the road led to Basle, from where he was to continue to play a role in Calvin's life. The Zwinglians were in the ascendant and when Viret arrived he faced hostile questioning. After a rough handling he returned to Lausanne expecting to lose his position.[29]

The situation in Berne, however, was vastly improved by the council's inspired decision to call Johannes Haller as chief preacher. Haller, an extraordinary figure who has never received much attention, drew together in his person many of the conflicting tendencies of the Swiss reformation. A native of the Bernese rural territories, he was, like Bullinger, the son of a priest. His father had fallen beside Zwingli at the Second Battle of Kappel in 1531 and the young Johannes was sent to study in Zurich and then at various universities in the German lands. He visited Luther and Melanchthon in Wittenberg before becoming a minister in Augsburg, where he remained until forced out by the victory of the Catholic armies of Charles V in 1547. His long years in the empire only enhanced his reputation among the Swiss, and in 1547 he was called to both Zurich and Berne. Bullinger wanted him as a colleague, and although Haller chose his native Berne, the Zurich reformer remained a close contact and correspondent until 1575, the year they both died. It was Haller who translated Bullinger's *Decades* into German – it was known as the *Hausbuch* – thereby making it a bestseller among Protestant communities across Europe and the New World.

Haller belonged to a new generation. He looked not to Zwingli, but to Bullinger, which meant that there was greater flexibility towards Calvin. His primary task, however, was to restore peace to the troubled Bernese church. With Pierre Viret and André Zébédée he had his hands full. Just as a resolution of the dispute between the two men appeared to be at hand, the contents of Viret's book became known in Berne. Haller recounted his exasperation to Bullinger.

> I had hoped that Viret's case was settled. But behold, while these things were taking place, he published a book in French on the power and practice of the ministry of the Word of God. . . . Zébédée translated certain excerpts into Latin and sent them to us. Once again, Viret has irritated everyone, for certain things are clearly contrary to us, and others doubtful, confused and obscure. With other things, although true, it is neither the time nor the place to bring them up. For it is not at all helpful now to stir up the hornets. Although he is otherwise pious, I fear that he will be released and dismissed.[30]

Haller would later lament to Bullinger that 'I have never seen more contentious men in my life'. The fact that Viret, the popular preacher and man of peace in Geneva, was regarded in Berne as quarrelsome and even seditious is indicative of the cultural divide that existed between the French- and German-speaking communities of the Bernese lands.

Calvin was far from an innocent bystander in these events. From the start he fully supported Viret and urged him to stand fast, even going so far, in the style of Farel, as to threaten him with divine punishment if he backed down. The Genevan reformer was waging his battle against Zwinglian theology and Bernese authority in the Vaud through its native son. It was a clever though explosive tactic.

Contact

Calvin was caught in an awkward position. He objected to the Zwinglian theology of the Bernese church, and his relations with Berne were poor. He referred to the Bernese ministers who opposed him as 'beasts', though essentially he regarded them as bit players. However, the cool winds blowing from Wittenberg required him to find some way of opening a dialogue with Bullinger on the Lord's Supper. He knew that his reputation was being sullied in Zurich by reports from the Vaud and Berne. Bullinger was unlikely to reach out to him, so he would have to grasp the nettle. At the end of April 1548 he communicated to Farel his intention that they should make the five-day journey to Zurich and meet Bullinger. An opportunity arose in June for Calvin, after seven years, to meet in person the head of the Zurich church. The Frenchmen were well received by the Zurich ministers, and the good impression they made did much to dispel the unease. Nevertheless, the Genevans were not allowed to feel they had arrived as equals: Bullinger was the senior man and Calvin was made aware of this. A charm offensive was necessary.

Around the table in Bullinger's house weighty matters, above all the sacraments, were discussed in Latin, and for both men the scales began to drop and mutual suspicions dissipate. It was the beginning of a personal relationship between two very different characters that would last until Calvin's death. Bullinger's growing warmth towards Calvin was expressed by the presentation to the Frenchman of a manuscript of his latest work on the Lord's Supper. Bullinger invited him to comment, a signal mark of a new friendship.

A letter written on his return to Geneva shows both Calvin's budding friendship and the lingering difficulties. Why, he wondered, had Bullinger not chosen to discuss the book while he was in Zurich when they would have been able to speak in a 'familiar' manner? For all the good will, the discussions had clearly had their awkward moments. 'And yet we are censured, as if we departed from the pure and simple doctrine of the Gospel. I should wish, however, to learn what that simplicity is to which we are to be recalled. When I was lately with you, I pressed this very point. But you remember, as I think, that I received no answer.'[31]

Calvin knew exactly where the problem lay.

> I have long ago observed, moreover, that our contact with Bucer acts as a deadweight upon us. But I beseech you, my Bullinger, to consider with what propriety we should alienate ourselves from Bucer, seeing he subscribes to this very confession that I have laid down. I shall not at present declare the virtues, both rare and manifold, by which that man is distinguished. I shall only say that I should do a grievous injury to the Church of God were I either to hate or despise him. I make no reference to the personal obligations under which I lie to him. And yet my love and reverence for him are such that I freely admonish him as often as I think fit.

Calvin was adamant that his loyalty to Bucer did not mean that he was a 'Bucerian'. He demanded that Bullinger recognize him on his own terms, with his own theology and plans for unity. In short, he was no agent of Strasbourg. The strategy worked. The favourable response from Zurich translated into support for the Frenchmen in Berne and Lausanne as Bullinger used his leverage to ensure Haller's friendly disposition towards both Viret and Calvin.

Storm Clouds

The positive developments in Zurich owed much to the Catholic resurgence of the 1540s. The summoning of the Council of Trent by Pope Paul III in 1545 signalled a co-ordinated Catholic response to the Reformation. In Italy the inquisitions in Rome and Venice were rooting out those sympathetic to Lutheran ideas, and in the papal curia itself the views of Cardinal Carafa and others dead set against doctrinal compromise with Protestantism held sway. Francis I, defeated by Charles V, renounced support for the German Protestant princes. At the same time, in the east the war against the Turks had gone quiet. A favourable moment had finally arrived for Charles V to turn on the German heretics. The Schmalkaldic League, beset by internal bickering and a clumsy organization, was about to turn military superiority into inglorious defeat.

In June 1546 the imperial diet opened in Regensburg without the participation of the Schmalkaldic League. By the end of the summer the armies of the emperor and the League began to manoeuvre. War broke out at the end of October and for the League it went from bad to worse. In order to defend Saxon lands most of southern Germany was left open to the forces of Charles V brought from Italy and the Spanish Netherlands. On 21 March 1547 Strasbourg capitulated and the Burgermeister Jakob Sturm was obliged to perform obeisance before the emperor. Strasbourg withdrew from the League, ensuring that Martin Bucer's days in the city were numbered. Accepting Archbishop Cranmer's invitation, he fled Strasbourg by stealth and was smuggled by agents to the Channel coast, crossing to the Protestant England of the young King Edward VI.

On 21 April the imperial forces scored their decisive victory at Mühlberg, leaving Johann Frederick, elector of Saxony, as Charles' prisoner. Two months later Philip of Hesse surrendered. At the beginning of September 1547 an imperial diet opened in Augsburg at which Charles reigned triumphant. Not only had he conquered the Protestant League, but his main European rivals, Francis I and Henry VIII, were dead. In June he had also managed to conclude a five-year peace treaty with Sultan Suliman I.

The disaster for Protestantism did not surprise Calvin. Coming from the Gallican tradition which defined itself in terms of the struggle against papal authority, he harboured no illusions about the strength and depth of the threat posed by Rome. The religious colloquies had persuaded him that the Catholics were not serious, and he was certain that efforts at compromise on the part of the Protestants would inevitably play into the hands of their opponents. During his time in German lands he had shrewdly assessed the leading princely and theological players and relayed his thoughts to Farel.[32] German Protestantism had paid a terrible price for supping with the devil, and worst of all were the Protestant princes, whose self-interest and lack of commitment to the Gospel appalled him. Luther was dead and Charles triumphant.

Calvin joined a wider Protestant assault on the Council of Trent alongside Bucer and Bullinger.[33] His most significant work was the *Acts of the Council of Trent with Antidote* of 1547 in which he juxtaposed the early decrees of the council with his commentary. Drawing on scripture and the church fathers, Augustine in particular, he offered a brutal assessment of the council's decisions. The *Acts of the Council* reflects his astonishing confidence in his own abilities. By placing the acts alongside his own commentary he demonstrated absolute certainty that the reader would see the superiority of his logic. The work was originally written in Latin and later translated into French, as Calvin addressed his native land, arguing that Trent was no true council.

> I will ask my French countrymen what price they set on the portion which they have contributed. They doubtless hold the kingdom of France to be one of the leading branches of the Church. Why, then, send only two bishops, one from Nantes, and another from Clermont, both equally dull and unlearned. The latter was not long ago deemed as ridiculous as a buffoon, and so libidinous that he was known to seek out dens of infamy with the scent of a pointer.[34]

Calvin systematically rejected the theological statements of Trent, in particular its decree on justification, though he allowed that a council was the optimal means of unifying the Church. He also agreed that the traditions of the Church were important, but all of this had been corrupted at Trent by the 'pope and his henchmen'. The success of Calvin's work was such that the leading German humanist and Catholic polemicist Johannes Cochlaeus wrote a refutation in which he labelled Calvin the worst of all heretics.[35]

Victory had not been entirely sweet for the Catholics. The imperial triumph in German lands was not good news for the papacy, which had never trusted Charles, viewed by many in Rome as too ready to compromise with Protestantism. Just as the Catholic troops were marching towards victory the council fathers at Trent issued decrees on original sin and justification that utterly repudiated Lutheran and Reformed teachings. There would be no more attempts to find theological compromise. This did not, however, reflect Charles' own position; his plans for reform of the empire included reaching out to the Protestants without compromising the essential tenets of the Catholic faith. A third way had to be found, and in late 1547 and early 1548 intensive work was undertaken to find a formula. The key Catholic figures were the Mainz suffragan bishop Michael Helding and Julius von Pflug, Bishop of Naumberg. By the end of February 1548 a document had been drafted that outlined the traditional elements of Catholicism. Although intended as a temporary solution, it was given additional force by the presence in southern German lands of Charles' Spanish troops. The Protestant electors of the Palatinate and Brandenburg secretly signed the Augsburg Interim, as it became known. To the horror of many of his contemporaries, including Calvin, Martin Bucer also signed.[36] Impressed by Calvin's attack on Trent, Bullinger asked the Frenchman to take on the Augsburg Interim, which Calvin described as an adulteration of the Christian faith. The co-operation between Zurich and Geneva in 1548 over the Interim opened the door to negotiations over the Lord's Supper.

By the end of the decade, Calvin and Bullinger shared a gloomy prospect of events in German lands. Calvin saw Charles V as a modern Nebuchadnezzar sent by God to punish the Church for its infidelity, and in the summer of 1548 offered a providential view.

> We have had no news from Germany since the capture of the Landgrave [Philip of Hesse], who has been suitably rewarded for his baseness. In the present state of affairs, I recognize our God's intention utterly to deprive us of a triumphant Gospel that he may constrain us to fight under the cross of our Lord Jesus. But let us be content that he returns to the early method of his dealings, in the miraculous preservation of his Church by his own power, without the help of an arm of flesh. The trial is hard, I confess, but our fathers have had the like, quite as depressing, and have never been shaken in their stability. Now is the time to put in practice the proverb, 'Let us hope and we shall see.' Besides, we need not be astonished that God has corrected us thus roughly, considering the life we have led.[37]

The sense of deserved punishment from the hand of God articulated Calvin's ambivalent attitude towards the German reformation. Luther's successors had proved unworthy of the departed prophet; Calvin despised the culture of political and religious compromise and the conduct of the so-called Protestant princes, who, in his view, were beneath contempt. Most spectacular was the bigamous marriage of Philip of Hesse to Margarethe von der Saale in 1540, to which Bucer had reluctantly agreed, as had Luther, though he later denied it. The marriage was a scandal that divided and discredited the Protestant cause. For this, Calvin entertained no doubts: God had vented his wrath. The game was over: the Lutheran church had been crushed and the Reformation had failed. It now fell to those who were left to continue, and this made unity among the Swiss churches all the more imperative.

Reaching Agreement

Events in the Pays de Vaud and the empire pushed Calvin and Bullinger together, but, even with growing warmth, finding agreement on the Lord's

1 John Calvin (1509–64). Line engraving from the sixteenth century.

12 A seventeenth-century line drawing of the massacre at Vassy, 1 March 1562, when French Protestants were murdered on the order of the Duke of Guise. The event sparked the religious war feared by Calvin.

Supper was difficult. The long years of dispute over that issue had taken their toll. There were also their very different Gallic and Swiss temperaments. Calvin was a man of action, always ready to express his views, respond quickly to events and travel, if required. Bullinger, in sharp contrast, was cautious and taciturn. Considered advice was his natural tone, not polemic, and he never travelled.

After Calvin's journey to Zurich, which had seemed to go well, he grew frustrated with Bullinger's silence.

> It is now six months since I returned your book, with annotations, such as you had requested me to make. I am surprised that I have received no reply from you since that time. When I was in your quarter, you reminded me that there was to be frequent exchange of letters between us. In the meantime, I have heard of some of your townsmen having at different times passed through this place [Geneva]. I have had no one going to you, so far as I remember. Should an opportunity of writing be at any time afforded you, I earnestly request you not to allow it to pass without availing yourself of it.[38]

Contact did resume with the exchange of texts and comments, but by early 1549 Calvin felt that matters were dragging and, quite frankly, that Bullinger did not fully trust him. Again and again he insisted that there was little that divided them and that the issue of the Lord's Supper could be quickly resolved.

But it could never be that simple. His publications on the Lord's Supper after returning to Geneva, including the *Short Treatise* and the commentary on 1 Corinthians, had underscored their differences, and these printed works were well known in Zurich. Was he now suggesting that the distinctions he had drawn between himself and Zurich a few years earlier were no longer significant? Calvin could not avoid drawing the conclusion that it was Bullinger's attitude towards him that remained a stumbling block.

> A preconceived opinion regarding me leads you to imagine and attribute to me what never occurred to my mind. Besides, while you are concerned to maintain your own opinions to the very last, whatever they may be, you sometimes consider more what is in harmony with them than what is the truth on the subject. If simplicity pleases you, I certainly take no delight in disguise and circumlocution. If you love a free declaration of the truth, I never had any mind to bend what I wrote so as to receive its acceptance with men. If there be any who have flattered Luther and others, I am not of that number.[39]

Elegantly put, but disputable. Although Calvin's theology was never developed to flatter others, the proximity of his thought to that of both Bucer and Melanchthon was not easily disguised. Once again the issue of Bucer came to the fore as Calvin defended his close association with a man so despised in Zurich, arguing that he was perfectly free to be friends with someone even if he occasionally disagreed with him, and this was the case with Bucer. Friendship permitted dissent as long as the common cause of the Word of God was shared. Bullinger, Calvin contended, demanded something he could not give, absolute agreement in order to have a relationship, and he repeatedly denied any suggestion that he was traducing the Zurichers behind their backs. 'It may indeed be that I have found fault with you in private letters to my friends, or that I have not concealed my conviction that what they censured was correctly done. There was always, however, such a mixture of praise to qualify any bitterness and to prove my good intentions.'[40]

There was another issue on which, in Zurich's eyes, Calvin stood on the wrong side – the renewal of the alliance between the Swiss Confederation and the French monarchy sought by Francis I's successor, Henry II, in the late 1540s. Once more, he and Bullinger viewed the matter from different perspectives. Calvin was adamantly in favour of the alliance as a means of exercising influence on a king increasingly persecuting the faithful in France, but Bullinger was vehemently opposed to the French monarchy. In 1521 opposition to the French alliance had been a central plank of Zwingli's reform movement in Zurich. The French were the principal recruiters of mercenaries, who were the source, Zwingli believed, of moral turpitude. Bullinger maintained Zurich's anti-French sentiments, though the mood in Basle and Berne was quite different.[41] These cities, geographically oriented towards the kingdom, believed that France offered the only viable protection against the conquering Charles V. Both Berne and Basle had consistently renewed their alliances with France from 1521, and the question of religion played no part.

In November 1548 Henry II instructed his ambassadors to find local men in the Confederation to work for the renewal of the alliance. Calvin was approached and willingly acted as an agent.[42] A key task was to change the mood in Zurich, and Calvin linked his negotiations with Bullinger on the Lord's Supper with the French question. Bullinger would have none of it. He was not prepared to contemplate a return to selling mercenaries to the French monarch, and the idea of making political arrangements with Henry II, who was openly persecuting evangelicals in France, was abhorrent to him. He was astonished that Calvin seemed prepared to do a deal with the antichrist. On what grounds, he argued, was one to expect any good from Henry II?

Following stuttering negotiations, an agreement on the Lord's Supper consisting of twenty-four articles was signed by Calvin and the ministers of the Zurich church in May 1549. Known as the Consensus Tigurinus, it has often been presented as a resolution of the differences between Zurich and Geneva. That it certainly was not. In order to achieve agreement Calvin had essentially allowed Bullinger to dictate the terms. The resulting document had little in common with Calvin's writings on the Lord's Supper. Nowhere was the sacrament spoken of as an instrument of God's grace. Bullinger's emphasis on the action of God in the sacrament and downplaying of the role of the physical elements is evident throughout.

What happened? Did Calvin cave in to Bullinger, or had he even changed his mind? It had been an extraordinary gamble to come to Zurich, and Calvin had risked humiliation in his bid to succeed where Bucer and others had failed. He wanted to move the Swiss, and in particular Zurich, out of their isolation and make them part of the wider Reformation movement. The only way to bring this about, he had recognized, was to be flexible for the sake of unity. He needed Bullinger to provide stability in the tumultuous relations with Berne, and he was trying to build a Protestant consensus to present to the French evangelicals. Perhaps he even hoped that agreement on the Lord's Supper would shift the Zurichers on the French alliance. What the events of the 1540s clearly demonstrate is that Calvin never regarded his theological formulations as non-negotiable. No one who had seen the consequences of Charles' victory could allow disputes over terminology to doom the Church. Calvin was prepared to shift to reach agreement in the cause of unity.

Nevertheless, this bold undertaking left Calvin profoundly troubled. He had strong reservations about the Consensus, and three months later in August he inserted another two articles more directly in line with his teaching. Remarkably, Bullinger accepted the amendments, largely because Calvin formulated them to permit multiple interpretations.[43] For the revised version Calvin wrote a preface in which he spoke of the unity between the Genevan and Zurich churches. The Consensus was not printed until 1551, but it was circulated among the Swiss churches as Bullinger and Calvin sought general agreement. This was to prove a great disappointment. Although Haller in Berne reported that the ministers had received the document favourably, they were not going to adopt it, and the reason was wounded pride. Berne had been bypassed in the negotiations and resented the new relationship between its old rival Zurich and its problematic client Geneva. Haller indicated to Bullinger that suspicion of Calvin among the Bernese magistrates obstructed acceptance. Basle likewise demurred. The church under Simon Sulzer, with his Bucerian leanings, was not theologically favourable to Bullinger, and subscription to the agreement was not a viable option. During the summer of 1549 both Calvin and Bullinger worked to change minds, but to no avail. The smaller Confederates Schaffhausen and St Gall agreed, but without Basle and Berne there was no consensus among the Swiss churches. Calvin's gamble to find unity had failed, and worse was to come.

The agreement with Bullinger was without doubt one of Calvin's greatest achievements. It brought together the two leading centres of Reformed faith as a powerful base of the Protestant Reformation after the defeat of Lutheranism in German lands. But it fell far short of what Calvin had hoped for. It did not unite the Swiss churches, and, as we shall see, it provoked a hostile storm among Lutherans. Calvin invested heavily in his commitment to church unity during the 1540s, as witnessed by his willingness to travel, despite illness and the pressing demands of a new church order in Geneva. Over the course of the decade he journeyed to Strasbourg in 1543, and to the German lands in 1545 to make a plea on behalf of the Waldensians. Along the way he stopped in Berne, Basle, Constance and Strasbourg. In 1546 he was in Neuchâtel, and then in Zurich in 1547 and 1548 to meet with Bullinger. During the years 1547 and 1548 he returned to Berne and Basle on both church and political business. He often served as an ambassador for the Genevan council carrying out fact-finding missions, as when he was in Basle and sought to determine the state of Charles V's army. In addition to these longer journeys Calvin was frequently in Neuchâtel and Lausanne. Like Bucer, he was prepared to trudge the dangerous roads of sixteenth-century Europe in pursuit of the unity of the Church. And like his mentor he was made to pay a heavy price.

CHAPTER ELEVEN

'Since Calvin Acts So Bravely, Why Does He Not Come Here?': France

Persecution

FROM THE dedication of the 1536 *Institutes* to Francis I, through his time in Strasbourg and participation in the religious colloquies, and ultimately beyond his return to Geneva, France was never far from Calvin's thoughts. The situation in the kingdom was alarming. The Edict of Fontainebleau of June 1540 authorized the courts of the crown to take over from the church the prosecution of heresy, making false belief a matter of sedition, a crime of divine and temporal *lèse majesté*. Ecclesiastical and secular authorities co-operated in the attack on heresy. In 1545, for example, the Paris Parlement sanctioned the list of censured texts which had been drawn up by the Sorbonne.[1] Protestant churches as such did not yet exist, but individuals and groups were hunted down.

Claude Le Painctre was in many ways the typical evangelical. A young man from an urban environment with a skilled, advanced trade, he had fled Paris in 1538 for Geneva, where 'the streams of the Gospel had been started and preached and spread to the land of France', before returning in 1541 to engage in missionary work. His opposition to Catholicism was not particularly theological, but was based on the rejection of outward acts such as the veneration of saints and the Virgin Mary.[2] Betrayed by fellow workers, he was detained and condemned to the fire, but not before he had had his tongue cut out.

Eustache Knobelsdorf, a Catholic German student in Paris, witnessed the executions in Paris in 1542.

I saw two burnt there. Their death inspired in me differing sentiments. If you had been there, you would have hoped for a less severe punishment for these poor unfortunates. . . . The first was a very young man, not yet with a beard . . . he was the son of a cobbler. He was brought in front of the judges and condemned to have his tongue cut out and burned straight afterward. Without changing the expression of his face, the young man presented his tongue to the executioner's knife, sticking it out as far as he could. The executioner pulled it out even further with pincers, cut it off, and hit the sufferer several times on the tongue and threw it in the young man's face. Then he was put into a tipcart, which was driven to the place of execution, but, to see him, one would think that he was going to a feast. . . . When the chain had been placed around his body, I could not describe to you with what equanimity of soul and with what expression in his features he endured the cries of elation and the insults of the crowd that were directed towards him. He did not make a sound, but from time to time he spat out the blood that was filling his mouth, and he lifted his eyes to heaven, as if he was waiting for some miraculous rescue. When his head was covered in sulphur, the executioner showed him the fire with a menacing air; but the young man, without being scared, let it be known, by a movement of his body, that he was giving himself willingly to be burned.[3]

There were dangers in other parts of the kingdom. Francis I had initially hesitated over what to do with the Vaudois (or Waldensians), known as the 'poor of Lyon', in the Luberon region of Provence.[4] By 1543 local Catholic pressure for their extermination boiled over, leading in 1545 to the royal order for the eradication of the villages of Cabrières and Mérindol.[5] French troops carried out the killings; the exact number who died has never been accurately determined, possibly two to three thousand, with others sent to Mediterranean galleys. In 1555 Jean Crespin, Calvin's colleague and the great martyrologist of the French reformation, published an account of the persecution in which the sacrifice of the Vaudois was cast in terms of the martyrs of the early church.[6] His narrative was taken up by other Protestant martyrologists, notably John Foxe.

The force of persecution was also dramatically felt with the crackdown on a group of lay evangelicals in Meaux, the city of the famous Briçonnet circle of the 1520s.[7] The Meaux conventicle, led by biblically literate laypeople, was undoubtedly a forerunner of the secret French churches of the 1550s.[8] Jean

Crespin argued that the group had modelled itself on Calvin's church in Strasbourg, meeting secretly on Sundays at the house of one of its leaders for scripture reading, psalm singing and prayers, and to celebrate the Lord's Supper.[9] Fourteen members were executed in 1546 while others were banished to other French cities, where they continued to propagate the evangelical faith.[10] The house where they had met secretly was levelled by royal officials to be replaced by a chapel where mass was celebrated. Was Meaux the entry point of Calvin's influence on France? This is still debated, but for Crespin, writing from Geneva, there was no doubt.

By the mid-1540s persecution of heresy was well established. The massacre of the Vaudois and the destruction of the church in Meaux marked a bloody end to Francis I's reign. Henry II succeeded to a troubled kingdom in 1547. Every year from 1540 to 1545 the average number of men and women investigated for heresy by the Parlements grew, but it was the period 1544–9 that witnessed the greatest number of executions before the wars of religion.[11] A central role was played by the infamous Chambre Ardente, founded in the year of Henry's accession and modelled on a tribunal established in Rouen two years earlier. It was composed of twelve counsellors appointed to deal with heresy cases.[12] Illuminated by torches, it was known as the 'burning chamber' and quickly became associated with the infamy of Henry II's persecutions, a sort of French black legend. One of its victims was a conventicle of evangelicals in Langres, where four people were executed in July 1548. After their trials eight more men and women were sent to their deaths. The records tell of their grim fate.

> [They were to be taken] in tipcarts from the prisons in Langres up to the great market place, to the place nearest and most convenient to the house of Taffignon . . . and at this said place to be lifted to those scaffolds that will be set up for this, and around those will be set a great fire, and in this the said Taffignon will be burned alive, and his body converted and consumed into ashes, and the said Mareshal, Boulerot, Michau, Royer, Séjournant, Cremer and Baillye to be strangled in the said gallows, and afterwards their bodies, together with the books found in their possession, will be burned. And it was declared that all and each of their goods be confiscated to the king.[13]

It is not known exactly how many people died in the persecution of the 1540s, though it was a relatively small proportion of those arrested.[14] Execution was the most dramatic and draconian punishment; most were required to attend mass or endure a public ritual of abjuration.

Determined to eradicate heresy, the king sought by his edict of 1549 to clarify the jumble of jurisdictions inherited from his father. Simple heresy was made the concern of the church, but where it spilled over into sedition, ecclesiastical and civil authorities were required to work together; the role of the judiciary was also greatly enhanced.[15] Yet Henry's new offensive likewise bogged down in conflicting legislation, corruption within the church, the impossibility of implementing laws and growing public disorder. Sterner measures were required, resulting in the Edict of Châteaubriant of June 1551, a lengthy document drawn up during a period of relative peace between France and the Habsburgs. New courts across the country were made directly dependent upon the crown; their brief was to prosecute heresy and exclude evangelicals from office-holding, reflecting the monarchy's concern at the extent to which 'heretics' had infiltrated the judiciary, even the Parlements.[16] The edict also outlined rigorous control of printing and book distribution. For common people, the hand of the law was most directly felt with the pressure to turn in neighbours. Incentives were offered, such as one-third of the property of the accused. Informing was made mandatory, the duty of loyal Catholics and Frenchmen. The sheltering of heretics was strictly forbidden and punishable. The list went on. It was obligatory to attend church. Bishops were each week to read out the articles of faith drawn up by the Sorbonne in 1543 to protect 'the integrity of the Catholic Church'. Only those licensed to preach were permitted and they were bound by the Sorbonne articles. All of this was to be supervised by the Parlements, which reported to the king.

The execution of heretics was a risky business for the authorities. While they might seek to cleanse the community and set a terrifying example, those who died bravely professing their faith might have an undesired effect on the crowds. They appeared as martyrs rather than criminals and their bravery bore witness to the truth. Their stories were retold across Europe in Protestant martyrologies, encouraging and edifying new generations.[17] In truth, the Chambre Ardente was not the ruthless and arbitrary tribunal of Protestant propaganda, but a well-calculated offensive against heresy that was both pragmatic and targeted in its approach. Its records do not permit easy assumptions about heresy or evangelicalism in France. Most of those who appeared were hauled up for blasphemy, possession of forbidden books, holding secret meetings or insulting the mass, the virgin and the saints. There is little evidence that they were in fact Protestants, and the exact nature of their beliefs is difficult to determine. Were they followers of Calvin? In the years before Protestant churches were established in France in the mid-1550s, this is hard to say. The viciousness of Calvin's attacks on many French evangelicals suggests that their religious views were fluid, and not what Geneva expected. Terms like 'Calvinist' and 'Zwinglian' were not badges worn with pride so much as insults used by opponents to indicate that the people were not Christians.

Much of our evidence for these events comes from the work of Jean Crespin. Living in Geneva, and closely connected to Calvin, Crespin was committed to an account that emphasized the influence of the reformer and city. Often dependent for his information on refugees who came to the city – and similarly inclined towards Calvin – his martyrology could not be comprehensive. It is full of tales from the Auvergne and Normandy, for example, but says nothing of La Rochelle. He shaped his accounts to offer a Geneva-centred view of the reformation in France. On that point royal officials seem to have agreed with him, for the city was clearly identified as the source of heresy.[18] Geneva was repeatedly mentioned in edicts. No one was to correspond or have any contact with persons in the city. In response to the growing numbers who had left the kingdom for Geneva and the Swiss Confederation towards the end of the 1540s, the Edict of Châteaubriant introduced strictures to make flight less attractive: the property and goods of religious émigrés were to be confiscated, cutting off the possibility of secure or prosperous exile.[19]

Calvin was present in France during the 1540s, not in person but through his writings in French. His rapid ascent to the status of the most read Protestant author in France was the result of a series of related factors. By the middle of the 1540s his vernacular works, including the French edition of the *Institutes*, his *Short Treatise on the Lord's Supper* and the *Catechism*, formed a coherent body of accessible theological ideas and spiritual guidance. He offered a lucid and compelling vision of the Church and the Christian life grounded in a comprehensive understanding of scripture. He was able to express this vision to his countrymen by shaping the French language to reach beyond the Latinate elite to common men and women who had embraced the evangelical faith. That he was a Frenchman was of the greatest significance. Calvin could not be discredited by the authorities as a dangerous foreigner, as was Luther. He had inherited the mantle of the great Lefèvre, and perhaps even of the medieval reformer Jean Gerson. His was the French voice of reform. He spoke to the people as one of their own, standing in the tradition of Gallican liberties and French humanism.

French Voice

Calvin wrote and spoke Latin with ease. In Basle, Strasbourg, Regensburg and Zurich this was his shared language with Grynaeus, Bucer, Melanchthon and Bullinger, and even with the French-speaking Farel and Viret he preferred to write Latin letters. It was the language not only of theology and international contact, but of the humanist sodality of reformers. It expressed the Renaissance terms of friendship in a precise manner, something that appealed to Calvin's exacting mind. His command of the language was total, and in both prose and conversation he could craft sentences to express his thought with accuracy and elegance. He chose his words, phrases and syntax with extraordinary care as he moved between the genres of polemic, instruction and exhortation. His language was economical, marked by the brevity he so admired, and within the Latinate fraternity he could, and did, assume on the part of his readers an extensive classical, biblical and historical knowledge.

But when it came to reproducing these thoughts in French Calvin faced a problem. The distinguishing characteristics of his Latin, conciseness and elegance, were virtually unknown in French literature of the sixteenth century. The works of his friend and colleague Guillaume Farel are a useful foil. Lengthy and wordy, they meandered through topics with numerous digressions, illustrations and explanations. There were no models in vernacular religious writing for the type of work Calvin wanted to produce for the faithful: the French language simply did not have the grammatical constructions necessary for brevity and nimbleness. What could be expressed with a few words in Latin required whole clauses and even sentences in French.[20] In addition, the goal of reaching a non-Latinate audience had other complications. The classical and historical references that abounded in the *Institutes* made little sense to those outside the humanist community. Either explanation or omission was necessary if the work was to fulfil its purpose of instructing the faithful in the essentials of the Christian religion.

Given his reputation as a great author, we need to remind ourselves that French was not Calvin's native tongue. As a boy, he had grown up speaking Picard, and with education Latin had become his written language. Naturally, he spoke French fluently, but to write it was a skill he had to acquire, and this was part of his crucial Strasbourg years, when his services were called upon. In 1540 he was asked to prepare a French translation for Charles V of a document written by Philip Melanchthon on behalf of the Schmalkaldic League. The emperor had little facility in Latin and no German whatsoever. Calvin also kept his French colleagues informed of events in the empire by translating Bucer's dispatches.

Calvin's sensitivity to the problems of translation emerged in the French *Institutes* of 1541, widely regarded as a landmark in the development of the language. He worked closely with the 1539 text to replicate the ideas but expressed them quite differently. He abandoned the rhythm of the Latin, which would require demonically long French sentences, in favour of clear, concise prose. Where he could, he retained the rhetorical elegance and force of the Latin, but, as Francis Higman has noted, this was achieved by mirroring the forms of the original language rather than by direct transfer.[21] The uniqueness of his approach is illustrated by two different translations of the 1539 *Institutes* into French: the first by Pierre de la Place, the second by Calvin. Whereas de la Place's attempt to translate the text literally came to a lamentable end in long-winded sentences, Calvin was much freer, choosing to adapt the Latin to a suitably comprehensible French style.[22] Calvin sought a French version of the Latin, not identical but faithful to the ideas.

Hatred in Print

Calvin began to publish more extensively in French during the 1540s as he tried to reach lay audiences in Geneva and, above all, in France. In particular, he cultivated his polemical voice with a series of tracts aimed at a gallery of opponents, including the resurgent Catholics and the Anabaptists, and those he would label Nicodemites. Polemic, for Calvin, was part of his enterprise to explain scripture, but it differed in form from the *Institutes* and the commentaries. It was not simply about denouncing enemies, though he did a good deal of that. Through dramatic contrasts and the casting of good against evil with no middle ground he portrayed the battle of true religion against idolatry.

Pressure for these vernacular works came from friends and colleagues, who exhorted him to speak to the unlearned. Language was crucial and Calvin developed a style in which he appropriated elements of popular culture through his use of vocabulary, proverbial sayings and examples drawn from daily life. His first efforts were simplified French versions of his commentaries on the epistles of Jude and to the Romans. In the course of the 1540s Calvin produced six major polemical works in French.[23] Crucially, he wrote directly in French without first drafting the works in Latin; only *On Scandals* was originally written in Latin.

Although we have little evidence for what Calvin preached during the 1540s, his evolving polemical forms surely mirrored the pulpit. The polemical tracts acted as sermons delivered at a distance. The reader was addressed directly and his or her attention demanded throughout. Calvin used all his powers of persuasion. Opponents were ridiculed and made to look like idiots, but humour and entertainment were only means to an end – the reader was to be edified and strengthened by the Word of God. Calvin laid out his plan clearly: those against whom he was writing were carefully identified with chaos and contradiction, while true doctrine was associated with order, which he as the narrator embodied.

Calvin's method is illustrated in the first and most famous of the tracts, his treatment of relics in 1543. After providing the views of Paul and Augustine, he introduces himself as standing alongside these great figures, speaking with their authority in the defence of true religion. Augustine, he says, had observed how common it was for the relics of martyrs to be carried around in a 'vile and sordid' traffic in order to fleece the ignorant populace who readily believed these bits of bones to be the remains of saints. The ancient abuse had raised its ugly head once more, Calvin warned, and the scandal of idolatry remained the same. 'When Christ ought to have been sought in his Word, sacraments, and spiritual influences, the world, after its wont, clung to his garments, vests, and swaddling-clothes.'[24]

One of Calvin's principal strategies was to appeal to his readers' common sense. Idolatry need not be proved wrong, for that is self-evident. What is required is for readers to be called to their senses, to be reminded of what they already know to be right: 'But when I have called attention to frauds that cannot be denied, every person, even those with the least prudence, will open their eyes and employ their minds to consider what had never occurred to them.'[25] The argument is straightforward: by cataloguing as many instances as he can, Calvin intended to demonstrate the ludicrousness of the claims of the Roman church to possess relics of the saints. If such preposterous assertions were true, then 'every Apostle has more than four bodies, and every saint two or three'. Further, 'even if one emptied out the churches and monasteries of one diocese,' he adds, 'there would be such a pile of rubbish that no one would be in any doubt that it was a fraud'. The conclusions to be drawn are not uncertain – there is only one correct answer.

Calvin also identified himself with his readers by drawing on his own experience.

I remember when I was a little boy what took place in our parish. On the festival day of St Stephen, the images of the tyrants who stoned him (for they are thus called by the common people) were adorned as much as that of the saint himself. Many women, seeing these tyrants thus decked out, mistook them for the saint's companions, and offered the homage of candles to each of them. Mistakes of this kind must frequently happen to the worshippers of relics, for there is such confusion amongst them that it is quite impossible to worship the bones of a martyr without danger of rendering such honours by mistake to the bones of some brigand or thief, or even to those of a horse, a dog, or a donkey.[26]

There is humour, usually sarcasm, but not always. Calvin was able to build a joke to an effective punchline. On the cross: 'In truth, if all the pieces that could be found were collected into a heap, they would form a good ship load, though the Gospel testifies that a single individual was able to carry it. What effrontery then to fill the whole world with fragments, which it would take more than three hundred men to carry?' Sometimes the humour is more an elegant aside, as when he speaks of the dish for the Pascal lamb, which is 'at Rome, and at Genoa, and at Aries'.

The constant refrain is the absence of evidence for the relics in either scripture or the writings of the early church fathers. In the final part of the treatise readers are exhorted to compare what they had heard about the relic pedlars with examples from the Bible. Were the Patriarchs dug up and venerated? In the earliest days of the Church Christians sought to rescue the bodies of martyrs from their persecutors, which was honourable, but this had degenerated into the idolatrous practice of consecrating remains instead of simply burying them. False worship must be identified and eradicated, ignorance is no justification. Christians must worship God rightly and that comes only from the knowledge of Christ as revealed in scripture. Anger, humour and ridicule lead to the Gospel.

'Profaned that Sacred Pledge of Eternal Life': The Nicodemites

During the 1540s Calvin sought to wrest control of the evangelical movement in France away from the Navarrists centred around Marguerite.[27] Calvin understood that to impress his influence on the disparate evangelical communities he had to define Christian behaviour in a culture of persecution. His own choice had been to flee his homeland, but in 1534 he had been a single young man without a career; arguably, he had not had to leave much behind. For those with families, property and positions, exile was not an attractive option, and to profess evangelical views openly carried the very real possibility of death. Many chose instead to dissemble, continuing to adhere to the outward forms of the Catholic religion by attending mass while secretly holding evangelical views. Calvin despised this practice, regarding it as a toxic mixture of the Gospel with false worship, and during the 1540s he waged a relentless campaign to discredit it as idolatry. He referred to this conduct as 'Nicodemism', so named from the leader of the Jews who visited Jesus at night for fear of reprisal. Calvin was not the first to use the term, but he made it infamous.

In the light of increased persecution in France the reformers were frequently consulted about how the faithful should act in such perilous circumstances. For Bucer and Capito the debate was shaped by their continuing hope for reconciliation between the Catholic and Protestant churches, which led them to a more lenient view of participation in Catholic services. The Strasbourgers also followed a tradition begun by the early reformers of offering support to those in France who were not prepared to break with the church. In contrast, Heinrich Bullinger in Zurich categorically denounced Catholic rites as idolatrous and forbidden to Christians. In the same vein, Farel and Viret believed that martyrdom was the test of a true believer.[28] Calvin was very much aware of the debate in Strasbourg during his stay, and on this issue he disagreed sharply with his esteemed mentor Bucer. Together with Bullinger, he called for an end to support what he saw as the lukewarm evangelicals in his native land.

For Calvin, Nicodemism was a form of conduct that had to be eradicated, and his *Epistolae duae* to Duchemin and Roussel of 1536 had begun a relentless campaign that would continue for well over a decade. The printed version opened with the prophetic words of 1 Kings 18:21: 'Elijah went before the people and said "How long will you waver between two opinions? If the Lord is God, follow him, but if Baal is God, follow him." But the people said nothing.' The text signalled Calvin's claim to the prophet's mantle and he reiterated his prophetic authority throughout his anti-Nicodemite writings of the 1540s, asserting that his task was to teach the doctrine of life (*vitae doctrinam*).[29] In 1540 he wrote to friends who had inquired about the propriety of attending Roman rites; in 1541 he enjoined the Duchess of Ferrara to an open confession of faith; in September 1540 he penned his *Short Treatise*, not printed till 1543.[30] The most important, however, was his *Answer to the Nicodemite Gentlemen* of 1544.

Who were these shadowy Nicodemites?[31] They are hard to track down as, naturally, it lay in the nature of dissembling not to leave footprints in the sand.

Antoine Fumée, who wrote to Martin Bucer and the ministers in Strasbourg in the early 1540s, was certainly regarded by Calvin as a Nicodemite.[32] Fumée argued that the Gospel was not sufficiently explained and that he continued to attend mass, while protesting his faithfulness to scripture and the church fathers. For this he did not apologize and presented a vigorous defence of the evangelical faith in the dangerous world of Catholic Paris. In 1543 he complained to Calvin that many Frenchmen sympathetic to his evangelical teaching found the Genevan reformer's insistence on a break with the Catholic church impossible: 'a number of people think your assertions are thoroughly wretched. They accuse you of being merciless and very severe to those who are afflicted; and say that it is easy for you to preach and threaten over there, but that if you were here you would perhaps feel differently.'[33] The charge that Calvin could declaim from behind the walls of Geneva was frequently repeated by his critics.

Calvin attacked what he saw as timorous Christians, without naming them. In his eyes, anyone who concealed his or her faith through feigning compliance with the Catholic church was a Nicodemite, falsely holding out the possibility of compromise between the idolatry of Rome and the purity of the Gospel. He was particularly keen to discredit the idea that participation in Roman rituals was a matter of indifference best left to the judgement of individuals. He did acknowledge that the major cause of Nicodemism was the fear of persecution and that most who fell into this camp were sincere evangelical Christians trying to survive.[34] Nevertheless, for Calvin compromise was deadly and precluded true Reformation.

There were gradations in Calvin's thought. He distinguished between dissimulation and simulation: the former was acceptable if one kept one's beliefs secret and did not act against them; the latter was unacceptable because one not only concealed beliefs but connived in what was false.[35] In other words, it was acceptable to conceal one's religious views as long as one did not engage in idolatry. Calvin rejected the idea that that one could participate in the mass without any attachment to it. Feigned idolatry was idolatry nonetheless, and he repudiated the argument that if a person did not inwardly accept false religion it did not matter to God how he or she acted. Calvin bridled at the suggestion of certain Frenchmen that in tolerating the mass their conduct reflected Paul's attitude towards Jewish ceremonies. Paul, he thundered, acted to bring about converts, not to curry favour with the world.[36] In so doing the Apostle sought to avoid offending the conscience, while the Nicodemites act to save their flesh.

The *Answer to the Nicodemite Gentlemen* of 1544 was Calvin's reply to others who believed that he had been too severe on women and men in France who had conformed. He listed and denounced four kinds of Nicodemite: those who use the faith to obtain church positions, but pretend to preach the Gospel; those who try to convert ladies at the court and in high places, but never take the Gospel seriously; those who try to reduce Christianity to a philosophy; and, finally, merchants and common people afraid of danger.[37] As Calvin's approach to evangelizing France depended on a strategy of winning over the nobility, he concentrated on the first three forms of Nicodemism.

The Nicodemism debate was so fierce because it was deeply personal. Calvin understood that his own reputation was on the line.

> I want to point out to them that it is great ingratitude on their part to employ the line they do: 'Since Calvin acts so bravely, why does he not come here, to see how he will do? He acts like the commanders who drive their troops into the breach to take the blows, while they stay far from the danger.' Well, in this way the ancient believers might have ridiculed all the exhortations of the apostles, when they urged them to endure continual persecutions for the name of Jesus Christ; to flinch not because of anything that might befall them; to lose their possessions joyfully; to endure the scorn of the world with a cheerful heart; and to die in faith, should such be the will of God. For they might have said, 'Go do it yourselves, and show us how it is done.'[38]

What immediately catches the eye is Calvin's sense that the evangelicals have shown him ingratitude, as well as his personal association with the apostles.

With savage irony Calvin turned his opponents' argument on its head by declaring them unworthy of the name Nicodemites, for Nicodemus had ultimately confessed openly his faith in Christ, which they fail to do. Persecution, he continued, is the rod of God upon the faithful for their sinfulness, testing and correcting, and they should respond in humility. Calvin invoked the example of David, who:

> when he was a fugitive in the land of the Philistines, although he was not constrained to practise idolatry, regretted nothing more than being deprived of the blessing of being able to assemble with the faithful to pray in their midst, to strengthen himself through the sacraments, and to hear the law of the Lord (Ps. 42:4). In comparison with that, he was not

concerned about being banished from the kingdom which God had given him, about being driven away from his relatives and friends, about being stripped of his wife. We do not read of him lamenting these things as he did about not having access to the temple of God.[39]

Suffering is God's will. True Christians must neither engage in illegal activities of any sort nor take upon themselves acts of iconoclasm. Their duty lies in fidelity to the Gospel and trust in God's providence, which remains beyond human comprehension.

The hostility of many in France to Calvin's hard line forced him to seek support from other reformers. Copies of his work, along with letters from France, were sent to Melanchthon, who, as we have noted, thought it unwise to pass them along to Luther. Melanchthon's writing on the issue of Nicodemism was subtle, avoiding strict arguments, though in tone generally sympathetic to Calvin. Given the precarious situation in the empire, Melanchthon was cautious in his discussion of the papists and the mass. Nevertheless, Calvin was quick to claim that he and Melanchthon were of one mind, despite minor differences. In Strasbourg, Peter Martyr Vermigli commented on the writings of Melanchthon and Bucer. Calvin printed the replies of Melanchthon, Bucer and Vermigli together with two letters of his own under the title *De vitandis superstitionibus*. In autumn 1549 approval of the work arrived from Zurich as part of the agreement on the Lord's Supper.

But there was no disguising the truth that Calvin's hard-line views on Nicodemism caused disquiet among other reformers, including his closest colleagues. In 1547 Pierre Viret wrote on Nicodemism by treating the biblical book of Esther wherein he spoke of crypto-Protestant nobles and magistrates.[40] Although Viret made many of the same arguments as Calvin on the need to emigrate or die for the faith, his tone was more sympathetic to those forced to live under the Roman church. Toleration of idolatry, according to Viret, was an error of weakness, not malice, and he displayed considerable sensitivity to the complexities of life in France for the evangelicals.[41]

The assault against Marguerite's circle continued in 1545 with Calvin's *Against the Libertines*, in which he savaged French and Flemish spiritualists at the Navarre court.[42] Calvin had grown distrustful of Marguerite's court in Nérac and had resisted their attempts to enlist him as an agent. Well educated, often literary and largely anti-dogmatic in character, the men surrounding her were influenced by Gérard Roussel, who to Calvin's disgust had become a bishop in Béarn in the south of France. Calvin distinguished between these

'Libertines' and the 'Nicodemites', but not in any positive sense. The former, for all their learning, were equally duplicitous, hiding their false belief behind apparent openness to new ideas. Their use of parables, allegory and incomprehensible language was, in Calvin's view, equivocation and cunning.[43] Calvin's polemic against them was fierce, though in his condemnation of 'Libertines' who continued to practise Catholic rites he carefully refrained from including the queen, concerned that Marguerite should continue to lend political support to the cause in France.

Many of those who found themselves attacked by Calvin were humanist writers and printers whose religious views could be described as Erasmian or Lefèvrian, and who might have had some sympathies with Geneva. To Calvin, however, they were free thinkers who with their speculative ideas and literary interests undermined the pure Gospel. In 1550 he rounded on such a group of figures he regarded as dangerous examples to the evangelicals in France. *On Scandals* denounced, among others, such eminent literary figures as Etienne Dolet, Clément Marot and François Rabelais, all of whom had prospered under the patronage of Marguerite of Navarre.

Etienne Dolet was a man of extraordinary talents: a humanist, author and printer who had once been arrested for killing a painter in a street brawl in Toulouse.[44] On more than one occasion he had been saved by the intervention of Francis I, who held him in high esteem, but eventually his luck ran out. Arrested in 1544 for heresy, he managed to escape briefly before being imprisoned in Paris for two more years. Tried and convicted by the Parlement of Paris, he was strangled and burned at the stake in the Place Maubert on his birthday in 1546. Dolet had written extensively and controversially about the Latin language, and his religious views, drawn from the New Testament, were, to say the least, eclectic. Despite the ridicule to which he was subjected in *On Scandals* by Calvin, Dolet himself a difficult man, had certainly been prepared to risk great danger for his religious and humanist beliefs. Clément Marot had been in Geneva where he had produced his famous work on the psalms, and was regarded as the most renowned and popular author in France.[45] In 1542 he wrote a poem advocating dissimulation and advised his readers in the face of persecution to avoid speaking like the Genevans. Despite this, he was able to return to Geneva where he worked with Calvin before being forced out to die a pitiful death, alone and without family, in 1544. His fate was not unlike those of many of the others Calvin denounced in France: hunted down for their heterodox views while discredited from Geneva. In the end dissembling did not protect them from the horrors of religious turmoil, as Calvin claimed. From Geneva there was no mercy.

It is common knowledge that Agrippa [von Nettesheim], Villanovanus [Michael Servetus], Dolet and their like have always proudly rejected the Gospel, as if they were so many Cyclops. They have finally lapsed so far into folly and madness that not only did they spread execrable blasphemies against the Son of God, but also, with regard to the question of the life of the soul, they held out that they were themselves no different from dogs and pigs. Others, like Rabelais, Deperius, and Goveanus, having sampled the Gospel, have been struck with the same blindness. And what is the reason for that except that they had previously profaned that sacred pledge of eternal life by making a mockery and a laughing-stock of it, with the impudence of the impious.[46]

For Calvin the core of Christianity was the proper worship of God. The decision that he could not live with false religion had been the defining moment of his life; exile had been his deliverance from idolatry. While explicitly not making himself a model, he insisted that others make that same choice, whatever the sacrifice. The vehemence with which he attacked the so-called Nicodemites reflected what was at stake. With their attitude of accommodation, they posed as great a threat as the Catholics. They undermined any reason for a Reformation and the consequence, most loathsome to Calvin, was a sham Christianity in which people's lives had little to do with the demands of the Gospel. Whether his own compromises of the previous decade weighed heavily as he bitterly admonished his backsliding countrymen is not known, but he was always at his most vicious when cornered.

'You Go There as to Your Inheritance': Martyrdom

The knowledge that his countrymen and women were dying for their faith haunted Calvin, particularly as he could put faces to many of their names. He had never seen himself as a martyr, and when persecution had touched his life he had fled. His consistent message remained that if possible Christians should avoid death or the pollution of idolatry by exile. But as the flames fanned across France he had to address the issue of martyrdom, most notably in 1552 when five students left Lausanne to return to their native France.[47] Shortly after their arrival in Lyon they were arrested, a shock to the Protestant world, and immediately the leading reformers, including Bullinger, Viret and Calvin, began writing on their behalf. Calvin launched a two-pronged strategy: via the Bernese council he sought to influence the French king and win their freedom;

at the same time he wrote to the students that they should prepare themselves for death.[48] He was in a difficult position. He would have saved the prisoners if he could, but once their cause was lost he was determined that they should die well.

Although the students could read Latin, Calvin wrote in French so that his guidance could benefit other religious prisoners. Martyrdom was a matter for the whole Church and he assured the students that they were being prayed for by the congregations of Geneva as well as by the faithful in all lands.[49] He instructed them in how they should conduct themselves under examination.

> Thus humbling yourself under the guidance of the Spirit of God, answer soberly, according to your knowledge, following the rule of scripture, 'I have believed, therefore I speak.' Yet do not let that stop you from speaking frankly and plainly, fully persuaded that he who has promised to give you a mouth and wisdom, which all your adversaries shall not be able to gainsay, will never fail you.[50]

They would find a model in the martyrs of the early church.

The students were reassured by Calvin that God gives special powers to martyrs, who particularly feel divine comfort: whoever dies for the faith will wear the crown of life. As consolation Calvin offered the text of Matthew 10:32–3: 'whosoever acknowledges me before men, I will also acknowledge him before my Father in Heaven'. The message was echoed by Viret, who wrote that while the five students would die in a material fire that would pass away, their judges would be committed to eternal flames.[51] All humans must submit to the will of God, and martyrdom is the most dramatic form of obedience – part of the duty to follow Christ. Calvin was clear that it can be God's will for the faithful to die; it strengthens the Church and wins converts, and the perseverance of the faithful in the face of their opponents was a holy example to the broader masses.

In May 1553, after all appeals for clemency had failed, Calvin wrote to the five prisoners to assure them of their salvation.

> In leaving this world we do not go away at a venture, you know not only from the certainty you have that there is a heavenly life, but also because from being assured of the free adoption of our God you go there as to your inheritance. That God should have appointed you his Son's martyrs is a token to you of super-abounding grace.

In July, shortly before their execution, Calvin's last letter contained the promise that he was with them in prayer.

> However, we must comfort ourselves in all our miseries, looking for that happy issue which is promised to us, that he will not only deliver us by his angels, but will himself wipe away the tears from our eyes. And thus we have good right to despise the pride of these poor blinded men, who to their own ruin lift up their rage against heaven. And although we are not at present in your condition, yet we do not on that account leave off fighting together with you by prayer, by anxiety, and tender compassion, as fellow members, seeing that it has pleased our heavenly Father, of his infinite goodness, to unite us into one body, under his Son, our head.[52]

Calvin's message to his countrymen was that they should be prepared to die for their faith. To compromise was to lose everything. Strangely, his harshest words during the 1540s were directed against those who regarded themselves as followers of the evangelical faith, and perhaps even of the Genevan reformer himself. There was a fundamental problem. The evangelical culture in France had survived by dissembling, as Calvin had himself during 1534. Persecution was erratic and not always well organized, but it was real and effective. People were dying for their faith. Calvin had chosen exile and had developed a visceral hatred for compromise; this put him at odds with the very people he sought to evangelize. During the 1540s he worked to discredit any form of conduct that fell short of a full and open confession of faith. That in his eyes meant a clean break with the demonic Roman church. It was a belief he would passionately maintain till the end of his life, and though thousands of men, women and children chose exile or death, for others that choice was too stark, and it cost him many followers.

CHAPTER TWELVE

The Years of Conflict

LIKE MOST middling cities of the sixteenth century, Geneva's foetid physical space was small, and its inhabitants rubbed shoulders daily in social interaction and commerce. Such was the age. It is recounted that when the humanist Erasmus passed through the squares of Basle he would cover his nose with a cloth on account of the stench.[1] In narrow streets, churches, market places and taverns friends and enemies were in constant contact, knowing nothing of our modern sense of privacy. Rumour and gossip were the daily fare of social discourse, and violence a common means of conflict resolution. If one reads the sermons of the ministers the impression given is of a cesspool of immorality, but in truth Genevans were no different from those living in any of the French, Swiss or German cities. All across Europe rulers and common people worried about what to do with the youth, in particular young men, the poor and foreigners. Fear of disease and the threat of fire from lightning, workshops or household hearths was constant. Most diseases were thought to be contagious, making the close proximity of people all the more a source of fear. What distinguished Geneva in this period was the sheer number of immigrants, who overwhelmed the local population. It turned a tense situation in which political factionalism was rife into a powder keg.

Refugees

By the middle of the 1540s refugees from France flowed through the gates of Geneva and flooded the city. Drawn by Calvin's reputation, by family and

friends, and by the promise of safety, these men and women radically transformed Geneva, and by 1546 their presence had become the dominant political
issue. In spring 1544 Calvin was allowed to hold a celebration of the Lord's
Supper for those who had arrived too late for Easter communion, but by 1546
things were turning ugly: it was not permitted for Genevans to rent rooms to
strangers without a licence and those who would not leave were threatened with
beatings. Efforts were made to pre-empt the arrival of refugees. A syndic was
sent to Mérindol in Provence, where the massacre of the Vaudois had taken
place and from where four thousand refugees had arrived in one year; he took
money for the local minister to support the faithful.[2] The Genevan approach
was to give the foreigners what they needed and then send them off. By 1546 it
became clear that this strategy was not working and the refugees were staying,
fuelling hostility from locals. On the whole, the newcomers faced a welcome
which was the common fate of religious refugees in the sixteenth century. They
were slandered as disease-ridden burdens on charitable institutions who took
local jobs and accommodation. It was the lot of refugees, from London
to Frankfurt, from Denmark to the Swiss Confederation, to be treated with
contempt and suspicion by those among whom they tried to settle. When the
Italian Protestant refugees from Locarno arrived in Zurich in 1555, encouraged
by Bullinger, they met waves of hostility from merchants and businessmen, who
saw them as unwelcome competition.[3]

For the native Genevans, however, the issue was not simply the number of
refugees, it was also the manner in which they quickly permeated the structures
of power. The foreigners sought integration, a reality most dramatically represented by John Calvin and his circle of French ministers. The ministers came
to stand for everything many Genevans despised and resented. Despite this,
the Genevans found a way to turn this influx into a windfall: the foreigners
were permitted to purchase bourgeois status in the city, and this proved something of a golden egg.[4] But the city found itself in a tightening bind. The sale of
bourgeois status was an essential means of income, but the leverage it provided
foreigners was unwelcome. By 1555 the coin generated by the purchase of these
rights amounted to almost 20 per cent of the city's revenues. In an attempt to
have it both ways, in 1551 the magistrates tried to forbid the right to vote for
twenty-five years for those who purchased bourgeois status, but the effort
failed.[5]

The refugees formed a distinct group, separate from native Genevans and
bound together by culture, family and their experiences of exile. Whereas some
Genevans felt the Reformed faith, with its intrusive Consistory, was being

forced on them, the refugees had come to Geneva by choice and on account of their religion. They were viewed by the locals as privileged and wealthy, purchasing property and maintaining a standard of living beyond the means of many Genevans. The contrast between the two communities was striking: the refugees had plenty of money and little property, while the Genevan elite had plenty of property and little cash. Precisely because the foreigners brought money into the Genevan economy they were able to act as financiers.[6] While there was little financial transaction between those Genevans who opposed Calvin and the foreigners, between Calvin's Genevan supporters and the French refugees there was much.[7] And the refusal of the French refugees to mix with the Genevans was another source of tension. They married among themselves, not locals, and their families were closely intertwined economically, conducting business, loaning money and witnessing transactions. Despite the edicts in France, many still had access to their wealth in the kingdom.

Yet the French were not a homogeneous body, and considerable social distinctions remained evident. While many of those who settled in the city were well educated and even aristocratic, others who sought protection from persecution came from humble backgrounds. In the 1550s the Genevan council permitted around five hundred refugees from Provence to settle in its rural areas.[8] The attitude of the council towards refugees who did not pose a political threat differed considerably from that towards the wealthy, urban French families.

Care of Body and Soul

Calvin and the other preachers repeatedly used the pulpit to remind the people of Geneva of their Christian duty towards those most vulnerable in society – the poor, the sick, the widowed and orphaned. In the 2 Corinthians commentary, Calvin uses Paul's statement that 'he that sows with blessings shall reap with blessings' to explain that almsgiving, although it lessens the goods of the giver, enriches the community. Paraphrasing Paul, he says it was as if the Apostle had declared, 'the more liberal you are to your neighbours, the more liberal you will find the blessing God pours forth on you'.[9] Following the *Ecclesiastical Ordinances*, care of the poor and sick in Geneva was the work of the deacons, whose office Calvin believed dated to the early church.[10] Under Calvin's guidance, the diaconate in Geneva was transformed from a stage towards ordination into a ministry of social welfare in its own right.[11]

During the 1540s care for the poor and sick was provided through a mixture of efforts.[12] The City Hospital tended to the needs of the locals, but for the vast numbers of immigrants the situation was different. Many of the refugees looked after their own privately, but a more organized system emerged in the form of bourses, one of which was known as the Bourse Française, a fund raised in the French community from wills and endowments.[13] The exact origins of the Bourse are not known, but Calvin was certainly involved. It probably had something to do with the bequest of David Busanton, a friend of Calvin's who died in 1545 leaving a considerable sum of money to the poor of Geneva and Strasbourg.

The Bourse was specifically intended to help refugees, many of whom would never have required assistance at home in France.[14] Through its extraordinary range of activities it looked after the diverse needs of the men, women and children who arrived in Geneva. It helped men retrain and obtain work, arranged apprenticeships for boys, looked after widows and found work for them, mostly in sewing. The type of jobs could vary enormously. Famously, Denis Raguenier was employed to copy the sermons of John Calvin. For at least eleven years till 1560 he was engaged by the Bourse to write down the reformer's sermons in shorthand and afterwards transcribe them in longhand.[15] The Bourse also acted as a marriage service in seeking new husbands for widows. Children had to be cared for and particular provision was made for widows with children. There was no separate orphanage, but the Bourse developed a system whereby children were sent to foster homes. It also gave money for men and women to return to France to bring family members to Geneva.[16]

The deacons of the Genevan church did just about anything and everything. They purchased clothing and firewood, provided medical care, and not infrequently were present at births. They arranged guardians for the children of the sick. Essentially, they attempted to meet any need. Their task was thankless. The deacons had to respond immediately to whatever crisis landed at their doors – a sudden influx of refugees could arrive unannounced. They had to deal with difficult benefactors and recipients and the records are full of the ingratitude of those whom they helped, as well as the hostility of locals. People often stole the items they were loaned, and violent threats against the deacons were not uncommon.[17] The deacons themselves were volunteers and therefore had to be men of means.

During the 1550s the Bourse relied upon a network of Frenchmen in the city who were formally excluded from political office, but who possessed a wide range of talents to offer the community. They were relatively wealthy and well disposed, and all of the early deacons were French-speaking foreigners.

Because they had to keep records, it was also important that they were versed in the skills of business accounting. The names of the deacons reveal them to be businessmen and usually close supporters of Calvin, such as his brother Antoine and Charles de Jonvilliers, his former secretary. As this was not a secular office, they were expected to be Christians of good standing. Calvin emphasized the role of women in caring for the sick and poor, though he did not think they should be designated deacons, an office held by men; the wives of deacons also appear occasionally in the records, tending to those who were in need and as benefactors after the deaths of their husbands.[18] The ministers of the city were firmly in control: they might tell the deacons what to do and the accounts of the Bourse passed under the eyes of the Company of Pastors.

'God Take the Preachers'

The factionalism endemic in the city since its break with Savoy rose to the surface once more in the late 1540s with the emergence of two distinct parties with profoundly different perspectives: the native Genevan families who saw themselves as defenders of the city's traditional liberties, and the French, made up of the ministers and their wealthy, often aristocratic, patrons who had come to Geneva. Resentment of the refugees in Geneva spread into the streets and meeting places, leading to arguments, protests and violence, often directed against the French ministers. To be sworn or spat at in the street was not an uncommon experience for Calvin and his colleagues. Calvin's letters and sermons frequently convey the impression that he and his embattled fellow ministers were locked in an apocalyptic struggle against the recalcitrant ungodly who rejected the Gospel and the discipline of the church. This is misleading. Without doubt, many Genevans hated what they saw as the intrusive work of the Consistory in their lives and relentless haranguing from the pulpits, all of which was carried out by people who had been offered refuge from persecution in their homeland. This, they believed, was a meagre return for their hospitality and generosity. But there was no groundswell of popular resistance to the ministers: in truth, the reforms took hold.

In 1550 the situation in Geneva was tense, but not hopeless. There was the usual run of disputes between individuals, often Genevans and Frenchmen, requiring the attention of the Consistory and the Small Council. These took the form of arguments over financial affairs, drunken brawling and sexual encounters, the usual fare of an early-modern urban community. Although Calvin and his fellow ministers continued to use the pulpit to denounce the conduct of Genevans, fuelling resentment, relations between the council and the clergy had by no means broken down. In the autumn of 1550 the ministers demanded the abolition of the celebration of the Lord's Supper at Christmas, Easter and Pentecost. They had been attempting for some time to distinguish the Reformed Lord's Supper from the mass by not holding it at the traditional times preferred by Catholics, and although this involved a break with the practice of the Bernese church, the Genevan magistrates concurred.[19]

Much more troublesome was a direct attack by the ministers on a traditional social and religious custom in Geneva: the choice of baptismal names for children.[20] To break adherence to established Catholic practices, from 1546 the Company of Pastors had produced a list of traditional names which it regarded as unsuitable, arguing that biblical names such as Daniel, Peter or Matthew should be adopted. In Geneva, like everywhere else in Catholic Europe, the names of saints, especially local ones, were an integral part of individual, familial and communal identity. In Geneva, for example, the name Claude was popular. This attack on traditional names was common across Reformation Europe and Calvin's actions in Geneva mirrored earlier efforts in Zurich and the other Swiss cities. It was part of the assault on lingering Catholic piety, or superstition as it was known to its opponents, rather than an attack on anything specifically Genevan. The reformers wanted to break the emotional bond with the veneration of saints, against which Calvin had written so strongly in 1543. There was a further purpose: to cleanse godparenting of elements regarded as superstitious and make parents, fathers in particular, more responsible for the spiritual guidance of their children. Crucially, the council backed Calvin when he introduced his list of proscribed names, and baptismal records demonstrate that the measure was implemented, though not without resistance.[21]

For many Genevans, this break with tradition was bewildering and disorienting, cutting them off from a vital part of their identity. Genevans quite naturally wanted to give their children names which linked them to their forefathers and mothers. It was the traditional right of a godparent to declare in public the name of a child and for child and godparent to be bound by that shared name. Godparenting was a matter not simply of religion, but of honour and status, and it had considerable economic benefits. The opposition to Calvin's innovations was vocal and by the end of 1550 resistance to the baptismal policy of the ministers in Geneva was stiffening.

The baptismal-names controversy was part of an escalating war of words between the clergy and certain elements of Genevan society. In 1550 Louis

Bandière spoke for many when he said, 'God take the preachers. They have consumed their goods and lands in France and want to take over here.' Further, 'the devil can take all foreigners, they can go and eat their God of paste elsewhere,' and 'the foreigners want to rule over us'.[22] (The 'God of paste' was a disparaging reference to the Lord's Supper. It was a verbal assault on the heart of Calvin's church.) When Bandière was reprimanded for his remarks he turned violent and struck a bystander. Some Genevans gave voice to their anger, often at worship services when ministers would reject point-blank the name proposed by the family and baptize the infant with something more acceptable. In February 1552 Balthazar Sept and Gaspard Favre complained to the Senate about the names, wondering whether Claude was acceptable.[23] Shortly thereafter Calvin was admonished for preaching too sharply on the subject. In October 1552 he refused to baptize one of Sept's children and the Genevan later complained to the Senate. When the ministers left the church Sept and others raged that 'these ministers have insulted us and we shall endure it no more'. Sept then challenged the right of one of the ministers to carry a sword. When the minister asked a syndic present to do something, he was rebuked. The incident very nearly turned violent. Sept and the other men involved were eventually jailed for a few days.

The council attempted to control this growing conflict in the city by declaring that certain names such as Gaspard and Melchior, traditional in Geneva, should not be refused by the ministers. It was a compromise which infuriated Calvin, who appeared before the magistrates to defend his list. Such 'common names', however, remained until 1555, when the Calvin party triumphed over its opponents, at which point they disappear from the baptismal registers.[24] The practice remained in force until well into the seventeenth century, when the prohibited names were no longer deemed a superstitious threat.

'To Defend Such a Man, I Say, Is the Extreme of Absurdity'

The Consensus Tigurinus with Bullinger in 1549 had been theologically problematic, and although intended to draw together the Swiss churches, both Basle and, crucially, Berne had refused to sign. Geneva had few friends. Precariously perched on the edge of Catholic French and Savoyard lands, it remained dependent on the protection of the Bernese. During the years 1548 to 1550 Genevan attempts to join the Swiss Confederation had come to nothing and the alliance between Berne and the city expired in 1550, though it was eventually extended for another five years. This alliance was one of the many sources of controversy within the city that could, and did, turn violent. The Bernese continued to believe that they had a right to intervene in Geneva's affairs and viewed with deep suspicion the growing number of French in the city. Under Calvin's leadership, the Genevan church had gradually yet relentlessly cast off Bernese rites and practices, and the influence of allies Pierre Viret and Theodore Beza in Lausanne on the French-speaking ministers was a sharp thorn.

The disintegration of Calvin's relationship with the Bernese began with the arrival of one French refugee who was certainly not sympathetic to the reformer. Jérôme-Hermès Bolsec was a Carmelite friar forced to leave France in 1545 on account of his evangelical preaching. From Paris he went to Ferrara and eventually settled just outside Geneva in 1550 in the Bernese-controlled village of Veigy, where he worked as a medical doctor, apparently healing the son of Calvin's friend Jacques de Falais, the Flemish nobleman who had converted to the Reformed faith and had moved close to Geneva. Bolsec attended the Friday Congrégation in the autumn of 1551 and publicly expressed grave reservations about Calvin's teaching on predestination, his insistence that before creation God had decided the fate of the elect and the damned. This, Bolsec argued, made God the author of evil. The accusation was neither new nor original, yet to state it openly in Geneva and in Calvin's presence was simultaneously audacious and idiotic. Whichever faction was in the ascendant, there was consensus on doctrine between the magistrates and ministers in Geneva and a theological quarrel was regarded by all as destabilizing and undesirable. An initial warning was followed by arrest in October 1551 and Bolsec languished in prison for over a month with no discernible sign of repentance. Realizing that he was fully committed to his views, the Genevan magistrates sought the opinions of the other Swiss cities. The collateral damage was extensive, for Bolsec had impugned not only Calvin's teaching, but also that of Huldrych Zwingli, the hero of the Swiss reformers. The Swiss were cautious in their advice to Geneva.[25] In principle, they supported silencing a rogue voice that might cause dissension within the church, yet none was prepared to contemplate an execution, the consequences of which were too unpredictable. Moderation was urged, a course the Genevans followed, and in late December 1551 Bolsec was banished from the city.

On one level the story is of little significance. As his later life would prove, Bolsec was a crank, if not a charlatan, and posed no serious theological threat to Calvin, who in turn treated him with utter contempt. The Genevan council entertained few doubts that Bolsec was a troublemaker who threatened communal order; his case was prosecuted before the magistrates, and not the ministers, and he never appeared before the Consistory.[26] Yet out of this curious episode arose unforeseen and unwelcome consequences for Calvin. As with other lesser opponents, he believed that Bolsec hardly merited a response. The former monk had, however, put into words the unease about the reformer's doctrine of predestination felt by many, including some of his closest allies, and Calvin would spend much of the 1550s on the defensive.

Most alarmingly, Calvin found himself at odds with Heinrich Bullinger. The official response from the Zurich church had expressed some surprise that it was being asked for an opinion on a matter addressed in the Consensus Tigurinus. There was nothing to be added except that the Zurich ministers felt that Bolsec had been treated too harshly by the Genevans. They prayed for peace and admonished their Genevan brethren to seek reconciliation with this miscreant. A personal letter from Bullinger to Calvin was more substantive.[27] He too was taken aback to be consulted on a doctrine he had so recently treated, apparently with Calvin's agreement, in his *Decades*. He interpreted the doctrine of predestination in terms consistent with the theological vision central to his pastoral work: God wills the salvation of all and does not desire the death of a sinner. Those who are damned are so because of their lack of faith, not because God wills it.[28] This was not Calvin's position, and Bullinger's response formed an implicit criticism of double predestination. God's election, Calvin never doubted, reflected the divine will that humanity be saved. Election, however, could not be separated from reprobation: the sovereign God decreed in a single moment who is saved and who is damned. This became known as Calvin's doctrine of double predestination, and it divided even his friends, who struggled to understand how a gracious God could will the eternal punishment of the vast majority of women and men. Bullinger did not deny the centrality of predestination; what concerned him was Calvin's fatal determinism, that those who are damned are so because God has decreed it, leaving nothing to be done. In one of his most remarkable statements to Calvin, Bullinger not only chastised him for his emphasis on predestination, but distanced himself from his predecessor Zwingli, something he almost never did.

> Now believe me, many are offended by your statements on predestination in your *Institutes*, and Jérôme [Bolsec] has drawn from them the same conclusion as he did from Zwingli's book on providence. In fact, it is my opinion that the Apostles touched on this sublime matter only briefly, and not unless compelled to do so and even in such circumstances they were cautious that the pious were not thereby offended, but understood God to desire well for

all men, and also to offer salvation in Christ, which itself can be received not only by one's own worth but by faith which is truly a gift of God.[29]

Bullinger believed that in his doctrine of predestination Calvin had gone beyond what even the Apostles were prepared to say, and in so doing was damaging the fabric of the Church. Bullinger, however, sought no controversy and argued that if Bolsec could be brought to a confession that salvation belonged to God's grace alone there should be reconciliation. He accepted Calvin's request that they keep their differences on this subject to themselves, though in private correspondence he continued to make clear his suspicion that Calvin backed a position that made God the author of sin.[30]

Calvin could not let such an accusation stand. The suggestion that a doctrine central to God's relationship with humanity was either a novelty or a precocious act of human folly stirred him to an angry reply.

> Your charging us with a lack of moderation and humanity was caused, we think, by your placing less confidence in our letter than you ought to have done. Would that Jérôme were a better man than our letter declared him to be! Would that he attributed all to the grace of God, as you seem to think. But for you to plead in defence of a man who seditiously disturbed a peaceful church, who strove to divide us by deadly discord, who, without ever having received the slightest provocation, loaded us with all sorts of abuse, who publicly taunted us with representing God as a tyrannical governor, or worse, that we had put the Jove of the poets in the place of God, – to defend such a man, I say, is the extreme of absurdity.[31]

Calvin was also offended by the linking of his theology to Zwingli's and drew a brutal comparison. 'Indeed I was astounded on finding from your letter that the kind of teaching which I employ is displeasing to many good men, just as Jérôme is offended by that of Zwingli. Wherein, I ask you, lies the similarity? For Zwingli's book, to speak confidentially, is crammed with such knotty paradoxes as to be very different, indeed, in point of moderation from what I hold.' Sensitive to the damage that could be done by a rift between them, Calvin concluded the letter with a reassertion of his friendship and requested that Bullinger attend to a member of his family who was studying in Zurich.

The Bolsec affair put a serious strain on relations between Calvin and the Swiss churches, and his correspondence with Bullinger ceased for almost a year. This was in part due to Bullinger's serious illness. He very nearly died from an attack of the plague and his recovery was extremely slow. When contact was resumed through a letter from Bullinger, Calvin expressed surprise that Bullinger should be concerned that the Genevan reformer had a negative view of him. In his long chat with the Zurich minister who delivered Bullinger's letter, Calvin wrote, 'mention was made of you, and of all your colleagues, but I uttered not one syllable, as far as I know, intended to convey an unfavourable opinion of you'.[32] And then he made a direct appeal to their friendship.

> I must first testify to you and solemnly declare that I am so far from regarding you as an enemy that I desire to remain bound to you forever by all ties of brotherly attachment. In assurance of this I praise you as nothing other than a loving and inseparable companion in the work of the Lord. Next, I want you to believe that I have neither written nor spoken anything but what was loving and honourable of a man who has publicly earned so much distinction in the Church, and who has always been my friend in private.

It is striking that Calvin even articulated the possibility that Bullinger might see him as an enemy. The roots of this remark lay with members of Bullinger's circle in Zurich, principally Theodor Bibliander, professor of Old Testament, who made no effort to conceal his criticism of Calvin, who in return spoke of his 'vile and perfidious character'.

Calvin was more candid with Farel. In anticipation of a lack of support from Basle he reflected caustically, 'Wait till they [the Basle church] make an absolute renunciation of the election of God.'[33] But in an almost Machiavellian vein he delighted in noting how providence had given him the advantage. 'For without being at the time aware of it, I, by the formula of our agreement [Consensus Tigurinus], have so bound them [the Swiss] that they are no longer at liberty to do damage to the cause. For, in other circumstances, as I am informed by one, they would have become the patrons of Jérôme.' This in short was Calvin's view of his relationship with the Swiss. With the Consensus of 1549 he had brought them to a point with which he could live, even if it by no means expressed the fullness of his theology. From this basis he could embark upon his two cherished, and related, goals: reconciliation with the Lutherans and the united support of the Protestant churches for their persecuted co-religionists in France. The Swiss saw things very differently. Despite their feeling that they had been outmanoeuvred by Bullinger and Calvin, the Basle and Bernese churches had eventually signed the agreement in 1551–2. The Consensus was now a fait accompli in which Bullinger had tamed Calvin and preserved their 'pure doctrine'. For the Swiss the Consensus was a ceiling rather than a floor, and, as the Bolsec case revealed, they were not prepared to negotiate.

Burning Calvin

If Calvin and the Genevan magistrates thought that by banishing Bolsec from the city they had effectively concluded the matter, they were gravely mistaken. Bolsec went to the Bernese lands where he not only continued to voice opposition, but quickly found numerous sympathizers, united not so much by theology as by their hatred of Calvin. The Bernese magistrates did nothing to relieve this new situation and Calvin grew more agitated. The heart of the matter was not Bolsec, who remained a peripheral figure of little consequence, but Berne's perception of Calvin and his supporters.[34] It was feared that Calvin and his agents Viret and Beza, as they were seen, were corrupting the French-speaking clergy and drawing them away from the discipline and theology of the established church. The focal point was the Academy at Lausanne, where Pierre Viret and Theodore Beza taught, which was perceived as a conduit of Calvin's pernicious teaching, above all predestination.

Calvin ruminated to Farel on the possibility of making a personal visit to persuade the Bernese magistrates that he was not exercising undue influence in the French-speaking lands, but decided it would do nothing more than inflame the situation.[35] He asked that Farel do what he could to make peace, and that included holding his tongue. He rightly believed that Farel's incendiary and abrasive preaching and writing were undermining their common cause. 'I beg and beseech of you to strive to restrain yourself that you may not afford Satan an opportunity that we see he so earnestly desires. You know that while we are not called upon to show too much indulgence to the foolish, we are nevertheless bound to give them something to allure them.' Calvin could be a brutal friend, but he knew what was at stake. 'Since the Lord commands us to ascend the pulpit not for our own edification, but for that of the people, you should so regulate the style of your teaching that the Word may not be brought into contempt by your tediousness.'

In the end, Calvin did go to Berne to make peace. He told the magistrates that he held them in the highest regard and had no intention whatsoever of undermining their authority over the church. He was reasonably well received, though many, including Johannes Haller, the head of the church in whom Calvin had once placed so much hope, remained wary of events in Geneva. The

Bernese lands, however, continued to be a safe haven for oppositional voices, not least those of Bolsec and André Zébédée, a long-time foe who had played a key role in the events leading to the Consensus. Meanwhile in Geneva the Bolsec case continued to reverberate. As Calvin was trying to restore harmony with the Bernese his doctrine of predestination was attacked again, this time inside the city. Jean Trolliet, who had been appointed by the syndics to review the defence against Bolsec drawn up by the ministers, had rounded on the clergy and denounced Calvin's teaching. Once more, the ministers and many leading Genevans descended into rancorous exchanges, leaving the syndics scrambling to establish peace. In the end, Trolliet apologized to the Small Council and was declared a good citizen. Calvin, for his part, received from the council the affirmation that his doctrine was acceptable.[36]

But the issue still would not go away. Hostile voices continued to be raised in Bernese lands against Calvin's teaching, and in 1554 Bolsec led such a fierce assault that the Genevan council was forced to write to Berne in protest.

> In a meeting of the classe of Morges, in the presence of a great many people, someone so slandered our brother, master John Calvin, that the rumour is common throughout the land that he is condemned as a heretic, as this word was also often repeated. Since then, Zébédée, the preacher at Nyon . . . speaking about the doctrine we hold and are ready to sign with our blood, said in the middle of the sermon that it was a heresy worse than all papism and that those who preach it are devils and that it would be better to maintain the mass. Meanwhile, one named Jérôme [Bolsec], who, as you know, was banished from the city of Geneva for his errors, had no trouble calling our brother Calvin heretic and antichrist.[37]

Despite the internal ruckus, the Genevan council was prepared to stand by Calvin, recognizing his extraordinary strength as a preacher and teacher, his considerable body of support and the pragmatic truth that theological discord would only put an unbearable strain on an already volatile situation.

Calvin's break with Berne was almost complete. He had virtually no contact with Johannes Haller, who had compared him to the 'two Martins', Luther and Bucer – by no means a compliment.[38] It is tempting to see the conflict between Calvin and Berne as the clash between a talented leading European reformer and a backward, provincial church, and to read Calvin's letters one could easily glean that impression. But this was not the case. Berne was a bulwark of the Reformation and for all their differences with Calvin its magistrates were equally committed to Protestantism. But they presided over a large territorial region consisting of diverse German- and French-speaking communities in which they struggled to maintain peace and order. For them Geneva was but one aspect. The Bernese magistrates were irritated by Calvin's attacks on their ministers, the abandonment of their liturgical rites in the city, the debate over baptismal names in Geneva and Calvin's linking of excommunication with the Lord's Supper.

Nevertheless, things grew uglier. In order to limit Calvin's influence, in 1554 the Bernese banned his writings in their lands, acting on the rumour that the *Institutes* was being taught at the Lausanne Academy. It was decreed that all of Calvin's books deemed contrary to the teaching of the Bernese church were to be burned.[39] Book burning was a powerful symbol of heresy. For most Protestants it conjured up the worst images of papal abuse and corruption, a very sign of the presence of antichrist, and for Protestants to burn the works of other Protestants was shockingly unthinkable. In May 1555 Calvin wrote a very long letter to the magistrates of Berne defending his theology, arguing that it was grounded in the Consensus to which all the Swiss churches, including Berne, had now agreed. He denied the charges of heresy, but did so with a sense of resignation that revealed his scepticism regarding the probability of improvement.

> This fiction [that Calvin is a heretic] is now so prevalent in your country that people speak of it as confidently as if it were the Gospel. Now I think it is not just, when I labour day and night in the service of the church, and for the maintenance of the truth, that I should reap such sorry thanks for my pains. It is true I shall never on account of the world's ingratitude cease to do what God commands me, nevertheless it is your duty to see that I be not wrongfully oppressed, since my labours, on the contrary, deserve that I should meet with encouragement.[40]

The dispute was less about theology than about personality. It is unlikely that many of Berne's magistrates were familiar with Calvin's works. The Frenchman embodied resistance against their authority, and he had to be dealt with.

The Fight in Geneva

The early 1550s saw Calvin battling several bush fires – the Bolsec controversy, bad relations with Berne and the baptismal-names dispute, as well as the ever present resentment of the ministers and their preaching by the Genevans. To add to the mix, 1551 brought a renewal of the argument in Geneva between the ministers and the magistrates over the authority of the Consistory. Calvin clashed openly on this subject with the leading syndic on the Consistory, Michel Morel. There was no shortage of prominent persons whose families had felt the firm hand of the disciplinary body, multiplying resentments and the desire to settle old scores. Such ill will only fuelled calls for both a limitation on the authority of the Consistory and recognition that its judgements could be appealed and overturned by the magistrates.[41]

How thoroughly politicized the Consistory was became apparent when Calvin's opponents, led by Ami Perrin, brought about a revision of the lay members, or elders, who served in the institution. From its inception in the early 1540s the magistrates who served on the Consistory were largely politically insignificant figures who were congenial towards the interests of Calvin and the French ministers. This changed in 1553 as men from the Perrinist party took up positions on the Consistory, threatening Calvin's position. This was part of an orchestrated move to limit the authority of the ministers in the city that included plans to prohibit them from speaking in the General Council.[42] At the same time the Perrinist party sought to clip the political wings of Calvin's supporters by excluding many of them from elections.

Dissension split the city into two warring parties. Against the backdrop of the various conflicts, including the Servetus case which arose that autumn, the defining confrontation concerned the handling of excommunication. One particular case deserves attention. Philibert Berthelier, who had been excommunicated by the Consistory, appealed to the Small Council on 1 September that he might attend the Lord's Supper.[43] Calvin appeared before a special session of the council to declare that he would rather die a hundred deaths than subject Christ to the disgrace of unworthy participation in the Lord's Supper. The syndics reviewed the matter and agreed that Berthelier had the right to make an appeal, though they told him not to receive the sacrament on 3 September, the autumn communion, a compromise that sent Calvin into spasms of anger. He denounced the decision from the pulpit and demanded a retraction from the syndics. He also declared at the communion service that he would defend the Table of the Lord with his life. Berthelier did not appear at the service.

The showdown was all the fiercer for taking place during the Servetus affair in Geneva, and Berthelier was widely believed, not least by Calvin himself, to be supporting the Spanish heretic to embarrass the reformer. Pending the resolution of the Servetus case, the syndics held off a final decision on

Berthelier until he petitioned once more in November to communicate in the Lord's Supper. Calvin and the other members of the Consistory were summoned before the syndics on 7 November to be told that denial of the Lord's Supper was a matter for the magistrates and that the Consistory had no choice but to acquiesce. Calvin protested and demanded to speak before the General Council. Once more the Swiss cities were to be consulted.

The debate over the powers of the Consistory was a defeat for Calvin, who had failed to win independent authority for the church in exercising discipline. He had not been able to persuade the magistrates to change their interpretation of the 1541 *Ordinances.* Indeed, it was such a reversal that he threatened to leave the city. The magistrates, however, were adamant that church discipline was firmly in their hands. Calvin found himself facing the defeat suffered by Martin Bucer in Strasbourg. Sensing that things could only get worse, he launched his own campaign by sending his friends Jean Budé to Berne and Zurich and Michel Cop to Biel and Basle to put his case to the leading churchmen. The responses were positive, if not uniformly supportive, of Calvin's interpretation of the *Ordinances.* He had again put the Swiss church leaders in an awkward position, for none of the cities possessed a disciplinary body with authority separate from the ruling magistrates. The Zwinglian polity had always envisaged the 'godly' magistrates as responsible for the handling of disciplinary matters and Bullinger had held closely to this, even though it frequently brought conflict with his political masters.[44] Nevertheless, Bullinger delivered firm support for Calvin, though Simon Sulzer from Basle was less committed, leaving Calvin so irritated that he stopped corresponding with Sulzer for over half a year.[45]

The year 1554 opened with stalemate in Geneva. Neither the magistrates under Perrin nor the ministers had sufficient muscle to deliver a knock-out blow against their opponents. The result was edgy and unwanted coexistence. Attempts at reconciliation were made, including a festive meal attended by both parties. Calvin reported to Viret in February that he had been privately reconciled with Perrin.[46] Despite the wine and food, however, peace did not hold. Berthelier was excommunicated once again following an argument with the Consistory. More significantly, he was arrested in June for striking a foreigner, an act indicative of the growing violence against the French in the city.

The turning point came with the elections of 1555 when the Perrinist party narrowly lost out to the supporters of John Calvin and the French ministers. The success of the Calvin party owed much to the perception within Geneva that the

Perrinists had failed to prevent the city from succumbing to social disorder. Years of violence and fractious arguments combined with convictions for notorious crimes such as sodomy gave many Genevans the uneasy feeling that perhaps the ministers had been correct in their thunderous sermons. Fear of disorder and divine punishment was a powerful motive in the early-modern world; Calvin and his colleagues had decried the immorality for years. But, what is more, they had also offered a solution. Obedience to the will of God would bring blessings to the community. The power of Calvin and his fellow ministers lay not in their talent for excoriation, but in their ability to create a vision of a godly community. In 1555 this was for many Genevans preferable to what they saw about them. In the highly charged atmosphere a sufficient number of people were persuaded that a different course was necessary and they swung the election. The Perrinists, with their close family networks and clannish behaviour, had become associated with 'inconclusive confrontation and disorder at the highest levels of Genevan government'.[47] The result was by no means a landslide and the situation in Geneva remained precariously perched on the edge of chaos.

Like the Perrinist party, Calvin's supporters sought to take hold of the Genevan government by putting their men in all the major political and judicial offices, but one very different tactic was also employed. To ensure that they would not be subject to the vagaries of elections, such as that which had undone the Perrinists, the victors moved quickly to entrench their position by admitting large numbers of Frenchmen to bourgeois status, thus packing the electoral roll. Between the elections of 1555 and 1556 approximately 130 Frenchmen acquired bourgeois rights.[48] The Perrinists had been defeated but remained a presence and as soon as they saw what was transpiring took action. In 1555 there were numerous violent clashes within the city between the two parties, but events came to a head after the Small Council, dominated by Calvin's supporters, refused the Perrinist demand to stop the admissions or at least to deny the Frenchmen the vote for ten years. On a May evening and fuelled by drink, the Perrinists took to the streets in protest against the Small Council. The event was more a brawl than an organized demonstration and at first the magistrates arrested only minor figures and left the main protagonists. Ami Perrin continued to attend the meetings of the Small Council, but over the course of the summer the victors consolidated their position. By the middle of June the Perrinists had been disfranchised, and in the following weeks they were arrested, fined and expelled.

Berne watched these events with consternation. The Perrinists, whom it had supported, had acted as an effective restraint on Calvin and his followers.

Geneva's alliance with Berne, extended to 1556, expired and negotiations for its renewal ploughed into the sand. Calvin made an ineffectual trip to Berne as part of an official delegation, but returned home empty handed. Berne and Geneva were now divided by theology and politics. For the most part the exiled Perrinists had gone to Berne, where they added to the congregation of opposition and fostered resentment. The situation grew dark and rumours swirled in Geneva of an impending invasion by the Bernese. The militia was bolstered and the walls reinforced. Reformation Europe looked to experience a new tragedy: intra-confessional warfare.

In the summer of 1555, as the Perrinists were being prosecuted in Geneva, Calvin responded to Bullinger's unease at rumours concerning the manner in which opponents were being treated and the Genevan reformer's role in these events. It was said that false confessions had been extracted from some of the Perrinists under torture and that Calvin had participated. Secondly, Calvin was portrayed, inaccurately, as opposed to the renewal of the Bernese alliance. The seriousness of these allegations was such that Calvin replied with one of his longest missives and a masterful apology. He did not deny that certain Perrinists had been put on the rack, and that they had confessed. What they had confessed under torture, Calvin the lawyer was careful to add, was consistent with what they later freely admitted. Following close on the execution of Servetus, which had brought Calvin infamy for his supposed cruelty and bloodlust, he was eager to demonstrate due legal process. It is a measure of the gravity of the situation that Calvin felt compelled to justify himself to Bullinger.

> Therefore when I saw the elder of two brothers already on the point of death, maliciously distorting and giving a false colouring to certain facts, I asked him in the presence of the whole people whether he had not, when there were neither judges nor witnesses present, of his own free will related to me the very same things which had been read over from the public acts of the court. He answered in the affirmative. I again asked him whether I had compelled him by threats, or allured him by wheedling promises to this confession. He replied unhesitatingly in the negative.[49]

Far from being the vindictive persecutor, Calvin stressed to Bullinger that he had sought a confession of faith and repentance as the two men faced the judgement of God. In this respect, he claimed to be successful, as both admitted that they had led shameful lives of moral degeneracy. They would not admit, however, to actions of sedition against the magistrates on behalf of the Perrinist party, though Calvin left Bullinger in no doubt of their guilt.

Calvin also pleaded innocent to charges that he had sought to undermine the Bernese alliance, despite the fact that so many slanders against him had arisen from those lands. He offered Bullinger a robust defence. 'Wherefore you have no need to harangue me greatly on the utility of the Bernese league for our city. Our whole Senate knows, and the majority of the people are not ignorant of how faithfully I have worked to defend it.' The Genevans were the wronged party, for they had always extended the hand of friendship to Berne, so wrote Calvin, and he encouraged Bullinger to use all his authority to work for peace between the parties in the bellicose atmosphere. 'The whole of the Bernese territory resounds with the talk of war, of the siege and sacking of this city. Certainly, not a day passes in which we are not menaced with new terrors, which, in truth, I consider to be vain.' The Bernese church, for Calvin, was the anti-model of the Reformation, an object lesson in the consequences of permitting civil rulers, untrained in exposition of scripture, to interfere in spiritual matters. It was a false rendering unto Caesar.

Victory in Geneva was never a forgone conclusion. Had the Perrinist party not lost control of the situation through its own blunders and internal rancorousness, Calvin might have been dislodged during the debates over church discipline. Certainly the Frenchman was at times despondent about his chances. Opposition in the city was considerable and well connected with outside powers. Yet Geneva was not the scene of a Tolkienesque battle between the forces of light and dark: Calvin certainly had his supporters and detractors, but these categories did not define the whole population. For many magistrates and citizens the overriding concern was true religion and stability in the city; when the Perrinists no longer appeared able to provide either they were pushed from their positions of power. The victory of Calvin's supporters is the most telling evidence for the degree to which the preaching in the city had won over the Genevans. The narrative of faith and salvation offered by the ministers, as well as their accounts of the depredations and moral turpitude of the world, did, contrary to the complaints of the pastors, bring the people to the churches to have their children baptized, to hear sermons and to participate in the Lord's Supper. A new Jerusalem it was not, as Calvin would daily remind his congregations – they were sinners in a sinful world – but it was a bracing tonic for a city worn out by conflict.

CHAPTER THIRTEEN

'There is No Form of Impiety that This Monster Has Not Raked Up'

The Hated Servetus

FOR MANY, the execution of Michael Servetus in Geneva has defined John Calvin's posthumous reputation. From the sixteenth century to this day detractors have seized this moment as confirmation of his tyrannical, intolerant character. In contrast, supporters frequently argue that the execution of a heretic in Geneva was no worse than what was taking place across Europe, where the Inquisition used torture, Anabaptists were drowned and Protestants went to the stake. On these terms the debate will never be resolved.

The events of 1553 had a history. There was bad blood between Servetus and Calvin, who had known of one another for at least twenty years. In 1534, at Servetus' request, Calvin had travelled to Paris at considerable personal risk to meet the Spaniard. Servetus did not keep the appointment, as Calvin would later remind him. Calvin's earliest theological work, the *Psychopannychia*, was at least in part directed against views attributed to Servetus and his circle in Paris. Calvin once said that if Servetus ever came to Geneva he would be burned, but that remark needs to be taken with a pinch of salt. Calvin could be cruel to opponents, and he did not hesitate to persecute them, but there is nothing to suggest that he actively sought to kill them. Heresy, however, was the gravest of dangers, as Calvin knew from personal experience. The accusations made by Pierre Caroli had almost derailed the reformation in Geneva in the 1530s and Calvin had been forced into a desperate struggle to establish his reputation. In the early-modern world heresy was not simply a matter of doctrinal error; it carried the stigma of moral corruption. It poisoned the community. The only known remedy was complete extirpation. One point on which both Catholics and Protestants were in full agreement was that a heretic could not be tolerated.

And Servetus was a known heretic. In 1546 he had sent his *On the Restoration of Christianity* to Calvin and expressed a desire for the two men to meet. Calvin exchanged a series of letters with the Spaniard, using his pseudonym Charles Despeville, before abruptly ceasing contact, having concluded that the Spaniard was beyond hope. 'Servetus lately wrote to me,' Calvin informed Farel, 'and included together with his letter a long volume of his delirious fancies, with the Thrasonic boast that I should see something astonishing and unheard of. He offers to come here if I agree. But I am unwilling to pledge my word for his safety, for if he does come, and my authority is of no avail, I shall never suffer him to depart alive.'[1] What he read horrified him. Among its offences were a denial of original sin and a bizarre and hardly comprehensible view of the Trinity. Christ, for Servetus, was not the eternal Son of God but a form taken by God to come to earth. And that was only the beginning. Virtually everything he wrote would have offended Protestants and Catholics alike. Servetus believed that the devil had created the papacy and that the end of the world would arrive when the Archangel Michael brought final deliverance, which the Spaniard held would be some time towards the end of the sixteenth century.

When Servetus published *On the Restoration* anonymously in 1553 he sent a copy to Geneva together with thirty letters he had written to Calvin without reply. By this point Calvin must have felt stalked by the Spaniard, who ranted against the Frenchman's teaching on the Trinity, calling it three Gods and the work of antichrist. This time Calvin took action. He informed the authorities in Vienne, a French city on the Rhône river twenty miles south of Lyon, where Servetus had been living as a medical doctor under the name Michel de Villeneuve, that they had a notorious heretic in their midst. Servetus was arrested and tried, but managed to escape. It was at that point that he appeared in Geneva at a church service where Calvin was preaching.

Why did he arrive? Calvin remarked to Farel that he had no idea 'with what design he came', but he admitted that Servetus had been detained on his recommendation.[2] Servetus' own explanation, given at his trial, was that he was travelling to Naples and stopped in the city for one night, hoping to remain unrecognized.[3] There was no obvious reason for him to have taken this risk: Geneva was an easily avoided route to Naples, and he knew perfectly well that Calvin had informed on him to the Catholic authorities of Vienne. Calvin had given Servetus every indication that he reviled him. In his words, 'those who spare heretics and blasphemers are themselves blasphemers'.[4]

It was not a mistake. Servetus' repeated attempts to make contact with Calvin bordered on obsession. His arrival in Geneva was a provocation shaped by an apocalyptic view that in the final days as the Four Horsemen rode across Europe he would confront the man he held responsible for turning the Reformation into a new Rome. Servetus had arrived to make his final stand. In Geneva he would give a full account of his views, and die a martyr. There would be no more flight or hiding – it was time to face his persecutors, and his most hated enemy.[5]

The timing could not have been worse. The dispute over excommunication raged in Geneva, with every prospect that Calvin might lose. During the summer of 1553 the atmosphere in the city was at fever pitch. The day after Servetus was arrested and in accordance with Genevan law, Calvin prepared a document outlining the Spaniard's life and teaching. Thirty-nine allegations were drawn from his writings concerning the Trinity, pantheism, baptism and the denial of immortality. Calvin's private secretary Nicolas de la Fontaine was placed in prison as surety should the charges prove false, only to be freed a few days later.[6] Such was dictated by law, and during de la Fontaine's voluntary incarceration Calvin appointed his brother Antoine in his place. The first hearings took place from 14 to 16 August and the formal process began on the 17th. Servetus was subjected to a series of interrogations on the basis of charges drawn up against him. First it was established that he had once been imprisoned in Basle for heresy, and letters written to Johannes Oecolampadius in 1531 were produced in which Servetus' case against execution for heresy was outlined.[7] Calvin related how Servetus had been forced to flee Strasbourg and Basle on account of his teaching. The first process drew to a close on 21 August with the council permitting Servetus books in order to prepare his defence and writing to Vienne in France to discover the reasons for his arrest there.

Although Servetus' quarrel was clearly with Calvin, the Frenchman's role in the process was limited. He was already enmeshed in the dispute with the magistrates over who possessed the right to excommunicate. This was a battle for control of the church. The rulers of Geneva were not about to permit Calvin to determine the course of the trial. The whole point was that they should decide whether the Spaniard lived or died. Calvin acknowledged as much in his letter to Farel.

Of the man's effrontery I will say nothing but such was his madness that he did not hesitate to say that devils possessed divinity. Indeed, that many gods were in individual devils, inasmuch as deity had been substantially communicated to those, equally with wood and stone. I hope that sentence of death will at least be passed upon him, but I desire that the severity of the punishment may be mitigated.[8]

Heresy was a capital offence, but Calvin did not want Servetus to die.

On 23 August the process resumed with Servetus required to answer thirty questions put to him by the city prosecutor, Claude Rigot, a member of the Perrinist party not well disposed towards him. Rigot rejected the terms of Servetus' plea to the council and argued that the prisoner did not need a lawyer as he could lie well enough without one.[9] He persisted in his cross-examination, suggesting to Servetus that he had been in contact with Jews and Muslims. In the meantime, a reply from Vienne requested that Servetus be returned to the city to face prosecution for heresy; Servetus pleaded to remain in Geneva. The Catholic officials had even thanked Calvin for his assistance in exposing Servetus.

The third part of the process was a discussion between Calvin and Servetus recorded in Latin. The following day Calvin prepared a statement of thirty-eight articles on which he and the Genevan ministers found Servetus' teaching heretical. Servetus replied that his views were defensible on the authority of the church fathers Irenaeus and Tertullian, and rebounded with a scathing attack on Calvin, denouncing him as an agent of the devil, and claiming that he had been misrepresented. Further, he declared that the Genevan magistrates should put Calvin to death, not him. Calvin replied with his *Brief Refutation*, signed by the other ministers. At the heart of the clash was Servetus' attack on Calvin's doctrine of God and humanity, and in particular his teachings on predestination and infant baptism. Calvin, for his part, objected vehemently to Servetus' representation of God's presence in the world in which he held, according to the reformer, that God is not separate from creation but embodied in it – a form of pantheism.

Once more the Genevan council decided to consult the other Swiss cities, and on 8 September Claude du Pan left the city with letters for Berne, Zurich and Basle. An indication of how bad things were in Geneva comes from Calvin's remark to Bullinger apologizing for the inconvenience of being drawn into the Servetus case. 'Indeed they [the council] cause you this trouble despite our admonitions, but they have reached such a state of folly and madness that they regard with suspicion whatever we say to them. So much so, that were I to allege that it is clear at mid-day they would immediately begin to doubt it!'[10]

Official letters from the council were accompanied by direct communications from Calvin to Haller, Bullinger and Sulzer. Calvin reminded Simon Sulzer in Basle of Servetus' visit to the city twenty years earlier and the damage done.[11] Calvin's letters to the Swiss churches reveal that he had acquired the measure of dealing with them. Applying his favourite principle of accommodation, he shaped each missive to suit the attitudes of his audience. Rather than present his own views directly, he reminded the Baslers of Oecolampadius and Bucer, whom Servetus had gravely offended. Similarly, he referred to Capito and the hostility of Berne, the city which had rejected Sulzer. He poked and prodded at soft points to goad the Basle church into stating its support. He had honed his skills in the endless negotiations of the 1540s and early 1550s. Without some cajoling on his part, Calvin feared that the advice to the magistrates from the Swiss cities might be so tepid as to be useless. The strategy worked. Zurich backed Geneva completely and Sulzer followed Bullinger's lead, responding with a clear denunciation of Servetus' errors. The letter was not as strong as Bullinger's, but it could have been worse, and by September, when du Pan returned, Calvin knew that the Swiss were onside.

While the Genevans awaited the replies of the Swiss, Calvin broadened the campaign against Servetus by writing to the ministers of the French community in Frankfurt.

You have doubtless heard of the name of Servetus, a Spaniard, who twenty years ago corrupted your Germany with a virulent publication, filled with many pernicious errors. This worthless man, after being driven out of Germany, and having concealed himself in France under a fictitious name, lately patched up a larger volume, partly from his former book, and partly from new figments which he had invented. This book he printed secretly at Vienne, a town in the neighbourhood of Lyon. Many copies of it had been conveyed to Frankfurt for the Easter fairs. The printer's agent, however, a pious and worthy man, on being informed that it contained nothing but a farrago of errors, suppressed whatever he had of it. It would take too long to relate with how many errors – indeed, prodigious blasphemies against God – the book abounds. Figure for yourselves a rhapsody patched up from the impious ravings of all ages. There is no form of impiety which this monster has not raked up, as if from the infernal regions. I had rather you should pass sentence on it from reading the book itself. You will certainly find on almost every single page something that will fill you with horror. The author himself is held in prison by our magistrates, and he will be punished before long, I hope, but it is your duty to see to it that this pestiferous poison does not spread further.[12]

From prison Servetus demanded clothes, books and access to a lawyer. He wanted a lawyer first and foremost because his French was not particularly good; his letters to the council in Geneva are full of Spanish, suggesting the difficulties he must have had in following his trial. He could speak to Calvin in Latin, but French was a problem even after years of living in Vienne.[13] In his petition to the council he wrote, 'You see that Calvin is at the end of his rope, not knowing what to say and for his pleasure wishes to make me rot here in prison. The lice eat me alive, my clothes are torn, and I have nothing for a change, neither jacket nor shirt, but a bad one. I have addressed you another petition which was according to God and to impede it Calvin cites Justinian.'[14] He was given clothes, at his own expense, and a copy of Calvin's *Brief Refutation*, which was probably less welcome. The books included the works of the church fathers Irenaeus and Pseudo-Clement of Rome, which Servetus read and annotated. Copies of these works remain in Geneva, along with Servetus' notes, which were placed before the council for its inspection.[15]

It was decided to write once more to the Swiss cities to seek their advice on a judgement against Servetus. This time Jaquemoz Gernoz left Geneva on 22 September bound for the Swiss cities laden with copies of Servetus' *Restitution*, the works of Tertullian and Irenaeus printed in Basle in 1528 and the discussion between Calvin and Servetus, as well as letters from the council to Swiss political leaders and churchmen. Gernoz made remarkable speed, travelling to Berne on 25 September, and arriving in Zurich on 29 September, where he remained for three days, and then journeying to Schaffhausen before reaching Basle on 9 October. All of the Swiss churches had responded with support, though there was no consensus on how Servitus should be punished. The Basle church declared that if reconciliation were not possible then Servetus should be put in prison where he could do no harm. But all agreed that the form of punishment should be left to the Genevan council. Having collected the replies Gernoz returned to Geneva on 18 October. The documents were translated and put before the council within a week.

To understand what happened next, we need to appreciate the force of the Swiss replies.[16] From Zurich Bullinger condemned Servetus as a demon from hell and wrote to Calvin that the Genevan church had been given a glorious opportunity to strike against heresy. Berne, so often at odds with Geneva, emphatically admonished the magistrates to rid the church of this pest. Even

Basle agreed that this heretic should be dealt with, but was not prepared to commit to any particular form of punishment. With such backing, the Genevan council was able to act. Servetus' fate was sealed

On 26 October the magistrates met for the last time to consider the Servetus matter, though, according to Calvin, Perrin attempted to stop the case. The council's decision was announced the following day: Servetus was unanimously condemned – he was to die. It was his teachings on the Trinity and infant baptism that were stated as his pernicious errors. Citing the unanimous decisions of the Swiss churches, the crime of heresy and the laws of Christendom, the council declared it had no choice. Calvin wrote to Farel that he had attempted at the last moment to alter the form of execution, which was to be death at the stake, but to no avail. The Frenchman had proposed the use of a sword. Calvin described how Servetus took the news. 'At first he was stunned and then sighed so as to be heard throughout the whole room; then he moaned like a madman and had no more composure than a demoniac. At length his cries so increased that he continually beat his breast and bellowed in Spanish, "Mercy! Mercy!" '[17] Servetus asked to speak with Calvin, a meeting the reformer alone has recorded. Calvin assured him that he harboured no personal animus and then, for the record, detailed his own exemplary conduct.

> I reminded him gently how I had risked my life more than sixteen years before to gain him for our saviour. I would faithfully do my best to reconcile him to all good servants of God. Although he had avoided the contest I had never ceased to remonstrate kindly with him in letters. In a word, I had used all humanity to the very end, until he being embittered by my good advice hurled all manner of rage and anger against me.[18]

This was the end. 'So following the rule of Paul', Calvin added, 'I withdrew from the heretic who is self-condemned.'

Calvin had wanted Servetus to recant, not die, and in that respect victory belonged to the Spaniard. Farel accompanied Servetus to the place of execution, attempting to the last to gain a confession that Christ was the true Son of God. Servetus walked in silence. Straw and leaves sprinkled with sulphur were placed on his head and he was chained to the stake. His arms tied behind his back, he had the fire shown to him before it was tossed on to the wood. According to one source Servetus shrieked in horror. His last words were 'O Jesus, Son of the Eternal God, have pity on me!' – crucially, not 'eternal Son of God'. In half an hour he was dead at the age of forty-four.

Almost a year after the execution, Philip Melanchthon wrote to Calvin, 'I have read your answer to the blasphemies of Servetus and approve of your piety and opinions. I judge also that the Genevan Senate acted correctly to put an end to this obstinate man, who could never cease blaspheming. And I wonder at those who disapprove of this severity.'[19] Calvin replied thanking him for his friendship and support in crushing the heretic.

Why had the Protestant reformers so readily agreed to the execution of Servetus? To address that question we have to shed modern sensibilities and enter the world of the sixteenth century. By the early 1550s the Protestant Reformation was facing a resurgent Catholic church which at the Council of Trent was clearly defining its theology and discipline. The Protestant churches continued to be severely damaged by accusations that they were spawning heresy and heretics. The unwanted Servetus case came at a vital moment when Protestantism was forced to define itself against heresy. Failure to condemn Servetus and his evident denial of fundamental doctrines of the Christian Church would have been catastrophic. Having waged a long battle against what he regarded as idolatry, Calvin could not have turned a blind eye. To the Protestant churchmen of the sixteenth century, of all the plagues that struck their cities heresy was the most heinous.

But what of Calvin personally? He certainly played an important role in the process, urging his Swiss colleagues to support a severe sentence. His visceral hatred of Servetus was all too clear. He was determined to triumph over this man, and in debate he demolished him. He wanted Servetus convicted and probably, by the end, dead. The trial only escalated their mutual hostility. But Calvin could not have Servetus executed. That was the decision of a council not well disposed towards the Frenchman and with which he was locked in battle over excommunication. Servetus provided an opportunity for the magistrates to demonstrate their authority over Calvin, and that is perhaps why his request that the condemned man be put to the sword was rejected. The magistrates understood clearly that harbouring or exonerating a heretic would blacken Geneva's name across Europe. Servetus was a dead man the moment he was recognized in the church service.

Calvin the Executioner?

As soon as the Servetus process began in Geneva, opposition to Calvin stirred. Its focal point was Basle. Although in his letter to Sulzer Calvin had asked that the Baslers be properly informed of what had happened, there were other sources of information, and they were frequently hostile. Rumours quickly spread that Servetus had been arrested with the help of Calvin, and when the humanist Celio Secundo Curione arrived back in Basle in the middle of September he brought information gathered during stays in Graubünden and Zurich on his return journey from Italy. Graubünden, what is today eastern Switzerland, contained numerous Italian evangelical communities which provided an important link between Italy and northern Europe. Many humanists in Basle were Italian refugees who saw this case as nothing less than a return to the persecution they had fled, and not a few harboured sympathies for Servetus' ideas.[20]

One such figure was Matteo Gribaldi, a former professor of law in Padau who had taken citizenship in Basle and was a close colleague of Bonifacius Amerbach.[21] Gribaldi's religious views were anti-Trinitarian in character and in sympathy with Servetus, whose works he had read, claiming he would never have known Christ otherwise. He had been in Geneva at the beginning of the process before returning to Basle with a negative account of Calvin and the trial. Echoing Servetus, he held that no one should be punished on account of false teaching, and that heretics should certainly not be put to death. Gribaldi had attempted to meet Calvin while in Geneva and discuss the matter, but the Frenchman had refused. When Gribaldi arrived in Basle he was greatly honoured and fêted along with his fellow Italian Curione with a civic banquet. Together with Curione, Amerbach, Castellio and the printers Oporinus and Pietro Perna, Gribaldi followed the Servetus case closely.[22] On 28 September 1553 Simon Sulzer wrote to Bullinger that feelings in Basle were strongly against Calvin: David Joris, the Dutch radical living incognito in the city, spoke openly of the pious Michael Servetus and wrote that if Servetus were really a heretic then he should be admonished fraternally.[23] When news of the execution reached Basle, Calvin was instantly vilified.

In the days following the execution several notable figures left Geneva to travel to Basle where they joined the chorus of dissent. One was Jean Colinet, a teacher at the Genevan grammar school despised by Calvin, who described him as having caused confusion in the Genevan church for five years; their relationship had not improved when Calvin learned that Colinet had labelled the Genevan clergy hypocrites. Colinet was dismissed from the Collège de la Rive on account of his support for his predecessor Sebastian Castellio – he had written a preface to one of the Savoyard's works. He was cited before the Consistory on the very day that Servetus was executed.[24] Next was Léger Grymoult, a former Augustinian from La Rochelle who had been arrested for heresy in France before arriving in Geneva in 1547, where he tutored the three sons of the prominent du Villard family. He had gone to Basle in 1552 to study at the university, where he came in contact with Amerbach, Martin Borrhaus, professor and rector of the university, and Castellio. Deeply attracted to Castellio's teaching, Grymoult began editing the Savoyard's writings. He was back in Geneva at the time of the execution and was shocked by what he witnessed. He left the city and went to Zurich, where he complained about the case before the mayor. The clergy of Zurich, however, were hostile and Grymoult was required to leave, returning to Basle. Another figure was the Dutchman Pieter Anastasius de Zuttere (Hyperphragmus) from Ghent, who had fled his homeland in 1551/2 and come into the Swiss lands. He claimed to have been in Geneva for the execution, though that is uncorroborated, and in 1557 he wrote a *History of the Death of Servetus* as well as verses in French about the Spaniard. He maintained he had rescued copies of Servetus' work, and following his flight from Geneva he stayed at the castle at Veigy with the nobleman Jacques de Falais, Calvin's former friend with whom he had fallen out dramatically in the early 1550s.[25]

In Basle another *History of the Death of Servetus* appeared, claiming to be drawn from eyewitness accounts.[26] Possibly written by Castellio, the detailed history analysed the motives of the participants: Ami Perrin, it was said, had not wished to be part of the bloodletting, while Calvin naturally came across very badly. After the holy death, when Servetus cried out, 'Jesus Christ, have mercy on me,' Calvin was said to have smiled. The second part of the text provided arguments against the execution of heretics and revisited some uncomfortable truths. Calvin had relied upon the judgement of the other Swiss churches, yet in matters of doctrine he had judged them, and not favourably. It was well known, the text proclaimed, that he had once joined with Luther in rejecting the teaching of Zwingli and Oecolampadius on the Lord's Supper. This was the same argument Bolsec had employed. In short, Calvin was accused of hypocrisy. He was named in killing Servetus, an act of mendacity as far removed from the teaching of Christ as possible and worthy only of the reviled Roman church. Calvin and Rome, the *History* continued, were akin to Herod and Pilate. Predestination was never far from the list of Calvin's execrable errors. If his teaching of double predestination was really true, and the author made clear his doubts, then the logical conclusion was that the faithful had nothing to fear from Servetus. Calvin had acted in desperation, determined that Servetus' body should not be honoured, just as the Jews had feared Christ. If Calvin really wanted to dispute with Servetus, he should have done so in a manner that permitted Servetus to reply.

In the period following the execution a 'Servetus party' emerged, not only in Basle, but also in Graubünden and Italian lands, largely composed of scholars. Many of these men were solitary figures on the margins. In Basle, however, there was a more coherent and recognizable body, including figures within the Italian community led by Curione, the Savoyard Sebastian Castellio, the circle around David Joris, and university students. Castellio complained that the official Basle response, which had supported Calvin, had been written by a small number of ministers who had excluded those such as himself, Curione and Borrhaus, whom Calvin did not trust. Calvin, Castellio was certain, had orchestrated the Basle reply and his malign influence was everywhere. Although Calvin's opponents were few in number, they possessed the enormous advantage of access to the printing press. With men like Oporinus and Perna onside, they could get their views into print and tell a very different story from Calvin's. The prevailing mood among these men was that the execution was a gross injustice for which they blamed not the Genevan council but Calvin himself. They chose to believe, in contradiction of the facts, that Calvin had been able to decide Servetus' fate. An ally of Calvin in Basle told Bullinger on 28 October that many claimed the Frenchman had behaved as though he were the executioner.[27]

Reluctantly Bullinger emerged as a pivotal figure, trusted by both the Italians and the Genevans and frequently consulted for his views and for information. As a result of the presence of leading scholars such as Konrad Gesner and Theodor Bibliander, a known critic of Calvin's theology, Zurich was regarded more favourably by the Italians than Geneva. Bullinger, Farel and Viret were all aware of this growing network of opposition and began to worry. Calvin wrote to Bullinger that he intended to defend himself, a tack the Zurich churchman supported, but with the admonition that Calvin should not name any of his opponents in Basle. There were many pious people in that city, Bullinger warned, and Calvin should not be seen to be writing against the whole church because of a few 'perversi'.[28] On 11 December Calvin appeared before the Genevan council and was granted permission to prepare his defence.

Writing with great speed, Calvin presented his response two weeks later to the council, which appointed four representatives to examine it. Entitled *Defence of the Orthodox Faith against the Errors of Michel Servetus* it was not his best work. The signs of haste were evident and the argument lacked his usual fluency. The message, however, was uncompromising. There was no greater error among servants of Satan than Servetus' false doctrine.[29] Calvin wrote that he had initially hoped that the sheer ridiculousness of Servetus' positions would have persuaded reasonable people to dismiss them, but sadly that had not happened. Calvin was aware of the miasmic nature of the opposition, and outlined three specific goals: to demonstrate the divergent and confused arguments among those who claimed to be Servetus' followers; to dispel the false rumours about his actions; and to deal with the spread of Servetus' views among the Italian exile community.[30] The central question, however, was the right of magistrates to punish a heretic. He quoted Servetus' works extensively but added that the Spaniard had not acted alone. There were other 'fanatics' who opposed the punishment of heretics, and by this he meant his old foe Castellio. Calvin accepted that God does not call Christians to kill, and that the Kingdom of God is advanced by preaching and not the sword, but robustly maintained the fundamental difference between coercing people to believe and defence of true doctrine and the Church. Indeed, Christ brought the sword of the Word, not violence, but the Bible provides authority for the use of force: in Acts 5 Peter had Ananias and Saphira punished with death for lying, while Paul rendered the magician Elymas blind, and even Christ himself used force to cleanse the temple. Princes have an obligation to preserve the unity of the Church with the sword, and Calvin attacked the idea that gentleness was appropriate in dealing with false teaching, for it fostered the misguided belief that error should be tolerated. The role of the magistrate was to maintain the order of the community by defending its foundation, true religion.[31]

Calvin's work was less an apology for his Trinitarian theology than an assault on his critics. Reception of the book was divided. In Berne Niklaus Zurkinden was especially critical, arguing that Calvin could have done the papists no greater service than follow their example in condemning opponents.[32] Zurkinden was a distinguished citizen, having served as secretary to the council and as governor of Noyon. He knew well the Pays de Vaud where he possessed an extended network of friends. Although close to Calvin and a crucial contact in Berne, in February 1554 he expressed his disquiet at the Frenchman's views concerning religious toleration.[33] Calvin complained to Bullinger that he was being portrayed by his opponents as an agent of death who sought to murder with his pen.[34]

Against the Doubters

At precisely this moment a book entitled *Concerning Heretics and Whether They Are to Be Persecuted* appeared in Basle written by one 'Martin Bellius' and directed against Calvin's principal arguments.[35] Bellius was a pseudonym for

Sebastian Castellio, the learned humanist driven from Geneva by Calvin in the early 1540s. *Concerning Heretics* was a collection of texts drawn from the writings of various reformers in which they opposed the death penalty for heretics, but the most significant part was the preface by Bellius. At its core was the warning that one should be very careful about who is named a heretic, for Christ himself had been executed on such a charge. Secondly, heretics should not be treated more harshly than church discipline requires. Magistrates were to punish thieves and murderers and protect the faithful, but their authority did not extend to theology. They should also not persecute anyone for the sake of faith. The last section of the book, by Basilius Montfortius (Castellio again), rejected Calvin's appeal to Deuteronomy, countering that the injunction to kill false prophets did not apply to heretics. The words of Christ that his enemies be tolerated till the end of time were to be followed; it did not fall to humans to divide the faithful from the unfaithful. Like Calvin's *Defence* the work was quickly translated into French, all the more worrying for Geneva.

The book was printed by Oporinus and financed by the Marquess Bonifacio d'Oria in Naples and it is possible that David Joris had a hand in its composition. Castellio could also call upon the support of Borrhaus, Amerbach and Thomas Platter, close friends and men well placed to provide him with intellectual and financial means. Amerbach was an executor of Erasmus' will and offered Castellio a regular, though modest, stipend from the Dutch humanist's estate. When Oporinus published the work he gave the place of publication as Magdeburg – possibly to invoke the authority of the city which had resisted Charles V's attempts to suppress heresy.[36] Calvin, however, recognized the elegant style of his hated adversary. 'A short time ago a book was also published clandestinely at Basle in which under feigned names Castellio and Curione argue that heretics ought not to be repressed by the sword. Would that the ministers of that church at length, though late, could arouse themselves to prevent the evil from spreading wider.'[37] At the start of 1555 Calvin spoke of the work once more as he wrote to the church at Poitiers, referring to Castellio and his followers as the 'New Academy' who, as followers of Socrates, sought 'in the unholy freedom of doubt to destroy the whole religion'.[38]

Three linked but distinct issues united Calvin's opponents: revulsion at the Servetus execution, rejection of the broader principle of punishing heretics, and hatred of his doctrine of predestination. Following Castellio's work the next provocation was Celio Secundo Curione's *Concerning the Amplitude of the Blessed Kingdom of God*, an attack on Calvin's doctrine of predestination that never mentioned the Frenchman by name.[39] In Geneva an anonymous letter in French appeared addressed to the syndic Vandel which condemned the teaching of Calvin and the Swiss reformers on predestination. The references to Calvin were highly personal and he appeared before the council in the summer of 1554 to state that he could not remain in office if the magistrates did not support him against these calumnies. The threat worked and the council stood behind him, though not quite as resolutely as he demanded.[40] The author of the letter has never come to light, but Calvin's narrowed eyes turned on Castellio.[41]

Although nothing had been done in Basle to prevent the publication of *Concerning Heretics*, by 1554 Calvin had gained some leverage in the city. When Castellio published a Latin translation of the Bible, his notes for Romans 9: 13 ('Just as it is written "Jacob I have loved, but Esau I have hated" ') formed a virulent attack on Calvin's doctrine of predestination. What gave the matter added urgency was news that the notes had been printed separately and were circulating in France in both Latin and the vernacular. Calvin demanded that the Basle authorities act, and they did. The notes were removed from the second edition of the Bible and Castellio was brought before the censors to face his one-time friend Martin Borrhaus, who was now supporting Calvin.[42]

The debate over the treatment of heretics remained unresolved, and despite growing pressure in Basle from censors in the 1550s Castellio and Curione persevered. Castellio prepared a bitter attack on Calvin's *Defence* in which he rejected every aspect of the Genevan's account of the Servetus trial. Unlike others, Castellio's purpose was not to defend Servetus' thought, which he recognized as heretical. That was not the point. The question was whether a heretic could be punished by civil officials. Like Calvin, Castellio was looking towards France, and their debate was anything but abstract. The question of whether rulers had the right to put heretics to death was of immediate consequence for evangelicals in France who looked to the king for protection. If the evangelicals were branded heretics then Calvin's argument played into the hands of the king and justified executions. Castellio's case for toleration and a separation of religious sentiments from civil authority was far more attractive to those facing persecution. Geneva was aware of the seductive appeal of Castellio's ideas and responded with venom.

Castellio's *Against the Book of Calvin* cast Servetus as a doubter, not as a man who sought to destroy true religion, and repudiated once more the idea that people should be put to death for the sake of doctrine.[43] It was not printed and remained in manuscript for another fifty years before appearing in the Dutch Republic in the early seventeenth century. Most likely, Castellio wrote it for circulation among his friends and supporters, though Geneva was aware of its existence and Calvin entrusted Theodore Beza with the response, a measure of his growing trust and confidence in his friend. Beza's *Antibellius*, printed by Robert Estienne in September 1554, attacked the 'Academicians' for employing the mask of toleration to conceal their betrayal of church reform.[44] The term 'Academician' had been used by Calvin previously against his opponents and was a reference to those members of Plato's Academy after the philosopher's death who cultivated scepticism. Cicero had belonged to this tradition, as did the young Augustine, who late in life repudiated scepticism in his *Against the Academicians*.[45] Beza described the modern Academicians as those who spoke of mildness and generosity but in truth undermined everything for which those who had borne witness to faith had suffered. He despised what he saw as their refusal to commit to doctrine under the guise of avoiding disputes, for this was nothing less than a betrayal of the Church. It was a work that could not go unanswered and Castellio took up his pen once more to refute the accusations, though he essentially repeated the arguments found earlier in *Concerning Heretics*. Once more the work remained unprinted, circulating instead in manuscript among a smaller circle.

The last phase of the polemical war between Calvin and Castellio lasted from 1556 to 1558 and was dominated by the doctrine of predestination. The campaign opened at the end of 1556 with the appearance of Theodore Beza's Latin New Testament in which he remorselessly attacked Castellio's translation for the manner in which it sought to render biblical stories and language in pagan forms.[46] Castellio, for example, believed that had Moses lived in ancient Rome he would have spoken as a great orator, so he rendered Moses' words in an elegant classical style, which Calvin and Beza found execrable. Two more contrasting views of scripture could not be found. Castellio, the humanist and spiritualist, saw the Bible primarily as a human, literary text which was dead apart from the Spirit. He could therefore take such extraordinary steps as to insert passages from the Jewish historian Josephus (37–c. 100) into the Bible to fill in the narrative. Nothing could have enraged Calvin more than such liberty with sacred scripture.

Matters deteriorated further in November 1557 when Philip Melanchthon wrote to Castellio expressing sympathy for the manner in which he had been treated.[47] No names were mentioned, but for Calvin this was nothing less than betrayal. Melanchthon had supported Calvin in the execution of Servetus, though some time later he had begun to change his mind. When he met Beza at a religious colloquy in Worms, he expressed his concern that some among

Calvin's circle were too given to doctrinal intransigence.[48] When Calvin learned of Melanchthon's offer of friendship to Castellio he became incandescent with rage. His wrath fell on Hubert Languet, a French colleague once the go-between for Basle and Wittenberg, whom he charged with deceiving Melanchthon and spreading Castellio's good name through France like poison. Calvin believed that Languet was a front man for his former secretary François Bauduin, who had been critical both of Calvin's earlier treatment of Castellio and of the doctrine of predestination.[49]

Calvin's last blast against Castellio, printed in January 1558, was his most vicious, describing the Savoyard as a thief, liar, and a traitor. Yet as the abuse heaped up there was a palpable sense of frustration that he, God's prosecutor, had not been able to finish off his opponent. He had never succeeded in having Castellio condemned in Basle, nor had he been able to discredit him. After all the hammer blows from Geneva, Castellio survived. He died one year before Calvin and was buried in the Basle Münster, a privilege accorded to university professors, but like his Genevan opponent his last months were marked by severe illness and relentless attacks from opponents. Exhausted and emaciated, he went to his grave at forty-eight, seven years younger than Calvin. Inside a year, the French reformation lost its two greatest literary figures, freed to reconcile in the next world.

The trial and execution of Michael Servetus made Calvin an international figure for all the wrong reasons. For his opponents, he had come to represent the failure of the Reformation, demonstrating the extent to which the Protestant churches, once founded on the principle of scripture alone and justification by faith, had degenerated into institutions of power and vested interests that served the state. Whatever the legal merits of the case and the truth of Calvin's role, the story assumed an extremely damaging life of its own. Opposition to Calvin, in the form of a diverse collection of persons, coalesced around the issue of Servetus and the right to execute heretics. They may have been small in number, but they proved highly effective in disseminating their views. Yet, for all the opposition, the attacks on Calvin following the Servetus case did not dislodge him, largely because the Swiss Reformed churches had backed him. The relationship with Bullinger cultivated in the 1540s sustained him through the dark years of the early 1550s as he faced the disputes over excommunication and Servetus. He may have grown sceptical of winning the Swiss to a more active role in the evangelizing of France, but he never forgot who kept him in Geneva.

CHAPTER FOURTEEN

Luther's Heirs

IF ONE were to admire Calvin for nothing else, his ability to sustain the relentless onslaught of the 1550s is astonishing. Generally 1555 is seen as the crucial moment of transition, when he and his supporters vanquished the Perrinists and took control of Geneva. Yet history can grace events with an inevitability by no means self-evident to the protagonists. Such was the case in Geneva. Victory remained balanced on a knife edge till the last moment, and for Calvin the maelstrom of politics in the city was accompanied by bitter feuds with opponents spread across German, Swiss and French lands. The enemies kept coming and the reformer was required to attack and defend in equal measure. Less spectacularly, but more ominously, by the middle of the decade the daily grind of work was taking a dreadful toll. Only forty-six years old, and deeply wounded by the backlash following the death of Servetus and the support for Sebastian Castellio, Calvin reflected in late 1555 on a life that he could hardly bear to live.

Believe me, I had fewer troubles with Servetus and have now with Westphal and his like than I have with those who are close at hand, whose numbers are beyond reckoning and whose passions are irreconcilable. If one could choose, it would be better to be burned once by the papists than to be plagued for eternity by one's neighbours. They do not allow me a moment's rest, although they can clearly see that I am collapsing under the burden of work, troubled by endless sad occurrences, and disturbed by intrusive demands. My one comfort is that death will soon take me from this all too difficult service.[1]

This Westphal was a little-known Hamburg Lutheran minister whose 1552 *Farrago of Confused and Divergent Opinions on the Lord's Supper Taken from the Books of the Sacramentarians* assembled selections from the works of a range of Protestant reformers, such as Karlstadt, Zwingli, Oecolampadius and Bucer, with the malign intent of demonstrating their disagreement on the Eucharist.[2] In particular, Westphal took aim at Calvin's *Short Treatise on the Lord's Supper* (1541) and his commentary on 1 Corinthians (1546), and inducted the Frenchman into what he regarded as a gallery of heretical rogues, alongside the hated Zwinglians. Theologically, Westphal adhered to the doctrine of ubiquity with its emphasis on the real presence of the resurrected Christ in the bread and wine. This, he believed, made him a true disciple of the departed Martin Luther against the corrupting forces of Melanchthon and Calvin, whose colours as a Zwinglian Westphal saw in the Consensus Tigurinus.

Luther's death and the defeat of German Protestants by Charles V led to a theological bloodbath. Lutherans split into two camps: the Philippists (named after Melanchthon) and the Gnesio (or true) Lutherans, both of which claimed the reformer's inheritance. Matters came to a head in 1548 when Melanchthon, with others, introduced what became known as the Leipzig Interim in Saxony permitting the reintroduction of certain Catholic rituals he regarded as having no effect on the faith. Such concessions to Rome enraged the Gnesio-Lutherans, who vilified Melanchthon. A leading figure was the talented and antagonistic Croat Matthias Flacius Illyricus, once one of Melanchthon's greatest prodigies and now his sworn enemy. Melanchthon spoke of having raised a viper in the nest. Westphal, a far less talented figure, was part of the northern German group of Lutherans which opposed Melanchthon's supposed collaboration with the Catholics and in 1549 he published an attack on the Wittenberg professor accusing him of having betrayed Luther. Calvin made an ill-advised venture into this debate that year, writing to the beleaguered Melanchthon and offering with one hand his friendship and the smack of a rebuke with the other.[3] Melanchthon, Calvin suggested, was prepared to accept too many Catholic practices for the sake of peace. If that was the case, Melanchthon's response to the letter from Geneva was anything but pacific: he is said to have ripped it up.

For almost thirty years following Luther's death the movement which bore his name became locked in a civil war. The Gnesio-Lutherans detested and reviled Melanchthon for numerous offences which seemed to run in opposite directions. He had conceded too much to the Catholics with the Leipzig

Interim and was suspected of harbouring Reformed ideas of the Lord's Supper. When Westphal turned on the Consensus Tigurinus his assault was only in part aimed at Calvin and Bullinger. They were not major players in the empire. It was primarily a means of attacking Melanchthon by associating him with heresy. A familiar story.

Calvin became aware of Westphal's text only in the spring of 1554 when Bullinger referred to a controversy in German lands in which the Consensus was under attack. Consumed with conflicts at home and abroad, not least with those concerning Servetus and Castellio, Calvin was hardly inclined to enter what must have seemed a minor fray and pondered aloud whether it was worthwhile responding. Nevertheless, he told Bullinger that, if the latter desired, he would set aside three days to write something.[4] Bullinger, eager to avoid controversy, thought the matter should rest, but Calvin warmed to the idea of a reply, presumably once he had read Westphal's work and had grasped its implications. In April he wrote once more to Zurich: 'Even though nothing can be imagined more insipid than that lightweight book of Westphal, nevertheless, since we see the souls of princes corrupted by such calumnies, and we recently had a sad example of it in the King of Denmark, it seems to be our duty to use all allowable means.'[5]

Calvin was referring to the plight of Dutch refugees from England under the leadership of the Polish nobleman John a Lasco, who had settled in Denmark only to be expelled by the king for refusing to accept the Lutheran doctrine and discipline of the Danish church.[6] Lasco had written to the reformers from Emden describing the desperate plight of the migrants and enclosed a copy of Westphal's attack on the Consensus Tigurinus.[7] This remarkable Polishman had played a prominent part in the origins of the conflict: in 1552 he had published a series of sermons critical of Luther's teaching on the Lord's Supper and supportive of the Consensus. Westphal was horrified that what he regarded as the purity of Luther's teaching was being impugned and that the Consensus might form the basis for future discussions between Lutherans and the Reformed. His *Farrago* was followed in 1553 by *Right Belief Concerning the Lord's Supper* in which he defended the Lutheran doctrine of ubiquity.[8] By the spring of 1554 Westphal's name regularly appeared in the news travelling between Geneva and Zurich: Beza wrote to Bullinger concerning Castellio, adding that he was now reading Westphal, another work of the devil.[9]

Calvin's disposition was clear. 'You will learn', he wrote to Farel, 'in what savage a manner these madmen conduct themselves, who, under the name of

Luther, attack us. Shortly you will receive more details, which I have not yet had the leisure to peruse.'[10] Westphal, he unwisely assumed, was a lone voice who did not represent the mainstream Lutheran thought embodied in Melanchthon's *Variata* of the Augsburg Confession. Calvin had willingly signed the *Variata* in 1540 and continued to believe that his doctrine of the Lord's Supper held nothing contrary to it. He was working with two misguided assumptions: that Westphal was an 'ape', a view shared by Bullinger, and that Lutherans on the whole were sympathetic to Calvin's views of the Lord's Supper.

Defending the Agreement

If there were to be a reply, Calvin was adamant, it would have to be in the name of all the Reformed churches. He was prepared to undertake it, but not alone. Bullinger began to accept the idea, no doubt fired by old enmities. 'The Lutherans', he wrote, 'a contentious and ruinous lot of men without understanding and culture, are persecuting us more than the papists. They are renewing an interrupted battle. . . . I doubt whether we should continue to gloss over their savage and illiterate writings. Westphal – that true Westphalian, a stupid and barbarous man – published another book on the Lord's Supper besides the *Farrago*, in which he lashed out at our orthodox teaching on the Supper.'[11] Bullinger offered to send his copy of the work to Geneva so that the two men could work together. With laconic understatement Calvin noted on the letter, 'he is beginning to think the matter over'. For once Calvin played the cool head. In reply to Lasco he explained the reformers' ambivalence.

Despite encouraging words to Lasco, Calvin was not fully persuaded that he wanted to take up the quill. The delicacy of the moment was evident. To enter into a debate with the Lutherans would gravely imperil hopes of further negotiations, but if he failed to defend the Consensus he would lose the Swiss. The speed at which he was producing texts on various topics must have taxed even Calvin's brain. He thought little of Westphal's writing and intellect, and wondered whether an acolyte might discharge the task, thinking of either Lasco or Pierre Viret. The response to Westphal, he wrote to Viret, 'does not require any singularly keen intellect, nor great learning, nor any meticulous application; it only needs faith and ordinary cleverness.'[12] In other words, a lesser man than Calvin could do it. What Viret made of this offer to use his 'ordinary cleverness' is not known, but after more than a decade of acting as Calvin's agent in the Vaud he would have been familiar with the expectation that he should pick up bones pitched from Geneva.

In fact Calvin did the work himself and sent a draft in September to Bullinger for comment. He warned the Zurich minister that the text was not especially polished and that there might be grounds for criticism. He cautioned Bullinger that not everything he read would please his eye. 'I have one fear that you might think that I have sometimes granted them more than I should. I have deliberately done this so that if any even now should remain opposed to us then their obstinacy is hateful. Also, so that the learned who are in agreement with us and whom I see to be less courageous than is fitting, may have an appropriate excuse.'[13] The last point was a reference to Melanchthon, whose silence in the affair was deafening. Westphal's tactic had been to contrast the language of the Consensus Tigurinus with Calvin's earlier writings on the Lord's Supper, where he had spoken in very different tones. Although he had never accepted the Lutheran doctrine of ubiquity, Calvin's affinity with Strasbourg and Melanchthon was evident to all. As previous opponents had done, Westphal presented Calvin's new-found closeness to Zurich as wholly inconsistent with his earlier antagonism towards Zwingli's theology. In the Consensus he had swallowed his words for the sake of agreement. Westphal may indeed have been a Westphalean, but he was not stupid: he confronted Calvin with the discrepancies in his own writings and the Frenchman had to do some fast talking. To achieve this, Calvin reckoned, he would have to abandon his slightly supine relationship to Zurich and defend the Consensus on his own terms.

Once more, Calvin's experience in dealing with the Swiss served him well, and his letter of 8 October to the Reformed churches was a *tour de force*. He presented their undeniable differences and disagreements in terms of the unity of Christ's Church. He both played to the sensitivities of the Zurich church concerning their rejection by Luther and made it clear that he was not prepared to abandon his own understanding of the sacrament. It was incumbent upon the Reformed churches to reply, because internal 'bickering' served only their opponents. And then, in a distinct Calvinian tone, he added, 'since all dissimulation is base and opens the way for many evils, let learned and prudent men decide whether they should counter those attacks that do so much damage to the Church'.[14] 'Bickering parties' was a gentle reference to the Swiss, whom Calvin regarded as too unwilling to engage in any meaningful discussion with the Lutherans, while the dissimulator was, without doubt, Melanchthon.

Calvin launched an attack on Westphal's use of the term 'sacramentarian', commonly employed by the Lutherans to defame the Zwinglians. If what was meant was an 'empty ritual' of the Lord's Supper, in which Christ is only present symbolically, then no one, he argued, could rightly be accused of this offence, for 'which of us does not maintain that there is something real figured under the sacred symbols?' This must have had the Zurichers shifting in their seats. The 'us' to whom Calvin referred were not simply those who had agreed to the Consensus, but also those who embraced the whole tradition of Swiss Reformed theology. Much of the force of Westphal's attack resided in his use of the old trick of compiling texts to illuminate disagreement among the Reformers. Castellio had done the same in *Concerning Heretics*, tendentiously linking 'soundbites' of the reformers to suggest a consensus.

This was a construct that Calvin knew he had to pull down. The differences between the reformers, he countered, lay not in theology, but in modes of expression.

> And yet I do not conceal that he [Westphal] afterwards collects different opinions which, though they are not in reality irreconcilable, do never-theless present the appearance of contradiction. But first, if an argument has been expressed by anyone incidentally he maliciously lays hold of it as if it were a full definition. Next, when every man has, and should be allowed to have, his own way of expressing himself, he unfairly, not to say barbarously, imposes on all the necessity not only of saying the same thing, but also in the same manner.

For Calvin to argue that the differences between the reformers over the Lord's Supper was merely a matter of expression was remarkable enough, but he pressed his claim further. 'Nor, if those excellent and distinguished servants of Christ, Zwingli and Oecolampadius were still alive would they change a single word in that resolution [the Consensus]. For that man of glorious memory, Martin Bucer, in a letter to me, when he had read it congratulated according to his piety the whole Church.'

Calvin the peacemaker, however, would only bend so far. His defence of the Swiss and their agreement came at a price, and it was high. He met the Swiss by praising Zwingli, something he never did publicly, but they had to accept the legacy of Bucer, whom Bullinger had cold-shouldered for almost twenty years. The Swiss were required to acknowledge a position on the Lord's Supper which favoured Calvin's spiritual interpretation of the sacrament as well as his admiration for Martin Luther, whom he was not prepared to reject. In other words, Calvin would embark on this task in the name of their churches if the

Swiss could bring themselves to talk to those true disciples of the Protestant faith among the Lutherans, for whom Westphal was an abhorrent monster.

While Calvin awaited the reply from the Swiss he offered Farel a candid assessment of what would happen.

> I shrewdly suspect the Bernese in their usual way will excuse themselves by alleging that they did not receive the permission of their senate. Timidity alone will not prevent them, but they will also abstain because they had rather foster dissent in silence than communicate frankly to one another what they think. If we obtain however at Zurich what I expect, they will have to be urged with importunity to give their adherence. It will then be your business to be quick with Bullinger that he may extort something. I do not doubt that we shall have the worthy [Ambrosius] Blaurer with us, and not only from his piety and learning will he support us, but from his singular courtesy and excessive affection for me, he will also extol with eulogiums the feeble tract which you too have praised too liberally. Nothing will retard the inhabitants of Basle except the bland temper of Sulzer, who takes pleasure in caressing and coaxing everybody. But God will direct all these things.[15]

When the Zurichers received Calvin's text they went through it with a fine-tooth comb. He had suggested in a collegial spirit that they might want to examine his words carefully, but his Swiss colleagues took the task with utter seriousness and the Zurich ministers drew up a long list of significant revisions. In particular they were alarmed by the harshness of Calvin's *ad hominem* attack on Westphal in which he described the German as a 'beast'. The Zurichers feared the impact of such name-calling on relations with those in the German lands who remained favourable to the Reformed church. Polemic was an art Calvin had long mastered to good effect, but on the whole he had previously avoided making it personal. With Westphal he had indeed mocked and ridiculed his opponent's character. He was himself still locked in battle with Castellio and the opponents of the Servetus execution in which his person was continuously impugned. These were ugly days.

Language was one thing, but Calvin's favourable account of Luther was almost too much for Zurich to endure. The Frenchman had attempted to demonstrate that Westphal was not faithful to Luther's teaching, an argument unlikely to sit well with Bullinger, who sharply reminded him that 'you ascribe to Luther a teaching, which, if alive, he would not acknowledge, nor which the Lutherans, so bewitched by that man's writings, acknowledge today. . . . Perhaps, dear brother, you do not know how crassly and barbarously Luther felt and wrote about this spiritual banquet.' And then to remind Calvin who was in charge, 'you have not been able to read or understand his books since he wrote most of this type in German'.[16] For Calvin's benefit the Zurichers provided Latin translations from German of what they regarded as the most offensive passages. Bullinger rather patronizingly suggested that Calvin was not familiar with the whole story.

A bundle of documents was returned to Geneva and by the middle of October Calvin had revised his text, only one week after receiving the reply. He was evidently somewhat bemused by the slightly schoolboy manner in which he had been treated, but did not allow irritation to get the better of him. In principle, the Zurichers had made it clear that they would stand by him, and, no doubt mindful of their timely support in the Bolsec and Servetus cases, he was more than ready to take his medicine. He removed much of the offensive language against Westphal, though he refused to avoid mentioning him by name. Likewise, he varied the language on Luther so as to be less inflammatory. To Bullinger he wrote, 'I have always followed your advice. . . . If this is still not satisfactory I am prepared to bury it [the work]. . . . If it is satisfactory we ought not delay in having it printed.'[17] On certain points, however, he was not prepared to yield ground. Although he modified his comments on Luther, admitting that the Wittenberg reformer had been far too polemical against the Swiss in his 'ill humour', he retained his praise, 'to promote what may best secure peace'.[18] Calvin also defended his favourable account of the Augsburg Variata as well as his description of Christ as 'really' present in the sacrament.

The short fifty-two-page book, written in the name of the Swiss ministers, appeared in early 1555 with the title *The Defence of the Sound and Orthodox Doctrine of the Sacraments*, printed by Robert Estienne. Calvin was pleased with his accomplishment and sent around copies of the *Defence* to friends in the Reformed churches, and their response was equally gratifying. His strategy, however, went beyond the boundaries of the Swiss Confederation. He had hoped to isolate Westphal from the other German Lutherans and this meant, above all, Melanchthon. Calvin desperately wanted Melanchthon's approval of the work and he wrote to him in March 1555, 'I now eagerly await your opinion.'

'Let Nothing Be Done from Contention'

It was John a Lasco who had drawn Calvin's attention to Westphal's first book, and the whole matter remained closely interwoven with the fate of those religious exiles who had left England following the accession of Mary in 1553. The reign of Edward VI had offered refuge to French evangelicals and an exile, or stranger, church had been founded in London to serve the community, as well as visiting merchants.[19] This came to an end with the king's death and the French went to Wesel on the Rhine, where they were led by François Perussel, former minister of the London exile church. Relations with the local Lutherans proved troublesome and Perussel sought Calvin's advice on whether it was acceptable for those of the Reformed faith to conform to Lutheran practices. Calvin, echoing the position of Melanchthon in the Leipzig Interim, replied that these were external matters of indifference.[20] The reply shocked Perussel, who thought that Calvin had misunderstood the doctrinal differences between the Reformed and Lutherans, and that such a compromise was unthinkable.[21] There was division in the community as Lasco had offered contradictory advice, stating that no compromise with the Lutherans was acceptable.

In the spring of 1554 the scene shifted to Frankfurt, where French exiles arrived to a fairly warm welcome. The initial group, under the leadership of Valérand Poullain, consisted of twenty-four families, but by the end of 1555 numbers had swelled to over five thousand, more than 10 per cent of the population. The Lutheran ministers in Frankfurt were horrified and did their best to stir local resentments, particularly among merchants, against the refugee community, the majority of which was French speaking and had come from London. In the spring of 1555 John a Lasco arrived to organize the community. For the Frankfurt magistrates the situation was complicated. The exiles were Reformed, not Lutheran, and this led to considerable tensions, but there were strong economic reasons for tolerating their presence. The exiles included many tradesmen who made an important contribution to the local economy. Philip Melanchthon, facing enormous pressure from opponents within the Protestant church, worked together with Calvin in support of the French refugee community. He wrote to the Frankfurt magistrates against the expulsion of the French from the city on account of doctrinal disagreement.[22] He was also keeping his circle of friends informed about Calvin's activities and the plight of the refugees.[23]

Westphal turned his sights on the Frankfurt community, which he described as full of vagabonds, Lasco in particular. A polemical war broke out which polarized the city and the situation grew dark for the refugees. In an attempt to placate the Frankfurt magistrates, Calvin dedicated to them his *Harmony of the Gospels*, for which he received a very positive response and forty gulden. The Frankfurt council was under mounting pressure from the Lutheran ministers in the city to do something about the Reformed exiles, and Calvin sought to intervene. During the winter of 1556 he wrote to the Frankfurt magistrates offering to travel to the city and mediate. He received a polite reply in which no mention of his offer was made. The hostility between the ministers and the exiles was mirrored by internal squabbling within the exile community itself, in particular around the figure of Poullain. Calvin was so concerned that he sent an emissary from Geneva in late 1555 bearing a letter that could have been written by a bishop to his flock.

Calvin once more assumed his Pauline voice. He was horrified by the manner in which the community was ripping itself apart: at issue were Poullain's autocratic behaviour and his refusal to brook criticism.[24] Even if there were problems, and Calvin professed not to be well informed, the refugees should reflect upon their place in the world. He gave them a sermon on what it meant to be in exile. When someone like Poullain, he wrote, who has laboured successfully in planting churches, arrives and claims an office, they should not obsess themselves with the intricacies of electing a minister. Such rules exist for when a church is established, but in exile the situation is more elastic. They should look for signs of God's grace and not divide over regulations or their own opinions. 'You are settled there as in borrowed lodgings. When people perceive how difficult it is to satisfy you, will your peevishness not irritate the kind magistrates who have received you with so much humanity?'[25] Calvin warned the Frankfurt community that it would destroy itself through dissension, particularly as the majority in the city were simply waiting for the right moment to expel them.

Despite Calvin's dire warnings, the situation among the Frankfurt exile community only worsened. By the spring of 1556 there was a growing chorus calling for Calvin to mediate personally, and in April he secured leave from the Geneva council and travelled to Frankfurt via Strasbourg. Before leaving Geneva he sent another pastoral admonition.

Thus, my brethren, I beseech you in the name of God, increasingly to put in practice this lesson of Paul's, 'Let nothing be done from contention, nor from lust of victory' as the word which he employs indicates. The moment each person backs his own quarrel people must of necessity come to a battle. Rather let each man admit his faults, and those who have been to blame submit of their own accord. Let people give up all attacks, which are good for nothing except to keep up mutual grudges. For if we can endure nothing that displeases us it would be necessary for each man to order his manner of life separately. It is for this reason that Paul, wishing to exhort the Ephesians to maintain unity of mind in the bonds of peace, and especially to bring them back to humility, meekness and patience, insists on their bearing with one another and supporting one another in love.[26]

When he arrived in the city in September he found two French-speaking exile communities angrily opposed, yet both invoking his name; a similar fate would befall him when the English community in Frankfurt acrimoniously split. Like Luther, Calvin had two unreconciled parties claiming his authority. He was not permitted to preach in the city for fear it would stir Lutheran opposition, but he joined a commission that included Lasco and several other ministers to examine the case. His status, personality and years of work on the Consistory and Company of Pastors in Geneva enabled him to broker a deal and obtain from the committee his desired resolution, which he had determined before his arrival in Frankfurt: Poullain was not to be publicly criticized but his resignation was essential to the restoration of peace. This was achieved, though it destroyed Calvin's relationship with Poullain, once a good friend.[27] It was a bittersweet peace at Frankfurt, for cessation of hostilities in the community was followed by defeat in Wesel, where the Reformed exile church under Perussel was closed down.

Cajoling Melanchthon

Calvin was a deeply divisive presence in German lands. His ability to establish peace in Frankfurt spoke to the respect he enjoyed among certain Lutheran officials. At the same time, he was deeply implicated in the battle between the Gnesio-Lutherans and the Philippists. The complexity of the situation was reflected in his association with Melanchthon himself. What Calvin wanted was something Melanchthon could not offer – an open alliance. Although the two men maintained a cordial, even friendly, relationship, their theological differences were significant. Melanchthon, under attack from the Gnesio-Lutherans, was not in a position to enter Calvin's dispute with Westphal. He had supported Calvin in the Servetus case, and for that the Genevan reformer had thanked him in his letter of March 1555, but he was not prepared to do the same on the Lord's Supper.[28] Where overt backing was not possible, he was able to offer a quiet word. Through his extensive contacts among churchmen and lay magistrates he worked with Calvin to support the religious refugees in

German lands.[29] It was an alliance often invisible to the naked eye, but it would bear fruit with the adoption of the Reformed faith in the Palatine electorate in 1561, opening the door to Calvinism in the German lands in the later decades of the century.[30]

Calvin's patience would not bear Melanchthon's apparent timidity. The Genevan wrote that he was certain the two men could resolve their differences over predestination and wanted Melanchthon to make a public statement of support on the Lord's Supper. The Zurichers were in agreement and there was a real chance for rapprochement. He even stressed the degree to which his *Defence* was in accord with Luther, but Melanchthon did not take the bait. In May 1555 Melanchthon replied, avoiding any commitment to open support, preferring to pray for the divided Church. He did not want Calvin to use his name in this propaganda war as he had done several years earlier over predestination and when Calvin once more urged Melanchthon's support in August the response was a silence that lasted three years.[31] At the same time as he was receiving Calvin's imploring letters there were others in the Lutheran churches urging Melanchthon to take a stand against the Reformed churches. Caught in the middle, he kept his own counsel.

While Calvin and Melanchthon were in contact during the summer of 1555 Westphal pushed the debate a stage further. No doubt delighted that he had roused a chief adversary to debate, he published *A Just Defence against the False Accusations of a Certain Sacramentarian*, which was printed in Frankfurt, the city of the English and French refugees. Once more he reviewed the various positions of those whom he named 'sacramentarians', concluding that they were united only in denying the presence of Christ in the Lord's Supper. Lasco sent a copy to Calvin with the warning that 'Westphal has written a most vicious book against you. . . . They say he attacks you with your own words!'[32] To this Peter Martyr Vermigli, the Italian reformer in Strasbourg greatly respected by Calvin, added that he too had heard of the work, which had probably been printed in Frankfurt to have maximum effect among the foreign churches in the city. He was also hearing from friends that Calvin was being vilified in Saxony.

Calvin was now in the heat of battle and there was no turning back. January 1556 brought from the press of Jean Crespin Calvin's second work entitled *A Second Defence of the Pious and Orthodox Faith concerning the Sacraments in Answer to the Calumnies of Joachim Westphal*. This time Westphal was named in the title and the work was blisteringly polemical, having ballooned in size to over 170 pages with a point-by-point refutation of Westphal's arguments. The volume was dedicated to the Saxon churches with the express hope of using the Consensus as a basis for agreement. To Westphal's damaging argument that he had changed his tune to win over the Zwinglians, Calvin responded in his dedication to the Saxon churches that the inconsistency was not his: 'who now sees not that the hatred which this man [Westphal] bears to those against whom he has once declared war is so implacable that he assails the very doctrine which he formerly favoured in order that he may have nothing in common with them?'[33]

The structure of the *Second Defence* was carefully laid out to defuse Westphal's central contention that the Reformed doctrine of the Lord's Supper amounted to nothing more than an empty sign.

> We detest the dishonesty of those who invidiously disseminate among the people that we take away the presence of Christ from the Supper and measure the power of God by our own sense. As if the sublime nature of this mystery, namely, that Christ, though remaining in heaven as to the locality of his body, yet descends to us by the secret agency of his Spirit so as to unite us with him and make us partakers of his life – did not transcend the reach of human intellect.[34]

Despite its length, Calvin was not entirely satisfied with his reply, which was harsher and less elegant than he might have liked. He reflected that 'many can bear witness that this book was hastily written. What the case required, and occurred spontaneously at the time, I dictated without lengthy consideration, and with a feeling so remote from gall (with which [Westphal] says I am thoroughly infected) that I afterwards wondered how harsher terms had fallen from me while I had no bitterness in my heart.'[35] Calvin made the same remark to the Zurichers, expressing surprise at how such language had poured out of his mouth.

During 1556 the dispute spread. On the Reformed side Bullinger added his contribution, which he sent to Calvin for approval, while among the Lutherans several stepped forward to write against the 'sacramentarians'. Calvin's hope of isolating Westphal was badly misplaced, for clearly most of the leading Lutherans identified with the Hamburg minister and not with the Genevan reformer, despite the latter's appeal to Luther. Calvin found himself facing the arrayed forces of the Saxon church, which, as Vermigli had heard, despised him. This was brought home to him in the manner of Westphal's reply in 1557. Calvin had written his *Second Defence to the ministers of Saxony*, but in a brilliant move Westphal turned the tables and assembled the views of the different German

Lutheran churches on the subject. Magdeburg and Bremen submitted detailed refutations of Calvin while a host of other churches, mostly from northern German lands, sent in confessions of faith, all of which were hostile to Geneva. Such was the weight of the assault that Bullinger declared to Calvin, 'you thought that those who followed the crass opinion of the presence of the body were few in number. ... Troop after troop is on the attack; they are bearing arms; everyone is rising up against us. Everyone is defending Westphalism!'[36]

Indeed, during 1557 Westphal continued to pour forth a torrent of polemic against the 'sacramentarians', demanding the expulsion of the exiles from Frankfurt, whom he described as 'sick sheep' in the flock. His letter to the Frankfurt council was translated into German, broadening the conflict to a wider, lay readership. At the same time his Latin polemic against Calvin sold well.[37] To his own work he added a tract by Melanchthon to counter any impression proffered by Calvin and others that the Wittenberg professor was on their side. The tracts proved so popular that in Wittenberg they sold out quickly.

This thrust of the sword found exposed flesh. Calvin was desperate to maintain the increasingly doubtful impression that he and Melanchthon were in agreement. He replied to Westphal for the last time in the summer of 1557, admitting to Farel that when it came to dealing with this man he could hardly control himself, though he felt compelled to make one final stand. His *Final Admonition* was enormous, twice as long as the *Second Defence*, and it addressed in detail the positions of Westphal and the Magdeburgians, who included the reformer Flacius Illyricus. Calvin wrote to Bullinger that he was particularly concerned about what he might make of it. Bullinger responded, 'I most eagerly read your book against the Saxons and many times while reading it I thanked God and you, and even now I send my deepest thanks. I like the book.'[38] Calvin argued that he had always approved of the Augsburg Confession, meaning, of course, Melanchthon's Variata, which he had signed in 1540. 'We teach nothing at variance with the Confession of Augsburg, and therefore they have no cause for quarrelling so bitterly, or rather, so savagely. If there is any doubt as to this, we appeal to Philip [Melanchthon] who wrote it. As the Magdeburgians speak hesitatingly in their reply, I, trusting to a good conscience, venture freely to repeat what I said. Let Philip, as often as it is thought proper, be called upon to explain his own meaning.'[39]

Although Calvin and Bullinger worked together opposing Westphal, the episode proved divisive. The two men had seen the matter in very different light. For Bullinger it was about defending the pure doctrine of the Reformed faith against yet another attack from the Lutherans, from whom he expected nothing other than vile polemic. Calvin, in contrast, had hoped that it would lead to some form of reconciliation, and from the start had urged the convening of a conference of the two parties. Bullinger refused to be drawn, an attitude that effectively pushed Calvin into spasms of rage and momentary loss of perspective. Calvin's rising temper can be seen in a letter to Farel.

> That he [Bullinger] thinks nothing should be attempted concerning a convention is neither new nor surprising to me, for I had anticipated this answer before I wrote. At the same time, however, you see how coldly and hesitatingly he gives me hopes of his protection, and that of the church of Zurich, which in the beginning he promised with an excess of generosity. But as I have undertaken the cause without counting upon the help of others, so now, though they deceive me, I will not desist. To confess the truth, a freer field will now be open to me and my alacrity is even increased. For you know how much I was obliged hitherto to concede to their fastidiousness.[40]

Written in anger, the letter reflects the man rather than his intentions. He was hurt by what he regarded as Bullinger's indifference to the risks he had taken to defend their agreement, and he took it personally. He had no intention of abandoning Zurich, whose support he needed. Nevertheless, there was a strong sense that his plans for unity among the Protestants were hedged in by the need to keep the Swiss onside.

Earlier in the year, Calvin had drawn an extraordinary comparison between himself and Martin Bucer, who had died in England in 1551, and whose presence Calvin felt during the 1550s. '[Bullinger] compares me to Bucer,' he wrote to Farel in 1557, 'whose over-activity was hurtful for this very reason, that he never frankly and prudently defended the good cause in a proper manner. My line of conduct however is entirely different, since I am not concerned to absolve my character from calumnies.'[41] The reformer of Strasbourg, according to Calvin, had severely damaged his efforts on behalf of church unity by seeking to please everyone and never saying what he really believed. Two years earlier, he had reflected to Peter Martyr Vermigli that:

> wishing to calm the violence of Luther and his partisans, he [Bucer] stooped in such a servile manner that he was entangled in continual confusion by single words. Another exigency forced him to shuffle; he wished to conceal the disgrace of his former imprudence, as I often let

him know. No one, I think, urged him with greater freedom and even sharpness in this cause to have the courage to declare more sincerely and without equivocal phrases what he felt to be the truth.[42]

The language reminds us of the manner in which Calvin compared himself to David and Paul, at once drawing our attention to similarities and differences. Bucer was Calvin's spiritual father and model of self-sacrifice in the service of Christ's Church. From the early days of the Seneca commentary, Calvin's way had been the Stoic path of freedom from reliance on others. To be the man of unity he had to show himself to be not Bucer but Calvin.

As persecution of Protestants in France intensified in the mid-1550s Calvin grew increasingly anxious to forge a united Protestant front to petition the French king. To achieve this was a tall order: he had to defeat Westphal and convince both Bullinger and Melanchthon that a conference of Protestant churches would be worthwhile. He wanted the Protestant world to speak with one voice and was perfectly willing to tolerate a degree of theological flexibility to achieve this. The greater cause, as he saw it, was unity. Doctrine was not dispensable, as the Westphal case had shown, but he believed that the distance between the Swiss churches and those who followed Melanchthon was not great. To Bullinger he wrote, 'I, on the contrary, though I admit that nothing is more pernicious than an obscure and ambiguous or equivocal conciliation, do not despair that sincere and candid moderation may be hit upon which will be dear to all honest men, and will destroy the influence of those hot-headed individuals, who with their tumultuous clamours disturb the peace of the world.'[43] While to Melanchthon, from whom Calvin expected so much, he was sharper.

> Though you shrink from noisy contests, yet you know what Paul proscribes by his example to all the servants of Christ. Certainly you cannot desire praise for greater moderation than that which was evidenced in him. When he then, who was endowed with so much forbearance, passed intrepidly through seditions, we cannot give way where the circumstances in our times are by no means so painful. But, in one word, you should carefully consider whether your all too obstinate silence might not leave a stain on your reputation in the eyes of posterity.[44]

He then concluded, 'if a means of pacification is sought for, our only hope lies in a conference which I doubt not that you desire, but I wish that you called for more courageously'.

An opening did appear in the form of the German Lutheran Duke of Württemberg, who showed some interest in a religious colloquy. Calvin seized the opportunity with alacrity and campaigned for its realization, but to no avail. The Swiss, and Bullinger in particular, had been outraged by the actions of Theodore Beza and Guillaume Farel, who had travelled through the German lands on behalf of the Swiss churches seeking support for the persecuted Waldensians and French evangelicals.[45] On 14 May 1557 in Göppingen they presented Christoph of Württemberg with a highly Lutheran confession that delighted many of the Germans and horrified the Swiss.[46] Later, in the autumn of 1557, Beza and Farel met Melanchthon at the Worms Colloquy and came to a theological agreement, unknown to both Zurich and Geneva.[47] To make matters much worse, at Worms, under considerable pressure from other Lutherans, Melanchthon formally condemned the Zwinglians. Bullinger and the Swiss hated the Augsburg Confession in all its forms, and despite Calvin's arguments to the contrary they attributed the document to Luther. Calvin was forced into rapid damage control: Zurich felt betrayed by both Geneva and Melanchthon, who, in their view, had revealed himself to be no better than Luther. Calvin wrote to Bullinger that Beza had been forced into the situation and had acted alone, while he shared the Zurich reformer's anger that Melanchthon had damned Zwingli's theology. The only explanation, Calvin added, was the weakness of an old man.[48]

Westphal was not to be silenced, and during 1558 he published several more lengthy attacks on Calvin, but the Genevan reformer had had enough. Preoccupied with the situation in France and with his own commentaries on the Old Testament, and seriously ill, he left the field of combat. The Reformed church was more isolated than ever. The long-standing dispute with the Lutherans over the Lord's Supper had reached a new low and there was absolutely no sign of reconciliation. But for Calvin himself it was a personal defeat. He had lost the battle with Westphal, whom he had so badly underrated. A large part of Westphal's success was to do not so much with his own theological acumen, though that was considerable, but with the manner in which he had effectively used Calvin's own words to demonstrate the shifting and perhaps even contradictory character of the Genevan's teaching on the Lord's Supper. In so doing he had managed to tear the tissue of alliance between Geneva and Zurich. He had made Calvin squirm hard to explain himself, something to which the great orator and writer was unaccustomed. Calvin generally mauled his opponents, but not this time.

CHAPTER FIFTEEN

European Reformer

WITH THE remarkable growth of 'Calvinism' in the second half of the sixteenth century it is tempting to assume that during his life Calvin enjoyed widespread influence across Europe. This was true, to an extent. His involvement with imperial religious politics and close association with the leading German and Swiss reformers and the refugee communities brought prestige and respect. His growing reputation drew students to Geneva, expanding a network of contacts across the continent and furthering the transmission of his ideas. Yet, though his name was honoured among supporters, and his works enjoyed astonishing popularity, it would be misleading to single him out. Heinrich Bullinger and Philip Melanchthon likewise had extensive contacts, and after long years of teaching in Zurich and Wittenberg their students and writings were to be found everywhere. Bullinger's voice was clearly heard in England, eastern Europe and France, where he was the most widely read non-French Protestant author. Melanchthon was the great teacher of the Reformation and his reputation was towering. Calvin's achievements stood alongside those of these men and by no means put them in the shade. Their influence was cumulative. By the mid-1540s a web of Protestant contacts extended from the court of Henry VIII through the German cities, principalities and universities into the Swiss Confederation, France and, increasingly, eastward into Austrian, Hungarian and Polish lands. It involved churchmen, political figures, merchants, book handlers, students and couriers; through letters, printed works, book fairs, diplomatic contacts and religious colloquies news and ideas were exchanged. Calvin, Bullinger and

Melanchthon were the most prominent figures, but they were part of a much larger enterprise.

Calvin was involved in the wider European Reformation in various ways. In his pursuit of unity he travelled extensively, frequently visiting Berne, Zurich and Basle, as well as journeying further afield to Frankfurt and Strasbourg. At home, he received a constant flow of visitors from France, the empire, Italy, Swiss lands and eastern Europe, all eager to share news and discuss diverse theological and church matters. Not untypical was Calvin abruptly concluding a letter to Bullinger with the remark that he had arrived home to find an unexpected and large number of guests waiting to dine with him.[1] Calvin was also part of a vast information network in which fellow reformers passed along rumours and stories in written accounts, known in Latin as 'nova', which were frequently included with personal letters. These were often drawn from official reports and diplomatic exchanges between princes and cities and might be collected together by book traders.[2] Heinrich Bullinger was Calvin's best source: Bullinger's range of correspondents was astounding, and he kept the Frenchman abreast of events across Europe, particularly in Italy, through his contacts in Graubünden, England and the great cities of the empire, such as Augsburg and Nuremberg. But there were other sources, including Ambrosius Blarer – the 'Apostle of Swabia' – Philip Melanchthon and Johannes Haller. One of the major duties of the reformers was to keep their colleagues informed and determine the veracity of their assembled material. Before, for example, Bullinger passed along correspondence and news reports to Geneva he would annotate them in his own hand, frequently adding further information that had come his way.

Students, refugees and visitors in Geneva sought out Calvin and he willingly gave of his time, though he frequently found it exhausting. When they returned to their homelands they remained in touch and sought his advice. By the end of the 1540s he actively looked to play the role of international reformer by writing to rulers and leading noblemen and women; he began dedicating works to these figures in which he offered guidance. Let us look to the examples of Britain, Poland, the Low Countries and the Palatinate.

England

While in Strasbourg Calvin became aware of events in England through Martin Bucer, who was part of the growing network of contacts between the Archbishop of Canterbury, Thomas Cranmer, and the southern German reformers that developed during the 1530s.[3] Bucer had dedicated his 1536 commentary on Romans to Cranmer.[4] At the same time, not to be outdone by Bucer, Heinrich Bullinger began his long and highly successful campaign for influence in England. Students were sent from Zurich to study at Oxford and Cambridge, including the young Rudolf Gwalther, later friend of Calvin and Bullinger's successor. Bullinger encouraged other Swiss reformers to make contact with Cranmer and by the end of the 1530s a web of personal and literary contacts was in place.

During these dark days for the Reformation in the empire England provided a ray of hope. Henry VIII had sought the opinion of leading Protestants when he was trying to procure a divorce from Katherine of Aragon, and the king's next wife, Anne Boleyn, was an active patron of evangelicals until her fall in 1536. By the end of the decade Thomas Cromwell, Henry's chancellor, was actively pursuing an alliance between England and the Schmalkaldic League, and this stirred interest among the German reformers. The atmosphere changed, however, with the promulgation of the *Six Articles* in 1539, when Henry appeared to turn his face against the evangelicals, leading Luther to abandon the hope he had previously placed in the monarch.

Martin Bucer, as ever, remained optimistic and counselled patience, encouraging Cranmer to continue reform. Philip Melanchthon wrote to Henry VIII in November 1539 presenting a systematic refutation of the *Six Articles* while tactfully not blaming the king for their content.[5] Cromwell was undaunted and continued to work for a marriage alliance between Henry and the Schmalkaldic League, having alighted on Anne of Cleves, a duchess of sufficient stature. The central problem was the demand of the German Lutherans that the English king accept the Augsburg Confession, which he was loath to do on account of certain theological misgivings. Henry was sincere in procuring the alliance, and his motives were more religious than cynically political.[6] When the marriage famously and spectacularly failed in 1540 he did not lose interest in being in contact with the German Lutherans. Likewise, he was not overly offended by his savaging at the hands of Melanchthon. He was convinced that on certain key points of doctrine such as justification by faith his religious views were in accord with the Lutherans', in particular with Melanchthon's.[7] This proved a misunderstanding.

Henry's miscalculation reminds us of how frequently figures of the Reformation mistook the degree of doctrinal agreement between themselves. Calvin had made this mistake with Melanchthon. In part the consequence of wishful thinking brought about by the necessity of theological agreement for any form of alliance, this also owed a good deal to the manner in which texts were written and read. Calvin, like most humanist writers of his age, read to extract that which was agreeable. When studying his beloved Augustine, he plundered the works for those parts of the church father's thought congenial to his own purposes. This was also true of Bullinger, Bucer and the other Protestant reformers. In this way, as we have seen, authors could be read as saying something not originally intended. The converse also applied: opponents' works were raked over to lift passages that could be condemned. This long-standing practice of the medieval church was intensified by the theological warfare of the sixteenth century.

When he returned to Geneva in 1541 England hardly figured in Calvin's thoughts. Through Bucer and Bullinger he received information, but he was neither well informed nor particularly interested. There were too many other concerns at home, in the empire and with France. When Edward VI came to the throne in 1547 Calvin joined the Protestant chorus of rejoicing without feeling any particular need to become involved. That slowly changed over the following years. Calvin developed a fascinating spiritual bond with Edward Seymour, Duke of Somerset, regent to the young Edward VI. And through Bucer Calvin also began corresponding with Thomas Cranmer.

The Godly Duke: Protector Somerset

The letters to Somerset were part of Calvin's campaign to make contact with prominent members of the nobility he identified as sympathetic to the Reformation. He continued to exchange letters with Marguerite of Navarre, Francis I's sister and patron of French evangelicals, and maintained the relationship with Renée of France begun in Ferrara in the 1530s.[8] The dedication of the 1536 *Institutes* to Francis I, which he revised and continued to have printed, signalled Calvin's belief in the power of rhetorical argument in addressing leaders. In England he rightly identified Edward Seymour, first Duke of Somerset, as the key player, and in 1548 sent the duke a letter instructing him in the nature of true religion and the role of the prince in its defence. Edward Seymour was the brother of Jane Seymour, Henry VIII's third wife, and served as lord protector of England from 1547 till his fall in 1549.[9] He had quickly established control over the young Edward VI, and from his position of power pursued a cautious policy of religious reform. Reformation, Calvin opined, brings not peace but warfare, for regardless of princes' good intentions in banishing idolatry and establishing true religion 'their faith may yet be tried by diverse temptations'.[10] God's will is to test the people and force rulers to look beyond the affairs of the world. Tumult is also a sign that the devil is constantly at work endeavouring to undermine the Church of Christ. 'This is the age of salvation when God's word has been revealed, but what have we made of it, very little. That is why God continues to punish us.'

Calvin related that he knew of the revolts in England and emphatically declared that rebellion against the king was to be suppressed with the sword, for it was no less than an attack against God; rulers must protect the Church and the faithful, and this, at times, requires force. The Church, for its part, rests upon sound doctrine, requiring sound confession of faith, with which Calvin provided Somerset.

> We hold God alone to be the sole Governor of our souls, that we hold his law to be the only rule and spiritual directory of our consciences, not serving him according to the foolish inventions of men. Also, that according to his nature he would be worshipped in spirit and in purity of heart. On the other hand, acknowledging that there is nothing but wretchedness in ourselves, and that we are corrupt in all our feelings and affections, so that our souls are a very abyss of iniquity, utterly despairing of ourselves. And that, having exhausted every presumption of our own wisdom, worth or power of well-doing, we must have recourse to the fountain of every blessing, which is in Christ Jesus, accepting that which he confers on us, that is to say, the merit of his death and passion, that by this means we may be reconciled to God.

Calvin's summary of faith was intended as a 'common formula' for the instruction of 'children and ignorant persons, serving to make them familiar with sound doctrine'. For the people to be educated there must be preachers 'to teach, to exhort, to reprove, as Paul says in speaking thereof to Timothy'. No church can survive without a catechism, for it 'is like the seed to keep the good grain from dying out, and causing it to multiply from age to age'. God works through princes 'for advancing and upholding the state of Christianity, yet God is pleased to declare his sovereign power by this spiritual sword of his Word, when it is made known by the pastors'.

Calvin expressed the concern of many continental reformers that the pace of change in England was too slow. While acknowledging that 'we must observe moderation, and that overdoing is neither discreet nor useful' and that 'forms of worship need to be accommodated to the condition and tastes of the people', Calvin told Somerset that he had heard that practices continued in England contrary to the Gospel. 'In prayer to God, we must not take an unbounded licence in our devotions, but observe the rule which Paul gives us (Romans 10), which is that we must be founded upon the Word of God. Therefore, such commemoration of the dead, which involves a commending of them to his grace, is contrary to the due form and manner of prayer, – it is a hurtful addition to the Supper of our Lord.' The Reformation must of necessity proceed with prudence, but was ultimately the work of God and beyond human comprehension. Moderation does not extend to permitting anything that is contrary to the divine will. The Church must have discipline to root out vice and disorder and protect the teaching entrusted to it. 'For as doctrine is the soul of the Church for quickening, so discipline and the correction of vices are like the nerves to sustain the body in a state of health and vigour. The duty of bishops and curates is to keep watch over that, to the end that the Supper of our Lord may not be polluted by people of scandalous lives.' Calvin's letter to Somerset mirrored his words to other princes and magistrates, but this time it found the mark. The protector responded positively and on 9 July 1549 Calvin reported to Farel that he had received a ring from the Seymour family, which he noted to be of modest value, and that Somerset had taken his letter well.[11]

The relationship between Calvin and Somerset took a more interesting turn after the protector's fall in 1549 as a result of his disastrous wars with Scotland and France, the failure of his domestic policies, and opposition to the power he had acquired. In 1550 Calvin sent his friend Nicolas des Gallars to England with two works for Somerset in which he offered the protector spiritual guidance. Somerset translated the works into English during his imprisonment and had them printed as *An Epistle both of Godly Consolacion and also of Advertisement* and *A Spyrytuall and most Precyouse Pearle*.[12]

Calvin's pastoral letter contained genuine compassion for Somerset; he saw the protector as the true voice of reform in a kingdom which had only half-heartedly embraced the Gospel. There was a profound sense of disappointment among those reformers who had found refuge in England. Martin Bucer, who had arrived in 1548 with the Hebraist Paul Fagius, had been shown favour by the king and Somerset, and also by Cranmer, but he soon grew disillusioned. Bucer wrote to Farel in January 1550 that none of the exiles, such as himself, Peter Martyr Vermigli and the Italian Bernardino Ochino, was permitted a voice in the reforms.[13] Frustration arose from the perceived compromises made in the Edwardian church, by Cranmer in particular. The archbishop, however, was quick to remind his guests of the hospitality which had been afforded them after Charles V's triumph in the empire, and drew their attention to the numerous compromises made by German evangelicals. This was a bitter truth, but it was harsher still for Bucer to learn, as he did from Calvin, that many of his fellow reformers on the continent believed that he was complicit in the compromises of the Edwardian church.[14] Bucer was isolated in England and poured forth his unhappiness to Calvin, whom he regarded as his most steadfast ally, and upon whom he relied for information. Early in 1549 Calvin wrote his former mentor a letter of spiritual encouragement, invoking once more the language of the journey. 'The Spirit of God, like a most brilliant torch, or rather like the sun itself, shines in full splendour, not only to guide the course of your life, even to its final goal, but also to conduct you to a blessed immortality. Draw then from this source, wherever you may wander, and as soon as he finds you a settled abode, you ought to make that your place of rest.'[15] In a few exquisite lines Calvin captured the soul of his teacher and mentor who had travelled endless miles in search of unity before languishing in exile. The reference to a place of rest had heightened poignancy as even death did not bring relief: during Mary's reign Bucer's body was exhumed and burned, and his tomb destroyed.

The limitations of Calvin's grasp of events in England were reflected in a letter to Farel from November 1550 in which he referred obliquely to Bucer's correspondence, remarking that he had heard things of which he 'could not approve'. By this he meant not only the slow pace of reform, but the influence of John a Lasco on the exile churches. Calvin offered a biting, and utterly unfair, assessment of the Pole, who 'can be so much influenced by the slightest breezes of court favour'. 'I fear', he added, 'its winds will drive him in all directions.' More daunting was the prospect of writing to the young King Edward himself.[16] Calvin claimed he was being urged to do so by various unnamed figures, most likely Cranmer, who was trying to rally international support and shift him away from Somerset. Calvin admitted, unusually, to considerable anxiety about writing as he hardly knew what to say. Unlike with France, the Swiss Confederation and the empire, he was dealing here with wholly unfamiliar terrain. He decided to dedicate his commentary on Isaiah to Edward, later changed to Elizabeth, and then he added another dedication to the king in his commentary on the canonical epistles.

Calvin's relationship with Thomas Cranmer was respectful, though distant. They corresponded without ever becoming friends, and their point of contact was probably Bucer. Cranmer had certainly read some of the Frenchman's works – he possessed a copy of the 1536 *Institutes*, translated into English by Cranmer's son-in-law and published by the archbishop's printer. There was also a decisive intervention in 1551 when the minister of the Glastonbury French community located on Somerset's estate, Valérand Poullain – Calvin's friend with whom he would later fall out over Frankfurt – warned Calvin sternly against protesting to the king about the fallen protector's impending execution.[17] Poullain acted on the instructions of Cranmer, who foresaw the ruinous consequences of Calvin's stalwart support for the disgraced man. Ignorance of English politics nearly allowed Calvin to stumble into a serious miscalculation. It would happen again when Elizabeth came to the throne.

In the last years of Edward's reign contact between Calvin and Cranmer increased as the archbishop looked to a wider union of European Protestantism under the leadership of the young king. Peter Martyr Vermigli, now regius professor of divinity in Oxford, was an enthusiastic exponent of a Protestant council to be held in England, and his influence on Cranmer was considerable.[18] The archbishop wrote to Melanchthon, Bullinger and Calvin soliciting their support, but the replies were not encouraging.[19] Neither Bullinger nor Melanchthon was prepared to travel, but from Geneva Calvin enthused,

> This thing also is to be ranked among the chief evils of our time, that the churches are so divided, that human fellowship is scarcely in any repute among us, far less that Christian intercourse of which all make a profession, but few sincerely practise. If men of learning conduct themselves with undue hesitation, the heaviest blame falls on the leaders themselves, who, engrossed in their own sinful pursuits, are indifferent to the safety and entire piety of the Church, or who, satisfied with their own private peace, have no regard for others.[20]

Calvin urged Cranmer to call such an assembly and gather the divided Protestant churches; this was the dream he had so relentlessly, and seemingly fruitlessly, pursued. He claimed he would cross 'ten seas' to attend.

By July the hyperbole had faded and Calvin admitted to Cranmer that perhaps the time was not yet right for a council. He praised the archbishop for his efforts in this regard before delivering a body blow.[21] The rest of the letter was a brutal rebuke for Cranmer's mishandling of the reformation in England. Calvin stirred the prophetic fire once used on him by Farel and Bucer. It was the type of mauling he usually kept for his friends, but Cranmer was not an intimate. Directed at a senior figure, the tone is astonishing.

> I, for my part, acknowledge that our cause has made progress during the short period the Gospel has flourished in England. But if you reflect on what yet remains to be done, and how very remiss you have been in

many matters, you will discover that you have no reason not to advance with haste. . . . For I need not inform you that I, as it were, take note of your assiduity, lest, after having escaped danger, you should become self-indulgent. But to speak freely, I greatly fear, and this fear remains, that so many autumns will be spent in procrastinating that the cold of a perpetual winter will set in. You are now somewhat advanced in years, and this ought to stimulate you to increased exertions, so as to save yourself the regret of having been consciously dilatory, and that you may not leave the world while matters remain in so disordered a condition. I say matters are still in a disorganized state, for external religious abuses have been corrected in such a way as to leave innumerable young shoots, which are constantly sprouting forth.

Calvin continued the assault, saying that his sources had told him that many aspects of the mass were retained in the English liturgy, and that the revenues of the church were being plundered, which he termed 'shameful'. He concludes with the signal that it was Peter Martyr Vermigli whom he most trusted in England and expressed his pleasure that Cranmer was listening to him. With Bucer gone, Calvin saw himself and Bullinger as the leaders of the true Reformation, and the Gospel demanded the correction of a vascillating archbishop.

The Stranger Churches

Apart from Calvin's contacts with Somerset, Genevan influence on the Edwardian church was limited, and Strasbourg and Zurich formed a more significant presence. Bullinger rather than Calvin was the principal continental figure. Calvin's presence, however, was not entirely negligible, and a particular bond with England was formed through the exile religious communities who set up churches under the protection of the young king. There were French communities in London and Glastonbury and the French churches made use of the 1542 Genevan liturgy in their worship.[22] In terms of theology, however, it was Strasbourg and Zurich whose voices carried influence.[23] The leaders of the foreign community in England, John a Lasco, Martin Micron and Jan Utenhove, had all spent time in Zurich and were close to Bullinger.[24] Their relationship with Calvin was much more distant, though Utenhove kept the Genevan reformer in touch with events in England.[25] The foreign churches in London adopted Bucerian and Zwinglian doctrines of the Lord's Supper and the Church. Lasco's tendency to draw eclectically from the work of others ensured that the Dutch exile community did not necessarily accept Calvin's teaching on predestination. In fact, the two men did not enjoy a good relationship and Calvin expressed to Farel his concern about the extent of the Polish reformer's impact in London.[26]

Calvin's greatest influence was on the French community, where his Genevan catechism and the Olivétan New Testament were used, and the *Form of Prayers* opened with a distinctively Genevan expression of predestination.[27] When a dispute arose within the French congregation and Calvin's name was invoked Lasco wrote to Geneva imploring the reformer to intercede.[28] Calvin replied brusquely, telling the community not to make a Jerusalem of Geneva and an idol of himself. He was not inclined to become actively involved in the exile churches in London.

Among many English evangelicals, however, Calvin's name was held in the highest regard. Bartholomew Traheron, later one of the Marian exiles, had studied in Zurich and Geneva during the 1540s. Concerned about the predestination quarrel, which had spread to England, he wrote to Heinrich Bullinger seeking support. The letter throws some light on Calvin's early reputation in England.

> I am exceedingly desirous to know what you and the other very learned men, who live in Zurich, think respecting the predestination and providence of God. If you ask the reason, there are certain individuals here that assert that you lean too much to Melanchthon's views. But the greater number among us, of whom I own myself to be one, embrace the opinion of John Calvin as being perspicuous and most agreeable to holy scripture. And we truly thank God that that excellent treatise of the very learned and excellent John Calvin against Pighius and one Georgius Siculus should have come forth at the very time when the question began to be agitated among us. For we confess that it has thrown much light on the subject. . . . We certainly hope that you differ in no respect from his excellent and learned opinion.[29]

'The Flames of Unjust Hate into Foreign Lands': Exiles and the Scottish Church

On 3 August 1553 a disconsolate Calvin informed Bullinger, 'The messengers regarding the death of the English king are more numerous than I could wish.

We are therefore mourning him just as if we were already certain of his death, or rather mourning over the fate of the Church, which has met with an incalculable loss in the person of a single individual. We are held at present in anxious suspense as to whether matters turn into confusion.'[30] The accession of Mary Tudor in 1553 following the abortive attempt to place Lady Jane Grey on the English throne led to an exodus of evangelicals to safe havens abroad. On 17 September 1553 around 160 French and Dutch exiles filled two ships and departed for the continent. As the experience of those who went to Lutheran Denmark cruelly exposed, a warm welcome was not assured, and confessional differences among Protestants provoked bitter controversy. Similarly, the continuing hostility between the Lutheran and Reformed churches claimed as victims the vulnerable refugee communities, as the troubles in Frankfurt demonstrated.

Many of those who led the exiles were men of enormous character and powerful convictions. In the cramped, dangerous conditions in which these women and men were forced to live conflict inevitably arose. Such was the case with the English exiles who made their way to Frankfurt in the summer of 1553, where they settled and shared a church building with the French community under Valérand Poullain. This was permitted as long as the two groupings shared beliefs and practices.[31] The form of worship used by the English was largely drawn from the 1552 Book of Common Prayer, with some revisions based on the practices of the French community. For their part, the French worshipped with a liturgy drawn up by Poullain, who had borrowed heavily from Geneva. John Knox arrived in Frankfurt in the autumn of 1554 from Geneva to serve as minister to the English congregation and immediately found himself in a difficult position. The English exile community in Strasbourg under Edmund Grindal and Bishop Richard Cox wanted greater conformity to the Book of Common Prayer, of which Knox was fairly critical, though he did not feel he had a free hand to change the liturgy radically. Calvin was consulted, and on 18 January 1555 replied paternally. In words similar to his message to the warring French community, he reminded the English where they were.[32] In exile, when everything was at stake it was nothing short of madness to quarrel over external practices.

Calvin's inclination was to treat the externals of worship with a charitable spirit, tempered against excessive tolerance of the 'stupid obstinacy' of people unable to part from familiar practices. There was much in the English liturgy he found distasteful; it had not been sufficiently purged of superstitious language, a point he had made to Protector Somerset and Cranmer. But there was more at stake than a minor squabble. What had been begun in England was in ruins, and it fell to the community in Frankfurt to build God's Church again.[33] This required no less than the exercise of the true freedom of the Church: the freedom which permits latitude in external matters without a return to popery; the freedom offered by the divine command to love one's neighbour. Taken directly from Paul's words to the Corinthians, Calvin's unequivocal message declared reform essential to the service of God, but demanded the spirit of love that promoted the community and avoided dissension.

In the end, an arrangement was concluded whereby a revised form of the Book of Common Prayer was retained until the end of April 1555.[34] The concord was brief, however, concluding with the arrival in Frankfurt from Strasbourg of Bishop Richard Cox and a group more inclined to the Prayer Book, in particular those elements most disliked by Knox. Upset by the flouting of the agreement, Knox preached an inflammatory sermon criticizing the *Book of Common Prayer* and attacking the failings of the Edwardian church. In his fervour he censured particular individuals, whom he named, and some of whom were present. The congregation polarized. In what Knox was convinced was a conspiracy against him, an opposing faction laid information before the Frankfurt magistrates concerning his writings. The supporters of Cox pointed out that elements of Knox's work *Faithful Admonition to the Professors of God's Truth in England* were potentially slanderous against Emperor Charles V, in particular a comparison with the Roman Emperor Nero. The nervous Frankfurt magistrates suggested that Knox leave the city, which he did in March 1555 after an emotional farewell sermon to his supporters.

Calvin was furious. He wrote to Richard Cox in May declaring that Knox, whom he specifically named, had been treated abysmally.[35] He claimed to have received reports from various sources about what had happened in Frankfurt, though he refused to mention specific individuals for fear of stirring greater conflict. It beggared belief, he thundered, that a member of an exile community could be denounced before the magistrates by fellow churchmen. Then came a crushing rebuke: 'It would have been better to remain in one's homeland than bring the flames of unjust hate into foreign lands.' Calvin intimated that he had played a role in advising Knox to be more flexible; the same was now expected of Cox.

In the autumn of 1555 a group of men, led by William Whittingham, followed Knox to Geneva, where they set up their own community and worshipped according to the Genevan rite.[36] The community elected Knox and Christopher Goodman as its ministers and the two men worked together well, becoming good friends. Knox was frequently away from Geneva and Goodman served the church, working closely with Calvin, who had a particular care for the English refugees. Both Knox and Goodman drew many lessons from the Genevan church, famously described by the Scotsman as the 'maist perfyt schoole of Chryst. . . . In other places I confesse Chryst to be trewlie preachit; but maneris and religioun so sinceirlie reformat, I have not yit sene in any uther place.'[37] The Genevan church became the largest and most important English community in exile and made good use of the burgeoning culture of print. The *Forme of Prayers* was drawn from the Genevan liturgy and was printed by William Whittingham together with Calvin's *Catechism* and some metrical psalms to become the first Reformed liturgy in English.[38] The *Forme* became the foundation of the *Book of Common Order* after the establishment of the Reformed church in Scotland in 1560.[39] The greatest achievement, without doubt, was the Geneva Bible, produced by a translation team that included Whittingham, Miles Coverdale, Christopher Goodman and Anthony Gilby, among others.[40] It was to become the Bible of Elizabethan England, the Bible of Shakespeare, and it retained its popularity long after the appearance of the King James version. From 1579 it was adopted as the official Bible of Scotland, and a copy was to be in every household that could afford it.

Calvin performed the same mentoring role for Knox, Goodman and the others that Bucer had so influentially carried out for Calvin himself almost twenty years earlier in Strasbourg. Arriving within six months of the victory over the Perrinist party, the exiles observed the workings of an established church with its teaching, worship and discipline. They attended Calvin's lectures on the Bible, entered his circle of intimates, relished conversation and engaged in scholarly activity. With the presence of Robert Estienne they not only had access to presses, but could learn from one of the great printing masters of Europe. Knox would remember Geneva as the happiest period of his life.

The troubles at Frankfurt ultimately had an enormous impact on the development of the British reformations. Knox and Goodman embraced Calvin's model of reform and were determined to make it the foundation of the reform of Scotland, which in 1560 became the first 'Calvinist' land. The influence of Geneva upon the northern kingdom was pervasive: its Bible, doctrine, liturgy and consistorial discipline. With the support of the nobility, the Scottish reformers enjoyed an opportunity without parallel in sixteenth-century Europe, and with bewildering speed they began construction of a new church. The Genevan model extended, however, only so far: the reformation of the kingdom proved far more difficult, and political. In the attempt to establish consistorial discipline the church had to make considerable compromises with the nobility.[41]

The Angry Queen

The death of Mary and the accession of Elizabeth in 1558 brought forth a collective alleluia from the Protestant churches of Europe. The exiles began to stream home; the English church in Geneva was soon depleted and Calvin encouraged his guests to return and begin the work of reforming the English church. He was himself quick to act, dedicating his commentary on Isaiah to Elizabeth and writing to William Cecil, the queen's chief adviser and key architect of the Elizabethan settlement of religion, in 1559. To Cecil Calvin offered some frank but familiar advice.

> You are bound gravely to ponder – that we are doing God's work when we assert the uncorrupted truth of his Gospel and holiness, and therefore it should not be carried out with laxity. From your position you can better ascertain how much progress it will be expedient to make, and where it may be fitting to adopt prudent moderation. However, remember that all delay, on whatever specious pretext, ought to be regarded by you with suspicion.[42]

Calvin believed that this time the English church could be properly reformed and he was determined to be a leading voice. But this was not to be.

In May Calvin wrote once more to Cecil, this time in utter disbelief. 'The messenger to whom I had given my commentaries on Isaiah to be offered to the queen, brought me back word that my homage was rather distasteful to her Majesty, because she had been offended with me on account of certain writings that had been published in this city.'[43] These 'certain writings' were all too well known: Knox's *First Blast of the Trumpet Against the Monsterous Regiment of Women* and Goodman's *How Superior Powers Oght to be Obeyd of their Subjects*. Both were printed in Geneva, though Knox's work did not give its place of origin. They concerned the rights of the people to resist a monarch and, most disastrously, questioned the legitimacy of a female ruler.[44] The production of these works in 1558 was perhaps the worst mistiming of the European Reformation. Elizabeth was incandescent with rage, so much so that

Goodman had to go into hiding when he returned to England. The queen's wrath turned on Geneva, the source of the execrable ideas, and on John Calvin, whom, she believed, had connived in this calumny.

Calvin was not slow to recognize the consequences, and in the same letter to Cecil he attempted an explanation by which he might distance himself from Knox's arguments.

> Two years ago, John Knox, in a private conversation, asked my opinion respecting female government. I frankly answered that because it was a deviation from the primitive and established order of nature, it ought to be held as a judgement on man for his dereliction of his rights, just like slavery – that nevertheless certain women had sometimes been so gifted that the singular blessing of God was conspicuous in them, and made it manifest that they had been raised up by the providence of God, either because he willed by such examples to condemn the weakness of men, or thus show more distinctly his own glory. I here instanced Huldah and Deborah. I added to the same effect that God promised by the mouth of Isaiah that queens should be the nursing mothers of the church, which clearly distinguished such persons from private women.

Elizabeth's response was not mere pique. The whole reformation in England was thrown into turmoil by her rage; the return of the exile communities to London was put in doubt, and there was considerable fear among the Reformed that they were in disgrace with the new queen. Anthony Ashe, charged with the negotiations to bring the community in Emden back to London, reported that the godly were out of favour and, most spectacularly, that there had been a house-to-house search for Knox's works.[45]

Elizabeth was not Edward, and her religious views differed considerably from her brother's. She had survived the reign of Mary, and, though a Protestant, her instincts were conservative. She was not going to be told what to do by anyone. Knox's tract, therefore, could not have been more offensive, or damaging. The results for Calvin were deeply troubling. His association with Knox precluded any involvement in the English religious settlement of 1559 which led to the Acts of Supremacy and Uniformity. The dream that the continental Reformed churches would have a decisive voice in the formation of the English church quickly vanished.

Calvin, for his part, did not remain inactive. He sent his close friend and colleague Nicolas des Gallars to England to lead the French church in London.[46]

On 18 March 1560, just as the city was facing its greatest demand for ministers from France, the French community had written to Calvin asking for a minister from Geneva. It was a clear indication of the importance Calvin ascribed to the London community that he was prepared to send des Gallars, who brought Genevan discipline to the French church, and who developed a close relationship with Bishop Grindal of London, responsible for the stranger churches. Grindal had co-signed the French letter to Geneva and asked Calvin and the church there to pray for the English nation. Des Gallars was very close to Calvin, who in his letter to England indicated that it was hard for him to part from this loyal colleague, who had once served as his secretary.[47] There were also other reasons for concern: Calvin was uneasy about the degree of royal control over the church. How was the church to be cleansed and restored if it walked to the heel of its political master?

Bishop Grindal wrote to Calvin that des Gallars was of great assistance to him and 'our churches'.[48] A sign of his favoured status was Grindal's invitation to des Gallars to preach twice a week in Latin to the London clergy. The bishop hoped that something of the discipline and order of the French and other stranger churches would influence the English congregations.[49] However, the newly arrived and largely inexperienced minister soon became enmeshed in a series of disputes with another leading exile, Pierre Alexandre, who had been close to Cranmer, and Grindal was forced repeatedly to intervene and reconcile the combatants. In a series of letters Calvin supported des Gallars in his new post, assuring him that he had a true friend in Grindal and providing information about his wife and children, who had remained behind in Geneva. The situation grew so awkward that des Gallars informed Calvin that in his present troubles in London it was best for him to avoid mentioning the name of the Genevan reformer. Indeed, it was not just Calvin who felt the lash of Elizabeth's anger: none of those figures associated with the English church in Geneva, such as Miles Coverdale and William Whittingham, ever rose to any position in the new order. Nothing was forgotten or forgiven.

In London, des Gallars set about establishing the Genevan model of a church, and this brought him into direct conflict with a familiar problem. What about those Frenchmen who had remained in England during Mary's reign and had dissembled? Once more the talk was of Nicodemites. Des Gallars followed Calvin's line and insisted that those who had dissembled must do public penance and repent before they could be received into the community.[50] He made discipline as he had understood it in Geneva central to the French church in London, and this proved highly divisive. He remained three years in England before leaving, having the found the climate uncongenial, but his legacy was lasting, for the London church continued to favour ministers who came from Geneva.

Calvin and England is a curiously enigmatic subject. He died only six years after the accession of the Protestant queen. Their relationship had begun disastrously and never recovered, yet that was only part of the story. Through the stranger churches, French and Dutch, Geneva continued to be a major presence in England, and Calvin's name most prominent. He and Heinrich Bullinger were the continental patriarchs of the British reformations. Those who had been in exile in Calvin's city never forgot the experience: it marked them for life. They remained committed to what they had been taught there and never felt comfortable in the compromised world of the Elizabethan settlement. Many of these 'Genevans' kept themselves apart from English churches in order to preserve discipline, preferring to attend the services of the Dutch and French churches in London with their Genevan-style discipline rather than their own parishes.[51] They belonged to the generation that had been shaped by the experience of exile and through their contacts with Geneva and Zurich they became part of the Reformed church, which had been rejected by the Lutherans. When they died, the legacy remained. The stranger churches were the principal line of contact to Geneva, the practical means by which correspondence was exchanged.[52] And Puritanism took from those churches Calvin's theology, which it made its own. We are now aware of the astonishing quantity of Calvin's works translated into English during the sixteenth century, far outstripping his contemporaries, even Bullinger.[53] The 1559 *Institutes* was printed in translation in 1561, but that was only the tip of the iceberg, for it was soon followed by the biblical commentaries, particularly during the 1570s. Calvin was long dead, but in England he was now reaching the lay audience he had so vigorously pursued.[54]

Refuge of Heretics: Poland

During the years 1547 to 1553 Protestantism flourished in the regions surrounding Kraków and Lublin, mostly in the form of local movements under the protection of noble families, as was so often the case in eastern central Europe.[55] In 1550 Francisco Stancaro, the Mantuan-born Hebraist, arrived with six clerics to establish a new order for the church in Lesser Poland.[56] The order was based on the articles for Archbishop Hermann von Wied's abortive reformation in Cologne. By 1554 the first signs of an organized Reformed church were in place. Crucial support against attempts by the Catholic church to crack down on heresy was offered by the nobility who by the mid-1550s had largely secured the authority to order worship on their estates as they saw fit. In Lithuania the Polish reformation scored a considerable victory in 1553 with the conversion of Mikołaj Radziwiłł, chancellor of the Duchy of Lithuania, who controlled the vast fiefdom around Vilna. Radziwiłł became the patron of Protestant preachers and his own religious outlook shifted away from Lutheranism towards the Reformed faith. The mid-1550s was a period of great optimism.

Once more, divisions within Protestantism flared up. In Royal Prussia the Lutherans and Bohemiah Brethren dominated while evangelicals in Lithuania looked to the Swiss. Infighting spread like wildfire and, with a king unwilling to act, the situation teetered on chaos. At this point a meeting of the Polish Reformed church in Pinczów in 1556 invited Calvin, Beza and Eustache de Quesnoy, a professor at Lausanne, to Poland. Geneva was increasingly seen as the model for reformation. Calvin was slow to reply, waiting almost a year, but ultimately declined, citing his duties in Geneva and commending John a Lasco, a native. 'I do not think', he wrote, 'that you would wish me to be violently torn from the station in which I am usefully employed.'[57] Lasco returned to Poland and sought to mediate between the Lutheran and Reformed parties on the Lord's Supper, and to prevent further controversy made no mention of Calvin's doctrine of predestination.[58]

Calvin's first contact with the Polish churches came through Francesco Lismanino, a Graeco-Italian brought up in Poland and confessor of Queen Bona Sforza, who was in Geneva during 1554 purchasing books. He encouraged Calvin to write to Sigismund II, the subtle, reflective ruler of Poland from 1548 to 1572 in whom Protestants had placed great hopes.[59] During his stay in Geneva Lismanino converted to the Reformed faith, possibly under Calvin's influence, and married. The extensive contact between the two men is revealed by Calvin's considerable knowledge of Sigismund's attitudes and spiritual dilemmas. The king was somewhat sympathetic to the evangelicals, but little had come of it, and he was loath to break with Rome for fear of scuppering his chances of receiving an enormous inheritance from his Italian mother, Bona Sforza.[60]

In writing to Sigismund, Calvin went beyond the usual admonition that the king should bring about the cleansing of Christ's Church, and alighted upon a particular problem: a reluctance to act against the structures and traditions of the Roman church.

As the Papists are always obtruding their hierarchy on us, so I doubt not they are fortifying themselves with the same weapon among you. For as they see that we have the great advantage over them in all the different articles of doctrine, when defeated they have recourse to this miserable argument – that though the state of the church is exceedingly corrupt, yet it is not lawful for laymen to meddle with its defects.[61]

Calvin then offered his attack on the papacy, arguing, among other things, that if Paul, when he urged the Ephesians to unify, had intended this to mean under the headship of one person, it was a remarkable act of forgetfulness that he neglected to mention it. Christ is the only High Priest and head of the Church. Calvin drew from the model of the early church.

The ancient church indeed instituted patriarchates, and to different provinces assigned certain primacies, that by this bond of concord the bishops might remain more closely united among themselves. Exactly as if, at the present day, one archbishop should have a certain pre-eminence in the illustrious kingdom of Poland, not to lord it over the others, nor arrogate to himself a right of which they were forcibly deprived, but for the sake of order to occupy the first place in synods, and cherish a holy unity between his colleagues and brethren.

The 'soul of a Church is purity of doctrine' and in this respect Rome was worthy of no greater veneration than Babylon. The king should not be fooled by the claims of the papacy to a continuous line of authority; that had been forfeited when it descended into apostasy. Then came a remarkable claim: 'But God himself brings the remedy in raising up fitting and upright teachers to build up the church, now lying deformed among the ruins of Popery. And this office, which the Lord laid upon us when he made use of our services in collecting churches, is one that is altogether anomalous.' This was the mature Calvin, fully aware of his own remarkable calling, and repeatedly invoking the authority of Paul and using his words; he had no hesitation in instructing a king.

As Lismanino was returning to Poland he stopped in Zurich, and Calvin provided him with a letter of introduction to Bullinger. Calvin had obviously grown fond of Lismanino, describing him in the most positive terms. 'But as the man, not otherwise very robust, has found the climate in these parts unfavourable, and that he may not have to struggle continually with bad health, he has determined to try a change of situation. But nowhere, as he thinks, could he take up his abode more conveniently than among you.'[62]

Lismanino also carried with him a copy of Calvin's letter to Sigismund, on which Bullinger might want to 'waste half an hour'. It was, Calvin commented laconically, written by one who 'knows the disdain of princes'.

In 1555 a meeting of the Polish diet, in a spirit more Erasmian than Protestant, proposed that the king should lead a national church. Sigismund was in favour of reforms, such as clerical marriage, vernacular translations of scripture, and the Eucharist in both forms, and a blueprint for reform of the Polish church was drawn up and sent to Pope Paul IV, who was not receptive.

The same year Polish Protestants also held their own synod at Secemin which led to the emergence of radical lines of thought that bedevilled the Reformation in the east. The leading figure was Peter Gonesius, who had been influenced by Matteo Gribaldi, the Basle professor of law who had led the attack against Calvin over Servetus. Gonesius was sympathetic to Servetus' ideas, as were many Polish students studying in Basle, and sent home accounts of the execution drawn largely from Castellio.[63] Gribaldi's rejection of infant baptism and his anti-Trinitarian views, which he had derived from Servetus, were in evidence through the voice of Gonesius. Anti-Trinitarianism, which largely took the form of rejecting the divinity of Christ, had been brought into Polish lands by radical thinkers, many of whom were Italians who had made their way north through Swiss lands. When Lasco returned to his homeland he found that these men had gained considerable influence. In response, he summoned the churches of Lesser Poland in August 1557 and the Genevan *Catechism* and order of discipline were adopted. A school modelled after the Lausanne Academy was also established in Pinczów.

By the end of the 1550s the situation in Poland had become extremely confused and splintered. In 1559 Stancaro returned from abroad and launched a debate on the doctrine of the Trinity that tore apart the Polish churches and precipitated an international crisis.[64] Lasco's death in 1560 deprived the Polish Reformed church of effective leadership to face the radical challenge. Bullinger was heavily involved in battling Stancaro's views and had written repeatedly to his Polish colleague to refute the Italian's radical separation of Christ's divine and human natures. Melanchthon and Calvin were also drawn in as anxiety grew about the state of the emerging Protestant church in the east.

In a letter of June 1560 Calvin complained about the conduct of Pier Paolo Vergerio and Stancaro. The Venetian Vergerio, once a papal nuncio, had adopted radical ideas in Graubünden and Basle, where he had lived, before travelling to Poland.[65] Calvin wrote that Vergerio 'keeps gadding up and down, and poisoning with his admixtures the pure doctrines of religion'.[66]

Stancaro, he added, 'has falsely put forward our names among you to screen himself'. Calvin also wrote to the Bohemian Brethren, the descendants of the Hussites, on 1 July 1560 urging them to make agreement with the Polish Reformed church for the sake of unity. He had a stern warning for those who did not unite against the radicals who were undermining the orthodox faith.

> At present, the pious brethren [the churches in Poland], deprived of your
> co-operation, have a much harder task to perform. If Satan directs the
> attacks of Stancaro, Giorgio Biandrata and others against Poland, is it not
> your duty to come to the rescue? If you neglect it, reflect on whether one
> day your brethren might fail to come to your aid. For it will not be always
> in your own power to escape contentions from which God has to this
> point exempted you.[67]

The Stancaro controversy raged during the early 1560s and placed the Reformed churches in dire straits, especially as Stancaro had taken a leaf from Westphal's book and drawn attention to the differences between Geneva and Zurich, largely to Calvin's detriment.[68] By 1561 Stancaro had been expelled from Poland and the danger seemed to have passed, but in fact worse was to come. Giorgio Biandrata, who had made trouble for Calvin in Geneva with his doubts about the doctrine of the Trinity, appeared in Poland in 1560. Calvin had dedicated a revised version of his commentary on Acts to a Polish nobleman, and in the preface referred to Biandrata as a follower of Servetus and 'worse than Stancaro'.[69] What made Biandrata so dangerous was that he enjoyed the support of many Polish noblemen, who regarded Calvin's judgement of the man as unjust. Following the Servetus case and the discovery of anti-Trinitarian views in the Italian church in Geneva, Calvin, in contrast to Bullinger, was deeply suspicious of Italians. And despite the correspondence from Poland, he refused to believe that Biandrata had repented of earlier errors. Biandrata left Poland he for Transylvania in 1563, but by that point the damage had been done. Most of the 'Reformed' ministers in the kingdom had strong anti-Trinitarian sympathies, and by the time of Calvin's death the once promising prospect for the Reformation in the east looked very gloomy.

The Netherlands

Although evangelicals emerged early in the Low Countries, repression played a significant role in ensuring that it was not until relatively late in Calvin's life that organized churches took shape. Calvin's direct influence on these Netherlandish churches was limited to only a handful of letters and just over a dozen ministers trained in Lausanne and Geneva. But, once more, numbers mask the varied ways in which the voice of Calvin and Geneva was heard. In 1543 a friend of Calvin in Strasbourg sent two hundred copies of his *Small Treatise* to the evangelical conventicles in Tournai and Valenciennes. The work was not popular. Calvin's demand that the faithful be prepared to face either exile or martyrdom was too strong a medicine for the communities.[70] In 1544 a request was received in Strasbourg from the evangelical conventicle in Tournai and, after consultation with Calvin, Pierre Brully was sent as minister. Brully was arrested, along with twelve others, and executed, bringing Calvin's involvement in the Netherlands to an abrupt halt. From 1545 onwards the repression of heresy in the Netherlands was brutal, and over the following fifteen years the flow of blood was unstaunched. Many of the victims were Anabaptists, but the religious world of the Netherlands was extraordinarily diverse and works written by all the major reformers circulated there.

Following the execution of Brully many Dutch evangelicals went into exile, first to Wesel in the Rhineland – a church very close to Calvin's heart, as we have seen[71] – and then to London and Emden. Calvin's great concern for these exile churches made them the conduits for his influence in the Netherlands. By the mid-1550s the repression was fuelling resistance to the Catholic church and fresh attempts to erect Reformed communities were made, most notably in Antwerp in 1556. The first minister of the community was Evrard Erail, sent to the city from Geneva. The church in Antwerp faced grave dangers and had to take a number of precautions to avoid persecution.[72] At the same time it became part of the network of Reformed exile communities in the north, including Wesel, Frankfurt and, especially, Emden. With the accession of Elizabeth in 1558, the Dutch community in London once again became a crucial link in the chain. These churches exchanged ministers and literature and assisted one another in the resolution of internal conflicts. Strasbourg was an important source of influence, but so too was Geneva, and most looked to Calvin for advice.

Calvin wrote to the church in Antwerp in December 1556 expressing his abiding concern, 'for, as you have affection for me, I am convinced that it gives you pleasure that I keep you in remembrance'.[73] The congregation had high expectations of Calvin, but he warned them against relying on his teaching; they should turn rather to reading God's Word and maintaining its doctrine. The force of the letter, however, lay in his exhortation to the community not to follow the pattern of the Nicodemites. Significantly, his *Answer to the Nicodemite Gentlemen* had been translated into Dutch in 1554, the first of his works to appear in that language.[74] The first Dutch version of the *Institutes*, in contrast, did not appear until 1560. Calvin's anti-Nicodemite treatises, printed in Emden, were intended to counter widespread dissembling among Dutch evangelicals. In his letter, Calvin added his powerful voice.

> No doubt, it is not everything to read and to hear, for our chief end is to give to God in all holiness and perfection, and though we cannot persevere in that course till we are stripped of this corruptible nature, yet we have to walk in uprightness of life, and serve with a pure conscience that God of mercy who has set us aside for himself. But because of our natural infirmities and because, surrounded as we are by so many temptations, we speedily lose sight of our high calling and thus fail to acquit ourselves of our duty, our natural inconstancy transporting us hither and thither all the while, we have much need to avail ourselves of the aids which God has afforded us. Therefore, my brethren, exercise yourselves not only by reading in private, but also by assembling yourselves in the name of Jesus Christ, in order to call upon God and receive profitable instruction, that you may advance more and more.

Calvin was dead by the time of the outbreak of the Dutch Revolt in 1566, the 'Wonderyear' marked so dramatically by open-air preaching and iconoclasm as Protestants first came out of hiding, then retreated again into secret meetings and exile. His influence remained pervasive, however. His works were translated and disseminated through the networks that held together the exile communities. Young men were sent to Geneva to train as ministers before returning home to preach. When the Dutch churches emerged from hiding in the 1570s they adopted consistorial church government largely in line with Genevan practice, though with important modifications. Calvin's catechism was widely held as the standard of Reformed teaching and was used throughout the churches.

Success in the Empire: The Palatinate

During the period of religious turmoil within the empire Count Frederick II, who reigned from 1544 till 1556, had attempted to maintain a middle course that preserved peace in the Palatine electorate. Although a loyal servant of the Habsburgs, he had come in contact with Martin Bucer in the 1520s and employed him as a chaplain. During the religious colloquies of the 1540s he had sought to mediate between the Catholic and Lutheran parties, and his own religious instincts were moderate. By the 1540s, however, he had moved significantly towards Protestantism and by the middle of the decade a new church order had been drawn up for the electorate. The crushing defeat of the Schmalkaldic League in 1547 and the imposition of the Interim forced Frederick once more to change direction. He accepted the Interim, though it was never implemented in his lands and he did not dismiss leading Protestant advisers. However, the Palatinate was without any significant theological leadership, and when Charles V was defeated in 1552 Protestantism was not automatically restored.

After 1555 the German cities were bound by the Augsburg Confession, which largely eliminated Reformed influence, while in the north, as we have seen, Lutheranism was increasingly split by the divide between the Philippists and the Gnesio Lutherans. What distinguished the situation in the Palatinate was the enormous respect in which Philip Melanchthon was held. He had long been associated with the electorate and his reputation was unmatched among both political rulers and clergy. In 1558, under Elector Otto Heinrich, the University of Heidelberg was completely reformed with Melanchthon's guidance. As a result students of Melanchthon, as well as men from the Swiss churches, came to occupy prominent posts from which they could offer intellectual and church leadership.

With the accession of Frederick III in 1559 the Palatinate came under another man whose religious views were largely Melanchthonian in character. The Gnesio-Lutherans lost their last foothold and both prince and university were of one spirit. In a difficult and tumultuous dispute over the Eucharist Frederick turned to Melanchthon, whose *Judgement* was enthusiastically received by all. Melanchthon reigned supreme, though he was to die shortly thereafter in 1560. With the loss of this sage figure, the Palatinate church looked to Calvin and Bullinger for leadership. Thus, for all the disappointment Calvin had expressed in Melanchthon, it was his old friend who had in the end prepared the way for his influence to enter the empire in a significant manner.

Among those who came to Heidelberg was Kaspar Olevianus, a native of Trier in Germany who had studied law in France where he was exposed to Reformed Protestantism.[75] During a period of study in Geneva Olevianus grew close to Calvin, whom he admired enormously. He arrived in Heidelberg in 1560 to serve as professor of theology and court preacher and he looked to reform the church along the Genevan model. He saw Calvin as his mentor, and the French reformer sent letters of instruction on how to implement church discipline.[76] Calvin set out in detail every aspect of Genevan practice – the instruction of children, the use of church discipline in defending the Lord's Table, and the examination of ministers – but with the admonition that Olevianus should take what he found prudent. Shortly after Olevianus' arrival a major controversy broke out in the Palatinate over the Lord's Supper, and the elector was put under enormous pressure by the Lutheran princes to expel the heretics, that is, the Reformed. Olevianus kept Calvin informed of events, reporting on the enormity of the hostility towards the Reformed theologians. The elector, a genuinely pious man, held firm and in 1562 introduced the first of the major reforms of the church, followed a year later by the Heidelberg Catechism, 129 articles written by Olevianus and Zacharius Ursinus.[77] The Catechism reflected Frederick's difficult position. Under the terms of the 1555 Peace of Augsburg only Lutheranism was tolerated in the empire. The Reformed faith was illegal. The Heidelberg Catechism was an attempt to draw together the various strains of Reformed Protestant thought within the bounds of the Augsburg Confession.[78] Born in Poland, Ursinus had boarded with Melanchthon in Wittenberg during his studies at the university. Having travelled through the empire, France and Swiss lands he came into conflict with Lutheran theologians who found his Reformed teaching suspect. In Zurich he developed a lasting friendship with Peter Martyr Vermigli, who recommended him to the elector.

The Catechism was to become one of the great documents of the Reformed faith, but it landed the elector in serious trouble. He was summoned before the imperial diet of 1566 to explain himself, and he declared that he had never read Calvin's works. By contrast the Catechism was enthusiastically greeted by the leaders of the Reformed churches. Its nature has, however, been long debated. Recent research has emphasized its composite character, drawn from the theology of Melanchthon, the Swiss reformers and Calvin.[79] This amalgam of Swiss Reformed and Melanchthonian thought that emerged in the Palatinate did demonstrate that for all the conflict it was possible to find the common ground for which Calvin had hoped.

Nevertheless, all did not go well. Not long after Calvin's death the Palatinate split on the old issue of church discipline. Olevianus was eager to introduce the Genevan consistorial system, though in 1564 a more Zurich-oriented model was implemented.[80] This led to a bruising dispute through the 1560s which pitted Geneva against Zurich, reminding us of the extent to which differences within the Reformed church had been contained by personal relations between Bullinger and Calvin.

The extent of Calvin's international influence cannot be measured by confessions, church ordinances or even letters. His works were widely read and his ideas appropriated in varying degrees even in lands that never saw a Reformation. Through personal contacts, his teaching and preaching in Geneva and his correspondence, he reached a vast and diverse body of individuals. His reputation among those who were sympathetic was immense, but he did not stand alone. He was read alongside the other great reformers, such as Bullinger, Melanchthon and Vermigli. He never attempted to impose his views on church organization, and never regarded Geneva, despite Knox's praise, as the gold standard. Calvin's international work grew from his abiding belief that the visible churches had to be unified in doctrine, not in outward forms. During his life he saw very little of that unity, but through the massive printing of his works he remained in death its most prominent advocate.

CHAPTER SIXTEEN

The 'Perfecte Schoole of Christe'

The Godly Community

JOHN KNOX'S description of Geneva's perfections might well have made Calvin bristle. He could hope that with the establishment of true doctrine, proper worship and godly discipline the city would be an example to the struggling reform movements across Europe, but it was not a blueprint. And Geneva was by no means perfect. The very suggestion mocked Calvin's view that the life of the church, and of individual Christians, is measured in a daily struggle against sin in which there is much failure. Sustained by the Word of God and fed by the Body of Christ, the faithful are almost home: they have one foot in the kingdom. Perfection comes in the next world. Until then women and men must live in imperfect communities locked in an unceasing struggle to maintain faithfulness to God's commandments. Calvin never underestimated the task. Yet he never offered a golden key. There was no one form of Christian community. As long as God's commandments are obeyed and Christians live together in love the external forms of community could vary according to necessity. This was Calvin's long-held view of accommodation. As he pointed out to the community in Frankfurt, exile made its own demands. The more important question, as it was for the Israelites, was whether obedience to God was preserved. This message made Calvin the most powerful voice of his generation. He had transformed the Erasmian and Reformation message of inner spirituality and the journey to salvation into a vision of church life that could be lived in the maelstrom of the early-modern world.

For all its horrors, that world, for Calvin, is God's creation. Evil is not in God's handiwork, but in human sinfulness. Men and women must face up to the reality and consequences of their existence; there is no flight. The chaos and sin do not threaten God's redemption or promises, of that the Christian can be assured. Calvin feared social unrest and insisted on order and structures of power. Rebellion and disorder were the fruits of sin. People must obey their rulers; they must fear them. Commerce and civil order are maintained through the necessary distinctions in society in which each part fulfils its role. In this respect Calvin held typical sixteenth-century views of society: there was no social mobility. He believed that people could change their vocations, but not their social rank, and he distrusted rash alterations. The nobility were the natural ruling class. There was one piece of the puzzle, however, that did not fit easily. Calvin's adherence to the social structures of the day is inverted in his account of his calling. He portrayed himself as David, chosen from humble background for high office. His prophetic and apostolic standing in Geneva and the wider church, he was certain, arose from a special dispensation from God. This justified his resistance to civil rule, as it did Bullinger's in Zurich. A commanding personality carried great weight in the Protestant churches, and although frequently presented as prophetic, it rubbed harshly against the authority of institutions.[1]

Society for Calvin was mixed. The faithful live among the godless, who outnumber them greatly, and this is God's will. Christians are not exempt from the vicissitudes of this life – indeed, suffering is God's testing – and the faithful are called to live in communities, not to exclude themselves. This was at the root of Calvin's objection to the Anabaptists and to any suggestion of moral perfection in this world.[2] Christians remain sinners and the piety of their Church is imperfect: love, repentance, forgiveness and restoration are the daily fare of life. And the institutions of the Church exist to deal with the constant cycle of sin and forgiveness. Teaching, worship and admonition must sustain the Christian life, just as the sacrament of the Lord's Supper, for Calvin, was a true feeding of Christians to maintain their faith.

Calvin's mind always turned to the community, and he never privileged the salvation of individuals – even the punishment of one person was to heal the whole body. Individual vocations serve the larger community, and social, commercial and legal bonds must be preserved with justice and equity. The body, following the commonplace metaphor of the sixteenth century, depended on the health of its individual members as they worked together: Christians, by which Calvin largely meant men, should engage with the world – study the arts, take part in the economic and political life of the community; they should use the courts when necessary, but only out of love. A well-ordered state is a gift from God, and Calvin praised the mechanical arts, agriculture, architecture and all manual occupations because these pursuits promote the welfare and preservation of human society.[3]

The hand of providence is ever present. God's mysterious rule of the world is beyond human comprehension, though its signs are to be read in scripture and creation. God reaches out to humanity, overcoming sin and disobedience, but the divine purpose remains unknown. Christians know that God cares for them, but the limitations of their knowledge keep them humble and attentive to the Word.[4] Desire to know more, Calvin thundered, is shameless pride and the error of those who decry predestination. God is utterly free to decide, and that decision flows from divine goodness. That God should choose anyone for salvation is an extraordinarily generous act and something for which Christians should be thankful. To probe for reasons was to fly too close to the sun.

The Church is persecuted and its members are a minority – nothing else was to be expected – yet it must not separate itself from the world because God works in creation. Everything is contingent until the final coming of Christ, and humans are charged with labouring to cultivate God's world, to sow peace and fellowship. Resignation to fate and delusions of perfection were equally abhorrent to Calvin.[5] God's providence is an excuse for neither inaction nor wickedness; it encourages joy among the faithful, and fortifies them to face the hardships of the world, but it is not an inoculation. The Gospel teaches God's everlasting kindness and love; it is the source of comfort, and that is its chief power. Christians should wait on God with patience and perseverance, and submit to the divine will.

The Weakened Flesh

In 1555 Calvin was forty-six years old, a widower and in failing health. The triumphalist view of history remembers his ascendancy in Geneva over the Perrinists in a manner akin to Moses parting the Red Sea. To Calvin, however, the world looked very different. By the middle of the decade the daily grind of work was taking a terrible toll on a physical frame hardly able to bear the load. In addition to the migraines and bowel problems that plagued him through much of his adult life, Calvin suffered from gout.[6] This excess of uric acid led to the gallstones of which he frequently complained in his letters. Political victory brought no release from physical pain; he began to suffer severe night sweats that induced the coughing up of blood, indicating pulmonary tuberculosis. It grew much worse. His bowel movements were full of parasites such as hookworms, which exacerbated blood loss and left him exhausted and anaemic. Coughing and fatigue frequently rendered him unable to dictate letters or tracts for weeks or even months at a time. He ate very little, usually once a day, and frequently fasted, all of which contributed to his physical degeneration. Friends described him as little more than skin and bones.

In the autumn of 1558 Calvin's health took a serious turn for the worse, as he reported to Melanchthon.

At first, when the fit came upon me as I was asleep or dozing it was not difficult for it to steal a march on me without my perceiving it, especially as it was accompanied by very troublesome and acute pains to which I am well accustomed from a long familiarity with them. But when the shivering fit once seized me at supper time I thought it quite sufficient to rid myself in my usual manner of my dyspepsia by a rigid fasting. ... Nearly six weeks have now elapsed since I became acquainted with the nature of my complaint, during which I have been in the hands of the doctors who keep me shut up in my bedroom and pretty much confine me to bed in which I am protected by a double coverlet.[7]

The detail lavished on Melanchthon, as on other friends, was not simply information. Calvin's own body was part of God's providence: his torments were his fate. He might not face martyrdom or persecution directly but his depredations connected him directly to his fellow Christians and the experiences of Paul, whose account of his afflictions on behalf of Christ and the Church profoundly moved the Frenchman. In 2 Corinthians Paul relates how, shipwrecked and beaten, he survived in extreme danger. Calvin asked 'whether anyone can be Christ's without undergoing so many evils, dangers and vexations. My answer is that all these things are not necessarily required of everyone but, where they are seen, a greater and more illustrious testimony is given. The man who is singled out by so many marks of distinction will not despise others who are less noble or less tried, nor will he be puffed up with pride.'[8] His broken body belonged to his special calling.

Painful Endings

Calvin was never a solitary figure. After the death of Idelette, he did not express any desire to marry again, and in contrast to other reformers never sought another wife, despite the obvious comfort he had derived from her love and support. His inclinations ran counter to his advice to other widowers that they should remarry. To some extent Idelette's place was taken by Calvin's brother Antoine and his wife, who moved into the house on rue des Chanoines. Without impugning his genuine affection for Idelette, what Calvin clearly wanted and needed was someone to look after him and keep the house.

Throughout the endless conflicts with political opponents, with Bolsec, Servetus, Westphal and the Italians, Calvin was sustained by a devoted circle of friends who tended to his physical and professional needs. It was a fluid body made up of men who arrived, mostly from France, drawn by his reputation, but its mainstays were Farel and Viret. In the 1550s, however, changes took place with the appearance of new faces such as Theodore Beza. Also, Calvin's relationship with Farel and Viret began to alter: the old triumvirate gave way to a circle of highly talented, well-educated men. They were individuals after his own heart, generally humanists who had studied law in France. He did not abruptly turn his back on old comrades, but in subtle, and sometimes painful, moments figures such as François Bauduin, François Hotman, Jean Girard and Valérand Poullain, once close colleagues, drifted to the margins.

The endless disputes of the 1550s were not confined to theological differences; they were deeply personal. In the heat of battle Calvin demanded full loyalty from friends and this could push them to breaking point. Jacques de Bourgogne (known as de Falais), second cousin of Emperor Charles V, had, together with his wife, converted with great notoriety to the evangelical faith in the 1540s.[9] The conversion of such high-ranking figures had immediately caught Calvin's attention, and he was not slow to grasp the propaganda opportunity, dedicating his commentary on 1 Corinthians to de Falais.[10] He encouraged the couple to come to Geneva, and was attentive to their needs to the point of unctuousness, even lambasting Valérand Poullain for failing to serve the de Falaises with adequate respect. He exhorted them to remain firm in their faith and set an example for others, in the hope of winning other noble converts. Strikingly, he addressed them separately, shrewdly assessing that Yolande de Brederode, Madame de Falais, was a person of strong character who had considerable influence on her husband. Calvin exchanged many letters with her offering spiritual advice and consolation.[11]

The relationship crashed when it emerged that de Falais' evangelical sympathies were different from Calvin's, and that he found much of the reformer's theology disturbing. Not only did he back Bolsec, who had lived in his home for a while and had tended to the nobleman medically, but he expressed sympathy for Castellio and other critics of Calvin's teaching on predestination. To make matters worse, de Falais had close links with Basle and its circle of Calvin's opponents. This was a recipe for confrontation. Calvin's enthusiasm for a noble supporter had initially blinded him to what was transpiring. When he finally realized that de Falais had defended Bolsec, his anger was volcanic. 'When you went to such lengths, after having been duly informed by me, your object in extolling him [Bolsec] so highly must have been to have us and our whole doctrine condemned, of which, he has shown himself so deadly, so furious, and so diabolical an enemy that he has not blushed to write: – The God of Calvin is hypocritical, mendacious, perfidious, unjust, the provoker and patron of crimes, and worse than the devil himself.'[12] The sense of betrayal was shattering.

> As it chanced, your friend immediately after, or the following day, asked me if I had seen you. I replied that I had, and that I was sorry for it, and I added that if you were to pass a hundred times I should avoid all contact with you more carefully than with the most avowed enemies, since in showing yourself so intimate with that man, you were, as I have since been informed, the panegyrist of Castellio, who is so perverse with all kinds of impiety that in truth I had a hundred times rather be a papist.

For Calvin, friendship was framed by faithfulness to the cause of Christ's Church, and while this permitted precious little room for sentiment, it was also grounded in personal loyalty. In 1558, after almost thirty-five years, the relationship with Guillaume Farel came to a tragic end. Farel, aged sixty-nine, proposed marriage to a young girl of about sixteen who, together with her brother and widowed mother, had been offered refuge in his house. Calvin was horrified by the scandal, even suggesting to friends that Farel was mentally unstable. Farel came to Geneva in late summer 1558 to plead for support, but in vain. Calvin wrote an extremely ill-judged letter to the ministers of Neuchâtel in September 1558 in which he claimed that their opponents would see this marriage as manna from heaven, confirming all their accusations of moral dissoluteness among the Reformed clergy.[13] It was nothing short of outrageous, according to Calvin, that such an old man should marry a young girl. He regarded the matter as beyond repair for the banns had been announced, but was clear that if his advice had been followed in the first place events would never have reached this lamentable stage. He wrote to Farel to explain himself further. 'When I told you to your face that I would come neither to your espousals nor to your marriage it was because it was not possible and I judged it inexpedient. I do not know what your new invitation can mean. Had I the greatest desire to comply with your wishes, I am nevertheless prevented by several causes.'[14]

The wedding went ahead on 20 December 1558 and Calvin's predictions about the consequences proved sadly prescient. In Paris the Protestant congregation was shocked. The man who had brought about the reformation in Geneva and introduced the marriage of clergy had caused a damaging scandal by marrying a woman fifty years younger than himself.[15] The Reformation had a disaster on its hands, and Calvin had to act. There was no possibility of a divorce. He claimed that Farel had succumbed to mental illness and was not of right mind, arguing that others should not put too much pressure on him lest he be driven to suicide. In so doing, Calvin brutally cut himself loose from his long-time friend and sought nothing more than damage limitation. The story became even more pathetic: the couple had a son, born in the year of Calvin's death, whom they called Jean. Was he named after the man who had turned his back on his friend?

There was silence between the two men until just before Calvin died, when he dictated a letter to Farel in which he seemed to offer a form of apology. Farel had travelled to Geneva one final time to see the dying Calvin, but all we know of their meeting is that they shared a late supper. One can only guess what was discussed between these two warriors. Farel remained an outcast: he was not informed of Calvin's death until nine days after his friend's passing.

With Pierre Viret there was no spectacular parting of the ways. Calvin never lost sight of his friend's considerable talents, but during the 1550s there developed a clash of personalities within Calvin's circle as well as contrasting responses to the situation in France. For Viret, part of the problem was his poor relationship with Theodore Beza, with whom he taught in Lausanne. Calvin's growing fondness and respect for Beza was evident in his willingness to charge the young Frenchman with important tasks such as the revision of the Bible translation and the response to Castellio. Beza was a fellow Frenchman and a member of a minor noble family, qualities that attracted Calvin, whose soft spot for the aristocracy was never disguised. Calvin also saw something of himself in

Beza: they were both deeply versed in humanist studies and the law; Beza had likewise left France following a conversion.[16] The two men were of one mind. In Beza, Calvin found a young man who might have been himself, and he groomed him for leadership, as Bucer had done in turn so many years earlier. After Calvin's death Beza would reveal himself as a brilliant – and independent – successor.[17]

For Pierre Viret, the rise of Beza did not auger well. The acrimonious closing of the Academy in Lausanne by the Bernese officials had been a severe blow, but the hyssop became all the more bitter when Viret discovered that Calvin blamed him. Viret and Beza had not enjoyed good relations in Lausanne, and on their arrival in Geneva it was the latter who was warmly welcomed. In August 1558, when Viret believed that he was being undermined by the relationship with Beza, Calvin wrote him a devastating letter in which he compared the conduct of the two in France. 'But I see no reason for your being so incensed that Beza embraces the counsels of those whom he regards as faithful and sincere servants of Christ, when you desire to be at liberty to repudiate the counsels of those who intend nothing other than what is best for you. Nor, if you are honest, ought you to be surprised that Beza subscribes to the counsel of those whom he feels to be more congenial to himself.'[18] The story is vaguely biblical: Calvin was rebuking one son, Viret, for not following his advice, and praising the other, Beza, for his obedience and prudence, not least in accepting his guidance.

Beza and Calvin were united by ideals that sealed their friendship. Both believed that the higher nobility were key to winning over France to the Reformation, both opposed iconoclasm and any form of resistance to authorities, though Beza's stance was more nuanced, and Beza was utterly loyal to Calvin's teaching on consistorial church structures and the doctrines of predestination and the sacraments. Calvin, for his part, relied on Beza's undoubted diplomatic skills when he sent him to the German lands to negotiate with the princes and then to France, where he was entrusted with sensitive missions to the king of Navarre and the church in Paris and to lead the Colloquy of Poissy. Heinrich Bullinger shared Calvin's high estimation of Beza, and after Calvin's death in 1564 the leaders of the Zurich and Geneva churches became close friends. It was Beza who arranged for Bullinger's *Decades* to be translated into French and printed in Geneva.

In Calvin's last years a distant, but not forgotten, name re-emerged. The son of François Daniel, with whom he had studied in Orléans and Bourges, and with whose family he had lived, had come to Geneva to study, clearly attracted to the Reformed faith. The young Daniel, rebelling against his father's wishes for him to study law, looked to Calvin as a mentor and intercessor. Calvin renewed contact with his old friend, who had remained within the Catholic church, and reported on the son's predicament. The letter is of interest for various reasons. Not only is it a rare moment of reflection on the early years and what had happened to his youthful circle of friends, but the theme of the missive – the responsibilities of a son to his father – must have drawn Calvin's mind to his own father. He admonished Daniel's son to stay the course. 'I reminded him of his duty,' Calvin reported to the father, 'and that he could not escape the charge of ingratitude unless he complied with your wishes.'[19] Had Calvin complied with his own father's decision that he should change to a more lucrative career in law out of fear of ingratitude? Youth, Calvin told Daniel, will not be readily told what to do. It is the duty of elders, insofar as they can, to guide and advise, and Calvin had acted as surrogate father. For, whatever career his old friend had chosen for his son, it was essential, in Calvin's eyes, that the young man be instructed in true religion. Daniel should not lament, Calvin added, that his son had left home and come to Geneva, for in the city he had grown in faith. With this came a pointed reminder of their separation. 'Would to God that in time you too could extricate yourself from the snares in which you are held entangled.' When friendship and principles collided Calvin's response could be sensitive. 'I shall always be ready,' his letter to Daniel concluded, 'for the love I bear to you, to aid him as far as my slender means will permit.'

In February 1560 Calvin wrote to Daniel once more with details of his support for the young student in Geneva, who plainly showed little inclination for the study of law. Calvin had loaned him money, a straightforward enough gesture. What lay behind the act, however, was his enduring fondness for Daniel and his family, a sentiment he openly displayed.

> The twenty-seven crowns he received from me have been paid back. I was ashamed, indeed, to accept them when I reflected on how long I have been in your debt. Nor, in truth, had I been a little richer would I have allowed a single penny to have been paid back to me. But I would have you believe that I am wholly at your service, and the little that I possess I shall always hold at the disposal of you and yours. Only will you allow me to send what I have long intended to do, a gold piece to each of your daughters as a kind of New Year's gift, that they, at least, may have some slight token of my gratitude?[20]

Vestiges of a previous life remained. We have no further evidence of contact.

'A Far-Fetched Consolation': The Psalms

Through the embattled years of the early 1550s Calvin turned to a book of the Bible from which he had long drawn comfort: the psalms. In this he was not alone, as sixteenth-century writers of all persuasions had found consolation and encouragement in the book described by the church father Ambrose as 'sweet beyond all others'. Lefèvre's publication of the psalms in 1509, in which the author sought to lead the reader to Christ, had set them alongside Paul's epistles at the centre of spiritual renewal in France.[21] Martin Bucer's 1529 commentary, similarly, was hugely influential within Protestant circles.[22] The psalms were present from the earliest days of Calvin's reforming career. In January 1537 he persuaded the council in Geneva to introduce the singing of psalms into worship, and in Strasbourg he was involved in their versification and setting to melodies. He had written prefaces for the editions of the psalms of 1542 and 1543 by Clément Marot, and for the revisions of the Olivetan Bible in 1545 and 1551, in which he spoke of their profound value to Christians in expressing the emotions of piety. During the 1550s Calvin lectured and preached on the psalms, frequently on Sunday afternoon.[23] Following the crucial elections of 1555 and the defeat of the Perrinist party he began writing his commentary on the psalms. 'I have been accustomed', he writes in the preface,

> to call this book not inappropriately, 'An Anatomy of all the Parts of the Soul' for there is not an emotion of which anyone can be conscious that is not here represented as in a mirror. Or rather, the Holy Spirit has brought to life all the grief, sorrows, fears, doubts, hopes, cares, perplexities, in short, all the distracting emotions with which our minds are agitated. The other parts of scripture contain the commandments which God enjoined his servants to announce to us. But here the prophets themselves, seeing they are presented to us as speaking to God, and laying open all their innermost thoughts and affections, call, or rather draw, each of us to the examination of ourselves. In particular, that none of our many infirmities and many vices may remain concealed.[24]

Calvin's exploration of the soul in the psalms commentary delves into all that it is to be human: the consequences of sin, the fear of God and the longing for salvation. The anguish of abandonment and the cruel prosperity of one's enemies appear alongside the thirst for justice. Calvin's biblical interpretation was never limited to drawing doctrine from scripture. It was his ability to express in words the emotional responses of the Christian to the Word of God that made him the most powerful of commentators. Much was gathered from personal experience. Calvin's own life of suffering found spiritual expression, and not merely privately but in the service of the community, the Church. Calvin could speak of the exilic life as one he knew, and of how it had brought him to God, but his writing was not autobiographical. The psalms and his insights were God speaking to the disparate and suffering Christians of the day. Calvin used the example of Israel and its exile in Babylon to address a city whose population had swollen to twenty-one thousand, but he was also speaking to the English, the French, the Dutch and the Poles. Those who knew exile were in the churches of Geneva to hear him preach, but they were also in far-flung lands where his words reached them in print and through the sermons of others.

Calvin sought to do justice to the historic setting of the Israelites while demonstrating that Israel is the Church.[25] The kingdom of David foreshadows the kingdom of Christ, and the experiences of the Israelites teach and inform the people of the sixteenth century: in Calvin's words, they look at themselves as in a mirror. With the Reformation, God has recalled the people from their Babylonian exile with the promise that they will once more be united. Yet God also consoles those languishing in seemingly hopeless predicament. God's election is their guarantee. It is the election not of particular individuals, but of the Church in which God dwells and which he will deliver.[26] The world is the theatre of God's glory most brilliantly seen in the Church, which lives in the certainty that it is grounded in God's covenantal promise and has God's protection. It will never perish.[27]

God is the dwelling place of those who have no home in the world. In psalm 102 Calvin picks up on the image of the owl to convey the experience of exile: 'As the soul is like a bird cut off from others, so are the Israelites in exile. Although the land is rich, they are cut off from their home and temple. It is described as solitary or alone because it has been bereaved of its mate, and so deeply affected are these little birds when separated from their mates that their distress exceeds almost all sorrow.'[28] Further, 'the people call out that they are abused and insulted by their enemies. The Holy Spirit has dictated this prayer to them as a means of defence.'[29] The psalms, then, are the articulation of Christians' deepest needs brought to expression by the Spirit.

Calvin repeatedly contrasts the experiences of the godly and godless. Psalm 90 offers a reflection on the fickle nature of humanity. Obsessed with long life and material comforts, and paying little heed to God until disaster strikes, humans deceive themselves that God's judgement can be avoided. Yet evil never goes unpunished. The ungodly, according to Calvin, feel God's wrath as a dog on a lead: they struggle to free themselves. The faithful, in contrast, see God's purpose in divine anger and respond in humility and with remorse. But wrath does not define God; it is, as the psalms repeatedly demonstrate, graciousness and forgiveness that reveal the full divine nature. 'Although in enriching us with his gifts he gains nothing for himself, he would have the splendour and beauty of his character manifested in dealing bountifully with us, as if his beauty were obscured when he ceases to do us good.'[30]

In Psalm 102 the Psalmist proclaims, 'But you oh Lord sit enthroned forever; your renown endures through all generations. You will arise and have compassion on Zion, for it is time to show favour to her; the appointed time has come.' With his sure command of rhetorical construction and acute pastoral sense, Calvin turns this into a searching and consoling meditation on God's relationship to humanity. 'When the prophet for his own encourage-ment sets before himself the eternity of God it seems, at first sight, to be a far-fetched consolation. For what benefit will accrue to us from the fact that God sits immutable on his heavenly throne when, at the same time, our frail and mortal condition does not permit us to remain stationary for a single moment?'[31] It is this glimpse of God, Calvin continues, that enables one to perceive the fleeting and illusory nature of life.

> But the inspired writer, calling to remembrance the promises by which God had declared that he would make the Church the object of his special care, and particularly that remarkable article of the covenant, 'I will dwell in the midst of you,' (Exodus 25:8) and, trusting to that sacred and indissoluble bond, has no hesitation in representing all the godly languishing as partakers of this celestial glory in which God dwells, though they were in a state of suffering and wretchedness.[32]

To those who had become the modern-day Israelites for their faith and looked to Geneva and Calvin, he offered this message.

> Although the Church had perished, he [the Psalmist] was persuaded that God by his wonderful power would make her rise again from death to

renovated life. This is a remarkable passage showing that the Church is not always so preserved as to appear to survive externally, but that when she seems to be dead she is suddenly created anew, whenever it so pleases God. Let no desolation, therefore, which befalls the Church deprive us of the hope that as God once created the world out of nothing, so it is his proper work to bring forth the Church from the darkness of death.[33]

This was Calvin's word to the 1550s: to the persecuted in France, the divided Christians in the empire, and refugees from Mary's England.

The Printing World

The blossoming of Genevan printing in the 1550s had three interlocking elements. First was Calvin himself. It has been estimated that Calvin printed at least 100,000 words a year from 1550 till his death fourteen years later.[34] The second was scripture: astonishingly, between 1536 and 1563 approximately 150 complete Bibles and New Testaments were produced in the city, feeding the needs of the French kingdom, where the publication of scripture in French had been proscribed by the Sorbonne in 1526. Finally, there was the Psalter, which was completed by Theodore Beza in 1562 and became a printing sensation. All of this revolved around Calvin, who was the star author in Geneva's burgeoning print firmament. Everyone understood that what he wrote made money, regardless of what one made of his teaching. His health was not only a spiritual matter, it had economic implications.

During the 1550s printing in Geneva was radically transformed. In 1548 Robert Estienne, royal printer in Paris, applied to the Bernese officials to settle in Lausanne.[35] He passed through Geneva in October 1549 and met with Calvin. Estienne had not yet fully embraced the evangelical cause, and Farel wrote a vicious letter denouncing the great printer. Calvin was more circumspect, understanding the enormity of the decision facing a man who risked losing everything in Paris. Estienne had strong connections with the Budé family, and his decision to visit was influenced by the number of noble families making their way to Geneva. When he found his works banned by Henry II, he knew it was no longer sufficient for him to read his Bible and pray. He faced exile.

Calvin, naturally, was deeply attracted to the idea of having a former royal printer produce his works, but Jean Girard, with whom the Frenchman had

had a stormy relationship during the 1540s, had backers among Calvin's opponents on the council. At the centre of the struggle was the lucrative market for Calvin's works in France, where his popularity was paid a perverse compliment by the Edict of Châteaubriant of 1551, which named Geneva as the source of seditious works. By 1552 Estienne had effectively replaced Girard as his principal printer, though ugly quarrels followed. Calvin intervened in 1554 to demand that as an author he should have final say over the granting of the printing privilege. 'Therefore he requested to be allowed to give his works to whomever he pleases, so that he can keep watch over his work and maintain his honour. Regarding Jean Girard, he will allow him to have the catechism, which will be more than enough for him to live on.'[36]

Jean Crespin was also active in Calvin's circle after his arrival in Geneva in 1548.[37] In many ways, Crespin was typical of a number of Calvin's closest friends. He came from a distinguished family of jurists in Arras and appeared to be on his way to a successful career in law. His studies at Louvain's trilingual humanist college, however, brought him into contact with Reformation ideas, and by the mid-1540s he was banned from his native Artois and forced to leave behind his pregnant wife. In 1545 he made his first visit to Geneva on his way to Strasbourg, but the stay was long enough to change his life. He was drawn to Calvin, not least because they shared views on the repugnancy of Nicodemism. Crespin returned to Geneva to stay in 1548 after he had collected his wife and daughter from France, as well as his considerable fortune, much of which had come to him through a generous dowry. As a wealthy, legally trained, well-educated Frenchman, Crespin soon fell in with the circle that included Antoine Calvin, Nicolas des Gallars, François Hotman, Charles des Joinvillers, Laurent de Normandie and Theodore Beza. And it was Beza who introduced Crespin to the printing trade, where his affluence served him well, enabling him, for example, to afford his own independent paper suppliers.

Crespin was a shrewd businessman, and the works of Calvin constituted about a quarter of his output. In particular he was given control over the vernacular texts, such as the *Catechism* and the *Form of Prayers*, both of which sold well. After some initial work for the reformer, he was given the task of producing his polemical tracts, which had an international distribution but proved less rewarding financially. Crespin did good business from Calvin, but he also played a key role in disseminating his writings to a wider, non-Latinate public. His great interest was theology for the people, and this became the core of his major achievement, his martyrologies, whose first edition arose from the death of the five students in Lyon. With his subsequent editions Crespin shaped Calvin's understanding of martyrdom into a church history and a defining mark of Genevan teaching.[38]

Although he admired Calvin enormously and followed his teachings, Crespin was not part of the close-knit circle of printers around him. With the Estienne family in particular he formed a fierce rivalry; at issue was the monopoly held by the Estiennes over the printing of Bibles, a privilege which gave rise to bitter resentment. Like the other printers, and Calvin himself on occasion, Crespin periodically fell foul of the council, and in 1560 he found himself languishing in prison for three days and fined for printing an unauthorized version of Calvin's commentary on Acts. His status in Geneva through both his role as a printer and his wealth made him a man to be reckoned with, and he was treated with respect. His importance to Geneva extended well beyond his relationship with Calvin. He had strong links with Reformed groups across Europe, particularly in the Low Countries, and very important connections in the German-speaking worlds, in both the Swiss Confederation and the empire.[39] He was close to Bullinger, whose works he printed in Geneva, and was also the major printer of Luther in Geneva during the 1550s, a profitable line brought to an abrupt end by the Westphal controversy.

Towards the end of Calvin's life others emerged, including his brother Antoine, who oversaw the final editions of the Latin and French *Institutes*, including proofreading, a job to which John, like most humanists, gave little time. Antoine also acted as marketing director, financed printing projects and oversaw sales. When Robert Estienne's son Henry proved a disappointment, it was Antoine who arranged permission from the council for another printer to be employed.[40] Antoine Vincent also became a close friend of Calvin, involved in printing his works.

In the 1550s there was also a shift in Calvin's financial backing. Between 1546 and 1554 his works were financed by the wealthy businessman René de Bienassis. After 1550 Bienassis' support for some of Calvin's enemies, including Bolsec, led to an unpleasant rift. The principal figure after 1550 was Laurent de Normandie, who assisted Calvin with his publications until the reformer's death. By 1554 de Normandie had in place a booksellers' company that dealt with Calvin's works, and he financed the *colporteurs*, the itinerant sellers of religious books, who carried the works of the Genevan presses into France.[41] In this, he was assisted by the Bourse Française, which was not only caring for the poor, but also subsidizing Geneva's missionary efforts.[42] Normandie also underwrote the Badius print house, where many of Calvin's

French works were printed, though from 1551 it was Estienne who was preparing Calvin's Latin works, which required a higher level of expertise. The organization of all these arrangements was problematic and frequent disputes marred the printing of Calvin's writings.

Before the defeat of the Perrinists, Calvin had often been required to submit to censorship of his writings, providing hostile magistrates with ample opportunity to complicate his life. Their refusal to print the Consensus Tigurinus, for example, infuriated him. Printing was a political business, and as their city was bordered by Savoy and Berne, the Genevan magistrates had to proceed with caution. Such was the situation in other major Reformed cities: both Zurich and Basle kept a close eye on what was printed, for scandalous or contentious works had very real consequences. Even after Calvin's victory the supervision of printing lay with the council, which jealously guarded its rights. On the whole, however, after 1555 there was a fair degree of trust and the council was not inclined to confront him, though periodically, to the Frenchman's extreme irritation, the magistrates would intervene.[43] For Calvin, it was not the income that concerned him, though Antoine did keep watch over that; he was determined that only works that served the Reformation should be printed in Geneva – in short, books of which he approved. He was frequently consulted by the council on whether to print certain works and gave advice on the granting of privileges, and when in 1560 three men were appointed to oversee the printing industry they were all close friends: Theodore Beza, Jean Budé and François Chevallier.[44]

'There's Calvin Who Makes Himself a Prophet'

Great preachers of the past such as Girolamo Savonarola in Florence and John Wesley in England may seem today somewhat bloodless on the printed page, for what most distinguished them is lost to us – their voice. Bland estimations of the Reformation speak of Protestantism as a religion of the book in contrast to the sensuous or affective religion of the Middle Ages. To enter Calvin's world and the world of sixteenth-century Geneva requires imagination, a sense of how the spoken word could move, anger, console and edify. Far from the solemn quiet of modern churches, preaching in the sixteenth century was somewhat akin to speaking in a tavern. Preachers had to compete with barking dogs, crying babies, general chatter and constant movement, even fist-fights. They required presence to command respect and their most important tool was their voice. Johannes Oecolampadius, the reformer of Basle and a widely admired scholar, was rendered impotent in the pulpit by a weak voice. Written texts of Calvin's sermons exist, but they are problematic. They were recorded by others and provide only an inkling of what it must have been like to hear him. He spoke with few or no notes, and often with only a copy of the Bible in front of him; sheer spontaneity was an essential part of the experience as he applied God's Word to that moment in the life of the people. It was also a matter of time. With his endless pressing engagements, Calvin simply did not have the luxury of preparing sermons, so he spoke extempore.

Nevertheless, when Calvin preached the people came. In the wake of the first war of religion in France, what must it have been like to hear these words?

> We have seen battles for such a long time. There is no end to them. And even apart from battles, we have seen how many people have been killed by wars. This has not been the case merely in one place and in a single army, but has gone on among princes who claim to be Christians and Catholics – and yet they are killing an infinite number of people. . . . One sees poor people dead among the bushes, and others who are left have to endure hunger and thirst, and heat and cold, and many deprivations – to such a degree that if you cut their throat, you would do them a favour. For they are suffering and will die ten times, so to speak, before death strikes the final blow.[45]

Calvin's sermons on Genesis from the late 1550s are full of resonances of the refugee situation in the city.[46] Over seventeen hundred men, women and children had arrived in Geneva in 1559 alone. Comparison of Calvin's sermons on Genesis with his commentary reveals how the reformer adapted his language and style for the people while making few theological concessions.[47] Accommodation did not mean dumbing down.

Calvin's authority as preacher is found in a discussion of Paul. In treating 2 Corinthians 4:3, he considers why Paul did not subject himself to the incorrect judgement of the Corinthians. Calvin identifies himself in the argument, appealing directly to God when the people are unjust. 'But when a faithful pastor sees that he is borne down by unreasonable and perverse affections, and that justice and truth have no place, he ought to appeal to God, and betake himself to his judgement-seat, regardless of human opinion, especially when he cannot secure that a true and proper knowledge of matters shall be arrived at.'[48] Calvin saw his relationship with Geneva paralleling Paul's with Corinth. The Apostle's exemplary conduct in justifying himself and teaching the Corinthians became Calvin's own defence. 'Paul, therefore, felt sin dwelling in him and confessed it. But as to his apostleship (which is the subject treated here) he had conducted himself with so much integrity and fidelity that his conscience did not accuse him of anything.'[49]

In his theological and pastoral work Calvin's example was Paul, but when he entered the pulpit it was the prophets of the Old Testament who loomed large. In 1552, preaching on Ezekiel, he quoted his opponents, to describe himself, 'There are some who say today, "There's Calvin who makes himself a prophet, when he says that one will know that there is a prophet among us. He's talking about himself. Is he a prophet?" Well, since it is the doctrine of God I am announcing, I have to use this language.'[50]

Like the prophets, Calvin spoke to particular moments in the life of the community. He once remarked of his opponents, 'They would like me to preach with closed eyes and take no notice of where I am or in which place, or at what time.'[51] Contemporary events are not often specifically mentioned, but the context was clear. He did not, however, hesitate to refer to individuals or groups present in the church, much to their consternation. In preaching, the ancient stories of the Israelites and the early Christians became the reality of the people.

When preaching, the ministers brought the Word of God to the circumstances of the community and of individuals, but listening was not passive. Calvin's whole concept of theology was focused on the application of scripture to the world; to hear the Word of God without responding was meaningless. 'Our faith should not be based on what we think, but on what God has promised us. Like Paul said, faith comes forth from hearing, not by listening to all the talk that men are producing, but by hearing the Word of God alone.'[52] Also,

> It is a good thing that we progress in continuous growth. We should not always stay at the same level. When we receive education today, we should profit from it according to the knowledge we have received. Tomorrow we will have another sermon and then a new lecture. Is that useless? Not at all! We should value the knowledge of God. In accordance with his teaching us as he pleases, we will be inspired even more to follow his holy will and persevere in the doctrine of his Word.[53]

The sermons give a sense of Calvin's rhetorical fluency. He held a mirror to his congregation and asked what they saw.

How often do we remind ourselves of the content of the sermons in order to benefit from it? How do we talk about it at home? Most of them seem to think it is sufficient to hear one sermon on Sunday as a rule. When they return, they only talk about wicked and worldly plans, instead of considering what was said in the sermon, so that they better remember what the subject has dealt with. 'No, no, they say, it only makes us depressed to think about that; let us not agonize over it.'

He added, 'They enjoy breakfast more than the testimony of their salvation.'[54]

How effective were Calvin's sermons? Part of his identification with the Old Testament prophets was the depressing sense that the message was having little impact. Calvin asked, 'For what is the cause that the Gospel has brought so little fruit among us?' He answered his own question: 'Because most of us are not interested and care little about it. Although the Gospel is being preached, and the service attended, it is only a habit. For when too much is said here, what does each one take with him of that?'[55] 'For this is difficult to endure for the servants of God, who desire the salvation of souls, and who require good development and order of the church. For we know what the task is that God has assigned us to do, when he commanded us to proclaim his Word. Therefore when we see such ingratitude in the world, namely that God's Word is despised and rejected, what else can we do but lament and sigh and have a mournful heart?'[56] The lot of the preacher and prophet was not only to be trained in sound doctrine, but also to be able to withstand attack and rejection. Calvin saw resistance as a sign of right preaching: a preacher must not avoid confrontation with the congregation; harsh words are often necessary. But with judgement comes repentance and forgiveness. Damnation cannot be preached for its own sake.

Lamentations about the indifference of the people to the message of ministers and priests could be heard across Protestant and Catholic Europe. To read Calvin's words alone is to gain the misleading impression of a battle against the stiff-necked Genevans. In fact, his appeal was quite magnetic, and his sermons drew large congregations, such that by the middle of the 1550s he was preaching at the morning and afternoon services in Saint-Pierre to accommodate the numbers. Calvin was the star, but he did not and could not work alone. He was desperately concerned that he should not become the object of a personality cult, and by the end of the 1540s had established a carefully planned system by which the ministers of the city shared services. This meant shifting responsibilities for services in the Genevan church, often also with the intention of preventing Calvin from being overloaded.[57] Each individual minister preached *lectio continua*, or progressively through each chapter of a book of the Bible, so the people could be following several preaching series at the same time. Duties were also shared: when one minister was performing the sacraments another would preach. Calvin probably left the baptism of babies to others when he preached, which also had the beneficial effect of enabling other ministers to hear his sermons. When Calvin was not preaching himself he would attend the sermons of other ministers – doubtless a daunting prospect for them.

Ministry of Reconciliation

Nothing has shaped Calvin's posthumous reputation more, with the exception of Servetus, than his belief in the disciplining of the Christian society – though, in contrast to his mentor Martin Bucer, he refused to make discipline a mark of the Church. Victory in 1555 allowed him greater room for manoeuvre, and the evidence suggests that during the last ten years of his life the Consistory became increasingly intrusive.[58] He himself continued to be a dominating presence at its meetings, interrogating men and women and issuing admonitions. We know that a surprisingly large part of Genevan society appeared before him and his colleagues – somewhere in the range of 7 per cent of the population each year. Such diligence on the part of the Consistory, it has been argued, resulted in few repeat offenders among the Genevans.[59]

Calvin's personality and mastery of the legal issues ensured his domination of the Consistory sessions.[60] When a case involved complicated matters of law or biblical interpretation he would often appear before the council on behalf of the Consistory. Capital punishment, for example, was a matter for the council and judgements were pronounced by one of the syndics.[61] The verdicts were then read out by the town crier.

The 1546 *Marriage Ordinances* had effectively put into law Calvin's conception of the institution. He argued for the freedom of the marriage contract and mutual consent of man and woman, a fundamental point he continually defended in his sermons. Consensual engagements were essential; children were not to be forced into unions by their parents. Likewise, newcomers to the city could become engaged only upon proof of character and eligibility and had otherwise to wait a year. The Consistory watched over such engagements to ensure the *Ordinances* were upheld. From 1546 it records the case of Pernodi, who 'was admonished that about four months ago he became engaged to a woman and keeps her with him without ever having married her, which is a scandal, and not according to God. He promised to do his duty and will marry her a week from Sunday.'[62] Cohabitation or premarital sex were forbidden on punishment of prison, yet neither practice was remarkable in Geneva; the Consistory dealt with many cases and Calvin preached relentlessly on the subject. Although his view of marriage was founded on consent he also argued that rape victims should marry their assailants so as not to fall into prostitution.[63]

Calvin's Consistory upheld the ideal of a family home with father, mother, children and young servants. In Geneva grounds for divorce followed those established in the other Swiss Reformed cities, and included polygamy, incest, contagious disease and physical deformity.[64] Parties could also sue for divorce on grounds of abandonment. Calvin insisted upon an open process in order to avoid the practice of the medieval church of granting private dissolutions. On the whole, however, marriage was for life and everything was done to bring husband and wife together. Calvin's work as a marriage counsellor has become evident.[65] Divorces were only reluctantly granted once every possible means of reconciliation had been exhausted. In this respect Geneva was by no means unusual: in Zurich warring spouses could be locked in a tower with bread and water until they worked out their differences.

There was not always agreement among members of the Consistory. Calvin, for instance, favoured annulment when confessional or considerable age differences existed between a couple. This, for example, would have been his preferred course of action with Farel. Adultery, as elsewhere, was a serious offence and punishable to varying degrees. Most draconian was execution, though that was limited to those whose conduct resisted all attempts at reform or which brought particular scandal, such as multiple lovers. From 1560 there was some hardening of attitudes and the biblical command to put adulterers to death was practised in Geneva, though infrequently. Four women and one man were executed before 1564.

The Consistory was prepared to intervene in the family.[66] While parents might make use of the Consistory and Small Council to impose discipline on their children – and the Consistory usually sided with the parents – these institutions also took action to protect the child in cases they recognized as abuse. Under Calvin's guidance religious instruction of the youth had shifted out of the home and into the church, though this did not prevent many youths from skipping catechism lessons.[67] In the early years after Calvin's return the penumbra of problems faced by the church was such that certain things had to be overlooked. By the 1550s, however, failure to attend catechism was no longer dealt with by admonition but with corporal punishment. In 1558 nine boys were beaten with rods for playing a form of hockey on ice. Truancy was such a problem that by the end of the 1550s officers were appointed to patrol the streets during catechism instruction. Cases record that on Sunday afternoons young men were missing catechism to participate in Papeguai, a martial competition involving archery and arquebus-fire to choose a king. One François des Eaux was summoned before the Consistory in 1560 for offering fencing lessons during catechism. Usually the schools were to administer the punishment, but fathers were also instructed to act against sons. We must bear in mind that there was probably still enmity towards Calvin in Geneva after 1555, but it would have been unwise to express it. Non-attendance was one possible form of protest.

Economic life, in Calvin's eyes, was part of the fallen world, and the human lust for material goods knew no bounds. He accepted that commerce was essential to Genevan life, but believed that it had to be regulated on account of the avaricious nature of the market. He was not opposed to the market per se and even became involved in financial transactions by recommending speculative investments to friends and by securing loans for recently arrived immigrants.[68] Reasonable profit was acceptable, but he lumped usury together with all other forms of corrupt business practices in which merchants fleeced innocent people. It was essential, therefore, that government act to prevent profiteering. Calvin proposed a 5 per cent revenue on commercial credit and supported the creation of a public bank. Along with this, however, he campaigned for the control of food prices, fair labour wages and better working conditions. In 1559 he interceded in a labour dispute between printers and journeymen, going before the council on behalf of the journeymen to ensure better pay.[69] Under his leadership the Consistory prosecuted usurers, fraudsters, price-fixers and thieves.[70] Early-modern business practices transformed radically over the sixteenth century and the ministers and laity of the Consistory would have struggled to adapt to the new culture of credit. In Geneva, loan sharks, pawnbrokers and merchants who sold a wide range of goods at hugely inflated prices were hauled before the Consistory and frequently banned from the Lord's Table.

The generation of wealth, for Calvin, could not be separated from care for the poor, and by this he did not simply mean a form of chequebook charity. Men and women as Christians, he believed, should engage in direct action on behalf of those suffering. Their duty was to serve the body, as he reminded them from the pulpit. The massive influx of French refugees during the 1550s transformed the commercial culture of Geneva. From 1555 Calvin preached more than two hundred times on Deuteronomy, and his themes often concerned the practical responsibilities of those in the city towards the refugees: landlords should not charge them higher rates, citizens should employ them, and magistrates should judge them as they did others. Even if it were more expensive to employ these Frenchmen on account of their skills, or lack of them, the Genevans should do so.[71] The economic world of an early-modern city was complex and changing, and in the case of Geneva it was profoundly affected by the vast infusion of people over the course of a decade. Calvin viewed economic matters in biblical terms: the market had to serve the overriding principle of Christian unity. It was an extremely uneasy relationship, as the records of the Consistory bear witness.

Teacher

Those who possessed Latin encountered Calvin the teacher, committed to the education of fellow ministers as well as candidates for the ministry. During the 1550s he lectured on the prophets of the Old Testament, his teaching recorded by secretaries. Jean Budé has left an account. 'When, some years ago, John Calvin undertook to expound the psalms of David, some of us who were hearers took notes for our private study. At length, however, we began to consider what a great loss it would be ... if the benefits of such lectures should be confined to so few hearers. It seemed possible [to rectify this] if instead of our usual practice, we tried to take down the lectures word for word.'[72] Over the next couple of years the system was refined in order that Calvin's lectures on the prophets could be effectively and accurately recorded. The Frenchman was for the most part satisfied, though he did remain uneasy about his extempore lectures on scripture being recorded and disseminated.

The educated audience in Geneva for Calvin's lectures consisted of ministers, scholars, *auditeurs* and those about to make the perilous journey to France to serve the emerging churches. The *auditeurs* probably came from the large influx of educated French refugees in the city, who would have had sufficient Latin to follow Calvin. In addition to the French there were refugees and visitors from other lands, such as England, Scotland, Poland and Hungary. Many members of the English church in Geneva during the 1550s attended, receiving instruction in a theology they would soon carry home. As with just about everything he did, Calvin had little time to prepare the lectures and worked from the text, relying on memory, rhetorical skills and his formidable ability to craft an argument. The results entranced his listeners.

Alongside the Consistory and the Company of Pastors, schools were, in Calvin's mind, essential to the building of Christian society. The need for education to prepare for service in the church and the civil government had been recognized in the *Ordinances* of 1541, eighteen years before the Academy was established. During the 1540s and 1550s local ministers were charged with the supervision of religious education and Calvin took on a significant role, including a heavy teaching load which he regarded as an essential part of his duty to expound scripture to different offices. Latin and Greek were available for some boys at the Collège de Rive, where, famously, Castellio had once served. What Calvin wanted, however, was an institution where instruction would be offered by masters selected by the ministers.[73]

This was not to come about until 1559 with the foundation of the Academy. For Calvin, this was Geneva's equivalent of the royal lectureships in Paris of 1530 – a triumph of Christian humanism. With the arrival of de Normandie and Estienne in the city, plans were drawn up for a college and attempts were made to find a building. Calvin began the search for learned teachers, above all a Hebraist and a Graecist essential to scriptural instruction. The Collège de Rive, which had served as a school since 1536, however, was in a poor state of repair; during the years from 1550 to 1556 the rector complained that the pupils were contracting illnesses while attempting to study within its dilapi-dated buildings. Money, not surprisingly, was ever the stumbling block: Calvin was unable to obtain sufficient financial support from the magistrates for the school.[74] The Lausanne Academy was his model, but by 1558 it had become embroiled in a battle with the Bernese magistrates, and was riven by internal agitation between Viret and Beza. In the end, the entire staff was dismissed, along with a good number of the French ministers in the Vaud. Beza had left the Academy in Lausanne shortly before its closure and come to Geneva. Most of the staff, students and ministers in Lausanne also made their way to Geneva, where they formed the core of the new Academy opened in 1559 under the rectorship of Theodore Beza.

Beza's address at the opening of the Academy was an elegant exposition of the Christian humanism he shared with John Calvin. Classical authors are an essen-tial part of the pursuit of wisdom, and much is to be learned from them in the fields of language, history, literature and philosophy. But they were pagans, not Christians, living without the light of Christ's revelation. Education serves the purpose of preparing young men for the study of scripture and service in the Church. They were to be industrious, as God demands much from them, avoiding vain intellectual curiosity and mindful of their providential role in the historic battle against antichrist.[75]

The Academy, a term rarely used at the time, consisted of two parts: the *schola privata* (Latin school) and the *schola publica* (upper school). The *schola privata* was in many ways more important for the native Genevans, who wanted a school for their children. Historians, however, have tended to focus on the *schola publica*, with its preparation of the ministers. The *schola privata* was given the new buildings, while the *schola publica* was moved to the chapel of Notre Dame la Neuve.[76] The importance of the school is seen in the amount spent by the council on the endeavour, running to almost 20 per cent of its budget in the years 1559–60. Here was Geneva's 'dissolution of the monasteries', for much of the money came from the sale of Perrinist estates, though the council also found additional means. Citizens were, for example, required to leave legacies to the Academy in their wills. Similarly, fines subsidized expenses, as when Jean Bochy printed Calvin's *Institutes* in Lyon in direct contravention of the printing rights held by Antoine Calvin.

In addition to educating the youth and future ministers of Geneva, the Academy was also a deeply confessional institution that served the needs of the church. Students were required to subscribe to the teaching of the Genevan church as expressed in the catechism. The Academy offered, for example, brief courses in Reformed theology and practice for those who had converted to Protestantism from Catholicism. In other cases, ministers who were already in France returned to refresh their education.[77] During the great expansion of French Protestant churches at the end of the 1550s Geneva was called upon to supply ministers. This was war-time production: ministers were sent out with only basic instruction. In the years after Calvin's death, however, and under the leadership of Beza, the education of ministers became more ordered.

Calvin's involvement with the Academy was significant. During the last years of his life he lectured three times a week, usually mid-afternoon for an hour. He spoke on the Bible, and, as we have seen, his audience contained many non-students. He never taught theology as a separate discipline: he taught scripture.[78] The driving force was Theodore Beza, who proved a talented and visionary rector. He saw the Academy as essential to establishing Geneva's place as a leader of the Church and he worked tirelessly to construct the new buildings, create a library and ensure that quality teachers were appointed. The Academy had arrived too late for Calvin to play a major role, but it was an essential part of his legacy. It provided the institutional framework to accompany his *Institutes*, which were intended to instruct the clergy. It seems no great irony, then, that the Academy opened in the very year that his final Latin edition of the *Institutes* appeared.

'Wonder at this Mystery': The *Institutes* of 1559

Calvin continually revised the *Institutes* in both Latin and French after his return to Geneva, constantly searching to make it a more effective tool of education. The history of the revisions is complex and need not detain us.[79] More relevant is the nature of the evolution. Each edition developed from Calvin's unceasing study of scripture, the church fathers and medieval and contemporary commentators. New material was added and only rarely was anything removed. As a result, the work grew and grew. Scholars have been able to trace much of Calvin's reading over the decades by the appearance of new references, biblical and theological, in subsequent editions. The theological disputes of the 1540s and 1550s, such as those with Bolsec, Servetus and Westphal, led to new formulations of ideas that were incorporated into the expanding text.

When Calvin was preparing his final Latin and French versions of the *Institutes* in 1558 he was seriously ill. According to Beza, he was spitting blood. It seems likely that he dictated the French translation of the work, though this remains unproven.[80] In the final Latin form of 1559 he divided the work into four books of Father, Son, Spirit and Church.[81] The first book deals with the doctrine of God; the second with redemption and Jesus Christ; the third with faith, justification, regeneration and predestination; and the fourth with the nature of the Church.[82] The central theological argument, nevertheless, remained the same: Calvin's formulation of the two-fold knowledge of God – God as creator and God as saviour.

What is the theological vision of the *Institutes?* It is utter hubris to think that this can be adequately summarized in a few lines. But what we do find is a drawing together of many of the themes developed in different works and contexts. God is revealed in the created order and all humans possess some sense of the divine. Through the theatre of glory, God, the supreme being beyond all comprehension, is knowable. This knowledge strips humanity of any excuse for not acknowledging God, but it is not sufficient for salvation. Scripture is essential to reveal God's redeeming action. God can only be known through Jesus Christ, who is revealed in the Bible. Calvin offers an explanation of the doctrine of the Trinity to defend the divine nature of Christ. He ends his treatment of God by discussing providence: the God who creates cares for creation.

In the second book, Calvin makes clear that humans can be saved only by external help, and that this is the work of Jesus Christ. Calvin speaks of the law which was given to Moses and addresses its three forms: it teaches, it is used to control the community, and it instructs the faithful to submit to the will of God. He treats the Old and New Testaments as fundamentally the same, though the superiority of the New is stressed. He argues for the essential role of Christ in salvation and for his human and divine natures.

In book three Calvin turns to faith, which reveals God's will towards humanity and the benefits of Christ's sacrifice. Faith brings the presence of Christ into the life of the believer, who is grafted onto the body of the saviour. This leads to the doctrine of justification by faith and regeneration. Through being united with Christ the believer receives all the benefits of Christ and this brings moral and spiritual improvement. Calvin then turns to predestination, which he treats as explaining the mystery of why some believe the promises of God and others do not. It is a doctrine of comfort, reassuring Christians that they are not responsible for their salvation and that God will never abandon them.

In the fourth book Calvin treats the Church, raising many of the points we have touched on earlier, including the presence of the elect and the damned in the visible Church. The sacraments of the Lord's Supper and Baptism are discussed, and much of what Calvin wrote against Westphal was brought into the *Institutes*. He was particularly concerned to explore the ways in which the spiritual presence of Christ could be described.

The 1559 *Institutes* was a masterpiece of organization and clarity, despite Calvin's serious illness. His goal in this work is to present a comprehensive account of doctrine in a clear, brief and persuasive manner. This doctrine, he maintains, is what the true Church has always taught. His purpose is to explain the teachings of the Church in the right order so that the faithful might understand. This does not replace scripture, but is intended to act as a guide to key topics to be found in the Bible. Here was a stunning vision of God, creation, humanity, salvation and the Church, but it was not Calvin's last word. It reflected the state of his thought at the end of the 1550s, his engagement with the world and his reading of scripture, all of which were dynamic.

Calvin shared with Melanchthon a concern for the right method and order of teaching, and was profoundly influenced by the latter's 1555 *Loci communes*.

He usually moved from general principles to more detailed treatment of topics. He was also deeply influenced by classical writers, above all Plato, whom he regarded as deeply religious and a master of pedagogy. The *Institutes* was to provide readers with a series of topics that would enable them to understand scripture and explain all essential points until doubt was removed from their minds and false teachings dismissed. This goal often put him at odds with his cherished ideal of brevity. He sought to define terms in the *Institutes* to enable readers to be absolutely clear about what was being said, a method he derived from Cicero and Plato.[83] These definitions were not simply intellectual categories of knowledge: they had a strong rhetorical element. They were to persuade an individual to embrace the teaching and transform his or her life. The knowledge of God's saving action is transformative.

The purpose is to bring people to God. And the constant revising of the *Institutes* reflects Calvin's continuing struggle to find a better way of educating and edifying. Even for the master of language and rhetoric this proved too much.

I urge my readers not to confine their mental interest within these too narrow limits, but to strive to rise much higher than I can lead them. For, whenever this matter is discussed, when I have tried to say all, I feel that I have as yet said little in proportion to its worth. And although my mind can think beyond what my tongue can utter, yet even my mind is conquered and overwhelmed by the greatness of the thing. Therefore, nothing remains but to break forth in wonder at this mystery, which plainly neither the mind is able to conceive nor the tongue to express.[84]

Obedience, submission, humility – these were the watchwords of Calvin's view of the Christian life as expressed from the pulpit, the printing press and in the Consistory meeting. He also spoke of almighty God who was revealed by creation and whose love extended to that creation. It was a hierarchical vision in which Calvin's personal authority as a prophet of the Church loomed large, and his presence in Geneva was towering, despite his failing body. But as the flames of reform were fanned across his native France, and the Protestant churches began to emerge from hiding, other voices rose up that spoke of resistance and fighting, of blood and subterfuge. Calvin could only watch as the movement that embraced his name quickly slipped from his grasp.

CHAPTER SEVENTEEN

Churches and Blood: France

'Do not doubt that our brethren of France hold the same opinions that are taught by me,' wrote Calvin to the Elector Palatine in 1558.[1] He was not being immodest. Although Farel and Viret, as well as Bullinger in translation, were widely read during the 1540s and 1550s, Calvin had clearly emerged as the dominant Protestant author in France. The kingdom was awash with publications transported by *colporteurs* and merchants from Geneva along the main arteries of France. By 1550, Calvin had cultivated close contacts with evangelical conventicles who looked to Geneva for spiritual leadership and material support. After the death of Marguerite of Navarre in 1549 the Frenchman was regarded by many as the undisputed leader of religious reform. In 1550 the regent at Nîmes, Claude Baduel, wrote to Philip Melanchthon, his former teacher in Wittenberg, that their only solace lay in 'the teaching of God's Word ... the Genevan church ... and John Calvin, who through that piety, sound teaching and strength of soul that you know so well, consoles us in our deepest misfortune frequently and powerfully with his letters'.[2] Calvin's was the voice of French reform. His *Institutes*, in Latin and French, the biblical commentaries and polemical works combined to form a coherent message of a faithful, present God whose will is inscrutable, but whose love for those suffering for the faith is beyond doubt. His vision was of a God to be worshipped with hands unsoiled by idolatry, a God who demanded self-sacrifice and self-denial. Calvin gave purpose to living under the cross – persecution was a sign of election, a powerful reminder that God would never abandon the faithful. 'It becomes you to turn your eyes during these great troubles,' he wrote to his countrymen, and rejoice that he has esteemed you worthy of suffering affliction for his Word rather than chastisement for your sins, which we all deserve should he not support us by his grace. And if he promises to console poor sinners who received patiently correction from his hand, be confident that the aid and comfort of his Holy Spirit will not fail you, when putting your trust in him you shall accept the condition to which he has subjected his children.[3]

Yet Calvin's relationship with his homeland was not untroubled. Every day from Geneva he must have looked to the west to the land he had left twenty years previously. His own experience as a reformer had been defined by the decision to go into exile. During the 1540s he had waged a rugged campaign against those evangelicals who, in his eyes, had faint-heartedly embraced the Gospel while refusing to make a clean break with the Roman church. In Geneva, with the aid of Crespin's martyrology, he had succeeded in constructing a model in which suffering, exile and death were the acceptable responses to persecution – there was no third way for those needing consciences assuaged. Many followed Calvin's call and chose exile, flooding Geneva and overwhelming its religious and political culture, culminating in the triumph of his supporters in 1555. But others, in large numbers, did not. Calvin was not unaware of the attractions of concealment in a culture where so many had lost their lives for their beliefs. And the appearance of organized churches from the mid-1550s under noble patronage was no guarantee of safety. Calvin was forced into a dialogue with a mentality he reviled.

The Great Expansion

Calvin's hopes for the conversion of France lay with the leadership of the high nobility, and this led him to place his trust in men such as Antoine of Navarre and the Prince of Condé, both of whom ultimately disappointed. The conversion of so many nobles during the 1550s to the Protestant cause dazzled, even blinded, him, given that he had always inclined to an exalted view of their status. His admiration, however, had its limitations; as an outsider, he did not grasp aspects of aristocratic culture, and this extended to their fickle relationship with religion. Conversion among the nobles, in particular, was a slippery business, and confessional allegiance was elastic. Similarly, the acceptance by a noble of the Reformed faith did not ensure the conversion of the entire household; it only opened the door to the possibility of change.[4] Religion was complex, and the nobles in France, as in Scotland and elsewhere, tended to cherry-pick what suited them and disregard what did not. Conversion also rarely involved surrendering their way of life: no amount of moralizing from Geneva would stop the dancing, music, feasts and pageants. The nobility lived by codes of honour at odds with Calvin's teaching, and if there was to be a relationship compromises had to be found. Calvin was aware of this and recognized that for the sake of the Gospel in France he would have to accept, or at least turn a blind eye to, the conduct of those on whom he had banked so heavily.

From 1555 Protestant churches in France began to appear in large numbers, together with spectacular conversions among the nobility. The two phenomena were linked: noble converts offered protection to the nascent churches. In this period of growth Calvin encouraged his countrymen to shift from clandestine meetings to open churches with ministers, sacraments and consistories.[5] He dispatched numerous letters and ministers to the disparate churches to lay down appropriate forms of belief and conduct. He urged the brethren in Paris to admonish one another and avoid dissension at all costs, warning that if they turned on each other they would be 'prey for the wolf'.[6] To the church in Poitiers Calvin recommended that they should not take unnecessary risks and should avoid detection by moving from one house to another. Each person must be prepared to allow his home to be used for worship. Significantly, Calvin did not dictate the form of the meetings, leaving that to God's guidance and local arrangements.[7] The church in Angers was given similar advice: the brethren should separate themselves from the abominations of antichrist without unduly imperilling lives. They were to preserve order and discipline and avoid contention. 'We have rejoiced to hear that you have already estab-lished a certain order and police to prevent scandals, and serve as a curb to yourselves. Beware of abolishing such a discipline, but strive to enforce it, and let each of you submit to it to show that the spirit of meekness prevails among you.'[8]

The successes were stunning, and by 1559 there were at least fifty-nine churches across the kingdom. The areas of greatest growth were Guyenne, Gascony, Normandy, Dauphiné and Languedoc, where the movement enjoyed noble support. Those most attracted to Reformed teachings were the urban middle class, and Paris saw the emergence of a significant body of adherents. The Protestant church in Paris numbered among its worshippers members of distinguished families. Success brought grave dangers, and in September 1557 a total of 130 men, women and children were arrested during a service in the

rue Saint-Jacques.[9] Some of the noblemen present were armed with swords
and fought their way out, leaving the others to be hauled off to prison. The
clash of swords and the helplessness of families starkly revealed a conundrum.
Was it legitimate to resist? Calvin wrote to the church in Paris offering
sympathy, but rigorously denounced violence. Rue Saint-Jacques was the first
organized violence against the Protestants in Paris, but not the last. The defeat
of the French army at Saint-Quentin in August by Spanish forces created a
poisonous atmosphere in the capital.[10] The Habsburg army stood less than a
hundred miles from Paris and fear gripped the city. Calvin was kept informed
of events by the ministers in Paris, who visited the imprisoned Protestants and
encouraged them in their faith.

The arrests in rue Saint-Jacques disrupted the Protestant movement, but by
no means stopped it. François d'Andelot de Coligny from the great Châtillon
family and a leading military figure had converted to Protestantism in 1556
and began evangelizing his estates in Brittany. Under instructions from Calvin
the Paris ministers assiduously cultivated the higher nobility, including
d'Andelot's brother, Gaspard de Coligny, Admiral of France. By the spring of
1558 things looked promising again for the Protestants in Paris. A series of
rallies was held on the left bank during May at which psalms were sung. At least
one was attended by Antoine of Navarre, who, as First Prince of the Blood, the
title of the most senior member of the royal house not a son of the monarch,
was the biggest prize of all. The King of Navarre, son-in-law of Marguerite,
however, proved a difficult, even fickle ally, self-indulgent and deeply wed to
the luxuries of court life, including dancing and feasting. All of this appalled
Calvin, but for the moment had to be overlooked. He did what he could, and
wrote numerous letters to Antoine urging him to take the lead in reforming
religion, though he recognized that the king did not share his commitment to
the cause.

> I am quite aware what important results the confession which you will
> make may have to disquiet you in your person, royal dignity, states,
> honours and property. But, whatever comes of it, you ought to consider,
> Sire, how much you are bound and indebted to Him, from whom you
> hold all which you possess, and from whom you expect what is yet far
> better, namely, the heavenly inheritance. The high rank in which you are
> placed does not exempt you, as you know, from the law and rule which
> is common to all the faithful, to maintain the doctrine of our Lord Jesus
> Christ in which lies all our happiness and our salvation.[11]

The prophetic admonitions were to have little effect.

François d'Andelot de Coligny's conversion, in contrast, was followed by zealous activity, particularly in the Loire region, where he played a key role in planting churches. His new religious fervour, however, met with the opprobrium of the court of Henry II and in 1558 he was placed under house arrest. Calvin knew of the events in Paris surrounding d'Andelot's confinement through letters from the minister Jean Macard, whom he had sent to the church there. He was extremely fond of Macard and admired his courage, amply displayed by the minister when he busied himself in visiting the imprisoned faithful and serving victims of the plague. The situation with d'Andelot was critical; Calvin was desperate not to lose this important convert when the Reformed churches needed noble protection. In full prophetic tone he wrote to d'Andelot, urging him to stand firm or suffer eternal consequences.

> Continue and stop your ears against those who endeavour to turn you from the simplicity of Jesus Christ, persons whom Paul classes with seducers to inspire us with horror for their deceits and allurements. You know that, though the confession of our faith may seem to be useless in the eyes of men, it is nonetheless well pleasing and precious in those of God. It remains for you to offer to him this complete sacrifice, since it has pleased him to consecrate you to his service.[12]

To Calvin's horror, d'Andelot did waver and offered a half-hearted recantation to save his skin.

Henry II was determined to do something about the presence in his kingdom of 'Lutherans', as they were known, but he was caught up in the endless wars against the Habsburgs. The Edict of Compiègne of July 1557 was a desperate measure to stop the rot. The death penalty was introduced for those who persisted in the Reformed faith, but fierce resistance arose from the Paris Parlement, where the Protestants had made considerable progress. With the Peace of Cateau-Cambrésis in April 1559, however, Henry was able to turn his face towards the heretics infecting his capital. Dramatically, the king personally attended a session of the Paris Parlement in June 1559 to learn why so little action had been taken to implement his edicts. Protestant members of the Parlement openly defied him, including Anne du Bourg, a magistrate and nephew of the chancellor, who spoke against him, against his fervent Catholic mistress and against the persecutions. Henry resolved that du Bourg should die.

Events, however, took another unexpected turn. At the end of June 1559 Henry II was seriously wounded in a jousting match, dying ten days later from a splinter that had penetrated his brain through the eye. The death of the king, who had so ferociously, if not entirely successfully, persecuted the Reformed, led to the collapse of royal authority. The French monarchy passed to a sickly boy of fifteen, Francis II under the control of his mother, Catherine de' Medici. The principal rivals in the kingdom were the Montmorency family, the richest landowners, to whom belonged Coligny and d'Andelot, and the Guises. Catherine, with two weak sons, had to negotiate between these powerful families that stood on either side of the confessional divide. Calvin sent the minister Antoine de la Roche Chandieu to the King of Navarre with the message that the way was now open to him to become regent. Antoine was not interested. Many were disappointed in Navarre, but Calvin continued to insist that only the First Prince of the Blood could act.

Such diffidence, frustrating in Geneva, was understandable given the extreme dangers faced by Protestants in Paris, where fear and death reigned. The Protestant minister Macard had been warned that a list of names of evangelicals was in possession of the Cardinal of Lorraine, a member of the Guise family, who was prepared to hunt down heretics.[13] By the summer of 1559 women and men were being executed in front of raucous crowds in the city, their tongues cut out to prevent them making a confession of faith before their death. Bodies of those who had been hanged were torn down by the spectators and dragged through the streets. The matter was not simply religion: the crowds were persuaded that heretics posed a serious threat to the moral order of the city.[14] As the trial of du Bourg came to its conclusion in December 1559 there were rumours that Protestants intended to raze the city. And when he was executed just before Christmas, extra precautions were taken to guard against any rescue attempt.

The Protestant churches were taking shape with the first national synod in Paris in 1559.[15] The synod was led by François de Morel, sent by Calvin to Paris, and Antoine de la Roche Chandieu, a member of a Burgundian noble family who had studied in Geneva under Calvin before becoming minister of the church in Paris. Although Geneva's status was fully acknowledged, the meeting in Paris had a mind of its own and Genevan positions were adapted for changing circumstances. As a result a distinctive direction emerged.[16] Calvin was opposed to a new confession of faith, preferring that the French church adopt the Genevan, but the ministers in Paris thought otherwise. Calvin reluctantly agreed and prepared a new version.[17] De Morel assured

Calvin that the synod added only five articles to the draft sent from Geneva, but in fact the final version had little of Calvin's original.[18]

The year 1560 was a high-water mark in the conversion of the nobility to the Reformed faith, and noblewomen played a crucial role. They included Jeanne d'Albret, wife of Antoine of Navarre and daughter of Queen Marguerite.[19] Jeanne sponsored Reformed preaching in Béarn and announced her conversion in 1560, a major triumph for the cause. In reply to a letter from her, Calvin wrote in early January expressing his great joy at her conversion.[20] Navarre and Béarn, which lay north of the Pyrenees, formed an independent kingdom which was joined to France by personal union when Jeanne's son became King Henry IV of France.

Other converts included Charlotte de Laval, wife of Admiral Coligny, and Madeleine de Mailly, Countess de Roye, whose daughter was married to the Prince of Condé, younger brother of Antoine of Navarre, and who was decisive in bringing about his conversion. Calvin remained in close contact with these women and never underestimated their importance, but these relationships were not uncomplicated. At precisely the moment when events in France were flourishing, Calvin had suffered a serious reverse in England, as we saw, with the tract by John Knox against female rulers. The mishap had forced him to clarify his position on the role of women. What emerged was subtle and revealing. Women, he had assured Cecil in England, had been raised up by God to serve as rulers, as the Bible amply demonstrated, but this was generally in times of emergency and served as a sign of God's wrath. While they were certainly legitimate and godly – Deborah was one such – the natural order was for men to rule. This attitude towards women in high office was evident in Calvin's correspondence with the noble ladies of France: on the whole, he limited his remarks to spiritual counsel and encouragement, and did not enter into matters of politics and theology.

Calvin's strategy doggedly remained to win over the feckless Antoine, and in 1560 he sent Beza to Nérac to encourage reform and fortify the wavering King of Navarre. Beza was at one with Calvin in this approach, and attempted to persuade Antoine and his brother Louis, Prince of Condé, to throw their weight behind the Reformed churches against the Guises.[21] In the end, Beza carried little influence with Antoine, but he did make an impression on Condé and on Jeanne, Antoine's wife. He also met the seven-year-old Henry, Prince of Navarre and future King Henry IV, and the two began a lifelong relationship that would shape the course of events after Calvin's death.

Conspiracy of Amboise

The death of Henry II, though welcome to Calvin, brought to the throne a weak boy king, Francis II, husband of Mary Stuart. With the accession of a minor rose the Guise regency and the Cardinal of Lorraine, who were determined to intensify efforts to exterminate the Protestants. The years 1559–60 saw new levels of arrests and executions. For some Protestant leaders the need to act was compelling.

The origins of the disastrous conspiracy against the Guises remain obscure and are debated among historians.[22] It was conceived by Jean du Barry, Sieur de La Renaudie, a young nobleman formerly in the service of the Guises; he travelled to Geneva in 1559 where he met Calvin, who thought little of him. With Beza, however, he struck up a better rapport, as he did with some of the other ministers, who were prepared to contemplate some form of action against the hated Guise family. After the departure from Paris of the minister François de Morel, Calvin's ally, other Protestant ministers involved themselves with the conspirators. Most active was Calvin's friend and former student François Hotman, now professor of law in Strasbourg. In early 1560 there were rumours that the whole of France was about to rise against the Guises, but Calvin would have no part in this and vehemently opposed clandestine action. He had a strong aversion to La Renaudie, who planned to launch an attack on the French court, seize young Francis II and assassinate the Guise regents. The plan was discussed with Condé, who would be the 'silent chief' but take no part in order to keep his hands clean; the intention was to put the Bourbons on the throne.

The conspiracy took its name from a botched attack on 17 March 1560 on the Château d'Amboise, where the king was residing. Chaos ensued and the conspirators were easily defeated by an army that lay in wait. La Renaudie was seized and over twelve hundred men were strung up. One of them was Sieur de Villemongis, who before his execution put his hands in the blood of his beheaded companions and declared, 'Here is the blood of our children, O Lord, for this You shall be avenged!'[23] Although nothing short of a catastrophe, the conspiracy created the first political martyrs of the Reformed movement.

The debacle placed Geneva and Calvin in a difficult position. The city had to declare swiftly that it had not been involved and knew nothing of the plotting. Calvin, worried that he might be implicated, was less than straightforward with the Genevan officials.[24] He was prepared to admit to discussions with La Renaudie, but fiercely maintained that he had not approved the plot. Although he initially denied having talked to Antoine de la Roche Chandieu, his close friend and minister in Paris, he eventually revealed that he had in fact done so.

The case that Calvin knew nothing is further weakened by evidence that the Company of Pastors was aware of the conspiracy in its final stages and even sent a representative to a meeting of the conspirators in Nantes. It is not known, however, whether the minister who was sent, François Boisnormand, was instructed by the Company to participate.[25] It is plain that Calvin knew more about the conspiracy than he was prepared to confess. He must have been aware of Beza's sympathies for the plotters. He claimed in his testimony that he would not have opposed the plan had it been led by the King of Navarre. Condé, Navarre's brother, had refused and Navarre seems to have known nothing of it.

Condé swore before the French court that he had not been involved and retired to his lands in Navarre, where he was joined by Hotman and Beza, sent by Calvin to Nérac to urge the nobles to lead the Reformation. A meeting held in August 1560 was attended by Antoine of Navarre, Beza and Hotman, and another plot was hatched, to free the southern lands where Protestants were strong. Events were beginning to turn violent as Protestants in Lyon took up arms. Catherine de' Medici feared war and called on Philip II of Spain for support, while King Francis II demanded that Condé be summoned to court. Antoine of Navarre, forced to decide between rebellion against the monarchy and obedience, chose the latter path, agreeing to bring Condé to court in October 1560, whereupon the prince was immediately arrested. By publicly accusing him of stirring revolt against Francis II, Catherine forced Navarre to renounce his claim to be regent.[26] At the same time, she desperately sought to prevent the Guises from executing Condé, as that would have precipitated war. In the end, she was saved by the death of her own son, Francis II, which terminated the Guise regency.

The Conspiracy at Amboise, though in itself a ludicrous and tragic event, left its mark on Calvin. His own thinking on the right of individuals to resist a tyrannical ruler had been consistently negative. He was also aware that many, including some in Geneva such as Beza, were thinking differently. In the past he had counselled patience and obedience, leaving it to God to punish, but that message was not resonating with the French in the wake of persecution and executions. In the months following the conspiracy Calvin was clearly thinking of ways in which individual resistance could be justified.[27]

The Great Mission

Beginning in 1555 Geneva began its most audacious missionary effort in France by sending ministers to serve in the nascent Protestant churches. In the years between 1555 and 1562 just under a hundred ministers left the relative safety of Geneva and the Vaud to face appalling risks; they travelled in clandestine manner to avoid detection, and knew that capture meant torture and death.[28] Most came from noble, bourgeois and artisan classes; there were no peasants to be found among them. A few were former priests.[29] Those of noble birth were of immense benefit to the movement with their ability to move in higher social circles and win converts. Ministers left Geneva for destinations all over the French kingdom, though mostly to the larger cities and to certain provinces, patterns determined by sympathetic patronage. The new churches across France sent desperate appeals to Geneva for ministers, far more than the city could supply. The predictable consequence was that many who bravely and eagerly returned to their homeland were not well trained and could not meet the expectations of the communities.

Calvin recognized the opportunities and the challenges and sought to educate the ministers as best he could in restricted circumstances by providing basic instruction in the Bible. As we have seen, his sermons and lectures were copied down by students, and by 1561 it was estimated that about a thousand students attended his daily lectures.[30] Before the founding of the Academy in 1559, the council established a library in the city where printers placed copies of their books for students to borrow. Many of these students lived in the homes of professors, such as Beza, giving them privileged access to leading teachers, a practice common across Reformation Europe: in Wittenberg and Zurich Melanchthon and Bullinger provided accommodation for students, refugees and visitors, and mealtimes were a continuation of classroom discussions. The city tended to the families of those ministers serving in France who had been forced to leave behind wives and children. Frequently students preparing for the ministry in Geneva took temporary jobs such as tutoring the children of prominent families; others worked as secretaries, such as des Gallars, François Bourgoing and Jean Cousin, all of whom were occupied in recording Calvin's sermons during their student years.

There were limits to what could be done. Geneva was a middling city with only a few churches, not nearly enough to offer places for those preparing to be sent to France. As a result, and with the support of Berne, fresh recruits received practical training in the Vaud, Lausanne and Neuchâtel. Pierre Viret, who in 1559 was to become one of the missionaries, was responsible for much of the preparation carried out in the Vaud. This was a seminal moment in the dissemination of Calvin's theology in France, for the ministers who were to shape hundreds of congregations across France were trained and instructed in the doctrine and discipline of Geneva. This could, and did, cause friction with Berne, particularly as the majority of the ministers sent out in the years 1558–9 had served in Bernese lands and left following the conflicts in Lausanne.[31] They were loyal to Calvin's teachings and it was his voice which rang in the ears of those who risked life and limb travelling covertly into the kingdom to serve the new churches.

For his part, Calvin was extremely solicitous of the new ministers. His high view of the ministry remained undiminished and he recognized that the movement depended on the ability of the ministers to teach true doctrine and administer the sacraments in a disciplined community. Circumstances, however, dictated flexibility. A formal process existed in Geneva for the selection of its own ministers in which candidates were required to expound a passage from scripture in the presence of the Company of Pastors before being presented by Calvin to the council and the parish churches.[32] For ministers heading to France there was not enough time: candidates were simply approved by the Company. Importantly, those sent out remained under the authority of the Company and were expected to obey its orders; further, they were to report back to Calvin and the other ministers about local events. Many of the requests from France, particularly after 1555, were initially addressed to Calvin personally, though increasingly they were directed to the Company, which assumed the role of a quasi-bishop for the clergy. Dealing with the multitudinous requests was a task divided among the leading ministers of Geneva, who worked as a team, with the person most familiar with the particular region of France in question taking the lead. At the start, for reasons of political delicacy, all of this was carried out in great secrecy, and the Company told no one of its decisions, not even the council. Calvin was heavily involved in this covert action, though by 1557 matters were discussed openly.[33] For all its involvement and commitment to the cause, Geneva, ever vulnerable to attack from France, could not be seen as supporting sedition, so it preserved the fiction of disinterest.

Calvin was involved in every aspect of this missionary activity. He taught scripture to the ministers, oversaw their pastoral training in Geneva, Neuchâtel and the Vaud, examined them and presented them to the council. From their communities they provided enormous amounts of information on local conditions, keeping Calvin and his colleagues abreast of developments. He also acted as mediator and judge in disputes that arose between the ministers and their congregations.

During the years 1560–1 the growth of the Reformed churches in France was nothing short of spectacular. In Rouen about 20 per cent of the population had embraced the faith.[34] The movement became aggressive: Catholic churches were desecrated, their sacraments mocked, and mob violence flared in urban centres. Calvin was mortified by what he heard and continued to admonish the new churches to obedience. Few seemed to be listening. Within the kingdom there was an ever shifting balance of power, but it was during the years 1561–2 that the Protestant influence peaked with around 150 ministers dispatched from Geneva.[35] The Vaud was stripped of clergy to serve the cause in France, leaving the Bernese struggling to provide for their French-speaking lands, and Geneva itself was short of preachers.[36] Ministers were sent all over France, but a large contingent went to Orléans, where Condé was amassing his armies. Almost all of Geneva's leading ministers, except Calvin and Nicolas Colladon, who taught in the Academy, visited France in this period. Even Farel travelled back to France in 1561, though the Genevan council attempted to prevent him as 'he was the first to announce the Gospel to us'.[37] Beza made numerous trips. Jean-Reymond Merlin was sent by the Company of Pastors to the court of Admiral Coligny to represent Geneva at the House of Châtillon and provided extensive reports to Calvin detailing his activities and the preparations for the Colloquy of Poissy. When Merlin attempted to stay longer his request was refused by Calvin, who needed him in Geneva to work on a translation of the Bible.

Colloquy of Poissy

When Catherine de' Medici became regent in 1560 following the death of Francis II she undertook a campaign to prise power from the ascendant Guises, led by the Cardinal of Lorraine. This, she believed, required an end to persecution of the Protestants, who were becoming alarmingly radical. Michel de l'Hôpital, her chancellor and a moderate, sought peace in the kingdom by proposing a church council. Together de l'Hôpital and Catherine managed to calm the situation sufficiently for the Protestant churches to be able to meet in some safety but they remained vulnerable to mob violence, and in April 1561 Antoine of Navarre issued a stern warning to the priests of Paris not to incite Catholics to violence.[38] The monarchy hedged, hoping to find a compromise, but antagonism only grew as Protestant preaching and Catholic processions clashed. Even children fought in the streets. By the end of the summer of 1561 Protestants were preaching in Paris.

The colloquy of Poissy of September and October 1561 was the work of Catherine de' Medici and de l'Hôpital. The queen's purpose was to promote concord. De l'Hôpital, seen by Protestants as a client of the Guise family, believed that the coexistence of the two religions was a price worth paying to end the violence destroying France. The Cardinal of Lorraine, the most powerful member of the Guise family, did for a while seem to favour religious compromise, and made positive noises about the Augsburg Confession of 1530, which remained the basis of the religious settlement in the empire. This was anathema to Calvin, who perceived in the cardinal's favourable references to the Confession an attempt to drive a wedge between the Reformed and German Lutherans, at least those Germans who still maintained a positive view of Calvin.[39]

Genevan ministers, including des Gallars (who arrived from London), de Morel, de Saint-Paul, Folion and Beza, led the Protestant delegation at Poissy. Calvin followed the proceedings intently and pushed for greater doctrinal precision. In truth, he entertained low expectations, not believing for a moment that the Catholics would ever agree to anything. In writing to Beza, who sent him reports from the colloquy, he even permitted himself a joke. 'While others are feeding our expectations so freely with favourable reports,' he commented wryly, 'it would hardly be surprising if you felt ashamed of your stinginess which has left us almost famished for want of news. If you desire to give pleasure to many people, learn from that school in which your name is currently celebrated and learn to lie a little more audaciously. For while others speak of marvels, you alone scarcely permit us a glimmer of hope.'[40] He wished to be present but invisible. He gave Beza clear instructions on what to say and do, but insisted that his name not be raised as it was too divisive.

As expected, the colloquy did not go well. Neither side listened to the other, and when Beza presented the Reformed doctrine of the Lord's Supper to the meeting he was greeted with cries of derision. The Lutheran Duke of Württemberg wrote to Antoine of Navarre encouraging him to adopt the Augsburg Confession, propelling Calvin into action with a dire warning of the consequences.[41] Calvin detected the malign influence of Catherine de' Medici, the Cardinal of Lorraine and the Duke of Guise behind every move and instructed Beza to accept no compromise. Although nothing came of the meetings, Calvin was effusive in his praise of Beza's deft handling of events.[42]

Poissy was an important moment for the Protestants. Beza had indeed distinguished himself and found admirers even among his opponents. His extensive travels across France and his engagement with the court gave him a different perspective on events. Never disloyal to Calvin, he was better attuned to the changing situation in the land his colleague had left almost three decades earlier. Calvin himself frequently complained about the unreliable nature of post and correspondence. Impressed by his performance at the colloquy, Catherine asked Beza to remain in Paris during the winter of 1561–2, where he served the Protestant church and was chaplain in the household of Jeanne d'Albret. On 10 December he preached to six thousand people in the rain. During this brief respite, Beza's books and those of other reformers were sold in Paris, and the Frenchman reported to Calvin that Catherine was full of good will towards the Reformed, writing, 'I assure you that queen of ours is better intentioned toward us than ever before.'[43]

For all Calvin's enormous influence through his writings and personal contacts with ministers, it was Beza and Pierre Viret who were the visible leaders of French Protestantism. Calvin was sensible of the accusations that he had remained in Geneva and left it to others to carry forward the movement in its crucial hours. It was a charge he felt compelled to answer.

'I Have No Desire to Return'

In the summer of 1561 Calvin's lectures on the prophet Daniel were printed in Geneva. Their arresting preface was addressed to the faithful of France and confronted a question that Calvin's opponents had never shied away from raising. Why had the most prominent figure of French Protestantism never returned to his homeland? The answer is somewhat perplexing.

> Although with little regret I have been absent these twenty-six years from that native land which I hold in common with you, and whose agreeable climate attracts many foreigners from the most distant quarters of the world, it would not be pleasing or desirable to me to dwell in a region from which the truth of God, pure religion and the doctrine of eternal salvation have been banished, and the very kingdom of Christ laid prostrate! Hence, I have no desire to return to it. Yet it would not be in accordance with either human or divine obligation to forget the people from which I spring and ignore all regard for their welfare.[44]

What was he saying? Was his point that he could not live in a land still marred by idolatrous worship? If so, what did that mean for the new French Protestant churches which had to share urban and rural space with Catholics?

Was it fear of death? Without doubt there were many in France who would have loved to arrest and try Calvin, though it would have been extremely risky to create such a martyr. In any case, martyrdom was a path he had always avoided. He had chosen exile and made it the foundation of his prophetic authority. Perhaps the vital clue is found in his final testament of 1564 when he speaks of having been lifted out of the 'horrible pit' of idolatry in France by God's grace. He had been called to teach salvation, and this was what he had done. In the preface to Daniel he anticipated his final testament by offering an apology of his life and ministry, claiming that he had never stopped seeking to rouse the people of France from the idolatry into which they had fallen. His role was to teach and speak from afar as had the prophets of the exiled Israelites.

In the book of Daniel Calvin claimed he held up a 'mirror' – once more, a favourite image – to the faithful in France in which 'we observe as in a living picture that when God spares and even indulges the wicked for a time, he forges his servants like gold and silver. Thus we ought not to consider it a grievance to be thrown into the furnace of trial while profane men enjoy the calmness of repose.' God, in other words, will ultimately deal with persecutors, but the faithful must not look for immediate deliverance, as that may not be God's will. If necessary, they must be prepared to die 'to vindicate God's glory'.

The preaching of the Gospel will bring tumult, Luther had spoken of that, and as the Word is resisted conflict cannot be avoided, but this does not justify violence on the part of the faithful. Calvin asserted his authority and staked his claim as the presiding voice.

> It is not necessary for me to relate how strenuously I have endeavoured to prevent all occasion for tumult. Indeed, I call all of you together with the angels to witness before the Supreme Judge of all men that it is no fault of mine if the kingdom of Christ does not progress quietly without injury. And I think it is owing to my carefulness that private persons have not transgressed beyond their bounds.

The prophecies of Daniel, Calvin told the French churches, speak to the realities of France and encourage the faithful to hold firm to the expectation of salvation, even when they have been failed by their political leaders.

> Although it is truly a matter of grief that so great a multitude should wilfully perish, and rush devotedly to their destruction, yet their foolish

fury need not disturb us. Another admonition of Daniel should succour us, namely, that certain salvation is laid up for all who have been found written in the book. But although our election is hidden in God's secret counsel, which is the prime cause of our salvation, yet since the adoption of all who are inserted into the body of Christ by faith in the Gospel is by no means doubtful, be content with this testimony, and persevere in the course which you have happily begun.[45]

Calvin defined his position. 'Since it is not lawful for me to desert the station to which God has appointed me, I have dedicated to you my labour as a pledge until at the completion of my pilgrimage our heavenly Father, in his immeasurable pity, shall gather me together with you to his eternal inheritance.' The time for him to return to France had passed; he was no longer physically able. His place was Geneva. It was a world he knew and a bastion from which he could speak to his native land. Although one could ponder what might have happened if he had returned to France to lead the Reformation movement personally – without doubt he would have topped the most-wanted list of the Sorbonne and Parlement – in truth, it would not have happened. Calvin was not a leader of movements. His brilliance was in writing, speaking and running institutions – in shaping churches, not planting them. Like Moses on Mount Nebo he looked west to the Promised Land, but it was Calvin himself, not God, who prevented him from crossing the Jordan.

'We Have Been Basely Betrayed'

By the start of 1562 Calvin was restless and irritable. He wrote to Beza expressing his displeasure with the manner in which his friend had been conducting negotiations while in France. Gone was the praise that he had lavished on Beza following the Colloquy of Poissy; now the two men were at odds over how to oppose the presence of images in the church.

I am surprised that in the first colloquy you did not perceive the snares in which you threw yourself. The method you adopted always displeased me, namely, making half of your cause rely on the testimony of antiquity. On this matter [of images] the agreement between us is like that between fire and water. But because you committed this slip not from error or want of reflection, I leave that decision free to you. The wound, however, which was beginning to form a scar is evidently bleeding again and compels me to profess how greatly I differ from you.[46]

One can allow that the letter was written in a bad moment, but Calvin's harsh and biting words to Beza carry the marks of other relationships. Most galling was that Beza had apparently wilfully taken a different view which could not be explained by either error or haste. That to Calvin was the disloyalty that tore the scab off the wound.

The situation at home was no better. In his usual reports on events in France to Bullinger Calvin drew attention to a proposed meeting in Berne of church leaders. His diagnosis was harsh.

> You have no occasion to solicit my co-operation, for I declare that all our prospects are ruined. I dispense with saying anything more. Being lately summoned to a synod at Neuchâtel, I begged to be excused lest those who feign need of my assistance should exclaim that I exceed my bounds. I am summoned to it a second time. I am uncertain what I shall do. This I know, that you are greatly mistaken in thinking that they desire to consult for the good of the church. I wish I were in the remotest corners of the earth when I see them so insultingly making sport of me.[47]

To Bullinger alone he confessed the humiliation he felt at being mocked, his isolation and his lingering sense of betrayal. Was it simply Calvin's perception, his hypersensitivity to criticism which clearly heightened with age, or were the other reformers turning on him as he suspected? There is no evidence for the latter. The letters to Beza and Bullinger speak of a man who was witnessing that which he had most feared in France – war. Events were slipping away from him.

Nobody was surprised by the outbreak of hostilities in France in the spring of 1562.[48] The tinder that lit the fuse was the massacre at Vassy on 1 March when Guise troops opened fire on five hundred Reformed worshippers, killing thirty. Events spun out of control as Catherine de' Medici desperately attempted to maintain peace by negotiating between Condé and the Guises. By April, however, violence had broken out across France with a series of massacres. Condé led an army of Protestant nobles that seized Orléans, and declared that he had taken up arms against the king and Catherine. Throughout the summer of 1562 Protestants engaged in acts of mass iconoclasm in which churches and cathedrals were ransacked. In July 1562 Protestants were declared outlaws who could be killed with impunity.[49] Catherine de' Medici looked to Philip II of Spain for support while Condé saw Elizabeth I of England as the Protestants' natural ally. Elizabeth did promise money and troops in return for the port of Le Havre, an arrangement that enraged many French.[50]

The war revealed Geneva's curious, even ironic, predicament. The city's official policy was neutrality. Prayers were said for the faithful, though there was considerable pressure from both Condé and the Bernese to provide more tangible support.[51] That Calvin's city should be admonished for not supporting the French is difficult to comprehend, but it takes us to the complexities of the situation, for from the late 1550s onwards Geneva faced the grim prospect of attack from Savoyard and French forces, and its defences were by no means impregnable. Subterfuge was the answer. Though the city itself did not officially raise any troops, many individual Genevans petitioned the council for permission to leave for France and serve in the Protestant armies. In July 1562, when troops from Berne passed through its territory on their way to France, Calvin suggested that the city organize a cavalry escort. The head of the escort asked for permission to continue into France and Calvin intervened to ensure that the horsemen were given leave to escort the troops across the frontier. Nobody asked any questions when the Genevan cavalry unit simply kept going.

The level of Calvin's active involvement in the war effort was remarkable, particularly given his infirmity. He regularly appeared before the council, and was asked by the magistrates to conduct negotiations with other cities. He and Jean Budé set about organizing money-raising schemes whereby loans were floated in Basle and Strasbourg. Although Geneva's role in financing the war was relatively small compared to more affluent Basle, Strasbourg and Lyon, Calvin remained the contact person for the network of figures connecting Condé and other French leaders to the churches in the empire and in the Swiss Confederation.[52] These armies needed money, and he wrote frantically to the French churches, frequently scolding them for their parsimony and reminding them of their obligation to help pay for German mercenaries. Once more a degree of elasticity is evident: Calvin opposed rioting, unregulated iconoclasm and individual resistance, all of which he associated with social disorder. However, in dire circumstances he was prepared to tolerate paying for mercenaries, which even Machiavelli found objectionable. 'The point in question', Calvin wrote to the church in Languedoc, 'is to find money to support the troops which Messire d'Andelot has levied. This is not the moment to enter into inquiries or disputes in order to find fault with mistakes that have been committed in times past.'[53] However reluctantly, he had accepted the need for religious war.

The first war came to a head with the battle of Dreux on 19 December 1562, the first time in over a century that two French armies had faced one another in anger. The battle swung back and forth before Condé's army was eventually defeated, and the slaughter was horrific. Calvin provided Bullinger with a report of the encounter, which depicted Condé as a hero betrayed by cowardly troops, particularly his infantry and mercenaries.[54] Beza had been present on the battlefield in his preaching gown and flourishing a Bible, a worthy Old Testament prophet.[55] He also reported to Calvin the death of Antoine of Navarre during the siege of Rouen. Antoine, Beza spat out, was a modern Julian the Apostate.[56]

An unexpected twist followed in February 1563 when the Duke of Guise was shot and killed by a Protestant nobleman, leaving the Guise family without a senior figure.[57] Coligny was still leading the Protestant forces from Orléans. Catherine moved to establish peace by forcing Condé, who had been imprisoned after Dreux, to sign the Peace of Amboise (19 March 1563). Reformed churches were permitted in certain areas, but not in Paris and its surroundings. Property taken from the Catholic church was to be restored. The resolution pleased few on either side. When the unfortunate town criers of Paris publicized the terms they were pelted with mud and excrement and fled in fear of their lives.[58] The Catholic monarchs of Europe, including the pope, were outraged by the compromises with the hated Reformed Protestants and protested to the young Charles IX. Calvin was equally incandescent, declaring the peace a complete sell-out. 'We have been basely betrayed by the other brother [Condé]', he wrote to Bullinger.[59]

In May Calvin, who blamed Condé for the treaty, wrote the prince a more politic letter. 'Respecting the conditions of the peace, I know very well, Monseigneur, that it was not easy for you to obtain such as you could have wished. Therefore, if many people desire they had been better, I pray you not to think it extraordinary, for in that respect they are exactly of your own opinion. Meanwhile, if God has thrust us back more than we imagined, it is our duty to humble ourselves under his hand.'[60] Calvin did not wish to lose his influence with the prince and followed with a lengthy address combining encouragement with explicit instructions. Not least, the prince was to avoid the trap set by those who would have him accept the Augsburg Confession, which Calvin politely described as 'neither fish nor fowl'.

Conflicting Voices

When Pierre Viret arrived in Geneva in early 1559 following his expulsion from Lausanne he had many critics. His struggle with the Bernese magistrates over church discipline had ended with his removal. From Zurich Heinrich Bullinger opined that Viret had acted mendaciously, and that in opposing Berne he had once more thrown the Vaud into turmoil.[61] Calvin was also cool, not least in comparison to his eager reception of Theodore Beza. His lack of warmth was curious, particularly as he had insisted that the Bernese magistrates be resisted and Viret's collaboration had cost him his position in the city, a sacrifice for which he received little thanks in Geneva. Calvin blamed Viret for being too confrontational. He also added the cruel remark that Beza's unpopularity in Lausanne had been on account of his loyalty to Viret against his better judgement.[62] Nevertheless, Viret made his way to Geneva and assumed duties, even replacing Calvin during the Frenchman's serious illness of 1559–60. He remained in the city for two years, working closely with Calvin in the Consistory, processing requests from France for ministers, teaching in the Academy and serving as secretary of the Company of Pastors. He was also involved with the Bourse Française.[63]

From 1559 Calvin's strategy was to send out close colleagues from Geneva to win over major figures: Beza went to Navarre to negotiate with Antoine of Navarre; Antoine de la Roche Chandieu went to Paris and Navarre; François de Morel was in Paris. Calvin remained obsessed with Antoine of Navarre, believing that as a dominant court figure and prince of the blood he alone could bring about a peaceful reformation. This remained his policy until Antoine clearly snubbed him. What Calvin chose to overlook was the degree to which French Protestantism had advanced by acts of iconoclasm and violence, something of which he wholly disapproved. Viret's attitude was entirely different: in contrast to Calvin's admonitions to patience and secrecy, he encouraged open, active worship and no compromises with Catholicism. From 1559 he launched a series of scathing attacks on the mass, which he regarded as the heart of a thoroughly corrupted body. He had reprinted tracts he had written almost twenty years earlier against the mass. This polemic put him on a collision course with Calvin, who believed he was attempting to destabilize France.

What was emerging in sharp relief were conflicting attitudes towards reformation and hostile political authorities. Calvin's long-standing view was to deny legitimacy to any form of resistance by individuals against persecuting rulers. As we have seen, his counsel was exile or martyrdom. Passive resistance was one matter, but to resist authority actively was deeply troubling for the leading reformers. Matters, however, proceeded at speed and Calvin, remarkably, was showing signs of modifying his position. The 1559 *Institutes*, revised in the midst of the great surge of French Protestantism, indicates that Calvin was prepared to consider resistance against a tyrant.[64] The coercion of evangelicals to engage in idolatrous worship weighed heavily on his mind. He acknowledged the conflict between obedience to the monarch and fidelity to God, and modified his previous position by suggesting that resistance against the ruler in these circumstances was permissible. The faithful were no longer simply to die martyrs as they could fight back.

Nevertheless, in his letters to French congregations he continued to advise caution. To the church at Valence he explicitly rejected resistance. 'You have to fortify yourselves not to resist the rage of the enemy by the aid of the fleshly arm, but to maintain with constancy the truth of the Gospel in which consists our salvation, and the service and honour of God, which we are bound to honour more than our own bodies and souls.'[65] He was critical of many of the ministers sent out from Geneva for their aggressive tactics: they preached in public, causing scandal, and participated in acts of iconoclasm. Repeatedly he asserted that he had given no authority to any person or congregation to wage a campaign of violence.[66]

So who was inspiring these men to attack Catholic churches and confront authorities? It was Viret and Farel, whose old ways, honed in the Vaud of the 1530s, had been translated to France. They continued to publish works in which iconoclasm and resistance were advocated. They summoned the faithful to action, not, as Calvin did, to wait on God's providence.

In September 1561 Calvin told the Genevan council that Viret's doctors were of the opinion that he would never recover from his illness if he remained in the city, and that it was better for him to take the warm waters of southern France. Other evidence suggests that Viret left Geneva perfectly healthy. If truth be told, he had had enough of Calvin and was no longer prepared to play the loyal lieutenant, particularly with Beza around. He travelled south, and quickly established himself as the chief superintendent of the Reformed churches. In this respect, his position paralleled the work being done by Beza in the north. This, perhaps, had been Calvin's plan: his two closest friends as leaders of the Reformed church in France. If it was, it did not work. Calvin had been kept in the dark about the exact nature of Viret's health and had no idea of his plans to head to Nîmes. He certainly had not expected

Viret to tour the new Protestant churches in the south advocating positions unpalatable in Geneva. He was furious, and feeling duped he complained to the council and Beza.

Viret's activities in the south were precisely those condemned by Calvin. In Bas-Languedoc he encouraged iconoclasm and churches were ransacked. The evangelical movement had thrived in the south during the 1540s and 1550s as a result of intense jurisdictional rivalries that prevented effective persecution.[67] What was needed was leadership, and Viret seemed the man. Calvin was shocked by the reports that made their way to Geneva. The extent to which he was out of touch is expressed in his letter to the French monarch of January 1561.

> With regard to the charge of stirring up disturbances and seditions, they [Protestant leaders] protest against ever having entertained any such intention, and declare, on the contrary, that they have employed all their influence to check and prevent them. Also, that they have never given advice to make any innovations, or attempted anything criminal with respect to the established order of the state, but have exhorted those who are disposed to listen to them to remain in peaceful subjection to their prince. And if any disturbances have arisen, it has been to their great regret, and certainly not by their having furnished any pretext for them. And so far have they been from countenancing any such enterprises, they would willingly have lent their aid to repress them.[68]

This was far from describing what Viret was up to. In his 1561 work *Le Monde à l'Empire* he demonstrated his impatience with Geneva's attitude towards events. His language was full of violence, alarming both Calvin and Beza, whom he had not consulted about the text. He concealed from Calvin the extent of his involvement in the iconoclasm in Nîmes. Calvin was still be consulted by the French churches on innumerable matters of discipline and conduct, but Viret offered a rival source, one much more in sympathy with those churches that found themselves in the hostile atmosphere of France. In January 1562 the Genevan council's patience began to wear thin and Viret was ordered to travel either to Paris or to Geneva and leave the south of France. He declined. During this year Lyon fell into the hands of Protestants and became a centre of Reformation printing. Viret made his way to Lyon and was eager to remain there. He was, however, still under the authority of the Company of Pastors and required permission to stay in France. Calvin was opposed to this and had him recalled. Viret returned to Geneva in February 1563, but only temporarily.

If the end of the first religious war was not bad enough, by 1562 there was serious dissent within the Reformed movement. Jean Morély's *Treatise on Christian Discipline* argued against the hierarchical nature of the church and in favour of a congregational model in which ministers were elected and questions of doctrine debated under the guidance of the Holy Spirit.[69] It was a radical rejection of the Genevan form of consistorial church government and caused a scandal. The book was condemned in Geneva by Calvin, godfather to one of Morély's children. Morély was summoned before the Consistory, but refused to return to Geneva, though he expressed a desire to come to the city for the baptism of his son. He was duly excommunicated and his *Treatise* publicly burned in Geneva in 1562. Why did this matter? Although Morély felt the full weight of Genevan disapproval, his ideas had broad appeal across France. Many local churches resented the growing centralization of the French church and the disappearance of their liberties. Before the national synods the essential character of the French Protestant churches was congregational. This was to be replaced by provincial and national structures. Morély's advocacy of local authority found important support among the nobility, including Jeanne d'Albret, Queen of Navarre. The reason for this was quite straightforward: many of the nobility did not take well to the principle of consistorial discipline whereby they might be admonished for behaviour they associated with their traditional rights. Morély's advocacy of congregationalism was more appealing and offered an attractive alternative to the position of Calvin and Beza. The Genevan leaders were quick to recognize the threat to a central plank of their church government, and they demanded that the ministers of France condemn Morély.

There was another, more personal, element to the story. Morély's *Treatise* was dedicated to Pierre Viret. The latter's sympathy for Morély again revealed the different world from which he hailed. Unlike Calvin with his inflated view of the nobility, Viret came from Swiss lands and believed in communalism. In the summer of 1563 Calvin and Beza wrote to him complaining of the chaos among the French churches.[70] The letter reflects the near panic in Geneva as the two men feared the worst: radical tracts were in circulation, communities were in conflict, and the command of the king was openly flouted. Viret, they commanded, should not act in any way contrary to royal authority and should prevent illegal gatherings.

Relations between Calvin and Viret were breaking down. On 2 September 1563 Calvin replied to a complaint from Viret that he was no longer kept informed, that he had been supplanted by Beza and that information was withheld from him. Although they seem to have patched things up before Calvin's death, Viret no longer represented Genevan views. He was the advocate of a congregationalism against Calvin's consistorial government; he spoke for action and resistance, while Calvin continued to preach obedience and patience. Calvin had invested heavily in Beza and his contacts with the court; Viret was the popular preacher with the common touch, and through his work in Languedoc he had exposure to the front lines of French Protestantism. He had never lost his background in the Vaud, where he and Farel had led the resistance to the Catholic church. Iconoclasm ran in his blood.

During the autumn and winter of 1561–2, as war loomed, Calvin preached on 1 Samuel. What the people heard was his unvarnished hatred of the French monarchy. A king, he was clear, was to be distinguished from a tyrant, yet, he reminded the congregation, there were now more tyrannical princes than ever.[71] The French court was a snake pit. The language was not new and the men and women present would not have been amazed to hear Calvin and the other preachers denounce kings and princes. Indeed, visitors to the city often remarked on the manner in which the nobility were handled from the pulpit.[72]

Once the war broke out Calvin continued to preach on the Old Testament, this time 2 Samuel, from which he expressed his horror of arms and conflict. The 2 Samuel sermons are filled with accounts of the sufferings of the innocent in times of war. As for the princes, their courts were 'always full of this filth and infection, as if they were public whore houses. There are always plenty of whoremongers who are so utterly licentious that they make a trade and business of it, as they say.'[73] At the same time, however, Calvin's thought was radicalizing. He proclaimed that France was ruled by 'murderers', and that God had struck down the man responsible for the carnage, Antoine of Navarre, who had been shot during the siege of Rouen. Antoine had switched sides and abandoned the Reformed faith, and Calvin, who had once placed so much trust in him, decried him as a traitor. Navarre had been shot by a private citizen, and this, for Calvin, was just punishment, reflecting his growing acceptance that such acts could be legitimate.

In the last years of his life Calvin lost the friendship of the two men with whom he had once formed a triumvirate dedicated to the evangelizing of France. The Geneva–Lausanne–Neuchâtel nexus had been a powerful force that culminated in the sending of ministers to France during the early 1560s. It broke down partially for personal reasons, but more importantly because there had always been a fundamental difference between the men. Farel and Viret had been effective revolutionaries: they had connected with the people to overturn established orders and introduce Reformation. They believed in protest and action, including violence. Calvin had never experienced that stage of religious change. In Basle, Strasbourg, the Vaud and Geneva he had arrived when new orders were already in place. Certainly, he had proved an ingenious organizer of a new regime, but his world was of law and order, of properly functioning institutions. His greatest achievement, arguably, was the Consistory, which married biblical teaching with social order in a legal framework. In France, he had believed that the nobility would lead the Reformation cause, as it was their place to rule. The nobles did not listen, and the plan failed. Calvin's name was revered across France and his teaching inspired and shaped an entire movement. But in the end that movement had to part company with him; the Protestants of France knew they had to fight for survival and the Genevan message of obedience, even though there were signs of change, was out of touch. It was the path of Farel and Viret that they would follow: violence and resistance together with prophetic righteousness. In the year remaining to him after the devastating disappointment of the Peace of Amboise, Calvin could only watch in the expectation of the bloodshed that would surely follow.

CHAPTER EIGHTEEN

Endings

The Last Year

THE END was protracted and painful. Calvin was dying, and knew it. Most often it was to Bullinger he turned, sharing news of France, of common endeavours, of events in England and beyond, and of his deteriorating health. His attempt to dislodge kidney stones reminds us of the unimaginable torments endured by our early-modern forebears.

At present, I am relieved from very acute suffering, having been delivered of a stone about the size of the kernel of a hazel nut. As the retention of urine was excruciating, on the advice of my physician I mounted a horse that the jolting might assist in discharging the stone. On my return home I was surprised to find that I emitted discoloured blood instead of urine. The following day the stone had forced its way from the bladder into the urethra. Hence still more tortures. For more than half an hour I attempted to relieve myself by a violent agitation of my whole body. It brought nothing, but I obtained slight relief by fomentations with warm water. Meanwhile, the urinary canal was so lacerated that copious discharges of blood flowed from it. It seems to me, however, that for the last two days I have begun to live anew since being delivered from these pains.[1]

Bedridden and able to work only by dictating to his secretaries, Calvin persevered as his health permitted. He preached and continued to attend sessions of the Consistory and Company of Pastors when he could, though others frequently filled in when he was unable. He concluded his lectures on the book of Lamentations in January 1563 and immediately began his study of the prophet Ezekiel. He also completed his sermons on 1 and 2 Samuel in which he powerfully decried the carnage of religious war in France. The presses brought forth a continuous stream of his works, including his harmony of the last four books of Moses and his lectures on Jeremiah, which he dedicated to Elector Frederick III of the Palatinate.

The Palatinate, in contrast to France, offered a pleasing prospect. The reforms under Frederick III which were led by several of Calvin's students had brought Geneva back into the world of German Protestantism. For this Calvin had much reason to thank the departed Melanchthon, who had proved a better ally than the Genevan had allowed. Calvin, as ever, was not prepared to rest; the struggle had to be doggedly pursued. The dedication to Frederick was an opportunity to warn against the dangers of Lutheranism (meaning the Gnesio-Lutherans) and their malign influence in both the empire and France.[2] Calvin reminded the elector of the very real differences between Lutheran and Reformed teaching on the Lord's Supper. The dedication contains one of his rare references to the word 'Calvinism', widely used by the Lutherans as a pejorative tag.[3] 'They can find no more horrific insult to attack your Highness, most honourable prince, than the term Calvinism.' He added wearily, 'from where this bitter hatred against me comes is clear enough'. Calvin expressed his anxiety about the printing of these lectures, as he had also done with the sermons, for they were not from his own hand, but had been recorded by others. In the end, he was satisfied. 'I hear of impartial and plain readers who declare that they have received much benefit from this kind of labour.' The modesty was rather artful, as Calvin had a much clearer, and higher, sense of what he had achieved. 'And if Jeremiah himself were now alive on earth', he pointed out to the elector, 'he would, if I am not deceived, add his recommendation for he would acknowledge that his prophecies have been explained by me honestly and reverently. Further, that they have been usefully accommodated to present circumstances.'[4] This, summed up in two sentences, was Calvin on the nature and substance of his life's work – as the prophet who makes the eternal prophecies speak to contemporary society.

Illness and the wrenching disappointment of the Peace of Amboise curbed but failed to tame Calvin's appetite for work. He followed events in France with a hawk's eye and continued to correspond with a range of figures. To Antoine de Crussol, head of the Protestants in Languedoc, he wrote that the faithful would have to wait for God's will to be revealed; it was God's desire 'to test his own with this defeat'.[5] Yet there was no self-deception. He was aware of death's approach and his letters increasingly dwelt on spiritual advice, frequently to noblemen and women. In May he was in communication with Antoine de Croy, Prince of Porcien and close friend of the Prince of Condé, who had worked with Beza.[6] The prince had expressed his desire to see Calvin once more, to which the reformer replied that he would probably be disappointed, though he would gladly fulfil his Christian duty by sending a letter of spiritual encouragement. Calvin proclaimed his delight in hearing of the prince's piety, but reminded him that in itself this was not enough. Reputations for piety were meaningless; the true Christian life is a battle fought anew each day against temptation and evil, the more so for a man of high rank. Previous achievements count for nothing. The struggle is not undertaken with physical weapons – though, in an allusion to the war, that may prove necessary – but in obedience to Christ. The fight against both visible and invisible enemies does not end until death, and Christians can never be sufficiently armed or complacent. The language was intentionally martial, befitting the status of the nobleman, yet Calvin expressed true affection for the prince, with whom he exchanged several letters during his final year. He concluded by expressing doubt that they should see one another again in this life, as Antoine desired, but added the assurance that they would meet in the kingdom of God.[7]

To others, Calvin's advice was more particular. Jean de Soubise in Lyon had refused to accept the Peace of Amboise. Despite his own feelings about the treaty, Calvin admonished de Soubise to obedience to the civil authorities and to wait patiently on the will of the Lord with a reminder of Paul's words to the Corinthians: 'And God is faithful; he will not let you be tempted beyond what you can bear.'[8] He continued in his duty to inform the Swiss churches of events in France, describing to Bullinger the situation in Lyon, where Catholic churches had recently been restored. The spectre of the Augsburg Confession, however, continued to haunt him as he feared the Protestant leaders might be tricked into accepting it if they did not follow his advice. The irony of his anxiety was unlikely to be lost on Bullinger, who had been angered by his signing Melanchthon's Variata of the Augsburg Confession twenty-four years earlier. The 1530 Confession had marked the moment when the Swiss were isolated from the German reformation, and its very name was reviled among the Zwinglians. That, however, was not a memory that either of the ageing reformers was prepared to revive in these final months, where a touching mutual concern prevailed over past differences. No two friends, a true odd couple, had done more for the European Reformation.

Passions had not, however, entirely burned out, and Calvin's wrath was directed at Condé, the betrayer of the French Protestants. Catherine de' Medici was more hostile than ever, he reported to Bullinger, and Condé did nothing. Coligny, for his part, was hardly better, preferring to sit at home rather than expose himself to any danger.[9] Calvin was also sensible of the perils faced by these men in the wake of defeat. Coligny, the Count of Rochefoucauld and Theodore Beza had been named as co-conspirators in the murder of the Duke of Guise and had produced a written defence that was printed and circulated. Calvin sent a copy to Bullinger with the news that the work had sold well in France. He asked that the Admiral's defence be printed in Zurich and further distributed.

From the end of the summer of 1563 Calvin's health went into rapid decline. He was unable to attend the September communion in Geneva, though he continued to receive guests in his home, where, according to Beza, he would discuss matters of the faith and the wider Reformation. As ever, Calvin was sought out by eager visitors, students, ministers and magistrates for his opinions, but his ability to accommodate the ceaseless flow of demands ebbed. The work continued, largely thanks to his assistants, and he began his commentary on the book of Joshua. When he could go out, he was carried to church in a chair, and still preached and conducted baptisms. The famous pulpit chair in Geneva is a historical fabrication, but it does remind us of Calvin's frailty. He continued to attend the Congrégation on Fridays, and when no longer able to speak publicly would give the exhortation to prayer at the conclusion of the session. Beza has left a moving account.

> The congregation was delighted to have him there. Many people thought it would be like the other times when he had been ill, and we had seen him recover against all hope, as it seemed. It is true that not only ministers, but friends too, urged him not to wear himself out by coming and working like this. But he would make excuses and say that it did him good and that time would hang too heavily on his hands if he stayed indoors all the time.[10]

Calvin performed his last public duties at the beginning of February 1564; from that point he was confined to bed, and his condition fluctuated. At the beginning of March the end seemed at hand, but there was one last recovery, and Calvin spoke humorously of having being granted a stay of execution. The ministers of the city visited him regularly to comfort and be comforted, though Calvin found it increasingly difficult to speak.

In Beza's account there is a revealing moment. Lying in bed, with the ministers of the Genevan church around him, Calvin read from the Bible and declared his dissatisfaction with some of the marginal notes. 'Having asked for his papers, he took them and read out long extracts to the assembled company. At his request, they gave him their opinion. As Calvin went on reading, it became obvious that his condition was deteriorating, but as he said he was enjoying speaking to them, none of the brethren dared urge him to stop reading, especially as they were afraid of upsetting him.'[11] The image is arresting: Calvin, as he was happiest, in the company of friends whom he enjoyed and needed, yet with their acknowledgement of his superiority to the extent of being afraid of him. To the end they were his disciples. That had always been Calvin's way.

Calvin made a couple more public appearances: once before the town hall to thank the magistrates and citizens for their good wishes and to introduce the new rector of the Academy, and once to attend the Easter celebration of the Lord's Supper in 1564. On both occasions he was borne in a chair. By April, he was on his death bed, encouraging the ministers of Geneva to continue in their duties and reflecting on his life, admitting that he had not expected much when he returned to Geneva in 1541. Everything, he urged, was to be attributed to God's providence. Beza's account is a meditation on the good Christian death, describing Calvin's last days as one continuous prayer. He parted in peace from his friends and colleagues without ever allowing emotions to get the better of him; all sentiments, such as old friendships, were sublimated to a faithful testimony before God. This was Calvin's humanist ideal of friendship, forged as a young student of law with its strictly observed reciprocal obligations and transformed to the service of the Church. It was how he had lived, and it was now how he would die. According to Beza, so many wanted to see him that his door could have remained open day and night. Calvin asked that people satisfy themselves with praying for him.

The end was quiet. 'A message was quickly sent to me,' Beza recounted, 'when I had only left him a little earlier. I hurried to the house as fast as I could, accompanied by several other brothers, but I found that he had already peacefully breathed his last. He passed away without a word or a groan or even the slightest movement. He seemed rather to have fallen asleep.'[12]

Most likely death was caused by septic shock brought on by the poisoning of his body by the kidney stones.[13] From Beza's perspective, however, the cause was less important than its nature. That Calvin died peacefully was a sign that he had died well. Similarly, in 1546 a death mask of Martin Luther had been produced to demonstrate that his end had not been marked by screaming as his soul was taken away by demons, as Catholic opponents had predicted. To die well meant to have sufficiently prepared for one's end by prayer and repentance, and all confessions, Protestant and Catholic, looked to the good death.[14]

Grief fell upon Geneva, and many wanted to see the body and look one last time at Calvin's familiar face. Signs of a cult, the very thing Calvin feared, quickly appeared, and to prevent its growth Calvin's body was buried the next morning in the cemetery of Pleinpalais. The body was wrapped in a shroud, placed in a wooden coffin and laid in an unmarked grave, as Calvin had requested. All of this was, as Beza remarked, to avoid 'unhealthy curiosity'. The burial was attended by syndics and much of the city, and the ceremony was suitably simple.

A Final Confession

Calvin's testament, brief as it was and composed at the end of April 1564, was his closing speech. With his own voice, not as Paul, David or Jeremiah, he addressed his spiritual state. His testament touches on what he regarded as the seminal aspects of his life, all of which were brought about by the gracious providence of God. He had been lifted out of the 'horrible pit of idolatry' into which he had been plunged. His conversion to the Gospel had cleansed him from the world in which he had lived, and God had 'been pleased to use me and my labours to teach and make known the truth of his Gospel'.[15] This justified his decision to stay in Geneva, where he could fulfil the office to which he had been divinely called. He makes no allusion to his exile from his native land, except to say that his 'true refuge' is in God's gracious adoption. This had also been his theme in the psalms commentary, where he spoke of exiles having no home other than in God.

In his testament Calvin drew attention to his shortcomings. 'But, alas, my desires and my zeal, if I may so describe it, have been so cold and flagging that I am conscious of imperfections in all that I am and do.' This could be deemed formulaic, but when read in the light of his autobiographical account in the psalms commentary of 1557 and of his letters, his recollections have greater resonance. This was Calvin's divided self: the confidence in his calling as a prophet and apostle set against his ever present sense of unworthiness and dissatisfaction. It was this friction that drove him ceaselessly to seek to improve his work, to write clearer, more insightful commentaries, to rework the *Institutes* to enhance their value in teaching, and to travel endless miles of dangerous roads in search of church unity. These were two sides of the same personality. It was his acute sensitivity to the gap between what was and what should be that distressed him. He knew there would be no Jerusalem on earth, but he never stopped trying to build it.

Expectations

Calvin had been preparing for death all his life. From the *Psychopannychia*, written as he was about to begin a life in exile at the end of 1534, to the final revisions of his *Institutes*, he spoke of the Christian life as a journey towards eternity. On Matthew 24:43 he wrote, 'God does not bestow the honourable title of his children on any but those who acknowledge that they are strangers on the earth, who not only at all times are prepared to leave it but move forward in an uninterrupted "course towards the heavenly life" .'[16] Life in this world must be shaped by hope and patience; hope is grounded in the certain promises of God as expressed to all humanity in the Word, while patience is the ability to wait for God to reveal the hidden purpose. The pilgrimage is a struggle against the evils of the world, and suffering is the Christian's lot. Only those who love God more than the world will prevail. But prevail they will, because God will never abandon them while they travail in a hostile land. For Calvin, to go forward is to struggle, to bear the cross of Christ; the Christian life is not about standing still. 'Although believers are now pilgrims on earth,' he wrote on Romans 5:2, 'yet by their confidence they surmount the heavens, so that they cherish their future inheritance in their bosoms with tranquillity.'[17]

Throughout life, the Christian must have his or her eyes on eternity at every moment, and this means longing for death. Through all Calvin's writing and sermons coursed the same urgent message: the Christian lives in the face of eternity. Everything that distracts from that reality must be shunned. Weighed down by a disease-ridden body, Calvin possessed a heightened sense of the fragility of existence. He was driven to work by the knowledge that his mortal flesh could give out at any moment. Every hour was to be sanctified by the service of God. In book three of the *Institutes* Calvin had written a meditation on eternity in which he spoke of the distinctive Christian understanding of death. God has placed men and women in the world and can take them away at any moment; only the fool thinks that it is possible to hide from God's hand. The ancient philosophers rightly, in Calvin's view, had contempt for the world and saw honour in death, but they could behold it only with despair. Because they lacked faith there was nothing in death but release from the world. The Christian longing for death arises from an understanding that it is not the end, but rather a further step along the path; death brings one closer to God, the true end of the journey. It is natural for humans to fear death, but for Calvin fear belongs to those who lack faith. For Christians it is a source of joy, for they have the confidence of faith, and insofar as they live in hope, they are already in the kingdom of heaven. He had described his conversion in terms of fear of God's judgement; now that fear gave him hope of eternity.

What happens after death? Calvin, unsurprisingly, was not given to speculation about the appearance of the next life, but he did believe that the Bible offered some clear instruction. At the moment of physical death the body and soul are separated: the body turns to dust in the grave while the soul proceeds to immediate judgement. The souls of the elect and the damned face their appointed fates: the elect enter into bliss while the reprobate are cast into the fire.[18] In this respect, Calvin's thought was thoroughly unremarkable among the Protestant reformers. Purgatory, the third place of Catholic theology where the sins of the faithful are expunged before entry into heaven, is rejected. There is, for Protestants, only heaven and hell. The question remains: if the souls pass immediately into bliss or punishment what of the Last Judgement when Christ will return to establish the New Jerusalem? Have not the souls already been judged? Protestants attempted various answers to this knotty point. Some spoke of souls falling asleep till the Last Judgement – this had been the argument Calvin had attacked in his *Psychopannychia*. His view, in harmony with Bullinger and others, was that there are two judgements: the first at the end of life and the second at the Last Judgement. The souls of the faithful enter into bliss, but not fully. They remain in a state of expectation till the final judgement, when all is revealed. Thus, for Calvin, the expectation that marks the life of a Christian continued in death.

Remembering Calvin

It was Calvin's wish that he be buried without memorial in order to avoid any form of posthumous personality cult. This time there was no death mask. It was the authority which had come from God, he believed, which had elevated him above others, not his person. Calvin had always been clear about this distinction. His experiences of exile were never presented as a model of conduct and he preferred to speak through biblical characters such as Paul and the Old Testament prophets. In this respect, his situation was very different from that of Martin Luther, who had been lauded at his funeral by Philip Melanchthon as the great hero of the Church.[19] Lutherans openly praised their reformer in sermons and tracts. Even Bullinger had extolled the dead Zwingli publicly.[20] In Geneva there were no sermons or orations in honour of Calvin's memory; no attempt was made to portray him as a titan of the Reformation.

Why the difference? When Calvin died in 1564 his friends were well aware of his reticence about his life. Yet at the same time opponents were already circulating works in which his character was traduced. Further, Castellio's writings on toleration, in which Calvin fared very badly, were being read in France with admiration. There was need of defence on two fronts: to guard against canonization of Calvin by his followers and to refute the calumnies of hostile writers. During the sixteenth century three attempts at biography were made in Geneva by his friends. Each reflected the complexities faced by his supporters in dealing with his memory.[21]

Theodore Beza wrote the first, printed as part of Calvin's commentary on Joshua of 1564 which appeared after the reformer's death. Brief and succinct, Beza paid little attention to the events of Calvin's life, choosing rather to portray him as a man who embodied his doctrine. The intention was to present Calvin as an edifying figure to encourage the beleaguered faithful, above all in France. Calvin's own trials and tribulations were to be regarded as exemplary, something the reformer had never intended, and his battles against heretics, with especial attention to the hated Sebastian Castellio, were dramatically cast. Beza had been an integral part of the Genevan campaign to demolish Castellio's reputation, and although the Savoyard had died two years earlier in 1562, his presence was still felt. Beza's initial, rather one-dimensional, Calvin was not considered satisfactory and within a year a second version of the reformer's life appeared, this time co-authored by Beza and Calvin's friend Nicolas Colladon. The work retained much of the same flavour – Calvin as chosen figure of God – but it was extensively reworked to present a more chronological account enhanced with anecdotes drawn largely from personal memories to make the reformer more human.

A third and final version had to wait ten years and was appended to an edition of Calvin's letters printed in 1575. Written in Latin and translated into French only at the end of the seventeenth century, this biography was intended for a limited audience, and that is exactly what it found. The edition was a publishing failure. This third life, the one best known to us, languished in obscurity after its poor reception, which seems hard to imagine as this final life of Calvin by Beza, which follows the Frenchman from his youth to his grave, is often our only source for important aspects of his biography.

Calvin's friends had good reason for proceeding to publish with haste. There were others who wanted to tell a very different story. Calvin's nemesis Jérôme Bolsec lived to have the last word, and penned two accounts ten years after the reformer's death.[22] Like many Catholics, he feared that the Protestant reformers were being accorded the status of saints, and he sought to destroy the reputation of Calvin and Geneva. In this, as Irena Backus has shown, he was extraordinarily successful. The dark picture he painted of Calvin proved far more influential than Beza's various attempts to portray the man of God. Calvin, in Bolsec's hands, represented everything bad about the Reformation. He was immoral, cruel, mendacious and a tyrant. The author claimed that he based his work on the most reliable sources, but the truth was very different. He simply manufactured stories to discredit Calvin: that he had been convicted of sodomy in Noyon, that he was sexually perverted and that he had died horribly from crab lice. The biography found a large audience and went through numerous editions in the sixteenth and seventeenth centuries.

A string of hostile Catholic biographies of Calvin appeared after his death dwelling upon the reformer's tyrannical and heretical tendencies. The most interesting of these is the life of Calvin produced by Jean-Baptiste Masson, who was a student of François Bauduin, Calvin's former secretary who had accused him of being a monster.[23] Although his portrayal of Calvin was negative, emphasizing his cruelty and his dictatorial nature, what distinguished Masson's work was his critical use of sources, a number of which came from Bauduin's time working for Calvin. Many of the verbal exchanges recorded in this *Life* came from Bauduin himself, for example when Masson reflected on Calvin's vices. 'Although he appeared modest and disposed to expose his thoughts simply, the appearance concealed pride and self-love. This is the vice that all founders of sects are prone to regardless of whether the sect is good or bad. Therefore Bauduin says quite rightly, "your colleagues complain about your arrogance and unbelievable haughtiness".'[24] As a result, many of the historical details to be found in Masson's work are more reliable than the Protestant hagiographies. Unlike Bolsec, Masson did not simply set out to demolish Calvin's character. He constructed a narrative in which Calvin became all the more dangerous for his prodigious talents. He was, in Masson's words, a remarkable author, who 'wrote as much and as well as any secretary if we consider the quantity, the conciseness, the sting, the rhetorical stress, the vigour of expression'.[25] The richness of the information serves only to underscore Masson's principal point: 'we have given this account of Calvin's life as neither his friend nor his foe. I will not be lying if I say that he was the ruin and destruction of France. If only he had died in childhood or had never been born! For he brought so many ills to his country that it is only just to hate and detest his origins.'[26]

Memories

When examining contemporary representations of John Calvin, whether paintings or engravings, the overwhelming image is that of an old man. Yet Calvin never became the venerable figure of the European Reformation. He was not even fifty-six when he died, which even by the standards of the day was not ancient. Bullinger, his elder, outlived him by eleven years; the sickly Philip Melanchthon survived to a greater age, as did Martin Luther, Martin Bucer and his friend Guillaume Farel. Calvin's punishing routine and recurring illnesses aged him and put him in an early grave.

Yet it was Calvin who was remembered. There are many reasons for this. One could begin with the stewardship of Theodore Beza, who ensured Geneva's continuing prominence as a centre of the Reformed faith as Zurich, Basle and later Heidelberg faded into the mist. More importantly, the rise of Calvinism, which extended across Europe and then to the New World, drew from its eponym a coherent body of theology, a model of church organization and a spiritual discipline. Although there were many modifications and variations, the figure of John Calvin remained central.

As in life, so in death. Calvin's legacy was also part of a changing world. By the time he died in 1564 a fundamental shift in the European Reformation was taking place.[27] The era of the second-generation reformers, those who had taken over from Luther and Zwingli, was coming to an end. The rapid changes and theological fluctuations of Calvin's life were giving way to clearly defined confessional states (Lutheran, Reformed, Catholic) which were drawing up articles of faith and catechisms to serve established churches. Calvin's discursive, humanist style, which he shared with his contemporaries, was replaced by new forms of argumentation that could be used in the schools and academies. The theology itself was not changing, and Calvin's thought remained crucial to the Reformed tradition, but the means by which it was taught reflected new requirements.[28] Moreover, as he had lived, in death Calvin did not stand alone. He was read, studied and interpreted in various contexts all within a wider stream of Reformed thought that included Bullinger, Vermigli and their successors. Just as he had wanted, he belonged to the community of churchmen.

Across Europe memories of Calvin took many forms. Students studied his books as part of the Reformed tradition, and laity and clergy read his writings in a wide range of vernacular languages. But his voice was heard not only by those who read his works: his interpretations of the Bible poured from pulpits in countries as varied as Scotland and Hungary, reaching men, women and children who would have known little of the Genevan reformer. His words were in turn recited by those learning the faith through the Genevan catechism. In innumerable ways, he shaped the lives of those who formed the growing churches of 'International Calvinism' after his death. For a man who lived his life in exile, the most fitting memorial came from a land he never saw. In 1583 Geneva was under military threat from the Duke of Savoy, and Beza sent a delegation to England to seek financial assistance. Despite Elizabeth's frostiness towards Calvin, the collection raised was extraordinarily generous, reflecting the gratitude of a nation for a city and a man that had once offered refuge and Christian teaching.[29]

Notes

Abbreviations

ARG   *Archiv für Reformationsgeschichte*

Beveridge, *Tracts and Treatises*   John Calvin, *Tracts and Treatises*, trans. Henry Beveridge, 3 vols (Edinburgh: Calvin Translation Society, 1844–51)

BHR   *Bibliothèque d'Humanisme et Renaissance*

Bonnet   *Letters of Jean Calvin*, ed. Jules Bonnet, trans. David Constable, 4 vols (Edinburgh: Constable, 1855–7)

BSHPF   *Bulletin de la Société de l'Histoire du Protestantisme Français*

CO   *Ioannis Calvini Opera quae supersunt omnia*, ed. G. Baum, E. Cunitz and E. Reuss, 59 vols (1863–1900); also published as vols 29–87 of *Corpus Reformatorum*

CR   *Corpus Reformatorum. Philippi Melanchthonis Opera Quae Supersunt Omnia*. eds C. G. Bretschneider and H. E. Bindseil (Halle: 1834–1860)

De Clementia   *Calvin's Commentary on Seneca's De Clementia*, ed. Ford Lewis Battles and André Malan Hugo (Leiden: E. J. Brill, 1969)

HBBW   Heinrich Bullinger, *Briefwechsel* (Zurich: Theologischer Verlag, c. 1973–)

HSP   *Proceedings of the Huguenot Society of Great Britain and Ireland*

Institutes   John Calvin, *Institutes of the Christian Religion*, ed. John T. McNeill, trans. Ford Lewis Battles, 2 vols (Philadelphia: Westminster Press, 1960)

Romans   John Calvin, *The Epistles of Paul the Apostle to the Romans and to the Thessalonians*, trans. Ross McKenzie (Edinburgh: Oliver & Boyd, 1960). v = verse.

SCJ   *Sixteenth Century Journal*

STC   A Short Title Catalogue of Books Printed in England, Scotland, and Ireland and of English Books Printed Abroad 1475–1640

Chapter 1: A French Youth

1. Commentary on psalms, Preface, *CO* 31:21.
2. See Hugh Cunningham, *Children and Childhood in Western Society since 1500* (London: Longman, 1995). Also still extremely stimulating on early-modern childhood is the

classic Philippe Ariès, *Centuries of Childhood: A Social History of Family Life*, trans. Robert Baldick (1962; repr. Harmondsworth: Penguin, 1973).

3. *Censura* to the *Retractationes et Confessiones* (Basle, 1528), 1:45. I am grateful to Arnoud Visser of St Andrews for this reference. He discusses the subject further in his 'Reading Augustine through Erasmus' Eyes: Humanist Scholarship and Paratextual Guidance in the Wake of the Reformation', *Erasmus of Rotterdam Society Yearbook* 28 (forthcoming).

4. Commentary on psalms, Preface, *CO* 31:19–21.

5. Commentary on psalms, Preface, *CO* 31:21.

6. The classic study of Calvin's early years remains Alexandre Ganoczy, *The Young Calvin*, trans. David Foxgrover and Wade Provo (Edinburgh: T&T Clark, 1987).

7. Suzanne Selinger, *Calvin against Himself: An Inquiry in Intellectual History* (Hamden, Conn.: Archon Books, 1984).

8. Bernard Cottret, *Calvin: A Biography*, trans. M. Wallace McDonald (Grand Rapids, Mich.: Wm B. Eerdmans, 2000), 11.

9. On school education, see Georges Huppert, *Public Schools in Renaissance France* (Urbana, IL: University of Illinois Press, 1984).

10. Thomas More, *Utopia*, trans. Clarence Miller (New Haven, CT: Yale University Press, 2001), 19.

11. Theodore Beza, *The Life of John Calvin* (trans. 1997; repr. Darlington: Evangelical Press, 2005), 16.

12. Alister McGrath offers some helpful insights on the nature of the University of Paris, and the doubts he expresses about Calvin at Collège de la Marche are instructive, but no convincing alternative to the accounts in Colladan and Beza have been offered. See Alister E. McGrath, *A Life of John Calvin: A Study in the Shaping of Western Culture* (Oxford: Blackwell, 1990), 23–7.

13. This incident is recounted in A. Lefranc, *La Jeunesse de Calvin* (Paris: Fischbacher, 1888), 61.

14. 17 February 1550, *CO* 13: 525–6.

15. On Maturin's pedagogy, see Elizabeth K. Hudson, 'The Colloquies of Maturin Cordier: Images of Calvinist School Life and Thought', *SCJ* 9 (1978): 57–78. Also Jules le Coultre, *Maturin Cordier et les origines de la pédagogie protestante dans les pays de langue française (1530–1564)* (Neuchâtel: Secrétariat de l'Université, 1926).

16. Quoted in Foster Watson, 'Maturinus Corderius: Schoolmaster at Paris, Bordeaux, and Geneva in the Sixteenth Century', *School Review* 12 (1904): 285.

17. E. A. Berthault, *Mathurin Cordier et l'enseignement chez les premiers Calvinistes* (Paris, 1876), 11f.

18. Hans R. Guggisberg, *Sebastian Castellio, 1515–1563: Humanist and Defender of Toleration in a Confessional Age* (Aldershot: Ashgate, 2002), 31–2.

19. Ganoczy, *Young Calvin*, 57–63.

20. André Tuilier, *Histoire de l'Université de Paris et de la Sorbonne* (Paris: Nouvelle Librairie de France, 1994).

21. McGrath, *Life of John Calvin*, 33.

22. On Lefèvre, see above, pp.12–13.

23. *Erasmi Opera*, 426, I, Colloquia p. 806 et seq. translated into French by Augustin Renaudet, *Préréforme et humanisme à Paris pendant les premières guerres d'Italie (1494–1517)* (Paris: Librairie Ancienne Honoré Champion, 1916), 267–8.

24. McGrath, *Life of John Calvin*, 31–50 offers an entirely speculative account.

25. R. J. Knecht, *The Rise and Fall of Renaissance France, 1483–1610*, 2nd edn (Oxford: Blackwell, 2001), 84.

26. Marie-Madeleine de La Garanderie, 'Guillaume Budé: A Philosopher of Culture', *SCJ* 19 (1988): 379–88. See also David O. McNeil, *Guillaume Budé and Humanism in the Reign of Francis I* (Geneva: Droz, 1972).

27. Claude de Seysell, *The Monarchy of France*, ed. Donald R. Kelley, trans. J. H. Hexter (New Haven, CT: Yale University Press, 1981).

28. Ehsan Ahmed, 'Wisdom and Absolute Power in Guillaume Budé's Institution du Prince', *Romantic Review* 96 (2005): 173–86; see also M. Martin, *Guillaume Budé, le livre de l'Institution du Prince* (Berne: Lang, 1983).

29. On Francis I's cultural legacy, see Janet Cox-Rearick, *The Collection of Francis I: Royal Treasures* (New York: Harry N. Abrams, 1996).

30. On France, see Jean-Claude Margolin, 'Humanism in France', in Anthony Goodman and Angus MacKay (eds), *The Impact of Humanism on Western Europe* (London: Longman, 1990), 164–201.

31. On Francis I's complex religious views, see R. J. Knecht, 'Francis I, "Defender of the Faith" ', in E. W. Ives, R. J. Knecht and J. J. Scarisbrick (eds), *Wealth and Power in Tudor England: Essays Presented to S. T. Bindhoff* (London: Athlone Press, 1978), 106–27.

32. Quoted in Léon-E. Halkin, *Erasmus: A Critical Biography* (Oxford: Blackwell, 1993), 114.

33. Eamon Duffy, *The Stripping of the Altars: Traditional Religion in England, c. 1400–c. 1580* (New Haven, CT: Yale University Press, 1992).

34. Christopher Elwood, *The Broken Body: The Calvinist Doctrine of the Eucharist and the Symbolization of Power in Sixteenth-Century France* (Oxford: Oxford University Press, 1999), 12–26.

35. Francis Higman, 'Theology for the Layman in the French Reformation', in his *Lire et découvrir: la circulation des idées au temps de la Réforme* (Geneva: Droz, 1998), 87.

36. See Brian Patrick McGuire, *Jean Gerson and the Last Medieval Reformation* (University Park, PA: Pennsylvania State University Press, 2005).

37. David S. Hempsell, 'Measures to Suppress "la peste luthérienne" in France, 1521–1522', *Bulletin of the Institute of Historical Research* 49 (1976): 296–329; Rodolphe Peter, 'La Réception de Luther en France au 16e siècle', *Revue d'Histoire et de Philosophie Religieuses* 63 (1983): 67–89.

38. Francis Higman, 'Premières réponses catholiques aux écrits de la Réforme en France, 1525–c. 1540', in P. Aquilon and H.-J. Martin (eds), *Le Livre dans l'Europe de la Renaissance* (Paris: Promodis Editions du Cercle de la Librairie, 1988), 361–77. Also Higman, 'Luther d'histoire et la piété de l'église gallicane: Le Livre de vraye et parfaicte oraison', *Revue d'Histoire et de Philosophie Religieuses* 63 (1983): 11–57.

39. Knecht, *Rise and Fall of Renaissance France*, 115.

40. Francis Higman, 'Le Levain de l'Evangile', in his *Lire et découvrir*, 16.

41. David Nicholls, 'Heresy and Protestantism, 1520–1542: Questions of Perception and Communication', *French History* 10 (1996): 186.

42. Higman, 'Le Levain de l'Evangile', 17–18.

43. On Luther's image, see Robert Kolb, *Martin Luther as Prophet, Teacher, and Hero: Images of the Reformer, 1520–1620* (Grand Rapids, MI: Baker Books, 2000).

44. Guy Bedouelle, *Lefèvre d'Etaples et l'intelligence des écritures* (Geneva: Droz, 1976). See also John Woolman Brush, 'Jacques Lefèvre d'Etaples: Three Phases of his Life and Work', in Franklin. H. Littell (ed.), *Reformation Studies: Essays in Honor of Roland Bainton* (Richmond, VA: John Knox Press, 1962), 117–28; Richard M. Cameron, 'The Attack on the Biblical Works of Lefèvre d'Etaples, 1514–1521', *Church History* 38 (1969): 9–24; Richard M. Cameron, 'The Charges of Lutheranism Brought against Lefèvre d'Etaples', *Harvard Theological Review* 63 (1970): 119–49.

45. Eugene F. Rice Jr, 'Humanist Aristotelianism in France', in A. H. T. Levi (ed.), *Humanism in France at the End of the Middle Ages and in the Early Renaissance* (Manchester: Manchester University Press, 1970), 132–49.

46. Guy Bedouelle, 'Jacques Lefèvre d'Etaples (c. 1460–1536)', in Carter Lindberg (ed.), *The Reformation Theologians* (Oxford: Blackwell, 2001), 4.

47. Anselm Hufstader, 'Lefèvre d'Etaples and the Magdalen', *Studies in the Renaissance* 16 (1969): 31–61.

48. Jonathan Reid, 'King's Sister – Queen of Dissent: Marguerite of Navarre (1492–1549) and her Evangelical Network' (PhD dissertation, University of Arizona, 2001), 182. The book, with the same title, is forthcoming from E. J. Brill.
49. Reid, 'King's Sister', 168.
50. Walter Bense, 'Noel Beda and the Humanist Reformation at Paris, 1504–1534', 3 vols (PhD dissertation, Harvard Divinity School, 1967).
51. Reid, 'King's Sister', 169.
52. Knecht, *Rise and Fall of Renaissance France*, 115–16.
53. The most significant new work on Marguerite is Reid, 'King's Sister'. See also Henry Heller, 'Marguerite of Navarre and the Reformers of Meaux', *BHR* 33 (1971): 279–310.
54. Michel Veissère, 'Guillaume Briçonnet, évêque de Meaux, et la réforme de son clergé', *Revue d'Histoire Ecclésiastique* 84 (1989): 657–72.
55. Heather M. Vose, 'A Sixteenth-Century Assessment of the French Church in the Years 1521–24 by Bishop Guillaume Briçonnet of Meaux', *Journal of Ecclesiastical History* 39 (1988): 509–19.
56. 'Die Stellung desr "Summaire" von Guillaume Farel innerhalb der frühen reformierten Bekenntnisschriften', in Heiko A. Oberman and others (eds), *Reformiertes Erbe: Festschrift für Gottfried W. Locher zu seinem 80. Geburtstag*, 2 vols (Zurich: Theologischer Verlag, 1992), 93–114.
57. Michel Veissère, 'Guillaume Briçonnet, d'après sa correspondance avec Marguerite d'Angoulême (1521–1524)', *Information Historique* 41 (1979): 34–7.
58. Reid, 'King's Sister', 69.
59. Christian Wolff, 'Strasbourg, cité du refuge', in Georges Livet and Francis Rapp (eds), *Strasbourg au coeur religieux du XVI siècle: hommage à Lucien Febvre* (Strasbourg: Librairie Istra, 1977), 321–30.
60. Higman, 'Le Levain de l'Evangile', 19.
61. On the actions of the Parlement, see Christopher W. Stocker, 'The Politics of the Parlement in Paris in 1525', *French Historical Studies* 8 (1973): 191–212.
62. Natalie Zemon Davis, *Society and Culture in Early Modern France: Eight Essays* (Stanford, CA: Stanford University Press, 1975).
63. Higman, 'Le Levain de l'Evangile', 26.

Chapter 2: Among the Princes of Law

1. Ganoczy, *Young Calvin*, 62–3.
2. Ibid., 64.
3. Henri Delarue, 'Olivétan et Pierre de Vingle à Genève', *BHR* 8 (1946): 105–18.
4. Michael L. Monheit, 'Guillaume Budé, Andrea Alciato, Pierre de l'Estoile: Renaissance Interpreters of Roman Law', *Journal of the History of Ideas* 58 (1997): 21–40.
5. Ganoczy, *Young Calvin*, 68.
6. Monheit, 'Renaissance Interpreters', 31–2.
7. On Alciati, see Donald R. Kelley, *Foundations of Modern Historical Scholarship: Language, Law, and History in the French Renaissance* (New York: Columbia University Press, 1970): 87–115. Also Paul Viard, *André Alciat, 1492–1550* (Paris: Societé Anonyme du 'Recueil Sirey', 1926).
8. See Monheit, 'Renaissance Interpreters', 27–31.
9. Jean-François Gilmont, *John Calvin and the Printed Book*, trans. Karin Maag (Kirksville, MO: Truman State University Press, 2005), 196–7; and Olivier Millet, *Calvin et la dynamique de la parole* (Paris: Champion, 1992), 42.
10. Cornelius Augustijn, Christoph Burger and Frans P. van Stam, 'Calvin in the Light of the Early Letters', in Herman J. Selderhuis (ed.), *Calvinus Praeceptor Ecclesiae: Papers of the International Congress on Calvin Research, Princeton, August 20–24, 2002* (Geneva: Droz, 2004), 140–1.

11. Beza, *Life of Calvin*, 20.
12. Denis Crouzet, *Jean Calvin: vies parallèles* (Paris: Fayard, 2000), 74.
13. Emile Doumergue, *Jean Calvin: les hommes et les choses de son temps* (Lausanne: G. Bridel, 1899), 1:18, 37–9.
14. Aimé-Louis Herminjard, *Correspondance des réformateurs dans les pays de langue française* (Geneva and Paris, 1866–97), 2:394.
15. I follow here the argument of Michael L. Monheit, ' "The Ambition for an Illustrious Name": Humanism, Patronage, and Calvin's Doctrine of Calling', *SCJ* 23 (1992): 267–87.
16. *De Clementia*, 10.
17. Monheit, 'Ambition for an Illustrious Name', 269–71.
18. Beza speaks of Calvin's diligence in studying scripture while a student in Bourges. Beza, *Life of Calvin*, 20.
19. Gilmont, *Calvin and the Printed Book*, 164.
20. A. N. S. Lane, *John Calvin: Student of the Church Fathers* (Edinburgh: T&T Clark, 1999), 44, 52.
21. Gilmont, *Calvin and the Printed Book*, 165.
22. *De Clementia*, 11.
23. The crucial work is Guenther Haas, *The Concept of Equity in Calvin's Ethics* (Waterloo, Ontario: Wilfrid Laurier University Press, 1997). See also Christoph Strohm, 'Methodology in Discussion of "Calvin and Calvinism" ', in Selderhuis (ed.), *Calvinus Praeceptor Ecclesiae*, 76–7.
24. Irena Backus, 'Calvin's Concept of Natural and Roman Law', *Calvin Theological Journal* 38 (2003): 16–19.
25. Ibid., 21–2.
26. *De Clementia*, 33.
27. Irena Backus, *Historical Method and Confessional Identity in the Era of the Reformation (1378–1615)* (Leiden: E. J. Brill, 2003), here especially summation on 99–101.
28. *De Clementia*, 77.
29. Ibid., 85.
30. Backus, 'Calvin's Concept of Natural and Roman Law', 20.
31. *De Clementia*, 109.
32. Strohm, 'Methodology in Discussion of "Calvin and Calvinism" ', 75,
33. Ibid., 76.
34. See Peter Goodrich, 'Laws of Friendship', *Law and Literature* 15 (2003): 23–52.
35. Anthony Grafton and Megan Williams, *Christianity and the Transformation of the Book: Origen, Eusebius, and the Library of Caesarea* (Cambridge, MA: Belknap Press, 2006), 54–5.
36. Calvin to François Daniel, May 1532, *CO* 10:20–1; Bonnet 1:38.
37. Monheit, 'Ambition for an Illustrious Name', 285f.

Chapter 3: 'At Last Delivered': Conversion and Flight

1. Ganoczy, *Young Calvin*, 71.
2. Max Engammare argues that the oft repeated assertion that Calvin studied Hebrew with Vatable in Paris and with Melchior Wolmar in Bourges in the years 1531–3 is without proof. 'Joannes Calvinus trium linguarum peritus? La question de l'Hébreu', *BHR* 58 (1996): 37. Calvin never mentions the name Vatable in his correspondence, 38.
3. Augustijn, Burger and van Stam, 'Calvin in the Light of the Early Letters', 141.
4. From ibid., 142.
5. *CO* 31:13–35.

6. Heiko A. Oberman, 'Subita Conversio: The Conversion of John Calvin', in Oberman and others (eds), *Reformiertes Erbe*, 281.
7. John C. Olin (ed.), *A Reformation Debate: Sadoleto's Letter to the Genevans and Calvin's Reply* (New York: Harper & Row, 1966), 87–8.
8. Ibid., 89.
9. Ibid., 90.
10. Willem Nijenhuis, 'Calvin's "Subita Conversio": Notes to a Hypothesis', in W. Nijenhuis (ed.), *Ecclesia Reformata: Studies on the Reformation* (Leiden: E. J. Brill, 1994), 2:3–23.
11. Oberman, 'Subita Conversio', 291.
12. François Wendel, *Calvin: The Origins and Development of his Religious Thought*, trans. Philip Mairet (1950; trans. London: Collins, 1963), 39.
13. Francis M. Higman, *Censorship and the Sorbonne: A Bibliographical Study of Books in French Censured by the Faculty of Theology of the University of Paris, 1520–1551* (Geneva: Droz, 1979), 40–5.
14. Nicholls, 'Heresy and Protestantism', 185.
15. Reid, 'King's Sister', 484–7.
16. R. J. Knecht, *Francis I* (Cambridge: Cambridge University Press, 1982), 243–4.
17. Nicholls, 'Heresy and Protestantism', 194.
18. Calvin to Daniel, Oct. 1538, *CO* 10:27–30; Bonnet 1:12–16.
19. J. Dupèbe, 'Un document sur les persécutions de l'hiver 1533–1534 à Paris', *BHR* 48 (1986): 406.
20. Wendel, *Calvin*, 41.
21. 'Academic Discourse Delivered by Nicolas Cop on Assuming the Rectorship of the University of Paris on 1 November 1533', trans. Dale Cooper and Ford Lewis Battles, in John Calvin, *Institutes of the Christian Religion, 1536 Edition*, ed. and trans. Ford Lewis Battles, revised edn (repr. London: Collins, 1986), 365.
22. Bernard Roussel, 'François Lambert, Pierre Caroli, Guillaume Farel, et Jean Calvin (1530–1536)', in Wilhelm H. Neuser (ed.), *Calvinus Servus Christi: die Referate des Congrès International des Recherches Calviniennes/International Congress on Calvin Research/Internationalen Kongresses für Calvinforschung; vom 25. bis 28. August 1986 in Debrecen* (Budapest: Pressabteilung des Ráday-Kollegiums, 1988), 32–5.
23. Beza, *Life of Calvin*, 15.
24. Wendel, *Calvin*, 41; see also Gilmont, *Calvin and the Printed Book*, 11.
25. Olivia Carpi-Mailly, 'Jean Calvin et Louis du Tillet, entre foi et amitié, un échange révélateur', in Olivier Millet (ed.), *Calvin et ses contemporains: actes du colloque de Paris 1995* (Geneva: Droz, 1998), 8–9.
26. Beza, *Life of Calvin*, 16.
27. Ganoczy, *Young Calvin*, 84–5.
28. Bonnet 1:18; *CO* 10:37–8.
29. See Barbara Sher Tinsley, *History and Polemics in the French Reformation: Florimond de Raemond, Defender of the Church* (Selinsgrove, PA: Associated University Presses/ Susquehanna University Press, 1992).
30. Florimond de Raemond, *Histoire de la naissance, progress et décadence de l'hérésie de ce siècle* (Paris, 1605), 889, quoted in Ganoczy, *Young Calvin*, 331.
31. Augustijn, Burger and van Stam, 'Calvin in the Light of the Early Letters', 142–5.
32. Carpi-Mailly, 'Jean Calvin et Louis du Tillet', 8.
33. On the Affair of the Placards, see L. Febvre, 'L'origine des Placards de 1534', *BHR* 7 (1945): 62–72; Donald R. Kelley, *The Beginning of Ideology: Consciousness and Society in the French Reformation* (Cambridge: Cambridge University Press, 1981); Francis M. Higman, 'De l'Affaire des Placards aux Nicodémites: le movement évangélique français sous François Ier', *Etudes Théologique et Religieuses* 70 (1995): 359–66.
34. Higman, 'Le Levain d'Evangile', 23.

35. On Zwingli see Lee Palmer Wandel, *The Eucharist in the Reformation: Incarnation and Liturgy* (Cambridge: Cambridge University Press, 2006); and her *Voracious Idols and Violent Hands: Iconoclasm in Reformation Zurich, Strasbourg, and Basel* (Cambridge, Cambridge University Press, 1995); also Bruce Gordon, *The Swiss Reformation* (Manchester: Manchester University Press, 2002), 71–5.

36. Knecht, *Rise and Fall of Renaissance France*, 144.

37. Gabrielle Berthoud, *Antoine Marcourt, Réformateur et pamphlétaire, du 'Livre des Marchans' aux Placards de 1534* (Geneva: Droz, 1973).

38. Paul Wernle, *Calvin und Basel bis zum Tode des Myconius, 1535–1552* (Basle: Friedrich Reinhardt Universitäts-Buchdruckerei, 1909), 7; Willem Balke, *Calvin and the Anabaptist Radicals* (Grand Rapids, MI: Wm B. Eerdmans, 1981), 26–7.

39. Capito to Calvin, *CO* 10:45–6.

40. Precise dating of the text eludes us, but it seems most likely that these revisions were made while he was finishing the *Institutes* during the winter, spring and summer of 1535 in Basle. Calvin's letter to Fabri is dated 11 September 1534, and the changes to the *Psychopannychia* are referred to in the past tense. The *Institutes* were also completed in that month, though they would not appear till spring of the following year. Writing in September 1535 to Christopher Fabri, minister in the Vaud and friend of Farel, Calvin noted, 'Word has been brought to me by someone, I know not who, at your request, that you did not entirely approve of some things in my treatise on the immortality of souls.' Bonnet 1:19.

41. In 1516 Pietro Pomponazzi (1462–1525) had published *The Treatise on the Immortality of the Soul* in which he maintained that according to Aristotle the human soul could not operate apart from the body and could not, therefore, survive physical death. The Fifth Lateran Council (1512–17) denounced this idea and decreed, without naming Pomponazzi, that the intellectual soul is immortal and individual to each person. Martin Luther roundly denounced the Council's doctrine, declaring that the soul is mortal and dies with the body to rise with Christ on the last day.

42. Roussel, 'François Lambert, Pierre Caroli, Guillaume Farel, et Jean Calvin', 35–52.

43. On Servetus, see Roland Bainton, *Hunted Heretic: The Life and Death of Michael Servetus, 1511–1553* (1953; repr. Gloucester, MA: Peter Smith, 1978).

44. Beza, *Life of Calvin*, 25. There is some question as to whether the meeting was to take place in 1533 or 1534. Beza says 1534, and this is followed by Doumerge and Bainton, *Hunted Heretic*, 81.

45. Beveridge, *Tracts and Treatises*, 3:418. The original is printed in *CO* 5:165–232.

46. Ibid., 435.

47. Ibid., 426.

48. Ibid., 427.

49. Ibid., 406.

50. Ibid., 426.

51. Ibid., 429–30.

52. Wes Williams, *Pilgrimage and Narrative in the French Renaissance: 'The Undiscovered Country'* (Oxford: Oxford University Press, 1998), 26–8.

53. Gilmont, *Calvin and the Printed Book*, 40.

Chapter 4: Exile in a Hidden Corner

1. Beza, *Life of Calvin*, 8.

2. *CO* 31:21.

3. *CO* 31:23.

4. On the Basle reformation, see Hans R. Guggisberg, *Basel in the Sixteenth Century: Aspects of the City Republic before, during, and after the Reformation* (St Louis, MO:

Center for Reformation Research, 1982); Gordon, *Swiss Reformation*, 108–12; and Amy Nelson Burnett, *Teaching the Reformation: Ministers and their Message in Basel, 1529–1629* (Oxford: Oxford University Press, 2007).

5. Gordon, *Swiss Reformation*, 122–35; Helmut Meyer, *Der Zweite Kappeler Krieg. Die Krise der schweizerischen Reformation* (Zurich: Hans Rohr, 1976).

6. On Erasmus in Basle, see R. J. Schoeck, *Erasmus of Europe: The Prince of Humanists, 1501–1536* (Edinburgh: Edinburgh University Press, 1993), 283f.

7. Myron P. Gilmore, 'Boniface Amerbach', in Myron P. Gilmore (ed.), *Humanists and Jurists: Six Studies in the Renaissance* (Cambridge, MA: Belknap Press, 1963), 146–77.

8. Sigrid Looss and Markus Matthias (eds), *Andreas Bodenstein von Karlstadt (1486–1541). Ein Theologe der frühen Reformation* (Wittenberg: Hans Lufft, 1998).

9. Edgar Bonjour, *Die Universität Basel von den Anfängen bis zur Gegenwart, 1460–1960* (Basle: Helbing & Lichtenhahn, 1983).

10. Peter G. Bietenholz, 'Printing and the Basle Reformation, 1517–1565', in Gilmont, *Reformation and the Book*, 235–63.

11. Ibid., 245.

12. Gilmont, *Calvin and the Printed Book*, 180–1.

13. Unfortunately there is no good English translation of Platter's diary. It is best to consult the modern German edition, Thomas Platter, *Lebensbeschreibung*, ed. Alfred Hartmann, 3rd edn (Basle: Schwabe, 2006).

14. Emmanuel Le Roy Ladurie, *The Beggar and the Professor: A Sixteenth-Century Family Saga*, trans. Arthur Goldhammer (Chicago: University of Chicago Press, 1997), 68–9.

15. See Martin Steinmann, *Johannes Oporinus. Ein Basler Buchdrucker um die Mitte des 16. Jahrhunderts* (Basle: Helbing & Lichtenhahn, 1967); Martin Steinmann, 'Aus dem Briefwechsel des Basler Druckers Johannes Oporinus', *Basler Zeitschrift für Geschichte und Altertumskunde* 69 (1969): 104–203.

16. Wernle, *Calvin und Basel*, 3.

17. Ibid., 4.

18. There is very little scholarly literature on Simon Grynaeus. His mathematical interests are covered in Charlotte Methuen, *Kepler's Tübingen* (Aldershot: Ashgate, 1998); his important relations with Cranmer are treated by Diarmaid MacCulloch in *Thomas Cranmer: A Life* (London and New Haven, CT: Yale University Press, 1996), 60–8.

19. Peter G. Bietenholz, *Basle and France in the Sixteenth Century: The Basle Humanists and Printers in their Contacts with Francophone Culture* (Geneva: Droz, 1971), 58.

20. Ibid., 59.

21. On Münster and Hebrew, see Stephen G. Burnett, 'Reassessing the "Basel–Wittenberg Conflict": Dimensions of the Reformation-Era Discussion of Hebrew Scholarship', in Allison P. Coudert and Jeffrey S. Shoulson (eds), *Hebraica Veritas? Christian Hebraists and the Study of Judaism in Early Modern Europe* (Philadelphia: University of Pennsylvania Press, 2004), 181–201. The most recent study of Münster himself is Matthew McLean, *The Cosmographia of Sebastian Münster: Describing the World in the Reformation* (Aldershot: Ashgate, 2007).

22. Engammare, 'Joannes Calvinus trium linguarum peritus?', 39.

23. Ibid., 41.

24. Gilmore, 'Boniface Amerbach', 146–77.

25. The Eucharist dispute between Zwingli and Luther is summarized in Gordon, *Swiss Reformation*, 71–5.

26. Martin Greschat, *Martin Bucer: Ein Reformator und seine Zeit, 1491–1551* (Munich: Beck, 1990), 115–26. On Capito, see James Kittelson, *Wolfgang Capito: From Humanist to Reformer* (Leiden: E. J. Brill, 1975). On the influence of Bucer and Capito among the Swiss, see Amy Nelson Burnett, 'The Myth of the Swiss Lutherans', *Zwingliana* 32 (2005): 45–70.

27. On the Schmalkaldic League, see Thomas A. Brady Jr, *Protestant Politics: Jacob Sturm (1489–1553) and the German Reformation* (Atlantic Highlands, NJ: Humanities Press, 1995), 143–203.

28. On the Wittenberg Concord, see Greschat, *Martin Bucer*, 142–52; Ernst Bizer, *Studien zur Geschichte des Abendmahlsstreits im 16. Jahrhundert* (1940, repr. Darmstadt: Wissenschaftliche Buchgesellschaft, 1962). A more recent and thorough interpretation is Amy Nelson Burnett, 'Basel and the Wittenberg Concord', *ARG* 96 (2005): 33–56.

29. Gordon, *Swiss Reformation*, 149.

30. On the development of the Olivétan Bible, see Max Engammare, 'Cinquante ans de révision de la traduction biblique d'Olivétan: les bibles réformées genevoises en français au XVIe siècle', *BHR* 53 (1991): 347–77, esp. 348–52.

31. Quoted in Gilmont, *Calvin and the Printed Book*, 113.

32. Ibid., 149.

33. I have used here the text of the prefaces in Irena Backus and Claire Chimelli (eds), *'La Vraie Piété': divers traités de Jean Calvin et 'Confession de foi' de Guillaume Farel* (Geneva: Labor et Fides, 1986).

34. Traudel Himmighöfer, *Die Zürcher Bibel bis zum Tode Zwinglis (1531)* (Mainz: Philipp von Zabern, 1995).

35. 'L'homme tout entire, avec ses appartenances, ses faits, ses pensees, ses paroles, sa vie, ont totalement deplu a Dieu.' Backus and Chimelli, *'La Vraie Piété'*, 26.

36. This theme is treated extensively and persuasively in Randall C. Zachman, *Image and Word in the Theology of John Calvin* (Notre Dame, IN: University of Notre Dame Press, 2007).

37. Ibid., 26.

38. Backus and Chimelli, *'La Vraie Piété'*, 27.

39. *CO* 31:23.

40. Richard Muller, *The Unaccommodated Calvin: Studies in the Foundation of a Theological Tradition* (Oxford: Oxford University Press, 1999), 25–6.

41. *CO* 31:23.

42. Muller, *Unaccommodated Calvin*, 103.

43. Jean-Daniel Benoît, 'The History and Development of the *Institutio*: How Calvin Worked', in G. E. Duffield (ed.), *John Calvin* (Appleford, Berkshire: Courtenay Press, 1966), 103.

44. John Calvin, *Institutes of the Christian Religion. 1536 edition*, trans. and annotated by Ford Lewis Battles (London: Collins, 1986), 1.

45. Ibid., 2.

46. Ibid., 5.

47. Ibid., 9.

48. Ibid., 43.

49. Ibid., 76.

Chapter 5: Violent Reformations and Tumult

1. F. Whitfield Barton, *Calvin and the Duchess* (Louisville, KY: Westminster John Knox Press, 1989).

2. Ganoczy, *Young Calvin*, 105.

3. Psalms commentary, *CO* 31:23–5.

4. See Heiko A. Oberman, 'Calvin and Farel: The Dynamics of Legitimation in Early Calvinism', *Journal of Early Modern History* 2 (1998): 33–60.

5. Carlos M. N. Eire, *War against the Idols: The Reformation of Worship from Erasmus to Calvin* (Cambridge: Cambridge University Press, 1986), 119–21.

6. Michael W. Bruening, *Calvinism's First Battleground: Conflict and Reform in the Pays de Vaud, 1528–1559* (Heidelberg: Springer Verlag, 2005), 112.
7. Ibid., 40.
8. Ibid., 111.
9. Gordon, *Swiss Reformation*, 58–9, 92–3, 96–7.
10. On the disputation, see the collection of essays in Eric Junod (ed.), *La Disput de Lausanne (1536): la théologie réformée après Zwingli et avant Calvin* (Lausanne: Bibliothèque Historique Vaudoise, 1988).
11. Emile-Michel Braekman, 'Les Interventions de Calvin', in Junod (ed.), *La Disput de Lausanne*, 149–58.
12. I absolutely agree with Bruening on this point, *First Battleground*, 141.
13. Ibid., 142.
14. Ibid., 151–2.
15. William G. Naphy, *Calvin and the Consolidation of the Genevan Reformation* (Manchester: Manchester University Press, 1994), 16–18.
16. E. William Monter, *Calvin's Geneva* (New York: John Wiley & Sons, 1967), 64. As Monter has observed, 'Geneva was merely a satellite in the orbit of Berne.'
17. This is well described in Thomas Lambert, 'Preaching, Praying and Policing the Reform in Sixteenth-Century Geneva' (PhD dissertation, University of Wisconsin-Madison, 1998), 34–8.
18. Lambert, 'Praying and Policing the Reform', 39.
19. Jeanne de Jussie, *The Short Chronicle: A Poor Clare's Account of the Reformation in Geneva*, ed. and trans. Carrie F. Klaus (Chicago and London: University of Chicago Press, 2006), 128.
20. Herminjard, *Correspondance*, 4:208; Gilmont, *Calvin and the Printed Book*, 46.
21. Gilmont, *Calvin and the Printed Book*, 30.
22. E. A. de Boer, 'Calvin and Colleagues: Propositions and Disputations in the Context of the Congrégations in Geneva', in Selderhuis (ed.), *Calvinus Praeceptor Ecclesiae*, 332.
23. In Zurich the *Prophezei* focused on the Old Testament. The Hebrew text was read, followed by the Greek of the Septuagint. On the basis of the exposition of the biblical passages a Latin translation was given that was turned into the vernacular as the basis for a sermon to the people. It was understood as a seamless progression from scholarly interpretation to pastoral application. On the *Prophezei* and its development in Swiss lands, see Gordon, *Swiss Reformation*, 232–9.
24. De Boer, 'Calvin and Colleagues', 332.
25. This point has been made persuasively by Frans Pieter van Stam, 'Die Genfer Artikel vom Januar 1537: aus Calvins oder Farels Feder?', *Zwingliana* 27 (2000): 87–101.
26. Ibid.
27. Randall C. Zachman, *John Calvin: Teacher, Pastor, and Theologian* (Grand Rapids, MI: Baker Academic, 2006), 134.
28. The topic is discussed in Irena Backus, 'What Prayers for the Dead in the Tridentine Period? [Pseudo-]John of Damascus, "De his qui in fide dormierunt" and its "Protestant" translation by Johannes Oecolampadius', in Oberman, *Reformiertes Erbe*, 2:13–24.
29. Calvin to Megander, Feb. 1537, *CO* 10:85–7; Bonnet 1:25.
30. Ibid.
31. Quoted in Cornelius Augustijn, 'Farel und Calvin in Bern 1537–38', in Peter Opitz (ed.), *Calvin im Kontext der Schweizer Reformation* (Zurich: Theologischer Verlag, 2003), 11.
32. Ibid., 13.
33. Calvin to Grynaeus, *CO* 10:106–9; Bonnet 1:32.
34. Calvin to Viret, Bonnet 1:29.
35. Myconius to Bullinger, *HBBW* 17:185.

36. Bullinger to Myconius, *HBBW* 7:203–5.
37. Calvin to Zurich Church, 30 Aug. 1537, *CO* 10:119–23.
38. Amy Nelson Burnett, 'Myth of the Swiss Lutherans', 45–70.
39. 1 Nov. 1537, *HBBW* 7:289.
40. *CO* 10:127–8. See also Frans Pieter van Stam, 'Das Verhältnis zwischen Bullinger und Calvin während Calvins erstem Aufenhalt in Genf', in Opitz (ed.), *Calvin im Kontext*, 28.
41. Calvin to Bucer, Jan. 1538, *CO* 10:137–44.
42. Augustijn, de Boer and van Stam, 'Calvin in the Light of the Early Letters', 156.
43. Quoted in ibid., 147.
44. Beza, *Life of Calvin*, 31.
45. *Johannes Calvini, Opera Selecta*, ed. Peter Barth, 5 vols (Münster: C. Kaiser, 1926–36), 1:290.
46. Ibid.
47. The title of the work is 'De christiani hominis officio in sacerdotiis papalis ecclesiae vel administrandis vel abiiciendis', *Opera Selecta* I:229–362.
48. Naphy, *Consolidation*, 27.
49. Monter, *Calvin's Geneva*, 66.
50. Naphy, *Consolidation*, 28.
51. Calvin to Bullinger, Feb. 1538, *CO* 10:153–4; Bonnet 1:42.
52. Frans Pieter van Stam, 'Farels und Calvins Ausweisung aus Genf am 23. April 1538', *Zeitschrift für Kirchengeschichte* 110 (1999): 215.
53. Ibid., 219.
54. Ibid.
55. Bruening, *First Battleground*, 163–4.
56. Van Stam, 'Farels und Calvins Ausweisung', 222–3.
57. Ibid.

Chapter 6: Discovering the Church

1. Van Stam, 'Farels und Calvins Ausweisung', 223.
2. Ibid.
3. Ibid., 224.
4. Ibid.
5. Ibid.
6. Bullinger to Niklaus von Wattenwyl, 4 May 1538, *CO* 10:195; also *HBBW* 8:126.
7. Van Stam, 'Farels und Calvins Ausweisung', 225.
8. Calvin to Bullinger, 20 May 1538, *CO* 10:200–1; Bonnet 1:45.
9. Ibid.
10. Calvin to du Tillet, 10 July 1538, *CO* 10:220; Bonnet 1:48.
11. Calvin to du Tillet, 10 July 1538, *CO* 10:221; Bonnet 1:49.
12. Calvin to Farel, 4 Aug. 1538, *CO* 10: 228–30; Bonnet 1:51.
13. Ibid.
14. Calvin to Farel, 20 Aug. 1538, *CO* 10:235–7; Bonnet 1:54.
15. Cornelis Augustijn, 'Calvin in Strasbourg', in Wilhelm H. Neuser (ed.), *Calvinus sacrae scripturae professor* (Grand Rapids, MI: Wm B. Eerdmans, 1994), 168.
16. Thomas A. Brady Jr, *Community, Politics and Reformation in Early Modern Europe* (Leiden: E. J. Brill, 1998), 192.
17. On Strasbourg, see M. U. Chrisman, *Strasbourg and the Reform: A Study in the Process of Religious Change* (New Haven, CT: Yale University Press, 1967); Thomas A. Brady Jr, *Ruling Class, Regime and Reformation at Strasbourg, 1520–1555* (Leiden: E. J. Brill, 1978); Laura Jane Abray, *The People's Reformation: Magistrates and Commons in*

Strasbourg, 1500–1598 (Ithaca: Cornell University Press, 1985); René Bornert, *La Réforme protestante du culte à Strasbourg au XVIe siècle (1523–1598): approche sociologique et interprétation théologique* (Paris: E. J. Brill, 1974).

18. Wendel, *Calvin*, 60.
19. Thomas A. Brady Jr, 'Martin Bucer and the Politics of Strasbourg', in Christian Krieger and Marc Lienhard (eds), *Martin Bucer and Sixteenth Century Europe: actes du colloque de Strasbourg (28–31 août 1991)* (Leiden: E. J. Brill, 1991), 134–5.
20. *CO* 10:226–9. Cited in John Witte Jr and Robert M. Kingdon, *Courtship, Engagement, and Marriage in John Calvin's Geneva* (Grand Rapids, MI: Wm B. Eerdmans, 2005), 97.
21. Calvin to Farel, 19 Mar. 1539, *CO* 10:347–8. Cited in Witte and Kingdon, *Courtship*, 109.
22. Calvin to Farel, 19 Mar. 1540, *CO* 12:30–1.
23. Calvin to Farel, Sept. 1540, *CO* 11:83–6. See discussion in Witte and Kingdon, *Courtship*, 99.
24. *CO* 15:205–7. See Witte and Kingdon, *Courtship*, 100.
25. The only comprehensive biography of Bucer remains Martin Greschat, *Martin Bucer: A Reformer and his Times*, trans. Stephen Buckwalter (1990; English trans. Louisville, KY: Westminster John Knox Press, 2004). Relatively recent research is found in Krieger and Lienhard (eds), *Martin Bucer and Sixteenth Century Europe*.
26. See Willem van't Spijker, 'Calvin's Friendship with Bucer: Did It Make Calvin a Calvinist?', in David Foxgrover (ed.), *Calvin and Spirituality: Calvin and his Contemporaries; Colleagues, Friends, and Contacts* (Grand Rapids, MI: CRC Product Services, 1998), 169–86; also his 'Bucer und Calvin', in Krieger and Lienhard (eds), *Martin Bucer and Sixteenth Century Europe*, 461–70; also Wilhelm Pauck, 'Calvin and Butzer', in Richard C. Gamble (ed.), *Articles on Calvin and Calvinism: Calvin's Early Writings and Ministry* (New York and London: Garland Publishing, 1992), 37–56.
27. Calvin to Bullinger, 12 Mar. 1539, cited in Zachman, *Calvin as Teacher, Pastor, and Theologian*, 23.
28. Ian P. Hazlett, 'Calvin's Latin Preface to his Proposed French Edition of Chrysostom's Homilies: Translation and Commentary', in James Kirk (ed.), *Humanism and Reform: The Church in Europe, England and Scotland, 1400–1643; Essays in Honour of James K. Cameron* (Oxford: Blackwell, 1991), 129–50.
29. Spijker, 'Bucer und Calvin', 464.
30. Calvin to Bucer, 15 Oct. 1541, *CO* 11:296.
31. Calvin to Farel, 24 Oct. 1538, *CO* 10:273–6; Bonnet 1:68.
32. Spijker, 'Bucer und Calvin', 465.
33. Farel to Calvin, 25 May 1551, in Preserved Smith, 'Some Old Unpublished Letters', *Harvard Theological Review* 12 (Apr. 1919): 212.
34. Calvin to Farel, 8 Oct. 1539, *CO* 10:396–400.
35. Muller, *Unaccommodated Calvin*, 120.
36. Ibid., 104.
37. Cited from Muller, *Unaccommodated Calvin*, 104.
38. Olivier Millet, 'Les "Loci communes" de 1535 et l'Institution de la Religion chrétienne de 1539–1541, ou Calvin en dialogue avec Melanchthon', in G. Frank and Martin Treu (eds), *Melanchthon und Europa* (Stuttgart: Thorbecke, 2001), 85–96.
39. Muller, *Unaccommodated Calvin*, 128.
40. Carpi-Mailly, 'Jean Calvin et Louis du Tillet', 135–48.
41. Bonnet 1:93.
42. Cited in Cottret, *Calvin*, 139.
43. Calvin to du Tillet, 20 Oct. 1538, *CO* 10:270; Bonnet 1:71.
44. Ibid.
45. James R. Payton Jr, 'Calvin and the Libri Carolini', *SCJ* 28 (1997): 477.
46. Calvin to ministers of Geneva, *CO* 10:251; Bonnet 1:59.
47. Monter, *Calvin's Geneva*, 67f.

48. Calvin to Geneva, *CO* 10:252; Bonnet 1:61.
49. Calvin to Geneva, *CO* 10:351; Bonnet 1:118.
50. Calvin to Geneva, *CO* 10:352; Bonnet 1:120.
51. Calvin to Farel, *CO* 10:361; Bonnet 1:127.
52. John C. Olin, *A Reformation Debate* (New York: Fordham University Press, 2000), 37.
53. Ibid., 43.
54. Ibid., 45.
55. Ibid., 54.
56. Ibid., 79.
57. Ibid., 87.
58. Brady, 'Martin Bucer and the Politics of Strasbourg', 135.
59. Wilhelm H. Neuser, 'Calvins Beitrag zu den Religionsgesprächen von Hagenau, Worms, und Regensburg (1540/41)', in L. Abramowski and J. F. G. Goeters (eds), *Studien zur Geschichte und Theologie der Reformation: Festschrift für Ernst Bizer* (Neukirchen-Vluyn: Neukirchener Verlag, 1969), 214.
60. Christopher Ocker, 'Calvin in Germany', in Christopher Ocker and others (eds), *Politics and Reformations: Histories and Reformations: Essays in Honor of Thomas A. Brady, Jr.* (Leiden and Boston: E. J. Brill, 2007), 323.
61. Augustijn, 'Calvin in Strasbourg', 170–1.
62. Calvin to Farel, cited in ibid., 171.
63. Cited in ibid.
64. Neuser, 'Calvins Beitrag', 230–1.
65. Ocker, 'Calvin in Germany', 331.
66. Ibid., 329.
67. Ralph Keen, 'Political Authority and Ecclesiology in Melanchthon's "De Ecclesiae Autoritate" ', *Church History* 65 (1996): 1–14.
68. Translated for the first time into English by Christopher Ocker in his 'Calvin in Germany', 341–4.
69. Ibid., 343.
70. Neuser, 'Calvins Beitrag', 236.

Chapter 7· 'Lucid Brevity' for the Sake of the Church· Romans

1. See John B. Payne, 'Erasmus: Interpreter of Romans', *SCJ* 2 (1971): 1–35, and T. H. L. Parker, *Commentaries on the Epistle to the Romans, 1532–1542* (Edinburgh: T&T Clark, 1986).
2. *Institutes* 1.13.1, quoted from David Wright, 'Calvin's Accommodating God', in Wilhelm H. Neuser and Brian G. Armstrong (eds), *Calvinus sincerioris religionis vindex; Calvin as Protector of the Purer Religion* (Kirksville, MO: Truman State University Press, 1997), 4. Helpful is Jon Balserak, *Divinity Compromised: A Study of Divine Accommodation in the Thought of John Calvin* (Dordrecht: Springer, 2006).
3. Strohm, 'Methodology in Discussion of "Calvin and Calvinism" ', 71.
4. R. Ward Holder, *John Calvin and the Grounding of Interpretation: Calvin's First Commentaries* (Leiden: E. J. Brill, 2006), 142.
5. David C. Steinmetz, 'Calvin and the Irrepressible Spirit', *Ex Auditu* 12 (1996): 105.
6. *Romans*, 2.1.
7. Nicole Kuropka, 'Calvins Römerbriefwidmung und der Consensus Piorum', in Opitz (ed.), *Calvin im Kontext*, 163.
8. *Romans*, 3.
9. For an excellent discussion of Calvin's exegetical approach, see Randall C. Zachman, 'Gathering Meaning from Context: Calvin's Exegetical Method', in his *Teacher, Pastor, and Theologian*, 103–30.

10. *Romans*, 3.
11. See David Steinmetz, 'Calvin and Patristic Exegesis', in his *Calvin in Context* (Oxford: Oxford University Press, 1995), esp. 135–7.
12. Commentary on Ezekiel 20:18, cited from Lane, *Student of the Church Fathers*, 36. On Calvin's relationship to the church fathers, see Lane's illuminating introduction.
13. Ibid., 29.
14. Muller, *Unaccommodated Calvin*, 39–61. Also David C. Steinmetz, 'The Scholastic Calvin', in Carl R. Trueman and R. Scott Clark (eds), *Protestant Scholasticism in Reassessment* (Eugene, OR: Wipf & Stock, 2005), 16–30.
15. Muller, *Unaccommodated Calvin*, 57.
16. Elsie Anne McKee, 'Exegesis, Theology, and Development in Calvin's Institutio: A Methodological Suggestion', in Elsie Anne McKee and Brian G. Armstrong (eds), *Probing the Reformed Tradition: Historical Studies in Honor of Edward A. Dowey, Jr* (Louisville, KY: Westminster John Knox Press, 1989), 155.
17. Ibid., 156.
18. Timothy J. Wengert, 'Philip Melanchthon's 1522 Annotationes on Romans and the Lutheran Origins of Rhetorical Criticism', in Richard A. Muller and John L. Thompson (eds), *Biblical Interpretations in the Era of the Reformation: Essays Presented to David C. Steinmetz* (Grand Rapids, MI: Wm B. Eerdmans, 1996), 118–40.
19. Kuropka, 'Römerbriefwidmung', 154.
20. Ibid., 159.
21. G. W. Pigman III, 'Versions of Imitation in the Renaissance', *Renaissance Quarterly* 33 (1980): 1–32.
22. Quoted in ibid., 30.
23. *CO* 20:77–8.
24. Philippians 2:3. John Calvin, *The Epistles of Paul the Apostle to the Corinthians, Ephesians, Philippians and Colossians*, trans. T. H. L. Parker (Edinburgh: Oliver & Boyd, 1965), 246.
25. V. 1:20, *Romans*, 31–2.
26. V. 1:19, ibid., 31.
27. V. 1:18, ibid., 30.
28. On Calvin's treatment of faith in the Romans commentary, see Barbara Pitkin, *What Pure Eyes Could See: Calvin's Doctrine of Faith in its Exegetical Context* (Oxford: Oxford University Press, 1999), esp. 42–55.
29. V. 3:4, *Romans*, 60.
30. V. 3:25, ibid., 76.
31. V. 4:20, ibid., 99.
32. V. 4:23, ibid., 100–1.
33. V. 9:11, ibid., 200.
34. V. 9:22, ibid., 211 (altered).
35. V. 7:2, ibid., 138.
36. On Calvin and the Jews, see Achim Detmers, *Reformation und Judentum: Israel-Lehren und Einstellungen zum Judentum von Luther bis zum frühen Calvin* (Stuttgart: Kohlhammer, 2001), esp. 239–79. Detmers demonstrates that Calvin had very little knowledge of Jews or their culture. See also Stephen G. Burnett, 'Calvin's Jewish Interlocutor: Christian Hebraism and anti-Jewish Polemics during the Reformation', *BHR* 55 (1993): 113–23.
37. V. 13:8, *Romans*, 284.
38. V. 15:1, ibid., 303.
39. V. 5:4, ibid., 305.
40. V. 15:25, ibid., 315.
41. V. 15:31, ibid., 318.

Chapter 8: Building Christ's Church

1. Calvin to Viret, 19 May 1540, *CO* 11:36; Bonnet 1:162–4.
2. On this see Oberman, 'Calvin and Farel', 40–1.
3. Zurich to Strasbourg, *CO* 11:233–4. The answer from Strasbourg to Zurich, *CO* 11:239–40. The letter in support of Calvin came from Basle, *CO* 11:236–7.
4. Calvin to Zurich church, 31 May 1541, *CO* 11:230–3; Bonnet 1:258–62.
5. Strasbourg to Geneva, 1 Sept. 1541, *CO* 11:266–8; the reply from Geneva of 17 Sept. 1541, *CO* 11:284–5.
6. See Naphy, *Consolidation*, 84–5.
7. William G. Naphy, *Plagues, Poisons and Potions: Plague-Spreading Conspiracies in the Western Alps ca. 1530–1640* (Manchester: Manchester University Press, 2002), 45.
8. Ibid., 46.
9. Ibid., 51.
10. Naphy, *Consolidation*, 87–8.
11. *Institutes* 4, 1:vii.
12. Willem Balke, *Calvin and the Anabaptist Radicals* (Grand Rapids, MI: Wm B. Eerdmans, 1981), 156–7.
13. See Irena Backus, 'These Holy Men: Calvin's Patristic Models for the Establishing of the Company of Pastors', in David Foxgrover (ed.), *Calvin and the Company of Pastors* (Grand Rapids, MI: CRC Product Services, 2004), 47.
14. Likewise, when it came to examination and ordination of ministers, the *Ordinances* laid out a system which Calvin justified on the basis of early church practices; Backus, 'Holy Men', 44–5
15. The members of the committee were Calvin, Claude Pertemps, Amy Perrin, Claude Roset, Jean Lambert, Potalia and Jean Balardut.
16. R. M. Kingdon, 'The Episcopal Function in Protestant Churches, XVIth–XVIIth Centuries', in Bernard Vogler (ed.), *Miscellanea Historiae Ecclesiasticae* 8, in *Bibliothèque de la Revue d'Histoire Ecclésiastique* 72 (1987): 214.
17. Lambert, 'Preaching, Praying and Policing', 186.
18. Ibid., 193.
19. Ibid., 198.
20. Erik A. de Boer, 'The Congrégation: An In-Service Theological Training Center for Preachers to the People of Geneva', in Foxgrover (ed.), *Calvin and the Company of Pastors*, 71.
21. Lambert, 'Preaching, Praying and Policing', 227.
22. De Boer, 'Congrégation', 71.
23. Lambert, 'Preaching, Praying and Policing', 234.
24. Ibid., 201–2.
25. Bruce Gordon, 'The Protestant Ministry and the Culture of Rule: The Reformed Zurich Clergy of the Sixteenth Century', in C. Scott Dixon and Luise Schorn-Schütte (eds), *The Protestant Clergy of Early Modern Europe* (Basingstoke: Palgrave Macmillan, 2003), 137–55; see also his 'The New Parish', in R. Po-chia Hsia (ed.), *A Companion to the Reformation World* (Oxford: Blackwell, 2004), 411–25.
26. Darlene K. Flaming, 'The Apostolic and Pastoral Office: Theory and Practice in Calvin's Geneva', in Foxgrover (ed.), *Calvin and the Company of Pastors*, 150–1.
27. Ibid., 153.
28. Ibid., 163.
29. Calvin to Myconius, Oct. 1541, *CO* 11:311.
30. See Naphy, *Consolidation*, 59–68.
31. Ibid., 70.
32. Ibid.

33. The Zurich church frequently resorted to moving ministers as a result of disciplinary problems, though this system became possible only once there were sufficient ministers; see Bruce Gordon, *Clerical Discipline and the Rural Reformation: The Synod in Zürich, 1532–1580* (Berne: Peter Lang, 1992), 216.
34. Calvin to Farel, 28 July 1542, *CO* 11:416–19; Bonnet 2:313–16.
35. Naphy, *Consolidation*, 72f.
36. Ibid., 73.
37. Ibid., 75.
38. Witte and Kingdon, *Sex, Marriage, and Family*, 1:66–8.
39. As Thomas Lambert has noted, 'Tears and angry eruptions were a regular part of Consistory sessions.' Lambert, 'Preaching, Praying and Policing', 247.
40. Ibid., 266.
41. Ibid., 269.
42. Ibid., 274.
43. Balke, *Calvin and the Anabaptist Radicals*, 165.
44. *Institutes* 4:12.9.
45. Jeffrey Watt, 'Women and the Consistory in Calvin's Geneva', *SCJ* 24 (1993): 429.
46. Naphy, *Consolidation*, 78.
47. See Elsie Anne McKee, 'Context, Contours, Contents: Towards a Description of Calvin's Understanding of Worship', in Foxgrover (ed.), *Calvin and Spirituality*, 66–92.
48. Lambert, 'Preaching, Praying and Policing', 287.
49. Ibid., 316.
50. Ibid., 341.
51. Christian Grosse, 'Places of Sanctification: The Liturgical Sacrality of Genevan Reformed Churches, 1535–1566', in Will Coster and Andrew Spicer (eds), *Sacred Space in Early Modern Europe* (Cambridge: Cambridge University Press, 2005), 68–9.
52. Lambert, 'Preaching, Praying and Policing', 213.
53. Grosse, 'Places of Sanctification', 70.
54. *Institutes* 1:9.13, cited in Grosse, 'Places of Sanctification', 73.
55. Lambert, 'Preaching, Praying and Policing', 217.
56. See the comment by Christian Grosse in his 'Places of Sanctification', 77.
57. Calvin to Farel, 11 Nov. 1541, *CO* 11:321–2; Bonnet 1:282–4.
58. Thomas J. Davis, 'Preaching and Presence: Constructing Calvin's Homiletical Legacy', in David Foxgrover (ed.), *The Legacy of John Calvin* (Grand Rapids, MI: CRC Product Services, 2000), 92–3.
59. Davis, 'Preaching and Presence', 97.
60. Ibid., 99.
61. Lambert, 'Preaching, Praying and Policing', 369.
62. In William Monter's wonderfully evocative phrase 'this happy ending did not prevent the Genevan revolution from continuing to devour her own children'. Monter, *Calvin's Geneva*, 74.
63. Calvin to Farel, Apr. 1546, *CO* 12:334; Bonnet 2:38–41.
64. Calvin to Farel, 4 July 1546, *CO* 12:355–7; Bonnet 2:47–9.
65. Calvin to Farel, 1 Sept. 1546, *CO* 12:377–8; Bonnet 2:56–8.
66. Monter, *Calvin's Geneva*, 77–80.

Chapter 9: Calvin's World

1. Calvin to Bullinger, 23 Nov. 1554, *CO* 15:318; Bonnet 3:96–8.
2. 2 Cor. 7:5, *CO* 50:86–7. John Calvin, *The Second Epistle of Paul the Apostle to the Corinthians and the Epistles to Timothy, Titus, and Philemon*, trans. T. A. Smail (Edingburgh: Oliver & Boyd, 1964), 96–7.

3. See Robert M. Kingdon, *Adultery and Divorce in Calvin's Geneva* (Cambridge, MA: Harvard University Press, 1995).
4. *Institutes* 1:17.10.
5. Graham Robb, *The Discovery of France: A Historical Geography, from the Revolution to the First World War* (London: W. W. Norton, 2007), 92.
6. Max Engammare, 'Plaisir des mets, plaisirs des mots: irdische Freude bei Calvin', in Neuser and Armstrong (eds), *Calvinus sincerioris religionis vindex*, 189–208.
7. Engammare, 'Plaisir des mets', 195.
8. Ibid., 196.
9. Zachman, *John Calvin as Teacher*, 240–2.
10. On Calvin's work environment, see Gilmont, *Calvin and the Printed Book*, 127f.
11. Engammare, 'Plaisir des mets', 200.
12. Ibid., 202.
13. D. R. Kelly, *François Hotman: A Revolutionary's Ordeal* (Princeton, NJ: Princeton University Press, 1983), 36.
14. Ibid., 143.
15. Ibid., 47.
16. Gilmont, *Calvin and the Printed Book*, 181.
17. See Andrew Pettegree, 'Genevan Print and the Coming of the Wars of Religion', in Andrew Pettegree (ed.), *The French Book and the European Book World* (Leiden: E. J. Brill, 2007), 89–106. See also his *Reformation and the Culture of Persuasion* (Cambridge: Cambridge University Press, 2005).
18. *CO* 13:520. Cited in Gilmont, *Calvin and the Printed Book*, 186.
19. Farel to Calvin and Viret, 1 Dec. 1541, *CO* 11:353.
20. Calvin to Farel, 16 Sept. 1541, *CO* 11:281–2; Bonnet 1:260–1.
21. Calvin to Bucer, 15 Oct. 1541, *CO* 11:296–300; Bonnet 1:264–71.
22. Calvin to Viret, 24 Oct. 1545, *CO* 12:193–4; Bonnet 1:10–11.
23. Calvin to Farel, 1 Sept. 1549. The work is not named in the letter, but it was most likely Farel's *Le Glaive de la Parole Veritable contre le Bouclier de Defense, duquel un Cordelier s'est voulu server*, which was printed in Geneva in 1550. *CO* 13:374; Bonnet 2:247.
24. Farel to Calvin, 25 May 1551; Smith, 'Some Old Letters', 212–13, altered.
25. Calvin to Farel, 11 Nov. 1541, *CO* 11:321–2; Bonnet 1:282–4.
26. Calvin to Myconius, 14 Mar. 1542, *CO* 11:376–81; Bonnet 1:288–96.
27. Willem Balke, 'Jean Calvin und Pierre Viret', in Opitz (ed.), *Calvin im Kontext*, 72.
28. Bruening, *First Battleground*, 179f.
29. On the Eucharistic debate in Berne, see Burnett, 'Myth of the Swiss Lutherans', 45–70.
30. On this see the discussion in Bruening, *First Battleground*, 181f.
31. Hans R. Guggisberg, *Sebastian Castellio, 1515–1563: Humanist and Defender of Religious Toleration in a Confessional Age*, trans. Bruce Gordon (Aldershot: Ashgate, 2002).
32. Calvin to Viret, Sept. 1542, *CO* 11:436–9; Bonnet 1:326–7.
33. Guggisberg, *Sebastian Castellio*, 34f.
34. Calvin to Viret, 8 Mar. 1546, *CO* 12:305–6; Bonnet 2:23–4.
35. Calvin to de Falais, 4 July 1546, *CO* 12:354–5; Bonnet, 2:49–50.
36. Calvin to Viret, 13 July 1546, *CO* 12:359; Bonnet 2:51.
37. Calvin to de Falais, 18 Sept. 1545, *CO* 12:169–71; Bonnet 2:5–6.
38. Calvin to Farel, 21 Aug. 1547, *CO* 12:580–1; Bonnet 2:123–5.
39. Calvin to Viret, 15 June 1548, *CO* 12:731–2.
40. Calvin to Viret, 7 Apr. 1549, *CO* 13:230–1; Bonnet 2:202–3.

Chapter 10: Healing Christ's Body

1. Randall C. Zachman, 'The Conciliating Theology of John Calvin: Dialogue among Friends', in Howard Louthan and Randall C. Zachman (eds), *Conciliation and*

Confession: The Struggle for Unity in the Age of Reform, 1415–1648 (Notre Dame, IN: Notre Dame University Press, 2004), 96–7.

2. Lane, *Calvin as Student*, 179–80.
3. Ibid., 180.
4. Timothy Wengert, 'We Will Feast Together in Heaven Forever: The Epistolary Friendship of John Calvin and Philip Melanchthon', in Karin Maag (ed.), *Melanchthon in Europe: His Work and Influence Beyond Wittenberg* (Grand Rapids, MI: Baker Books, 1999), 26–8.
5. Ibid., 28.
6. Ibid., 30–1.
7. Greschat, *Martin Bucer*, 199.
8. On developments in the empire, see Brady, *Protestant Politics*, esp. 206–91.
9. Calvin, 'On the Necessity of Reforming the Church', in Beveridge, *Tracts and Treatises*, 2:245.
10. Gordon, *Swiss Reformation*, 173–4.
11. Genevan Catechism, Beveridge, *Tracts and Treatises*, 2:89.
12. See the discussion in Thomas J. Davis, *The Clearest Promises of God: The Development of Calvin's Eucharistic Teaching* (New York: AMS Press, 1995), 148f.
13. Ibid., 151.
14. Ibid., 120f.
15. Calvin, 'A Short Treatise on the Lord's Supper', in Beveridge, *Tracts and Treatises*, 2:159–60.
16. Ibid., 154.
17. On Calvin's relations with the Swiss, see Bruce Gordon, 'Calvin and the Swiss Reformed Churches', in Andrew Pettegree, Alastair Duke and Gillian Lewis (eds), *Calvinism in Europe, 1540–1620* (Cambridge: Cambridge University Press, 1994), 64–81.
18. Calvin to Farel, 26 Feb. 1540, *CO* 11:23–6.
19. Calvin to Viret, 19 May 1540, *CO* 11:35–7; Bonnet 1:162–4.
20. See Anthony N. S. Lane, 'Was Calvin a Crypto-Zwinglian?', in Mack P. Holt (ed.), *Adaptations of Calvinism in Reformation Europe: Essays in Honour of Brian G. Armstrong* (Aldershot: Ashgate, 2007), 21–41.
21. Wim Janse, 'Calvin's Eucharistic Theology: Three Dogma-Historical Observations' (conference paper, Calvin International Congress, Emden, 2006).
22. Melanchthon to Bucer, 28 Aug. 1544, in Heinz Scheible (ed.), *Melanchthons Briefwechsel* (Stuttgart-Bad Cannstatt: Frommann Holzburg, 1977–), 34:120.
23. Calvin to Farel 10 Oct. 1544, *CO* 11:754–5; Bonnet 1:404–5.
24. Calvin to Bullinger, 25 Nov. 1544, *CO* 11:772–5; Bonnet 1:405–10.
25. Calvin to Melanchthon, 21 Jan. 1545, *CO* 12:9–12; Bonnet 1:410–16.
26. Calvin to Luther, 21 Jan. 1545, *CO* 12:7–8; Bonnet 1:416–18.
27. Bruce Gordon, 'Holy and Problematic Deaths: Heinrich Bullinger on Zwingli and Luther', in Marion Kobelt-Groch and Cornelia Niekus Moore (eds), *Tod und Jenseitsvorstellungen in der Schriftkultur der Frühen Neuzeit* (Wolfenbüttel: Harrassowitz, 2008), 47–62.
28. Pierre Viret, *De la vertu et usage du ministère de la Parolle de Dieu et des sacraments* (Geneva: Jean Girard, 1545).
29. Bruening, *First Battleground*, 188–9.
30. Johannes Haller to Bullinger, 8 Aug. 1548, *CO* 13:24; cited in ibid., 190.
31. Calvin to Bullinger, 26 June 1548, *CO* 12:727–31; Bonnet 2:154–9.
32. This is discussed in Oberman, 'Calvin and Farel', 39–41.
33. Theodore W. Casteel, 'Calvin and Trent: Calvin's Reaction to the Council of Trent in the Context of his Conciliar Thought', *Harvard Theological Review* 63 (1970): 91–117.
34. Beveridge, *Tracts and Treatises*, 3:27.
35. Casteel, 'Calvin and Trent', 114.

36. Heiko A. Oberman, 'The Pursuit of Happiness: Calvin between Humanism and Reformation', in John W. O'Malley, Thomas M. Izbicki and Gerald Christianson (eds), *Humanity and Divinity in Renaissance and Reformation* (Leiden: E. J. Brill, 1993), 259.
37. Calvin to de Falais, 14 July 1548, *CO* 13:8–9.
38. Calvin to Bullinger 11 Sept. 1548, *CO* 13:51–2.
39. Calvin to Bullinger, 21 Jan. 1549, *CO* 13:164–6; Bonnet 2:196–8.
40. Ibid.
41. Bruening, *First Battleground*, 203.
42. For a full treatment of the French alliance, see ibid., 52–6.
43. Davis, *Clearest Promises of God*, 43.

Chapter 11: 'Since Calvin Acts So Bravely, Why Does He Not Come Here?': France

1. Francis Higman, *Censorship and the Sorbonne: A Bibliographical Study of the Books in French Censured by the Faculty of Theology of the University of Paris, 1520–1551* (Geneva: Droz, 1979), 62–3.
2. Davis, *Society and Culture in Early Modern France*, 7.
3. A. Munz, 'Deux exécutions à Paris pour cause d'hérésie. Lettre d'un jeune catholique allemande, témoin oculaire, 1542', *BSHPF* 6 (1858): 420–3. David Watson, 'The Martyrology of Jean Crespin and the Early French Evangelical Movement, 1523–1555' (PhD thesis, University of St Andrews, 1997), 85.
4. Gabriel Audisio, *Procès-verbal d'un massacre: les Vaudois du Luberon (avril 1545)* (Aix-en-Provence: C.-Y. Chaudoreille, 1992). Also his *The Waldensian Dissent: Persecution and Survival, c. 1170–1570* (Cambridge: Cambridge University Press, 1999).
5. Euan Cameron, *The Reformation of the Heretics* (Oxford: Oxford University Press, 1984), 237–9.
6. Jean Crespin, *Histoire mémorable de la persécution de Mérindol et Cabrières* (Geneva: J. Crespin, 1556); J. F. Gilmont, *Bibliographie des éditions de Jean Crespin, 1550–1572* (Verviers, Librairie P. M. Gason, 1981), 1:55–7, 59.
7. Henry Heller, *The Conquest of Poverty: The Calvinist Revolt in Sixteenth-Century France* (Leiden: E. J. Brill, 1986), 63–9.
8. M. Royannez, 'L'Eucharistie chez les évangeliques et les premiers réformés', *BSHPF* 125 (1979): 572.
9. On Crespin's method, see Catharine Randall Coats, 'Reconstituting the Textual Body in Jean Crespin's Histoire des martyrs (1564)', *Renaissance Quarterly* 44 (1991): 62–85.
10. Benedict, *Christ's Churches Purely Reformed: A Social History of Calvinism* (New Haven, CT: Yale University Press), 132–3.
11. William Monter, 'Les Exécutés pour hérésie par arrêt du Parlement de Paris (1523–1560)', *BSHPF* 142 (1996): 200.
12. N. Sutherland, *The Huguenot Struggle for Recognition* (New Haven, CT: Yale University Press, 1980), 42.
13. Nathanael Weiss, *La Chambre Ardente: étude sur la liberté de conscience en France sous François Ier et Henri II (1540–1550)* (1889; repr. Geneva: Slatkine, 1979), 202. Cited in Watson, 'Martyrology', 118.
14. William Monter, *Judging the French Reformation: Heresy Trials by Sixteenth-Century Parlements* (Cambridge, MA: Harvard University Press, 1999).
15. Sutherland, *Huguenot Struggle*, 43.
16. Ibid., 44–5.
17. The essential work is Brad S. Gregory, *Salvation at Stake: Christian Martyrdom in Early Modern Europe* (Cambridge, MA: Harvard University Press, 1999).

18. I am grateful to Andrew Pettegree for sharing this information. Recent work done in St Andrews has demonstrated that Geneva was second only to Paris in the volume of religious works printed in French.
19. Sutherland, *Huguenot Struggle*, 47.
20. Higman, 'Calvin and the Art of Translation', 374.
21. Ibid., 376.
22. Gilmont, *Calvin and the Printed Book*, 120; Millet, *Calvin et la dynamique*, 829f.
23. *The Treatise on Relics* (1543), *Answer of John Calvin to the Nicodemite Gentlemen Concerning their Complaint that He is too Severe* (1544), *Against the Anabaptists* (1544), *Against the Libertines* (1544), *Against Cordelier* (1547) and *Against Astrology* (1549).
24. John Calvin, 'On Relics', in Beveridge, *Tracts and Treatises*, 1:331.
25. Ibid., 334.
26. Ibid., 167.
27. Reid, 'King's Sister', 562f.
28. Peter Matheson, 'Martyrdom or Mission: A Protestant Debate', *ARG* 80 (1989): 165.
29. David Wright, 'Why was Calvin So Severe a Critic of Nicodemism?', in David F. Wright, Anthony N. S. Lane and Jon Balserak (eds), *Calvinus Evangelii Propugnator: Calvin, Champion of the Gospel; Papers Presented at the International Congress on Calvin Research, Seoul, 1998* (Grand Rapids, MI: CRC Product Services, 2006), 71–2.
30. Eire, *War against the Idols*, 241. See also his 'Prelude to Sedition? Calvin's Opposition to Nicodemism and Religious Compromise', *ARG* 79 (1985): 120–45.
31. Francis Higman has found ten works by 'Gallican Catholics' whom Calvin would term 'Nicodemites', which largely agree with Luther and reject papal authority: Francis Higman, 'The Question of Nicodemism', in W. Neuser (ed.), *Calvinus Ecclesiae Genevensis Custos* (Grand Rapids, MI: Wm B. Eerdmans, 1984). Thierry Wanegffelen has argued for a third way in France in the 1540s – those who believed in the possibility of evangelical reform within the Catholic church. These were non-confessional Christians, who were for the most part evangelical Catholics: Thierry Wanegffelen, *Ni Rome, ni Genève: des fidèles entre deux chaires en France au XVIe siècle* (Paris: Champion, 1997). Among the Protestant reformers, Wolfgang Capito had strong Nicodemite sympathies, and a letter of his circulated arguing that the Roman church was a true church.
32. David Wright, 'Why was Calvin So Severe', 67.
33. Herminjard, *Correspondance*, 9:126, n. 1316.
34. Eire, *War against the Idols*, 252.
35. Ibid., 256.
36. Perez Zagorin, *Ways of Lying: Dissimulation, Persecution, and Conformity in Early Modern Europe* (Cambridge, MA: Harvard University Press, 1990), 73.
37. Eire, *War against the Idols*, 243.
38. 'Answer to the Nicodemite' in John Calvin, *Come Out from Among Them: 'Anti-Nicodemite' Writings of John Calvin*, trans. Seth Skolnitsky (Dallas, TX: Protestant Heritage Press, 2001), 116.
39. Ibid., 123.
40. The work was entitled *Epistre envoyee aux fidèles conversent entre les chrestiens papistiques* (1543). Zagorin, *Ways of Lying*, 103.
41. Viret, *Admonition et consolation aux fidèles* (Geneva, 1547).
42. *Contre le secte phantastique et furieuse des libertines que se nomment spirituelz. Response à un certain holandais.* Ioannis Calvini, *Opera omnia*, series IV, vol. 1 (Geneva: Droz, 2005).
43. David Wright, 'Why was Calvin So Severe', 78.
44. Etienne Dolet, *Correspondance: répertoire analytique et chronologique suivi du texte de ses letters latines*, ed. Claude Longeon (Geneva: Droz, 1982).
45. Reid, 'King's Sister', 577. See also M. A. Screech, *Clément Marot: A Renaissance Poet Discovers the Gospel* (Leiden: E. J. Brill, 1994).

46. *Concerning Scandals by John Calvin*, trans. John W. Fraser (Edinburgh: Saint Andrew Press, 1978), 61.
47. The names of the students were Martial Alba, Bernard Seguin, Charles Faure, Pierre Navihères and Pierre Escrivain.
48. Mirjam G. K. van Veen, ' ". . . Les Sainctz Martyrs . . ." Die Korrespondenz Calvins mit fünf Studenten aus Lausanne über das Martyrium (1552)', in Opitz (ed.), *Calvin im Kontext*, 127–45.
49. Ibid., 131.
50. Calvin to Martin Drimont, 10 Jan. 1553, *CO* 14:466–9; Bonnet 2:366–9.
51. Van Veen, 'Les Sainctz Martyrs', 134.
52. Calvin to Five Students, 7 July 1553, *CO* 14:561–4; Bonnet 2:393–5.

Chapter 12: The Years of Conflict

1. See Johan Huizinga, *Erasmus and the Age of the Reformation*, trans. F. Hopman (New York: Dover Publications, 2001), 118–19.
2. Naphy, *Consolidation*, 123. On the refugees from Provence, see Gabriel Audisio, 'The First Provençal Refugees in Geneva (1545–71)', *French History* 19 (2005): 385–400.
3. See Mark Taplin, *The Italian Reformers and the Zurich Church, c. 1540–1620* (Aldershot: Ashgate, 2003).
4. Naphy, *Consolidation*, 124.
5. Ibid., 127–8.
6. Ibid., 133.
7. Ibid., 136.
8. Audisio, 'First Provençal Refugees', 390.
9. Calvin, *Commentary on II Corinthians*, 9:6, 121, *CO* 50:108.
10. Elsie Ann McKee, *John Calvin on the Diaconate and Liturgical Almsgiving* (Geneva: Droz, 1984); Robert M. Kingdon, 'Calvin's Ideas about the Diaconate: Social or Theological in Origin?', in Carter Lindberg (ed.), *Piety, Politics, and Ethics: Reformation Studies in Honor of George Wolfgang Forell* (Kirksville, MO: Truman State University Press, 1984), 167–80; Glenn S. Sunshine, *Reforming French Protestantism: The Development of Huguenot Ecclesiastical Institutions, 1557–1572* (Kirksville, MO: Truman State University Press, 2003).
11. Sunshine, *Reforming French Protestantism*, 100.
12. Jeanine Olson, *Calvin and Social Welfare: Deacons and the Bourse Française* (Selinsgrove, PA: Susquehanna University Press, 1989), 33.
13. Sunshine, *Reforming French Protestantism*, 99.
14. Olson, *Social Welfare*, 37–9.
15. Ibid., 47.
16. Ibid., 44.
17. Ibid., 75.
18. Ibid., 80.
19. Naphy, *Consolidation*, 168–9.
20. See William G. Naphy, 'Baptisms, Church Riots and Social Unrest in Calvin's Geneva', *SCJ* 26 (1995): 87–97, and Karen E. Spierling, *Infant Baptism in Reformation Geneva: The Shaping of a Community, 1536–1564* (Aldershot: Ashgate, 2005), 140–52.
21. Spierling, *Infant Baptism*, 147–8.
22. Naphy, 'Baptisms', 93.
23. Ibid., 95.
24. Spierling, *Infant Baptism*, 150–1.
25. Uwe Plath, *Calvin und Basel in den Jahren 1552–1556* (Basle and Stuttgart: Helbing & Lichtenhahn, 1974), 28, 35.

26. Naphy, *Consolidation*, 171.
27. Cornelis P. Venema, *Heinrich Bullinger and the Doctrine of Predestination: Author of the 'Other Reformed Tradition'?* (Grand Rapids, MI: Baker Academic, 2002), 59. See also his 'Heinrich Bullinger's Correspondence on Calvin's Doctrine of Predestination, 1551–1553', *SCJ* 17 (1986): 435–50.
28. Venema, *Heinrich Bullinger*, 60. See also, Peter Opitz, 'Bullinger's Decades, Instruction in Faith and Conduct', in Bruce Gordon and Emidio Campi (eds), *Architect of Reformation: An Introduction to Heinrich Bullinger* (Grand Rapids, MI: Baker Academic, 2004), 101–16.
29. Bullinger to Calvin, 1 Dec. 1551, *CO* 14:214–15, cited in Venema, *Heinrich Bullinger*, 61–2.
30. Venema, *Heinrich Bullinger*, 63.
31. Calvin to Bullinger, 22 Jan. 1552, *CO* 14:215–54; Bonnet 2:214–15.
32. Calvin to Bullinger, Apr. 1553, *CO* 14:513–14; Bonnet 2:384–6.
33. Calvin to Farel, 22 Feb. 1552, *CO* 14:289–90.
34. Bruening, *First Battleground*, 216–17.
35. Calvin to Farel, *CO* 14:289–90.
36. Naphy, *Consolidation*, 175.
37. Quoted from Bruening, *First Battleground*, 218.
38. Bruening, *First Battleground*, 219.
39. Ibid., 220.
40. Calvin's letter to Berne, 4 May 1555, *CO* 15:550–1; Bonnet 3:176–81.
41. Naphy, *Consolidation*, 173–4.
42. Ibid., 178.
43. The story is recounted in ibid., 184–5. See Christian Grosse, *L'Excommunication de Philibert Berthelier: histoire d'un conflit d'identité aux premiers temps de la Réforme genevoise (1547–1555)* (Geneva: Société d'Histoire et d'Archéologie de Genève, 1995).
44. Hans Ulrich Bächtold, *Bullinger vor dem Rat. Zur Gestaltung und Verwaltung des Zürcher Staatswesens in den Jahren 1531 bis 1575* (Berne: Peter Lang, 1982) treats a wide range of problems between Bullinger and the council. See also Gordon, *Swiss Reformation*, 251–7.
45. Plath, *Calvin und Basel*, 110–11.
46. Calvin to Viret, 8 Feb.1554, *CO* 15:18.
47. Naphy, *Consolidation*, 191.
48. Ibid.
49. Calvin to Bullinger, July 1555, *CO* 15:676–85; Bonnet 3:207–16.

Chapter 13: 'There is No Form of Impiety that This Monster Has Not Raked Up'

1. Calvin to Farel 13 Feb. 1546, *CO* 8:283.
2. Calvin to Farel, 20 Aug. 1553, Bonnet 3:417.
3. Roland H. Bainton, 'Servetus and the Genevan Libertines', *Church History* 5 (1936): 141–2.
4. Commentary on Deuteronomy, *CO* 8:476. Cited in Bainton, *Hunted Heretic*, 170–1.
5. Bainton, *Hunted Heretic*, 176.
6. Ibid., 168.
7. Platt, *Calvin und Basel*, 58f.
8. Calvin to Farel, 20 Aug. 1553, *CO* 14:590; Bonnet 3:417.
9. Bainton, *Hunted Heretic*, 190.
10. Calvin to Bullinger, 7 Sept. 1553, Bonnet 3:427.

11. Plath, *Calvin und Basel*, 54–5.
12. Calvin to Frankfurt ministers, 27 Aug. 1553, Bonnet 3:422.
13. Extracts of Servetus' letters to the Small Council in Geneva are found in Roland H. Bainton, *Michel Servet: hérétique et martyr, 1553–1953* (Geneva: Droz, 1953), 119–20.
14. Cited in Bainton, *Hunted Heretic*, 197.
15. Irena Backus, 'Servet Michel et les Pères anté-nicéens', in Valentine Zuber (ed.), *Michel Servet (1511–1553), hérésie et pluralisme XVIe–XXIe siècles* (Paris: Champion, forthcoming). I am grateful to Professor Backus for allowing me to read her paper in advance of publication.
16. The judgements of the magistrates and ministers of Zurich, Basle, Berne and Schaffhausen are in *CO* 8:808–23.
17. Cited in Bainton, *Hunted Heretic*, 209.
18. Ibid., 210.
19. Melanchthon to Calvin, 14 Oct. 1554, *CO* 15:268.
20. Most striking were the verses entitled 'Carmen in Calvinum', *CO* 15:239–44 by Camilio Renatus.
21. Plath, *Calvin und Basel*, 74.
22. Ibid., 73.
23. On the formation of Joris' thought, see Gary K. Waite, *David Joris and Dutch Anabaptism, 1524–43* (Waterloo, Ontario: Wilfrid Laurier University Press, 1990).
24. Plath, *Calvin und Basel*, 84.
25. Ibid., 86–7.
26. Ibid., 88.
27. Guglielmo Grataroli, a medical doctor, made this comment to Bullinger, *CO* 14: 657.
28. 28 Oct. 1553, *CO* 14:683.
29. Plath, *Calvin und Basel*, 121.
30. *CO* 8:461.
31. *CO* 8:474.
32. The classic study of this exchange remains E. Bähler, *Nikolaus Zurkinden von Bern, 1506–1588: Ein Vertreter der Toleranz im Jahrhundert der Reformation* (Zurich: Beer, 1912), 134f. See Guggisberg, *Sebastian Castellio*, 80.
33. Zurkinden to Calvin, 10 Feb. 1554, *CO* 15:19–22.
34. Calvin to Bullinger, 29 Apr. 1554, *CO* 15:124.
35. Guggisberg, *Sebastian Castellio*, 81–96.
36. I am grateful to David Whitford for this suggestion.
37. Calvin to Bullinger, 28 Mar. 1554, *CO* 15:94. Bullinger wrote to Calvin on the very same day, praising his work against Servetus, and placing before him a series of issues relating to the English church. *CO* 15:90.
38. Calvin to church at Poitiers, 31 July 1554, *CO* 15:200.
39. Markus Kutter, *Celio Secondo Curione: sein Leben und sein Werk, 1503–1569* (Basle and Stuttgart: Helbing & Lichtenhahn, 1955), 185.
40. Plath, *Calvin und Basel*, 169.
41. The letter is lost, but has been reconstructed from other correspondence; see Plath, *Calvin und Basel*, 170.
42. Hans Guggisberg, 'Tolerance and Intolerance in Sixteenth-Century Basle', in Ole Peter Grell and Robert W. Scribner (eds), *Tolerance and Intolerance in the European Reformation* (Cambridge: Cambridge University Press, 1996), 153.
43. Guggisberg, *Sebastian Castellio*, 105f.
44. Ibid., 110–14.
45. John Heil, 'Augustine's Attack on Skepticism: The Contra Academicos', *Harvard Theological Review* 65 (1972): 99–116.
46. Marie-Christine Gomez-Girand and Olivier Millet, 'La Rhétorique de la Bible chez Bèze et Castellion d'après leur controverse en matière de la traduction biblique', in

Irena Backus (ed.), *Théodore de Bèze (1519–1605): actes du colloque de Genève (septembre 2005)* (Geneva: Droz, 2007), 429–48.

47. Bruce Gordon, 'Wary Allies: Melanchthon and the Swiss Reformation', in Maag (ed.), *Melanchthon in Europe*, 58–60.
48. Guggisberg, *Sebastian Castellio*, 143.
49. Mario Turchetti, *Concordia o Tolleranza?: François Bauduin (1520–1573)* (Geneva: Droz, 1984), 375f.

Chapter 14: Luther's Heirs

1. Calvin to Johannes Wolf, 25 Dec. 1555; Rudolf Schwarz, ed., *Johannes Calvins Lebenswerk in seinen Briefen* (Tübingen: J. C. B. Mohr, 1909), 2:118–19. Not in *CO*. Wolfe (Wolphius) had written to Calvin on 3 December commending a Polish visitor and congratulating the Frenchman on defeating Servetus. *CO* 15:877–8.
2. On Westphal see Joseph N. Tylenda, 'The Calvin–Westphal Exchange: The Genesis of Calvin's Treatises against Westphal', *Calvin Theological Journal* 9 (1974): 182–209.
3. Wengert, 'We Will Feast Together', 35–6.
4. Tylenda, 'Calvin–Westphal Exchange', 184.
5. *CO* 15:124. Quoted from Tylenda, 'Calvin–Westphal Exchange', 185.
6. Beza to Bullinger, 4 Apr. 1554, *CO* 15:96–7.
7. The literature on Lasco is extensive; see primarily Diarmaid MacCulloch, 'The Importance of Jan Laski in the English Reformation', in C. Strohm (ed.) *Johannes à Lasco: Polnischer Baron, Humanist und europäischer Reformator* (Tübingen: Mohr Siebeck, 2000), 315–45; Michael S. Springer, *Restoring Christ's Church: John a Lasco and the Forma ac ratio* (Aldershot: Ashgate, 2007); Henning Jürgens, *Johannes a Lasco in Ostfriesland: Der Werdegang eines europäischen Reformators* (Tübingen: Mohr Siebeck, 2002).
8. Lasco to Calvin, 13 Mar. 1554, *CO* 15:81–4. Lasco describes in detail the attack against the Reformed doctrine of the Lord's Supper: *CO* 15:83.
9. Herwarth von Schade, *Joachim Westphal und Peter Braubach* (Hamburg: Wittig, 1981), 27–30.
10. Calvin to Farel, 25 May 1554, *CO* 15:140–1; Bonnet 3:39.
11. Bullinger to Calvin, *CO* 15:157–8.
12. *CO* 15:208; Tylenda, 'Calvin–Westphal Exchange', 190.
13. *CO* 15:255–6; Tylenda, 'Calvin–Westphal Exchange', 192.
14. Calvin to Swiss Churches, 6 Oct. 1554, *CO* 15:256–8; Bonnet 3:79–86.
15. Calvin to Farel, 1 Nov. 1554, *CO* 15:297–8; Bonnet 3:90.
16. *CO* 15:273–5; Tylenda, 'Calvin–Westphal Exchange', 93.
17. *CO* 15:318; Tylenda, 'Calvin–Westphal Exchange', 194.
18. Calvin to Zurich ministers, 13 Nov. 1554, *CO* 15:304–7; Bonnet 3:89–94.
19. The major study of the subject is Andrew Pettegree, *Foreign Protestant Communities in Sixteenth-Century London* (Oxford: Clarendon Press, 1986).
20. Calvin to Perussel, 27 Aug. 1554, *CO* 15:218–19; Bonnet 3:66.
21. Andrew Pettegree, *Marian Protestantism: Six Studies* (Aldershot: Ashgate, 1996), 66–7.
22. *CR* 9:179–80. Melanchthon had given the same advice to the magistrates in Wesel.
23. See, for example, his letter to Ulrich Mordeisen in Leipzig of 18 Jan. 1556: *Corpus Reformatorum*, ed. Karl Gottlieb Bretschneider and others (Halle, 1834–1907), 8:666.
24. Pettegree, *Marian Protestantism*, 70.
25. Calvin to Church in Frankfurt, Dec. 1555, *CO* 15:895–8; Bonnet 3:240–3.
26. Calvin to French Church in Frankfurt, *CO* 16:210–13; Bonnet 3:257–9.
27. Pettegree, *Marian Protestantism*, 76–7.
28. Wengert, 'We Will Feast Together', 37–41.

29. Hubert Languet discussed Melanchthon's role in the dispute, *CR* 9:484–5.
30. See Bodo Nischan, *Prince, People, and Confession: The Second Reformation in Brandenburg* (Philadelphia, PA: University of Pennsylvania Press, 1994).
31. Wengert, 'We Will Feast Together', 39.
32. Lasco to Calvin, *CO* 15:774; Tylenda, 'Calvin–Westphal Exchange', 198.
33. John Calvin, 'The Calumnies of Joachim Westphal', Beveridge, *Tracts and Treatises*, 2:231.
34. Ibid., 234.
35. Tylenda, 'Calvin–Westphal Exchange', 203.
36. Ibid., 205.
37. Pettegree, *Marian Protestantism*, 79.
37. Beveridge, *Tracts and Treatises*, 2:231.
38. Tylenda, 'Calvin–Westphal Exchange', 207.
39. Beveridge, *Tracts and Treatises*, 2:425–6.
40. Calvin to Farel, 9 Dec. 1555, *CO* 15:861–2; Bonnet 3:239.
41. Calvin to Farel, 24 Sept. 1557, *CO* 16:638–9; Bonnet 3:368–9.
42. Calvin to Peter Martyr Vermigli, 18 Jan. 1555, *CO* 15:386–9; Bonnet 3:121–6.
43. Calvin to Bullinger, 30 May 1557, *CO* 16:501–2; Bonnet 3:332–4.
44. Calvin to Melanchthon, 3 Aug. 1557, *CO* 16:556–8; Bonnet 3:335–8.
45. Cameron, *Reformation of the Heretics*, 196–8.
46. The Confession is printed in *CO* 16:469–72. Bullinger's outraged response is *CO* 16:479. See also F. Aubert, H. Meylan and A. Dufour (eds), *Correspondance de Théodore de Bèze* (Geneva: Droz, 1962), 2:73–5, 82f., 86–94, 238–42, 251.
47. Gordon, 'Calvin and the Swiss Reformed Churches', 79.
48. Calvin to Bullinger, 23 Feb. 1558, *CO* 17:60–2.

Chapter 15: European Reformer

1. Calvin to Bullinger, 7 Sept. 1553; Bonnet 2:426.
2. Rainer Henrich, 'Bullinger's Correspondence: An International News Network', in Gordon and Campi, *Architect of Reformation*, 235–7.
3. MacCulloch, *Thomas Cranmer*, 174f.
4. Ibid., 175.
5. John Schofield, *Philip Melanchthon and the English Reformation* (Aldershot: Ashgate, 2006), 130–1.
6. See Rory McEntegart, *Henry VIII, the League of Schmalkalden, and the English Reformation* (Woodbridge, Suffolk: Boydell Press, 2002).
7. Schofield, *Philip Melanchthon*, 133–4.
8. Charmarie Jenkins Blaisdell, 'Calvin's Letters to Women: The Courting of Ladies in High Places', *SCJ* 13 (1982): 67–84.
9. The essential work on Somerset is Ethan Shagan, 'Popular Politics and the English Reformation: New Sources and New Perspectives', *English Historical Review* 115 (2000): 121–33, and his subsequent monograph, *Popular Politics and the English Reformation* (Cambridge: Cambridge University Press, 2003).
10. Calvin to Protector Somerset, 22 Oct. 1548, *CO* 13:77–90; Bonnet 2:168–84.
11. Calvin to Farel, 9 July 1549, *CO* 13:324–5; Bonnet 2:224.
12. *An epistle both of Godly consolacion and also of aduertisemente written by Iohn Caluine the pastour and preacher of Geneua, to the righte noble prince Edwarde Duke of Somerset, before the time or knowledge had of his trouble, but delyuered to the sayde Duke, in the time of hys trouble, and so translated out of frenshe by the same Duke hymselfe, in the tyme of his impriesonmente.* [Imprinted at London : By [W. Baldwin? in the shop of] Edward Whitchurche, the .v. day of Aprill, 1550] *STC* 4408.

13. MacCulloch, *Thomas Cranmer*, 470.
14. Ibid.
15. Calvin to Bucer, Feb. 1549, Bonnet 2:198–9.
16. MacCulloch, 'Importance of Jan Laski in the English Reformation', 315–45.
17. MacCulloch, *Thomas Cranmer*, 498.
18. This influence is demonstrated in Torrance Kirby, 'Synne and Sedition: Peter Martyr Vermigli's "Sermon concernynge the tyme of rebellion"', *SCJ* 39 (2008): 419–40.
19. MacCulloch, *Thomas Cranmer*, 501–2; 20 Mar. 1552, *CO* 14:306.
20. Calvin to Cranmer, Apr. 1552, *CO* 14:312–14; Bonnet 2:330–3.
21. Calvin to Cranmer, July 1552, Bonnet 2:341–3.
22. Pettegree, *Foreign Protestant Communities*, 69.
23. On the influence of England, see Carrie Euler, *Couriers of the Gospel: England and Zurich, 1531–1558* (Zurich: Theologischer Verlag, 2006).
24. D. Rodgers, *John à Lasco in England* (New York: Peter Lang, 1994); J. ten Doornkaat Koolman, 'Jan Utenhoves Besuch bei Heinrich Bullinger im Jahre 1549', *Zwingliana* 14 (1974–8): 263–73.
25. Utenhove to Calvin, 5 Feb. 1550, reported to Geneva on Somerset's fallen state. *CO* 14:45–46.
26. Pettegree, *Foreign Protestant Communities*, 70–1.
27. *La forme des prieres ecclesiastiques Auec la maniere d'administrer les sacremens, & celebrer le mariage, & la visitation des malades, et aussi la maniere de confirmer & imposer les mains aux ministres, anciens, & diacres. LVCII. Seigneur, enseigne nous a prier.* [London: s.n.], 155; and *Doctrine de la penitence publique Et la forme d'icelle ainsi comme elle se practique en l'Eglise des estrangiers à Londres, deuant qu'on vienne à l'excommunication. Ensemble aussi la forme d'administrer la saincte Cene* [London: s.n., 1552]. See Pettegree, *Foreign Protestant Communities*, 71.
28. Lasco to Calvin, Apr. 1551, *CO* 14:107–8. On 7 June Lasco then wrote to Bullinger from London concerning the Lord's Supper and the warm reception accorded the Zurich reformer's *Decades, CO* 14:127–9.
29. Cited in Carl R. Trueman, *Luther's Legacy: Salvation and the English Reformers, 1525–1556* (Oxford: Oxford University Press, 1994), 216–17. 10 Sept. 1552, *CO* 14:359–60.
30. Calvin to Bullinger, 3 Aug. 1553, 4 Aug. 1553, *CO* 14:584; Bonnet 2:396–7.
31. See Euan Cameron, 'Frankfurt and Geneva: The European Context of John Knox's Reformation', in Roger Mason (ed.), *John Knox and the British Reformations* (Aldershot: Ashgate, 1998), 51–73.
32. Calvin to Church at Frankfurt, 13 Jan. 1555, *CO* 15:393–4; Bonnet 4:117–19.
33. Ibid.
34. Cameron, 'Frankfurt and Geneva', 60.
35. Calvin to Richard Cox, 31 May 1555, *CO* 15:628–9.
36. The great work on the community remains Charles Martin, *Les Protestants Anglais réfugiés à Genève au temps de Calvin, 1555–1560* (Geneva: A. Julien, 1915). See also Dan G. Danner, *Pilgrimage to Puritanism: History and Theology of the Marian Exiles at Geneva, 1555–1560* (New York: Peter Lang, 1999).
37. David Laing (ed.), *The Works of John Knox* (Edinburgh: Bannatye Club, 1856), 4:240.
38. William Maxwell, *The Liturgical Portions of the Genevan Service Book used by John Knox while a Minister of the English Congregation of the Marian Exiles at Geneva, 1556–1559* (Edinburgh: Oliver & Boyd, 1931). Also R. C. D. Jasper and G. J. Cuming (trans. and eds), *Prayers of the Eucharist: Early and Reformed* (London: Collins, 1975), 250–1.
39. Known as the *Book of Our Common Order in the Administration of the Sacraments and Solemnization of Marriages and Burials of the Dead*, it was adopted by the General Assembly in 1562 and then expanded in 1564.
40. See Maurice S. Betteridge, 'The Bitter Notes: The Geneva Bible and its Annotations', *SCJ* 14 (1983): 41–62.

41. On the Scottish Reformation, see Margo Todd, *The Culture of Protestantism in Early Modern Scotland* (New Haven, CT and London: Yale University Press, 2002); Michael Graham, *The Uses of Reform: 'Godly Discipline' and Popular Behavior in Scotland and Beyond, 1560–1610* (Leiden: E. J. Brill, 1996); and, most recently, Jane E. A. Dawson, *Scotland Re-Formed, 1488–1587* (Edinburgh: University of Edinburgh Press, 2007), esp. 200–39.
42. Calvin to Cecil, 29 Jan. 1559, *CO* 17:419–20; Bonnet 4:15–17.
43. Calvin to Cecil, May 1559, Bonnet 4:46–8.
44. Jane E. A. Dawson, 'Trumpeting Resistance: Christopher Goodman and John Knox', in Mason (ed.), *John Knox and the British Reformations*, 130–53. On Knox's view of female monarchy, see Robert M. Healey, 'Waiting for Deborah: John Knox and Four Ruling Queens', *SCJ* 25 (1994): 371–86.
45. Pettegree, *Marian Protestantism*, 145.
46. Jeannine E. Olson, 'Nicolas des Gallars and the Genevan Connection of the Stranger Churches', in Randolph Vigne and Charles Littleton (eds), *From Strangers to Citizens: The Integration of Immigrant Communities in Britain, Ireland and Colonial America, 1550–1750* (Portland, OR: Sussex Academic Press and The Huguenot Society of Great Britain and Ireland, 2001), 38–47.
47. Ibid., 41.
48. Patrick Collinson, *Archbishop Grindal, 1519–1583: The Struggle for a Reformed Church* (London: Cape, 1979), 134.
49. Patrick Collinson, 'Protestant Strangers and the English Reformation', in Vigne and Littleton (eds), *Strangers to Citizens*, 58.
50. Olson, 'Nicolas des Gallars', 42.
51. Collinson, 'Protestant Strangers', 62.
52. Patrick Collinson has remarked that 'as the Elizabethan Puritan movement gathered momentum, from the 1560s through to the 1580s, the stranger churches were admired and even envied as examples of everything which the Elizabethan church was not'. Collinson, 'Protestant Strangers', 61.
53. This comes from the work of Francis Higman, 'Calvin's Works in Translation', in Pettegree, Duke and Lewis (eds), *Calvinism in Europe*, 82–99.
54. Higman, 'Calvin's Works in Translation', 97.
55. On Poland, see Stanislas Lubieniecki, *History of the Polish Reformation and Nine Related Documents*, ed. George Hunston Williams (Minneapolis, MN: Fortress Press, 1995); and Janusz Tazbir, *A State without Stakes: Polish Religious Toleration in the Sixteenth and Seventeenth Centuries* (1967; repr. New York: The Kosciuszko Foundation and Twayne Publishers, 1973).
56. James Miller, 'The Origins of Polish Arianism', *SCJ* 16 (1985): 229–56.
57. Calvin to Polish Nobles, 17 Mar. 1557, *CO* 16:420–1; Bonnet 3:317–19.
58. Miller, 'Origins of Polish Arianism', 232.
59. James Miller, 'The Polish Nobility and the Renaissance Monarchy', *Parliaments, Estates, and Representation* 3–4 (1983–4): 65–87.
60. Miller, 'Origins of Polish Arianism', 231.
61. Calvin to Sigismund, 5 Dec. 1554, *CO* 15:329–36; Bonnet 3:99–109.
62. Calvin to Bullinger, 9 Feb. 1555, *CO* 15:425; Bonnet 3:132–3.
63. Miller, 'Origins of Polish Arianism', 236.
64. George H. Williams, *Radical Reformation*, 3rd edn (Kirksville, MO: Truman State University Press, 2000), 655–65.
65. See Anne Jacobson Schutte, *Pier Paolo Vergerio: The Making of an Italian Reformer* (Geneva: Droz, 1977).
66. Calvin to Lusan, 9 June 1560, *CO* 18:100–1; Bonnet 4:112–14.
67. Calvin to Bohemian Brethren, 1 July 1560, *CO* 18:126–8.
68. Taplin, *Italian Reformers*, 179–83.

69. Ibid., 182.
70. Andrew Pettegree, *Emden and the Dutch Revolt* (Oxford: Oxford University Press, 1992), 19.
71. On Wesel, see above, 243.
72. Guido Marnef, 'The Changing Face of Calvinism in Antwerp, 1550–1585', in Pettegree, Duke and Lewis (eds), *Calvinism in Europe*, 143–59.
73. Calvin to Church at Antwerp, 21 Dec. 1556, *CO* 16:337–9; Bonnet 3:302–5.
74. Marnef, 'Changing Face of Calvinism', 148.
75. Lyle D. Bierma, *German Calvinism in the Confessional Age: The Covenant Theology of Caspar Olevianus* (Grand Rapids, MI: Baker Academic, 1996).
76. Calvin to Olevianus, 25 Nov. 1560, *CO* 18:235–7.
77. Lyle D. Bierma (ed.), *An Introduction to the Heidelberg Catechism: Sources, History, and Theology* (Grand Rapids, MI: Baker Academic, 2005).
78. Lyle D. Bierma, 'The Sources and Theological Orientation of the Heidelberg Catechism', in ibid., 78.
79. Ibid.
80. Benedict, *Christ's Churches Purely Reformed*, 214f.

Chapter 16: The 'Perfecte Schoole of Christe'

1. See the stimulating discussion of prophecy in Max Engammare, 'Calvin: A Prophet without a Prophecy', *Church History* 67 (1998): 643–61.
2. Susan E. Schreiner, *The Theater of His Glory: Nature and the Natural Order in the Thought of John Calvin* (1991; repr. Grand Rapids, MI: Baker Academic, 2001), 84.
3. Ibid., 94.
4. William R. Stevenson Jr, *Sovereign Grace: The Place and Significance of Christian Freedom in John Calvin's Political Thought* (Oxford: Oxford University Press, 1999), 133.
5. Ibid., 145.
6. Charles L. Cooke, 'Calvin's Illnesses', in Timothy George (ed.), *John Calvin and the Church: A Prism of Reform* (Louisville, KY: Westminster John Knox Press, 1990), 62–3.
7. Calvin to Melanchthon, 19 Nov. 1558, *CO* 17:384–6; Bonnet 3:481–5.
8. Calvin, *2 Corinthians*, 152.
9. The relationship is well described in Françoise Bonali-Fiquet, *Jean Calvin, Lettres à Monsieur et Madame de Falais* (Geneva: Droz, 1991).
10. *CO* 12:260–1. The letter is undated, but de Falais marked it 'received 6 February 1546'.
11. A good example is a letter from Calvin to Madame de Falais from late summer 1545, *CO* 12:172–4, in which he encourages her to endure with patience the sufferings of the world.
12. 'Deus Calvini est hypocrite, mendax, perfidus, iniustus, fautor et patronus scelerum,' Calvin to de Falais, without date 1552, *CO* 14:448.
13. Calvin to ministers of Neuchâtel, 26 Sept. 1558, *CO* 17:351–3; Bonnet 3:473–5.
14. Calvin to Farel, Sept. 1558, *CO* 17:335–6; Bonnet 3:47–8, 475–7.
15. Oberman, 'Calvin and Farel', 43–9.
16. Scott M. Manetsch, 'The Journey towards Geneva: Theodore Beza's Conversion, 1535–1548', in David Foxgrover (ed.), *Calvin, Beza, and Later Calvinism: Calvin Society Papers 2005* (Grand Rapids, MI: CRC Product Services, 2006), 38–57.
17. See the recent work on Beza from the anniversary of his death in Irena Backus, *Théodore de Bèze* (Geneva: Droz, 2007).
18. Calvin to Viret, 28 Aug. 1558, *CO* 17:308–9.
19. Calvin to Daniel, 6 Dec. 1559, *CO* 17:680–1; Bonnet 3:86.
20. Calvin to Daniel, Feb. 1560, *CO* 18:16; Bonnet 3:98.

21. Guy Bedouelle, *Le Quincuplex Psalterium de Lefèvre d'Etaples: un guide de lecture* (Geneva: Droz, 1979).

22. R. Gerald Hobbs, 'How Firm a Foundation: Martin Bucer's Historical Exegesis of the Psalms', *Church History* 53 (1984): 477–91.

23. Barbara Pitkin, 'Imitation of David: David as a Paradigm for Faith in Calvin's Exegesis of the Psalms', *SCJ* 24 (1993): 846.

24. Commentary on psalms, Preface, *CO* 31:15.

25. Wulfert de Greef, 'Calvin as Commentator on the Psalms', in Donald K. McKim (ed.), *Calvin and the Bible* (Cambridge: Cambridge University Press, 2006), 104.

26. Herman J. Selderhuis, 'Church on Stage: Calvin's Dynamic Ecclesiology', in David Foxgrover (ed.), *Calvin and the Church* (Grand Rapids, MI: CRC Product Services, 2002), 49. See also Herman J. Selderhuis, 'Calvin as Asylum Seeker', in Wilhelm H. Neuser, Herman J. Selderhuis and Willem van't Spijker (eds), *Calvin's Books* (Heerenveen: Groen, 1997), 283–300.

27. Selderhuis, 'Church on Stage', 57.

28. Psalm 102 v.6, *CO* 32:63.

29. Psalm 102, *CO* 32:64.

30. Psalm 90 v.16.

31. Psalm 102 v.13, *CO* 32:66.

32. Psalm 102 v.12, *CO* 32:66.

33. Psalm 102 v.18, *CO* 32:70.

34. Gilmont, *Calvin and the Printed Book*, 3–4.

35. Elizabeth Armstrong, *Robert Estienne, Royal Printer: An Historical Study of the Elder Stephanus* (Cambridge: Cambridge University Press, 1954), 211f.

36. Gilmont, *Calvin and the Printed Book*, 186.

37. Gilmont, *Jean Crespin*, 39f. Gilmont's detailed biography remains the standard work.

38. David Watson, 'Jean Crespin and the Writing of History in the French Reformation', in Bruce Gordon (ed.), *Protestant History and Identity in Sixteenth-Century Europe* (Aldershot: Scolar Press, 1996), 2:39–58.

39. Gilmont, *Jean Crespin*, 119f.

40. Robert M. Kingdon, 'The Business Activities of Printers Henri and François Estienne', in G. Berthoud and others (eds), *Aspects de la propagande religieuse* (Geneva: Droz, 1957), 258–75.

41. Gilmont, *Calvin and the Printed Book*, 188.

42. Olson, *Calvin and Social Welfare*, 53–5.

43. Gilmont, *Calvin and the Printed Book*, 268.

44. Ibid., 188.

45. John Calvin, *Sermons on 2 Samuel, Chapters 1–13*, trans. Douglas Kelly (Edinburgh: Banner of Truth Trust, 1992), 85.

46. Max Engammare, 'D'une forme l'autre: commentaires et sermons de Calvin sur la Genèse', in Selderhuis (ed.), *Calvinus Praeceptor Ecclesiae*, 122–8.

47. Ibid.

48. Calvin on 2 Corinthians 4:3, *CO* 50:49.

49. Calvin on 2 Corinthians 4:4, *CO* 50:50–2.

50. Engammare, 'Prophet without a Prophecy', 649.

51. Wilhelmus H. Th. Moehn, *God Calls Us to His Service: The Relation between God and His Audience in Calvin's Sermons on Acts* (Geneva: Droz, 2001), 188–9.

52. Ibid., 198.

53. Ibid., 199.

54. Ibid., 204–5.

55. Ibid., 193.

56. Ibid., 226.

57. This has been examined by Elsie McKee in her 'Calvin and his Colleagues as Pastors: Some New Insights into the Collegial Ministry of Word and Sacraments', in Selderhuis (ed.), *Calvinus Praeceptor Ecclesiae*, 9–42.

58. This is the conclusion of Robert Kingdon in his *Adultery and Divorce*, 180–1.

59. Ibid.

60. Witte and Kingdon, *Sex, Marriage, and Family*, 1:24.

61. Ibid., 70–1.

62. Cited in ibid., 432.

63. Ibid., 121.

64. The most informative works on marriage and divorce in the sixteenth century remain Thomas Max Safley, *Let No Man Put Asunder: The Control of Marriage in the German Southwest: A Comparative Study, 1550–1600* (Kirksville, MO: Truman State University Press, 1984) and Joel F. Harrington, *Reordering Marriage and Society in Reformation Germany* (Cambridge: Cambridge University Press, 1995).

65. See Robert M. Kingdon, *Adultery and Divorce in Calvin's Geneva* (Cambridge, MA and London: Harvard University Press, 1995).

66. Jeffrey Watt, 'Childhood and Youth in the Genevan Consistory Minutes', in Selderhuis (ed.), *Calvinus Praeceptor Ecclesiae*, 43–64. The material which follows draws on his work.

67. Watt, 'Children and Youth', 53f.

68. Ibid., 136.

69. Ibid., 140.

70. This is extremely well treated in Mark Valeri, 'Religion, Discipline, and the Economy in Calvin's Geneva', *SCJ* 28 (1997): 123–42.

71. Ibid., 138–9.

72. Pete Wilcox, 'Calvin as Commentator on the Prophets', in McKim (ed.), *Calvin and the Bible*, 108.

73. Gillian Lewis, 'The Genevan Academy', in Pettegree, Duke and Lewis (eds), *Calvinism in Europe*, 35–63.

74. Karin Maag, *Seminary or University?: The Genevan Academy and Reformed Higher Education, 1560–1620* (Aldershot: Ashgate, 1995), 8.

75. Lewis, 'Genevan Academy', 40; Maag, *Seminary or University?*, 15–16.

76. Maag, *Seminary or University?*, 11.

77. Ibid., 23.

78. Ibid., 116.

79. See above all Muller, *Unaccommodated Calvin*, 118–39.

80. Wendel, *Calvin*, 118.

81. This is well treated in Zachman, *Teacher, Pastor, and Theologian*, 86–94.

82. A helpful summary is to be found in McGrath, *Life of John Calvin*, 151–74.

83. Zachman, *Teacher, Pastor, and Theologian*, 90.

84. *Institutes* 4:17.7, cited from Zachman, *Teacher, Pastor, and Theologian*, 101.

Chapter 17: Churches and Blood: France

1. Calvin to Elector Palatinate, 21 Feb. 1558, *CO* 17:54; Bonnet 3:403.

2. Jonathan Reid, 'France', in Andrew Pettegree (ed.), *The Reformation World* (London and New York: Routledge, 2000), 221.

3. Calvin to Brethren of France, June 1559, *CO* 17:570–4; Bonnet 4:49–54.

4. I am grateful to Malcolm Walsby for sharing his knowledge of this topic with me. See his *The Counts of Laval: Culture, Patronage and Religion in Fifteenth- and Sixteenth-Century France* (Aldershot: Ashgate, 2007).

5. Benedict, *Christ's Churches Purely Reformed*, 134f.

6. Calvin to Church of Paris, 28 Jan. 1555, *CO* 15:412–13; Bonnet 3:127–9.

7. Calvin to Church at Poitiers, 9 Sept. 1555, *CO* 15:754–6; Bonnet 3:138–51.
8. Calvin to Church in Angers, 9 Sept. 1555, *CO* 15:757–8.
9. Barbara B. Diefendorf, *Beneath the Cross: Catholics and Huguenots in Sixteenth-Century Paris* (Oxford: Oxford University Press, 1991), 50–1.
10. Ibid.
11. Calvin to Antoine, King of Navarre, 8 June 1558, *CO* 17:196–8; Bonnet 3:423–6.
12. Calvin to d'Andelot, 12 July 1558, *CO* 17:251–3; Bonnet 3:437–40.
13. Diefendorf, *Beneath the Cross*, 52.
14. As Barbara Diefendorf has observed, 'We must remember that the "Lutheran heresy" was not for sixteenth-century Parisians a mere failure of religious orthodoxy; it was a threat to the social order and a danger to the entire community. The Protestants were believed not only to be religious deviants, but also immoral and seditious.' Ibid., 54.
15. Sunshine, *Reforming French Protestantism*, 26–31.
16. Ibid., 30.
17. Ibid., 27.
18. Glenn S. Sunshine, 'Reformed Theology and the Origins of Synodical Polity: Calvin, Beza, and the Gallican Confession', in Fred Graham (ed.), *Later Calvinism: International Perspectives* (Kirksville, MO: Truman State University Press, 1994), 141–58.
19. David M. Bryson, *Queen Jeanne and the Promised Land: Dynasty, Homeland, Religion and Violence in Sixteenth-Century France* (Leiden: E. J. Brill, 1999). More judicious is the older biography, Nancy Lyman Roelker, *Queen of Navarre: Jeanne d'Albret, 1528–72* (Cambridge, MA: Harvard University Press, 1968).
20. Calvin to Jeanne d'Albret, 16 Jan. 1561, *CO* 17:315–16. On the Reformation in Béarn, see Mark Greengrass, 'The Calvinist Experiment in Béarn', in Pettegree, Duke and Lewis (eds), *Calvinism in Europe*, 119–42.
21. Scott Manetsch, *Theodore Beza and the Quest for Peace in France, 1562–1598* (Leiden: E. J. Brill, 2000), 20.
22. N. M. Sutherland, 'Calvinism and the Conspiracy of Amboise', *History* 47 (1962): 111–38.
23. Kelly, *François Hotman*, 112.
24. Robert M. Kingdon, *Geneva and the Coming of the Wars of Religion in France, 1555–1563* (Geneva: Droz, 1956), 64.
25. Ibid., 72.
26. Knecht, *Rise and Fall of Renaissance France*, 287.
27. W. Nijenhuis, 'The Limits of Civil Disobedience in Calvin's Last-Known Sermons: Development of his Ideas on the Right of Civil Resistance', in Nijenhuis, *Ecclesia Reformata*, 2:84–5.
28. The classic study of these ministers remains Kingdon, *Geneva and the Coming of the Wars of Religion*.
29. Ibid., 7.
30. Ibid., 14–15.
31. Ibid., 22.
32. Ibid., 26.
33. Ibid., 32.
34. See the essential study Philip Benedict, *Rouen during the Wars of Religion* (Cambridge: Cambridge University Press, 1981).
35. Kingdon, *Geneva and the Coming of the Wars of Religion*, 79.
36. Calvin reported on this to Beza in a letter of 27 Aug. 1561, *CO* 18:649–50; Bonnet 4:224–5.
37. Kingdon, *Geneva and the Coming of the Wars of Religion*, 81.
38. Diefendorf, *Beneath the Cross*, 57–8.
39. The matter is confusing as Calvin often spoke favourably of the Confession, but what he meant was Melanchthon's *Variata*, which he had signed in 1540, a highly revised and altered version of the 1530 original.

40. Calvin to Beza, 10 Sept. 1561, *CO* 18:682; Bonnet 4:227.
41. Calvin to Antoine of Navarre, Aug. 1561, *CO* 18:659–61; Bonnet 4:212–14.
42. Calvin to Beza, 24 Sept. 1561, *CO* 18: 737–8.
43. Manetsch, *Theodore Beza*, 22–3.
44. Commentary on Daniel, Preface, *CO* 18:615.
45. *CO* 18:623.
46. Calvin to Beza, 18 Feb. 1562, Bonnet 4:286.
47. Calvin to Bullinger, 12 Mar. 1562, *CO* 19:327–9; Bonnet 4:262–5.
48. Above all, see Mack P. Holt, *The French Wars of Religion, 1562–1629* (Cambridge: Cambridge University Press, 1995), esp. 50–75.
49. Knecht, *Rise and Fall of Renaissance France*, 306.
50. D. J. B. Trim, 'The "Secret War" of Elizabeth I: England and the Huguenots during the Early Wars of Religion, 1562–1577', *HSP* 27 (1999): 189–99.
51. Kingdon, *Geneva and the Coming of the Wars of Religion*, 117.
52. Ibid., 118–19.
53. Calvin to church in Languedoc, Sept. 1562, *CO* 19:550–1.
54. Calvin to Bullinger, 16 Jan. 1563, *CO* 19:637–41; Bonnet 4:286–90.
55. Manetsch, *Theodore Beza*, 25.
56. Beza to Calvin, 14 Dec. 1562, cited in ibid.
57. N. M. Sutherland, 'The Assassination of François Duc de Guise, February 1563', *Historical Journal* 24 (1981): 279–95.
58. Diefendorf, *Beneath the Cross*, 72–3.
59. Calvin to Bullinger, 8 Apr. 1563, *CO* 19:690–3; Bonnet 4:297–301.
60. Calvin to Condé, 10 May 1563, *CO* 20:12–15; Bonnet 4:309–13.
61. Bullinger to Viret, 3 Mar. 1559, *CO* 17:469–70.
62. Calvin to Viret, 27 Aug. 1558, *CO* 17:308. Oberman, 'Calvin and Farel', 57–8.
63. Olson, *Calvin and Social Welfare*, 50–9.
64. This is discussed in David M. Whitford, 'Robbing Paul to Pay Peter: The Reception of Paul in Sixteenth Century Political Theology', in R. Ward Holder (ed.), *The Reception of Paul in the Reformation* (Leiden: E. J. Brill, forthcoming). I am grateful to the author for permitting me to read his paper in advance of publication.
65. Calvin to Valence, 22 Apr. 1560, *CO* 18:63.
66. Oberman, 'Calvin and Farel', 54–6.
67. Ray Mentzer, 'Heresy Proceedings in Languedoc', *Transactions of the American Philosophical Society* 74 (1984).
68. Calvin to King of France, 28 Jan. 1561, *CO* 18:343–5; Bonnet 4:167–70.
69. Benedict, *Christ's Churches Purely Reformed*, 136–7. Philippe Denis and Jean Rott, *Jean Morély et l'utopie d'une démocratie dans l'église* (Geneva: Droz, 1993); Robert M. Kingdon, 'Calvinism and Democracy: Some Political Implications of Debates on French Reformed Church Government, 1562–1572', *American Historical Review* 69 (1964): 393–401.
70. Calvin and Beza to Viret, 1 Aug. 1563, *CO* 20:123.
71. Nifenhuis, 'Limits of Civil Disobedience', 86f.
72. Max Engammare, 'Calvin monarchomaque? Du soupçon à l'argument', *ARG* 89 (1998): 207–26.
73. The sermon is on 2 Samuel 11. Calvin, *Sermons on 2 Samuel*, 485.

Chapter 18: Endings

1. Calvin to Bullinger, 2 July 1563, *CO* 20:53–4. A filbert is closely related to a hazelnut.
2. Calvin to the Elector of the Palatinate, 23 July 1563, *CO* 20:72–9.
3. Ibid., *CO* 20:76

4. Ibid., *CO* 20:77–8.
5. Calvin to Antoine de Crussol, 7 May 1563, *CO* 20:8.
6. Calvin to Prince Porcien, *CO* 20:11–12.
7. Ibid., *CO* 20:12.
8. Calvin to Jean de Soubise, 25 May 1563, *CO* 20:30–1 (1 Cor. 10:13).
9. Calvin to Bullinger, 18 July 1563, *CO* 20:63–4.
10. Beza, *Life of Calvin*, 99.
11. Ibid., 100.
12. Ibid., 118.
13. Cook, 'Calvin's Illnesses', 66.
14. See Bruce Gordon and Peter Marshall (eds), *The Place of the Dead: Death and Remembrance in Late Medieval and Early Modern Europe* (Cambridge: Cambridge University Press, 2000), esp. 1–16.
15. Beza, *Life of Calvin*, 103.
16. Matthew 24:43, *CR* 73:678.
17. *Romans*, 105.
18. See Heinrich Quistorp, *Calvin's Doctrine of the Last Things* (Richmond, VA: John Knox Press, 1955).
19. See James Michael Weiss, 'Erasmus at Luther's Funeral: Melanchthon's Commemorations of Luther in 1546', *SCJ* 16 (1985): 91–114.
20. On Bullinger's praise of Zwingli, see Daniel Bolliger, 'Bullinger on Church Authority: The Transformation of the Prophetic Role in Christian Ministry', in Gordon and Campi (eds), *Architect of Reformation*, 159–80; also Gordon, 'Holy and Problematic Deaths'.
21. Irena Backus, *Life Writing in Reformation Europe: Lives of Reformers by Friends, Disciples and Foes* (Aldershot: Ashgate, 2008), 130–8. The following draws heavily on Professor Backus' work.
22. Ibid., 153–62.
23. On Masson's biography of Calvin, see ibid., 181–6.
24. Masson, 'Vita calvini', cited in ibid., 179.
25. Ibid., 183.
26. Ibid., 181.
27. On this see Richard Muller, *After Calvin: Studies in the Development of a Theological Tradition* (Oxford: Oxford University Press, 2003).
28. Ibid., 16.
29. 'Memoires et Procedures de ma Negociation en Angleterre (8 October 1582–8 October 1583) by Jean Malliet, Councillor of Geneva', ed. Simon Adams and Mark Greengrass, in Ian W. Archer (ed.), *Religion, Politics, and Society in Sixteenth-Century England* (Cambridge: Cambridge University Press, 2003), esp. 141–64.

Select Bibliography

This bibliography of secondary literature is determined by what I thought might be most useful to the reader. It also offers me the opportunity to acknowledge with gratitude the work of scholars from whom I have learned a great deal. Given the intended audience, the literature listed below is in English or cited in translation. Works in French and German are found in the Notes. I have not repeated books and articles in subsequent chapters after their initial reference.

For readers wishing to pursue their interests in John Calvin, I would recommend the following. The collected essays in Donald K. McKim (ed.), *The Cambridge Companion to John Calvin* (Cambridge: Cambridge University Press, 2004), are an accessible treatment of aspects of Calvin's life and work by leading scholars. William J. Bouwsma, *John Calvin: A Sixteenth-Century Portrait* (New York and Oxford: Oxford University Press, 1988) offers a provocative, if overly psychological, examination of Calvin. Jean-François Gilmont, *John Calvin and the Printed Book*, trans. Karin Maag (Kirksville, MO, Truman State University Press, 2005) is a valuable discussion of Calvin's life and work regime by an expert. William G. Naphy, *Calvin and the Consolidation of the Genevan Reformation* (Manchester: Manchester University Press, 1994) remains the essential work on developments in Geneva. Richard A. Muller, *The Unaccommodated Calvin: Studies in the Foundation of a Theological Tradition* (Oxford: Oxford University Press, 1999) is challenging, but offers the most illuminating treatment of Calvin's theology in context. Also highly recommended is Randall C. Zachman, *Image and Word in the Theology of John Calvin* (Notre Dame, IN: University of Notre Dame Press, 2007), and his *John Calvin: Teacher, Pastor, and Theologian* (Grand Rapids, MI: Baker Academic, 2006), which draws together the author's essays on various aspects of Calvin's work. Extremely helpful is David C. Steinmetz, *Calvin in Context* (New York and Oxford: Oxford University Press, 1995). John Witte Jr and Robert M. Kingdon, *Courtship, Engagement, and Marriage in John Calvin's Geneva* (Grand Rapids, MI: Wm B. Eerdmans, 2005) is an excellent introduction to the institutional world of Calvin's Geneva, as is Robert M. Kingdon, *Adultery and Divorce in Calvin's Geneva* (Cambridge, MA: Harvard University Press, 1995).

On the development of Calvinism after the reformer's death, essential is Philip Benedict's *Christ's Churches Purely Reformed: A Social History of Calvinism* (New Haven, CT and London: Yale University Press, 2002). Also the essays in Andrew Pettegree, Alastair Duke and

Gillian Lewis (eds), *Calvinism in Europe, 1540–1620* (Cambridge: Cambridge University Press, 1994), and Graeme Murdock, *Beyond Calvin: The Intellectual, Political and Cultural World of Europe's Reformed Churches, c. 1540–1620* (Basingstoke: Palgrave, 2004).

Chapter 1: A French Youth

The classic work on Calvin's youth remains Alexandre Ganoczy, *The Young Calvin*, trans. David Foxgrover and Wade Provo (Edinburgh: T&T Clark, 1987). Bernard Cottret, *Calvin: A Biography*, trans. M. Wallace McDonald (Grand Rapids, MI: Wm B. Eerdmans, 2000) is slightly eccentric but stimulating. See also Cornelius Augustijn, Christoph Burger and Frans P. van Stam, 'Calvin in the Light of the Early Letters', in Herman J. Selderhuis (ed.), *Calvinus Praeceptor Ecclesiae: Papers of the International Congress on Calvin Research, Princeton, August 20–24, 2002* (Geneva: Droz, 2004). The educational world of France is treated in Georges Huppert, *Public Schools in Renaissance France* (Urbana, IL: University of Illinois Press, 1984). For a comprehensible and readable background to French religious and political culture, see R. J. Knecht, *The Rise and Fall of Renaissance France, 1483–1610*, 2nd edn (Oxford: Blackwell, 2001). Also Knecht's *Renaissance Warrior and Patron: The Reign of Francis I* (Cambridge and New York: Cambridge University Press, 1994). More specifically on institutions, see Christopher W. Stocker, 'The Politics of the Parlement in Paris in 1525', *French Historical Studies* 8 (1973): 191–212. On French Humanism, Jean-Claude Margolin, 'Humanism in France', in Anthony Goodman and Angus MacKay (eds), *The Impact of Humanism on Western Europe* (London: Longman, 1990), 164–201. Important studies include David O. McNeil, *Guillaume Budé and Humanism in the Reign of Francis I* (Geneva: Droz, 1972) and Marie-Madeleine de La Garanderie, 'Guillaume Budé: A Philosopher of Culture', *SCJ* 19 (1988): 379–88. Extremely informative is Guy Bedouelle, 'Jacques Lefèvre d'Etaples (c.1460–1536)', in Carter Lindberg (ed.), *The Reformation Theologians* (Oxford: Blackwell, 2001), 19–33. Fundamental is Jonathan Reid, *King's Sister – Queen of Dissent: Marguerite of Navarre (1492–1549) and her Evangelical Network* (Leiden: E. J. Brill, forthcoming). On Meaux, see Henry Heller, 'The Briçonnet Case Reconsidered', *Journal of Medieval and Renaissance Studies* 2 (1972): 223–58. On the Sorbonne, J. K. Farge, *Orthodoxy and Reform in Early Reformation France: The Faculty of Theology of Paris, 1500–1543* (Leiden: E. J. Brill, 1985). A very helpful essay on French evangelicals is David Nicholls, 'Heresy and Protestantism, 1520–1542: Questions of Perception and Communication', *French History* 10 (1996):182–205. Much of Francis Higman's important work on French evangelical printing has been collected together in his *Lire et découvrir: la circulation des idées au temps de la Réforme* (Geneva: Droz, 1998).

Chapter 2: Among the Princes of Law

On the legal culture in France, see Michael Monheit, 'Guillaume Budé, Andrea Alciato, Pierre de l'Estoile: Renaissance Interpreters of Roman Law', *Journal of the History of Ideas* 58 (1997): 21–40, and Donald R. Kelley, *Foundations of Modern Historical Scholarship: Language, Law, and History in the French Renaissance* (New York: Columbia University Press, 1970). Calvin's activities in this period have been carefully reconstructed in Cornelius Augustijn, Christoph Burger and Frans P. van Stam, 'Calvin in the Light of the Early Letters', in Selderhuis (ed.), *Calvinus Praeceptor Ecclesiae*, 139–57. On Calvin and the Seneca commentary, see Michael L. Monheit, ' "The Ambition for an Illustrious Name": Humanism, Patronage, and Calvin's Doctrine of Calling', *SCJ* 23 (1992): 267–87. On Calvin's relationship to classical philosophy, see Irena Backus, *Historical Method and Confessional Identity in the Era of the Reformation (1378–1615)* (Leiden: E. J. Brill, 2003). The definitive study of Calvin's use of rhetorical and literary forms is Olivier Millet, *Calvin et la dynamique de la parole* (Paris: Champion, 1992).

Chapter 3: 'At Last Delivered': Conversion and Flight

On Calvin's conversion, Heiko A. Oberman, 'Subita Conversio: The Conversion of John Calvin', in Heiko A. Oberman, Alfred Schindler, Ernst Saxer and Heinz Peter Stucki (eds), *Reformiertes Erbe: Festschrift für Gottfried W. Locher zu seinem 80. Geburtstag* (Zurich: Theologischer Verlag, 1992), 279–95 and Willem Nijenhuis, 'Calvin's "Subita Conversio": Notes to a Hypothesis', in his *Ecclesia Reformata: Studies on the Reformation* (Leiden: E. J. Brill, 1994), 2:3–23. On the Placards, Donald R. Kelley, *The Beginning of Ideology: Consciousness and Society in the French Reformation* (Cambridge: Cambridge University Press, 1981). On the background to the disputes over the Lord's Supper, see Lee Palmer Wandel, *The Eucharist in the Reformation: Incarnation and Liturgy* (Cambridge: Cambridge University Press, 2006).

Chapter 4: Exile in a Hidden Corner

Bruce Gordon, *The Swiss Reformation* (Manchester: Manchester University Press, 2002) provides crucial background. On Basle, Hans R. Guggisberg, *Basel in the Sixteenth Century: Aspects of the City Republic before, during, and after the Reformation* (St Louis, MO: Center for Reformation Research, 1982); Amy Nelson Burnett, *Teaching the Reformation: Ministers and their Message in Basel, 1529–1629* (Oxford: Oxford University Press, 2007); and Peter G. Bietenholz, 'Printing and the Basle Reformation, 1517–1565', in Jean-François Gilmont (ed.), *The Reformation and the Book*, trans. Karin Maag (Aldershot: Ashgate, 1998), 235–63. On Basle humanism, Matthew McLean, *The Cosmographia of Sebastian Münster: Describing the World in the Reformation* (Aldershot: Ashgate, 2007). The negotiations of the 1530s are treated in Amy Nelson Burnett, 'Basel and the Wittenberg Concord', *ARG* 96 (2005): 33–56. The crucial work on Bucer is Martin Greschat, *Martin Bucer: A Reformer and his Times* (Louisville, KY: Westminster John Knox Press, 2004). On events in the empire, unsurpassed is Thomas A. Brady Jr, *Protestant Politics: Jacob Sturm (1489–1553) and the German Reformation* (Atlantic Highlands, NJ: Humanities Press, 1995). On the development of Calvin's writing, see Muller, *The Unaccommodated Calvin*; Gilmont, *John Calvin and the Printed Book*; and Jean-Daniel Benoît, 'The History and Development of the *Institutio*: How Calvin Worked', in G. E. Duffield (ed.), *John Calvin* (Appleford: Courtenay Press, 1966), 102–7.

Chapter 5: Violent Reformations and Tumult

The most important new book on Berne and the Vaud is Michael W. Bruening, *Calvinism's First Battleground: Conflict and Reform in the Pays de Vaud, 1528–1559* (Heidelberg: Springer Verlag, 2005). On Calvin and Renée, F. Whitfield Barton, *Calvin and the Duchess* (Louisville, KY: Westminster John Knox Press, 1989). The long and complex relationship with Farel is well treated in Heiko A. Oberman, 'Calvin and Farel: The Dynamics of Legitimation in Early Calvinism', *Journal of Early Modern History* 2 (1998): 33–60. The iconoclasm of the reformation in the region is discussed in Carlos M. N. Eire, *War against the Idols. The Reformation of Worship from Erasmus to Calvin* (Cambridge: Cambridge University Press, 1986). An excellent discussion of the background to and introduction of the reformation remains E. William Monter, *Calvin's Geneva* (New York, London and Sydney: John Wiley, 1967). A Catholic view of events is the valuable Jeanne de Jussie, *The Short Chronicle: A Poor Clare's Account of the Reformation in Geneva*, ed. and trans. Carrie F. Klaus (Chicago and London: University of Chicago Press, 2006). Also invaluable is Thomas Lambert, 'Preaching, Praying and Policing the Reform in Sixteenth-Century Geneva' (PhD dissertation, University of Wisconsin-Madison, 1998).

Chapter 6: Discovering the Church

On Strasbourg, see, M. U. Chrisman, *Strasbourg and the Reform: A Study in the Process of Religious Change* (New Haven, CT: Yale University Press, 1967); Thomas A. Brady Jr, *Ruling Class, Regime and Reformation at Strasbourg, 1520–1555* (Leiden: E. J. Brill, 1978); Laura Jane Abray, *The People's Reformation: Magistrates and Commons in Strasbourg, 1500–1598* (Ithaca, NY: Cornell University Press, 1985). Important is Cornelis Augustijn, 'Calvin in Strasbourg', in Wilhelm H. Neuser (ed.), *Calvinus sacrae scripturae professor*, (Grand Rapids, MI: Wm B. Eerdmans, 1994), 166–77. Bucer is treated in Martin Greschat, *Martin Bucer: A Reformer and his Times* (Louisville, KY: Westminster John Knox Press, 2004), and Amy Nelson Burnett, *The Yoke of Christ: Martin Bucer and Christian Discipline* (Kirksville, MO: Truman State University Press, 1994). On Calvin and Bucer, see Willem van't Spijker, 'Calvin's Friendship with Bucer: Did It Make Calvin a Calvinist?', in David Foxgrover (ed.), *Calvin and Spirituality: Calvin and his Contemporaries: Colleagues, Friends, and Contacts* (Grand Rapids, MI: CRC Product Services, 1998), 169–86; also, his 'Bucer und Calvin', in Krieger and Lienhard (eds), *Martin Bucer and Sixteenth-Century Europe: actes du colloque* [Strasbourg 1991], 2 vols (Leiden: E. J. Brill, 1993), 2: 461–70. Also, Thomas Brady Jr, 'Martin Bucer and the Politics of Strasbourg', in Krieger and Lienhard (eds), *Martin Bucer and Sixteenth Century Europe*, 134–5. Calvin's involvement in the religious colloquies has recently been comprehensively examined in Christopher Ocker, 'Calvin in Germany', in Christopher Ocker and others (eds), *Politics and Reformations: Communities, Polities, Nations and Empires: Essays in Honor of Thomas A. Brady, Jr.* (Leiden and Boston: E. J. Brill, 2007), 313–44. See also Brady's important collection of essays, Thomas A. Brady Jr, *Community, Politics and Reformation in Early Modern Europe* (Leiden: E. J. Brill, 1998). On Melanchthon's opposition to compromise, Ralph Keen, 'Political Authority and Ecclesiology in Melanchthon's "De Ecclesiae Autoritate" ', *Church History* 65 (1996): 1–14.

Chapter 7: 'Lucid Brevity' for the Sake of the Church: Romans

On Calvin and biblical interpretation and relations with the church fathers, see David C. Steinmetz, *Calvin in Context* (New York and Oxford: Oxford University Press, 1995); A. N. S. Lane, *John Calvin: Student of the Church Fathers* (Edinburgh: T&T Clark, 1999); John L. Thompson, *John Calvin and the Daughters of Sarah: Women in Regular and Exceptional Roles in the Exegesis of Calvin* (Geneva: Droz, 1992); also John L. Thompson, 'Calvin as Biblical Interpreter', in Donald K. McKim (ed.), *The Cambridge Companion to John Calvin* (Cambridge: Cambridge University Press, 2004), 58–73; Elsie Anne McKee, 'Exegesis, Theology, and Development in Calvin's Institutio: A Methodological Suggestion', in Elsie Anne McKee and Brian G. Armstrong (eds), *Probing the Reformed Tradition: Historical Studies in Honor of Edward A. Dowey, Jr* (Louisville, KY: Westminster/ John Knox Press, 1989), 108–15; Randall C. Zachman, 'Gathering Meaning from Context: Calvin's Exegetical Method', in his *Calvin as Teacher*, 103–30; and R. Ward Holder, *John Calvin and the Grounding of Interpretation: Calvin's First Commentaries* (Leiden: E. J. Brill, 2006). Extremely helpful is Barbara Pitkin, *What Pure Eyes Could See: Calvin's Doctrine of Faith in its Exegetical Context* (New York and Oxford: Oxford University Press, 1999). On Calvin's language of accommodation, see Jon Balserak, *Divinity Compromised: A Study of Divine Accommodation in the Thought of John Calvin* (Dordrecht: Springer, 2006).

Chapter 8: Building Christ's Church

On Calvin and the Swiss, Bruce Gordon, 'Calvin and the Swiss Reformed Churches', in Pettegree, Duke and Lewis (eds), *Calvinism in Europe*, 64–81. William G. Naphy, *Plagues,*

Poisons and Potions: Plague-Spreading Conspiracies in the Western Alps ca. 1530–1640 (Manchester: Manchester University Press, 2002) treats the culture of fear in Geneva. On the meetings in Geneva, see Erik A. de Boer, 'The Congrégation: An In-Service Theological Training Center for Preachers to the People of Geneva', in David Foxgrover (ed.), *Calvin and the Company of Pastors* (Grand Rapids, MI: CRC Product Services, 2004), 57–87. On Calvin and the office of minister, Darlene K. Flaming, 'The Apostolic and Pastoral Office: Theory and Practice in Calvin's Geneva', in Foxgrover (ed.), *Calvin and the Company of Pastors*, 149–72. John Witte Jr and Robert M. Kingdon, *Sex, Marriage, and Family in John Calvin's Geneva*, vol. 1: *Courtship, Engagement, and Marriage* (Grand Rapids, MI: Wm B. Eerdmans, 2005), and Robert M. Kingdon, *Adultery and Divorce in Calvin's Geneva* (Cambridge, MA: Harvard University Press, 1995) on institutional reform and social history. Also Jeffrey Watt, 'Women and the Consistory in Calvin's Geneva', *SCJ* 24 (1993): 429–44. Christian Grosse treats worship in 'Places of Sanctification: The Liturgical Sacrality of Genevan Reformed Churches, 1535–1566', in Will Coster and Andrew Spicer (eds), *Sacred Space in Early Modern Europe* (Cambridge: Cambridge University Press, 2005), 160–80. Also Elsie Anne McKee, 'Context, Contours, Contents: Towards a Description of Calvin's Understanding of Worship', in Foxgrover (ed.), *Calvin and Spirituality*, 66–92. On preaching, Thomas J. Davis, 'Preaching and Presence: Constructing Calvin's Homiletical Legacy', in David Foxgrover (ed.), *The Legacy of John Calvin* (Grand Rapids, MI: CRC Product Services, 2000), 84–106.

Chapter 9: Calvin's World

D. R. Kelly, *François Hotman: A Revolutionary's Ordeal* (Princeton: Princeton University Press, 1983) is essential. On print culture, see Andrew Pettegree, 'Genevan Print and the Coming of the Wars of Religion', in Andrew Pettegree (ed.), *The French Book and the European Book World* (Leiden: E. J. Brill, 2007), 89–106. Also Andrew Pettegree, *Reformation and the Culture of Persuasion* (Cambridge: Cambridge University Press, 2005). On the Eucharistic debate in Berne, Amy Nelson Burnett, 'The Myth of the Swiss Lutherans: Martin Bucer and the Eucharistic Controversy in Bern', *Zwingliana* 32 (2005): 45–70. The essential work on Castellio is Hans R. Guggisberg, *Sebastian Castellio, 1515–1563: Humanist and Defender of Religious Toleration in a Confessional Age* (Aldershot: Ashgate, 2002).

Chapter 10: Healing Christ's Body

'The Conciliating Theology of John Calvin: Dialogue among Friends', in Howard Louthan and Randall C. Zachman (eds), *Conciliation and Confession: The Struggle for Unity in the Age of Reform, 1415–1648* (Notre Dame, IN: Notre Dame University Press, 2004). The most important essay on Calvin's relationship with Melanchthon is Timothy Wengert, 'We Will Feast Together in Heaven Forever: The Epistolary Friendship of John Calvin and Philip Melanchthon', in Karin Maag (ed.), *Melanchthon in Europe: His Work and Influence beyond Wittenberg* (Grand Rapids, MI: Baker Books, 1999), 19–44. On Calvin's teaching of the Lord's Supper, Thomas J. Davis, *The Clearest Promises of God: The Development of Calvin's Eucharistic Teaching* (New York: AMS Press, 1995). Recently, Anthony N. S. Lane, 'Was Calvin a Crypto-Zwinglian?', in Mack P. Holt (ed.), *Adaptations of Calvinism in Reformation Europe: Essays in Honour of Brian G. Armstrong* (Aldershot: Ashgate, 2007), 21–41. The literature on Calvin and Trent is fairly old, but reliable: Theodore W. Casteel, 'Calvin and Trent: Calvin's Reaction to the Council of Trent in the Context of his Conciliar Thought', *Harvard Theological Review*, 63 (Jan. 1970): 91–117. Heiko A. Oberman, 'The Pursuit of

Happiness: Calvin between Humanism and Reformation', in John W. O'Malley, Thomas M. Izbicki and Gerald Christianson (eds), *Humanity and Divinity in Renaissance and Reformation* (Leiden: E. J. Brill, 1993), 251–83.

Chapter 11: 'Since Calvin Acts So Bravely, Why Does He Not Come Here?': France

Nicola M. Sutherland, *The Huguenot Struggle for Recognition* (New Haven, CT and London: Yale University Press, 1980) is a readable and thoughtful survey. On book culture, Francis Higman, *Censorship and the Sorbonne: A Bibliographical Study of the Books in French Censured by the Faculty of Theology of the University of Paris, 1520–1551* (Geneva: Droz, 1979). Natalie Zemon Davis, *Society and Culture in Early Modern France: Eight Essays* (Stanford, CA: Stanford University Press, 1975) remains an essential read on French religious culture. Euan Cameron, *The Reformation of the Heretics: The Waldenses of the Alps, 1480–1580* (Oxford: Oxford University Press, 1984) is the most important work on the relationship between the Waldensians and the Reformation. Henry Heller, *The Conquest of Poverty: The Calvinist Revolt in Sixteenth-Century France* (Leiden: E. J. Brill, 1986) treats the French reformation from a social history perspective. Also highly informative is Ray Mentzer, *Heresy Proceedings in Languedoc, 1500–1560*, (Philadelphia, PA: American Philosophical Society, 1984). On Crespin, helpful is Randall Coats, 'Reconstituting the Textual Body in Jean Crespin's Histoire des Martyrs (1564)', *Renaissance Quarterly* 44 (1991): 62–85. William Monter, *Judging the French Reformation: Heresy Trials by Sixteenth-Century Parlements* (Cambridge, MA: Harvard University Press, 1999). Brad S. Gregory, *Salvation at Stake: Christian Martyrdom in Early Modern Europe* (Cambridge, MA: Harvard University Press, 1999) is essential reading for a wider, comparative understanding of martyrdom. Peter Matheson, 'Martyrdom or Mission: A Protestant Debate', *ARG* 80 (1989): 154–71 explores the different attitudes among Protestant reformers. The issue of Nicodemism is freshly approached in David F. Wright, 'Why was Calvin So Severe a Critic of Nicodemism?', in David F. Wright, Anthony N. S. Lane and Jon Balserak (eds), *Calvinus Evangelii Propugnator: Calvin, Champion of the Gospel; Papers Presented at the International Congress on Calvin Research, Seoul, 1998* (Grand Rapids, MI: CRC Product Services, 2006), 66–90. The standard work remains Carlos M. N. Eire, *War against the Idols: The Reformation of Worship from Erasmus to Calvin* (Cambridge: Cambridge University Press 1986). See also his 'Prelude to Sedition? Calvin's Attack on Nicodemism and Religious Compromise', *ARG* 79 (1985): 120–45. For a broader, comparative approach, see Perez Zagorin, *Ways of Lying: Dissimulation, Persecution, and Conformity in Early Modern Europe* (Cambridge, MA: Harvard University Press, 1990).

Chapter 12: The Years of Conflict

On refugees coming to Geneva, Gabriel Audisio, 'The First Provençal Refugees in Geneva (1545–71)', *French History* 19 (2005): 385–400. Mark Taplin, *The Italian Reformers and the Zurich Church, c. 1540–1620* (Aldershot: Ashgate, 2003) is the definitive work on the radicals and the Swiss churches. Elsie Anne McKee, *John Calvin on the Diaconate and Liturgical Almsgiving* (Geneva: Droz, 1984) is the essential study of the office. Jeanine Olson, *Calvin and Social Welfare: Deacons and the Bourse Français* (Selinsgrove, PA: Susquehanna University Press, 1989) is the major study of social care in Geneva. William G. Naphy, 'Baptisms, Church Riots and Social Unrest in Calvin's Geneva', *SCJ* 26 (1995): 87–97 examines the interplay of religion and factional politics. Recently, Karen E. Spierling's important monograph *Infant Baptism in Reformation Geneva: The Shaping of a Community,*

1536–1564 (Aldershot: Ashgate, 2005) explores both the theological and social dimensions of the sacrament. Cornelis P. Venema, *Heinrich Bullinger and the Doctrine of Predestination: Author of the 'Other Reformed Tradition'?* (Grand Rapids, MI: Baker Academic, 2002) is illuminating on the relationship of Calvin and Bullinger.

Chapter 13: 'There is No Form of Impiety that This Monster Has Not Raked Up'

On Servetus, Roland H. Bainton, *Hunted Heretic: The Life and Death of Michael Servetus, 1511–1553* (1953: repr. Gloucester, MA: Peter Smith, 1978) remains the best study in a field where there are many bad ones. See also Roland H. Bainton, 'Servetus and the Genevan Libertines', *Church History* 5 (1936): 141–2. On Joris and radical thought, Gary K. Waite, *David Joris and Dutch Anabaptism, 1524–43* (Waterloo, Ontario: Wilfrid Laurier University Press, 1990). In addition to his definitive biography of Castellio, see Hans Guggisberg, 'Tolerance and Intolerance in Sixteenth-Century Basle', in Ole Peter Grell and Robert W. Scribner (eds), *Tolerance and Intolerance in the European Reformation* (Cambridge: Cambridge University Press, 1996), 145–63. Bruce Gordon, 'Wary Allies: Melanchthon and the Swiss Reformation', in Maag (ed.), *Melanchthon in Europe*, 45–69 treats Melanchthon's relations with many of Calvin's opponents.

Chapter 14: Luther's Heirs

On the Westphal controversy, see Joseph N. Tylenda, 'The Calvin–Westphal Exchange: The Genesis of Calvin's Treatises against Westphal', *Calvin Theological Journal* 9 (1974): 182–209. Also Joseph N. Tylenda, 'Calvin and Westphal: Two Eucharistic Theologies in Conflict', in Wilhelm H. Neuser, Herman J. Selderhuis and Willem van't Spijker (eds), *Calvin's Books* (Heerenven: Groen, 1997), 9–22. On Lasco, see Diarmaid MacCulloch, 'The Importance of Jan Laski in the English Reformation', in Christoph Strohm (ed.), *Johannes à Lasco: Polnischer Baron, Humanist und europäischer Reformator* (Tübingen: Mohr Siebeck, 2000), 315–45 and Michael S. Springer, *Restoring Christ's Church: John a Lasco and the Forma ac ratio* (Aldershot: Ashgate, 2007). Andrew Pettegree, *Foreign Protestant Communities in Sixteenth-Century London* (Oxford: Clarendon Press, 1986) treats the sacramentarian debate, while Bodo Nischan, *Prince, People, and Confession: The Second Reformation in Brandenburg* (Philadelphia, PA: University of Pennsylvania Press, 1994) examines the further development of Calvinism.

Chapter 15: European Reformer

Diarmaird MacCulloch, *Thomas Cranmer* (London and New Haven, CT: Yale University Press, 1996) is excellent on the archbishop's European connections. John Schofield, *Philip Melanchthon and the English Reformation* (Aldershot: Ashgate, 2006), and Rory McEntegart, *Henry VIII, the League of Schmalkalden, and the English Reformation* (Woodbridge, Suffolk: Boydell Press, 2002) are very helpful on England. Charmarie Jenkins Blaisdell, 'Calvin's Letters to Women: The Courting of Ladies in High Places', *SCJ* 13 (1982): 67–84. Ethan Shagan, 'Popular Politics and the English Reformation: New Sources and New Perspectives', *English Historical Review* 115 (2000): 121–33; and his *Popular Politics and the English Reformation* (Cambridge: Cambridge University Press, 2003) are the essential works on Somerset. See also D. Rodgers, *John à Lasco in England* (New York: Peter Lang, 1994) and Carl R. Trueman, *Luther's Legacy: Salvation and the English Reformers, 1525–1556*

(Oxford: Oxford University Press, 1994). An excellent overview is found in Euan Cameron, 'Frankfurt and Geneva: The European Context of John Knox's Reformation', in Roger Mason (ed.), *John Knox and the British Reformations* (Aldershot: Ashgate, 1998), 51–73. Dan G. Danner, *Pilgrimage to Puritanism: History and Theology of the Marian Exiles at Geneva, 1555–1560* (New York: Peter Lang, 1999) offers a recent examination of their life and work. Maurice S. Betteridge, 'The Bitter Notes: The Geneva Bible and its Annotations', *SCJ* 14 (1983): 41–62 treats the development of the Bible and its significance. Margo Todd, *The Culture of Protestantism in Early Modern Scotland* (New Haven, CT and London: Yale University Press, 2002) is outstanding on the Scottish reformation, as is Michael Graham, *The Uses of Reform: 'Godly Discipline' and Popular Behavior in Scotland and Beyond, 1560–1610* (Leiden: E. J. Brill, 1996). Jane E. A. Dawson, *Scotland Re-Formed, 1488–1587* (Edinburgh: University of Edinburgh Press, 2007) is a new and accessible history of Scotland in the sixteenth century. Also Jane E. A. Dawson, 'Trumpeting Resistance: Christopher Goodman and John Knox', in Mason (ed.), *John Knox and the British Reformations*, 130–53 and Robert M. Healey, 'Waiting for Deborah: John Knox and Four Ruling Queens', *SCJ* 25 (1994): 371–86 on Knox's tract and Calvin. Jeannine E. Olson, 'Nicolas des Gallars and the Genevan Connection of the Stranger Churches', in Randolph Vigne and Charles Littleton (eds), *From Strangers to Citizens: The Integration of Immigrant Communities in Britain, Ireland and Colonial America, 1550–1750* (Portland, OR: Sussex Academic Press and the Huguenot Society of Great Britain and Ireland, 2001), 38–47 is helpful. In the same volume, Patrick Collinson, 'Europe in Britain: Protestant Strangers and the English Reformation', 57–67. See also Patrick Collinson, *Archbishop Grindal, 1519–83: Struggle for a Reformed Church* (London: Cape, 1979). On the spread of Calvin's works, Francis Higman, 'Calvin's Works in Translation', in Andrew Pettegree, Alastair Duke and Gillian Lewis (eds), *Calvinism in Europe, 1540–1620* (Cambridge: Cambridge University Press, 1994), 82–99. Poland is well treated in James Miller, 'The Origins of Polish Arianism', *SCJ* 16 (1985): 229–56, and George H. Williams, *Radical Reformation*, 3rd edn (Kirksville, MO: Truman State University Press, 2000). Andrew Pettegree's two works, *Foreign Protestant Communities in Sixteenth-Century London* (Oxford: Oxford University Press, 1986) and *Emden and the Dutch Revolt* (Oxford: Oxford University Press, 1992) are essential reading on the stranger communities and refugees. Guido Marnef, 'The Changing Face of Calvinism in Antwerp, 1550–1585', in Pettegree, Duke and Lewis (eds), *Calvinism in Europe, 143–59* is crucial on the early formation of the Dutch churches. Also Guido Marnef, *Antwerp in the Age of Reformation: Underground Protestantism in a Commercial Metropolis, 1550–1577*, trans. J. C. Grayson (Baltimore, MD and London: Johns Hopkins University Press, 1996). Lyle D. Bierma, *German Calvinism in the Confessional Age: The Covenant Theology of Caspar Olevianus* (Grand Rapids, MI: Baker Academic, 1996) provides a lucid and helpful treatment of the Palatinate, as does Lyle D. Bierma, 'The Sources and Theological Orientation of the Heidelberg Catechism', in Lyle D. Bierma et al. (eds), *An Introduction to the Heidelberg Catechism: Sources, History, and Theology* (Grand Rapids, MI: Baker Academic, 2005), 75–102.

Chapter 16: The 'Perfecte Schoole of Christe'

Max Engammare, 'Calvin: A Prophet without a Prophecy', *Church History* 67 (1998): 643–61 is a typically insightful examination of Calvin. Highly recommended is Susan E. Schreiner, *The Theater of His Glory: Nature and the Natural Order in the Thought of John Calvin* (1991; repr. Grand Rapids, MI: Baker Academic, 2001). See also William R. Stevenson Jr, *Sovereign Grace: The Place and Significance of Christian Freedom in John Calvin's Political Thought* (Oxford: Oxford University Press, 1999). On Calvin and the psalms, Barbara Pitkin, 'Imitation of David: David as a Paradigm for Faith in Calvin's Exegesis of the Psalms', *SCJ* 24 (1993): 843–63; and Herman J. Selderhuis, 'Church on Stage:

Calvin's Dynamic Ecclesiology', in Foxgrover (ed.), *Calvin and the Church* (Grand Rapids, MI: CRC Product Services, 2002), 46–64. Old but still informative is Elizabeth Armstrong, *Robert Estienne, Royal Printer: An Historical Study of the Elder Stephanus* (Cambridge: Cambridge University Press, 1954). On Crespin's understanding of history, David Watson, 'Jean Crespin and the Writing of History in the French Reformation', in Bruce Gordon (ed.), *Protestant History and Identity in Sixteenth-Century Europe,* (Aldershot: Scolar Press, 1996), 2:39–58. Important on Calvin's preaching is Wilhelmus H. Th. Moehn, *God Calls Us to His Service: The Relation between God and His Audience in Calvin's Sermons on Acts* (Geneva: Droz, 2001). Elsie Anne McKee in her 'Calvin and his Colleagues as Pastors: Some New Insights into the Collegial Ministry of Word and Sacraments', in Selderhuis (ed.), *Calvinus Praeceptor Ecclesiae,* 9–42, examines the organization and provision of worship. For a broader perspective on marriage in early-modern Europe, Thomas Max Safley, *Let No Man Put Asunder: The Control of Marriage in the German Southwest: A Comparative Study, 1550–1600* (Kirksville, MO: Truman State University Press, 1984), and Joel F. Harrington, *Reordering Marriage and Society in Reformation Germany* (Cambridge: Cambridge University Press, 1995). Jeffrey Watt, 'Childhood and Youth in the Genevan Consistory Minutes', in Selderhuis (ed.), *Calvinus Praeceptor Ecclesiae,* 43–64, throws new light on society in Calvin's Geneva. Mark Valeri, 'Religion, Discipline, and the Economy in Calvin's Geneva', *SCJ* 28 (1997): 123–42 is excellent on the church and the changing economic world. On education, see Gillian Lewis, 'The Genevan Academy', in Pettegree, Duke and Lewis (eds), *Calvinism in Europe,* 35–63, and the definitive Karin Maag, *Seminary or University?: The Genevan Academy and Reformed Higher Education, 1560–1620* (Aldershot: Ashgate, 1995).

Chapter 17: Churches and Blood: France

Jonathan Reid, 'France', in Andrew Pettegree (ed.), *The Reformation World* (London: Routledge, 2000) is an excellent overview. Barbara B. Diefendorf, *Beneath the Cross: Catholics and Huguenots in Sixteenth-Century Paris* (Oxford: Oxford University Press, 1991) remains essential reading. Nancy Lyman Roelker, *Queen of Navarre: Jeanne d'Albret, 1528–72* (Cambridge, MA: Harvard University Press, 1968) is the best on the queen who played a crucial role. See also David M. Bryson, *Queen Jeanne and the Promised Land: Dynasty, Homeland, Religion and Violence in Sixteenth-Century France* (Leiden: E. J. Brill, 1999). Mark Greengrass, 'The Calvinist Experiment in Béarn', in Pettegree, Duke and Lewis (eds), *Calvinism in Europe,* 119–42, treats the distinctive place of Navarre. Scott Manetsch, *Theodore Beza and the Quest for Peace in France, 1562–1598* (Leiden: E. J. Brill, 2000) is now essential on Beza. N. M. Sutherland, 'Calvinism and the Conspiracy of Amboise', *History* 47 (1962): 111–38 on the disastrous enterprise. Malcolm Walsby, *The Counts of Laval: Culture, Patronage and Religion in Fifteenth- and Sixteenth-Century France* (Aldershot: Ashgate, 2007) examines the place of a key family. Robert M. Kingdon, *Geneva and the Coming of the Wars of Religion in France, 1555–1563* (Geneva: Droz, 1956) is still the standard work on the missions to France. Our understanding of the emergence of Protestant churches is now informed by Glenn S. Sunshine, *Reforming French Protestantism: The Development of Huguenot Ecclesiastical Institutions, 1557–1572* (Kirksville, MO: Truman State University Press, 2003). Philip Benedict, *Rouen during the Wars of Religion* (Cambridge: Cambridge University Press, 1981) is a classic study and highly recommended. Mack P. Holt, *The French Wars of Religion, 1562–1629* (Cambridge: Cambridge University Press, 1995) provides a well-written and informed examination of the roots and course of the wars. D. J. B. Trim, 'The "Secret War" of Elizabeth I: England and the Huguenots during the Early Wars of Religion', *HSP* 27 (1999): 189–99 discusses English involvement. See also N. M. Sutherland, 'The Assassination of François Duc de Guise, February 1563', *Historical Journal* 24 (1981): 279–95. On resistance, David M. Whitford, 'Robbing Paul to Pay Peter: The

Reception of Paul in Sixteenth Century Political Theology', in R. Ward Holder (ed.), *The Reception of Paul in the Reformation* (Leiden: E. J. Brill, forthcoming).

Chapter 18: Endings

On the culture of death, see Bruce Gordon and Peter Marshall (eds), *The Place of the Dead: Death and Remembrance in Late Medieval and Early Modern Europe* (Cambridge: Cambridge University Press, 2000). Calvin on death is treated in Heinrich Quistorp, *Calvin's Doctrine of the Last Things* (Richmond, VA: John Knox Press, 1955). The crucial work on biographies of Calvin is Irena Backus, *Life Writing in Reformation Europe: Lives of Reformers by Friends, Disciples and Foes* (Aldershot: Ashgate, 2008). On the development of Calvinism and Reformed theology, indispensable is Richard Muller, *After Calvin: Studies in the Development of a Theological Tradition* (Oxford: Oxford University Press, 2003).

Index